THE MEMORY WORK OF JEWISH SPAIN

INDIANA SERIES IN SEPHARDI AND MIZRAHI STUDIES

Harvey E. Goldberg and Matthias Lehmann, editors

THE MEMORY WORK OF JEWISH SPAIN

DANIELA FLESLER AND
ADRIÁN PÉREZ MELGOSA

INDIANA UNIVERSITY PRESS

This book is a publication of

Indiana University Press
Office of Scholarly Publishing
Herman B Wells Library 350
1320 East 10th Street
Bloomington, Indiana 47405 USA

iupress.org

Manufactured in the United States of America

Cataloging information is available from the Library of Congress.
ISBN 978-0-253-05010-6 (hardback)
ISBN 978-0-253-05012-0 (paperback)
ISBN 978-0-253-05011-3 (ebook)

1 2 3 4 5 25 24 23 22 21 20

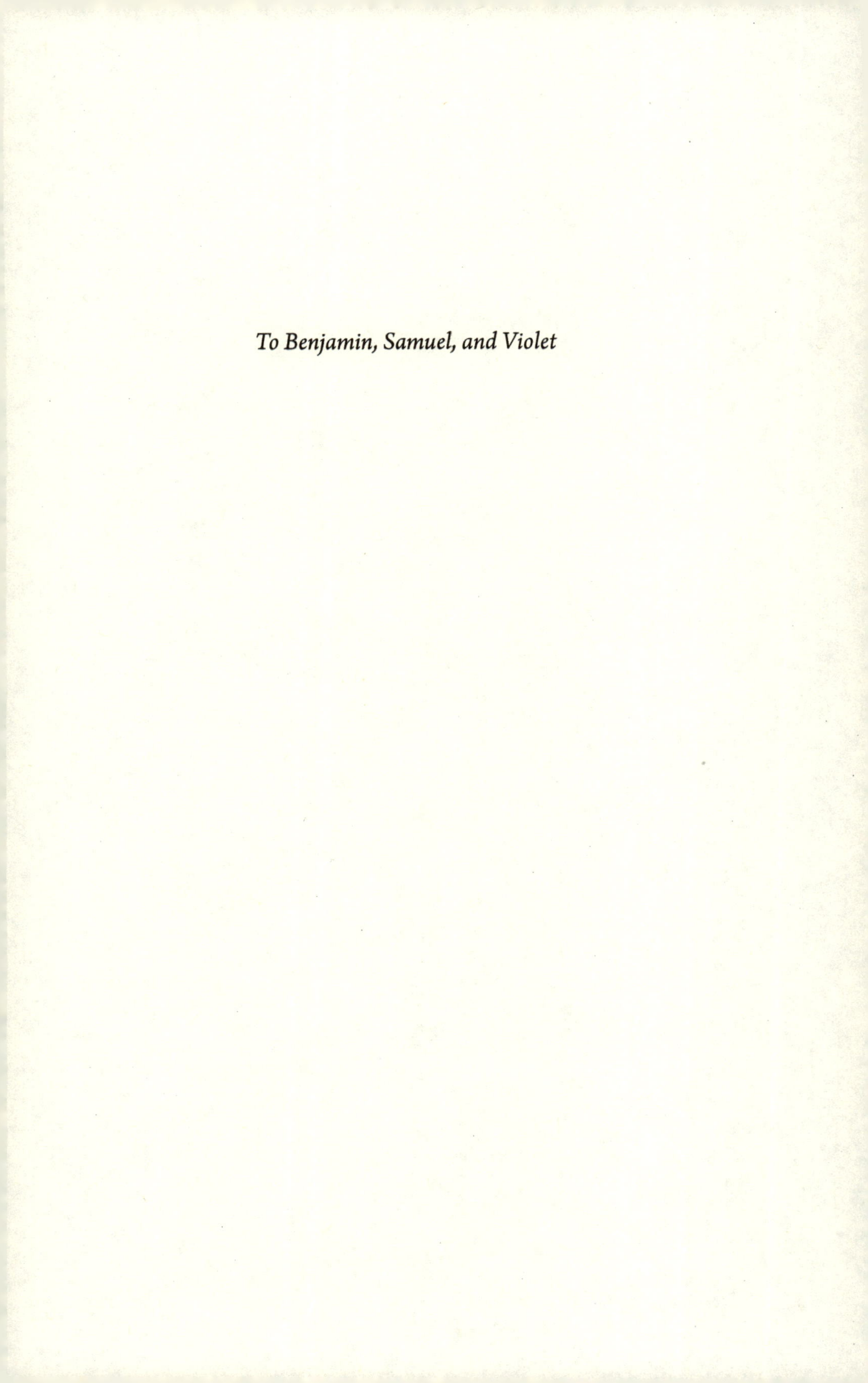

To Benjamin, Samuel, and Violet

CONTENTS

ACKNOWLEDGMENTS

THIS BOOK IS THE PRODUCT of a double journey of discovery. The first involved extensive travel within the emerging geography of towns, institutions, and people engaged in the reactivation of a variety of memories of historic Jewish presences in Spain. The other consisted of an intellectual voyage through the research and interpretation of the many tasks that the memory of Jewish Spain has been asked to perform throughout history by a variety of social actors both within and outside of Spain. At every step in these journeys, we have benefited from the generosity of many people whose advice, friendship, and hospitality have made this book possible. To all of them, whether they are named here or remain anonymous due to our faulty memories, go our deepest thanks.

Very early on, Solly Wolodarsky became a mentor and guide in both of these journeys. Either by pointing us in the right direction, providing personal connections, or by conversing with us about his own writings and thoughts on Jewish Spain, Solly's influence is present throughout this book. We know he would have been so happy to see it in print. Esther Bendahan generously opened the doors of her house to us, shared her deep knowledge and insights about Sephardi history and literature, and introduced us to readings and people that became key to the book's development. We are so grateful for her friendship and support. One of the people we met thanks to Esther was Daniel Quintero, whose portrait of Samuel Halevi we had long admired. We thank Daniel and Jane Young for the long conversations, the insights about Daniel's work, and their friendship.

Early in our fieldwork, Marciano de Hervás shared with us his own research and insights about the Jewish and *converso* history of Hervás. His work played a key role in our understanding and analysis of Hervás's evolving festival.

Jacobo Israel Garzón always found time to answer our questions and shared his expertise on the intricacies of past and present Jewish communities in Spain and Morocco. Miguel de Lucas answered our many questions in Centro Sefarad–Israel in Madrid. Conversations throughout the years with many other people in Spain have shaped this project. We thank them for their generosity and their time: Assumpció Hosta Rebés in Girona; María Teresa Yurba in Toledo's Casa de Jacob; Anun Barriuso and José Manuel Loureiro in Madrid; Miguel Nieto, Pedro García, Jesús Sanabria, and Teddy Ramírez in Hervás; José Luis Chao, José Ramón Estévez, and Miguel García in Ribadavia; Lorenzo Rodriguéz in Castrillo Mota de Judíos; and Oriol Saula in Tárrega. As we were completing the last revisions of the manuscript in August 2019, we received the news of Santiago Palomero's passing. As director of the Museo Sefardí in Toledo, Santiago shared with us his wealth of knowledge and passion about the museum in several interviews throughout the years. We feel honored to have met him.

The research group Geneaologías de Sefarad has provided, since our first meeting in Soria in 2015, the perfect forum to share our research and writing. The intellectual camaraderie and warm friendship of Stacy Beckwith, Rina Benmayor, Michal Friedman, Dalia Kandiyoti, Tabea Linhard, and Asher Salah have illuminated our journeys. Special thanks go to Stacy and Tabea, who read the whole manuscript and provided us with erudite advice, and to Dalia Kandiyoti, Michal Friedman, and Allyson González, who read different chapters and greatly improved them as a result. We feel honored and humbled to contribute our piece to the puzzle we are all trying to figure out. We also deeply thank Alejandro Baer, Jo Labanyi, and Susan Martin-Márquez for their help, expertise, and inspiring work, which have accompanied us throughout the years.

This book would not have been written if not for the tireless support, intellectual exchange, and friendship of our dear colleagues at Stony Brook. Lou Charnon Deutsch read and edited with utmost patience early drafts of each long chapter. Kathleen Vernon was our chair while we completed the writing of most of the manuscript. Her advocacy on our behalf and her support were invaluable at many key moments. We deeply thank Lou and Katy for being the best mentors one could dream of. Gene Lebovics's work on French and US museums and Daniel Levy's work on collective memory were pivotal to the development of the book. We cannot thank them enough for their generous reading of early drafts of our work and their friendship and support. Our colleagues from inside and outside the department of Hispanic Languages and Literature: Lena Burgos-Lafuente, Paul Firbas, Joseph Pierce, Víctor Roncero López, Lilia Ruiz Debbe, Sally Sabo, Javier Uriarte, Aurelie Vialette, Lisa Dietrich, Vicky Hesford, E. Ann Kaplan, Shirley Lim, Sara Lipton, Judith Lochhead, Peter

Manning, Andrew Newman, Susan Schekel, Josh Teplitsky, Tracey Walters, Kathleen Wilson, and many others provided key insights, bibliography resources, and enthusiastic support throughout the years. Bill Piper has been a wonderful editor and reader, and his enthusiasm and good humor made the countless revisions worthwhile. While the best in this book may come from the contributions and inspiration we have received from all these colleagues and friends, we are the only ones responsible for any shortcomings it may have.

We deeply thank our families and close friends in Spain, Argentina, and the United States for always being there for us. Esther Pérez Melgosa accompanied us through some of our early trips to Hervás, Ribadavia, Toledo, and Segovia, providing help exactly when it was needed. Special thanks go to Celia Chactong for her unwavering support, no matter the circumstances. Many times with joy, many others with tired steps, our children, Ben, Sam, and Violet, have accompanied us from one town to another, into museums, out of historical buildings, and from one interview to another. Often, with the spontaneous access to deeper truths available to children, they decided that all the new people they were meeting on our trips were relatives from branches in our extended families they were just getting acquainted with for the first time. We thank them for their patience and joy, and we thank our collaborators and colleagues for their kind understanding that this project has been not only an intellectual endeavor but also a family affair.

Several of our research trips to Spain were made possible by Stony Brook University's FAHSS initiative and Distinguished Travel Awards. We thank our dean, Nicole Sampson, and our provost, now interim president, Michael Bernstein, for their support. We were able to complete most of the writing thanks to the time and support provided to Adrián from a Fall 2016 Humanities Institute at Stony Brook Faculty Fellowship and the support provided to Daniela from a 2014–15 ACLS Fellowship and a 2017–18 NEH Fellowship. Our deepest appreciation also goes to Ashante Thomas, Dee Mortensen, and the editors of the Indiana Series in Sephardi and Mizrahi Studies for their support of this project, and to Jamie Armstrong for her impeccable editing.

An early draft of parts of chapter 2 was published as "Marketing *Convivencia*: Contemporary Tourist Appropriations of Spain's Jewish Past" in *Spain Is (Still) Different: Tourism and Discourse in Spanish Cultural Identity,* edited by Eugenia Afinoguénova and Jaume Martí-Olivella (Lanham, MD: Lexington Books, 2008), and an early draft of parts of chapter 5 as "Hervás, *Convivencia,* and the Heritagization of Spain's Jewish Past" in *Journal of Romance Studies* 10, no. 2 (2010), 53–76. To all these individuals and institutions, we send our deepest gratitude.

THE MEMORY WORK OF JEWISH SPAIN

INTRODUCTION

The Memory Work of Jewish Spain

IN THE 1920S, SPANISH WRITER Rafael Cansinos Assens (1882–1964) titled one of his short stories "Amnesia ofensiva" [Offensive amnesia]. Its protagonist, a Sephardi Jew visiting Spain "from the Orient," confronts his local interlocutors with the painful paradox that in Spain, "no hay antisemitismo porque no hay semitismo, nos habéis olvidado y eso es lo más triste. Para vosotros no existimos" [there is no antisemitism, because there is no Semitism; you have forgotten us and that is the saddest thing. We do not exist for you] (Cansinos Assens 162). As a writer who tried to "reconnect" with Judaism after learning of his family's *converso* descent, Casinos Assens himself fell prey to this form of amnesia. His works, admired by his contemporaries, remain all but forgotten in the current canon of Spanish literature. In the context of early twentieth-century Spain, his notion of "offensive amnesia" reinterpreted the apparent absence of antisemitism among the people his protagonist meets as a peculiarly insidious form of prejudice, the result of a protracted and collective effort to systematically forget and erase the country's Jewish past.

Cansinos Assens's protagonist strives in vain to find concrete evidence of that past in Spanish cities that he identifies as "the settings of the old tragedy." Yet what distresses him the most is the fact that his interlocutors, those who inhabit streets, buildings, towns, and landscapes where Jewish people once lived, have developed a selective blindness, a specific forgetfulness toward that past. And by forgetting the Jews who lived there, they absolved themselves of any blame for their absence (Cansinos Assens 159–60).

And yet, the fact that Cansinos Assens could write about this amnesia in the 1920s was partly due to the fact that the Iberian Jewish past and the existence of peoples who were descendants of those Iberian Jews had become a topic of public discussion in Spain. As Allyson González argues, Cansinos Assens's own Jewish self-identification speaks of a time of profound change, of "complex desires for personal and national regeneration" (421–22). Since the mid-nineteenth century, historians in Spain had been reassessing the place of Jews in Spanish history (Friedman, "Reconstructing" and "Jewish History"; Bush). In 1860, in the context of the Hispano-Moroccan War, numerous articles in the Spanish press had commented on the fact that, upon entering the city of Tetuán, Spanish troops had encountered Jews who spoke to them in "old Spanish" (González García, *El retorno*). By the 1920s, the movement known as philosephardism had become well-established. The philosephardi campaigns sought to expand Spain's influence in the Mediterranean and advance its colonial ambitions in Morocco through the cultivation of links with Sephardi Jews. If philosephardism tried to remap the Sephardi communities of the eastern Mediterranean and Morocco into an imagined cartography of diasporic Spain, Cansinos Assens's story attempts to recontextualize Spain as a Jewish territory. As he walks in Toledo and Segovia, the story's protagonist sees faint traces of that Jewish past, although the people who live next to them do not have the means to see them. He registers the silence, oblivion, and resistance with which his interlocutors regard these traces and attempts to map these cities into a larger global Sephardi cartography.[1]

In 2015, almost one hundred years after Cansinos Assens wrote those lines, a popular Spanish television series, *El Ministerio del tiempo* [The ministry of time], uses the Iberian Jewish past as the foundational element of its central plot. In the series, a group of agents from a secret ministry with access to a series of "time portals" strive to thwart efforts from a variety of enemies to alter Spain's past and, therefore, its present. The fourth episode of the series, "Una negociación a tiempo" [A deal on time], reveals the origin of these "time doors." The doors were once an ancient secret held by Rabbi Abraham Levi, a (fictional) medieval Spanish Jew who recorded their location, access points, and protocols in the (also fictional) *Book of the Doors*. In 1491, while facing prosecution from the Inquisition, Levi gave the treasured book to Queen Isabel in exchange for her protection. Chief inquisitor Tomás de Torquemada eventually ordered Levi's execution by going behind Isabel's back, a detail the series makes a special effort to highlight, thus saving Isabel from suspicion of not having kept her word.[2] The episode centers on Levi's fictionalized present-day descendants and their threat to sue the Spanish government for the breach of Isabel's agreement with Levi. The descendants' lawyer, Aaron Stein, characterized by his arrogance and "marked American accent" (per the script), threatens to publicly reveal the ministry's secret existence unless Spain pays Levi's descendants $100 million and returns the book to them.

Throughout the episode, a clear-cut contrast develops between two Jewish characters: one is Levi, portrayed as a wise, venerable, and principled rabbi who lived in medieval Spain, where he discovered the time portal and wrote the *Book of the Doors*. The other is Stein, a self-interested present-day American lawyer who, propelled by economic interest, blackmails the resource-limited and well-meaning Spanish government. In this episode's culminating scene, agents of the ministry go back in time to rescue Levi from being burned at the stake and bring him to the present to face Stein. In a solemn voice, in Hebrew, the rabbi from the past admonishes the Jewish lawyer from the present to stop bringing shame to God with his demands.

This sharp contrast in the characterization of Levi and Stein condenses a current and widespread popular perception of Jews in Spain. On the one hand, present-day Jews, associated with the United States and Israel and mostly thought of as Ashkenazi (as in the surname *Stein*), embody the antisemitic tropes of self-interest, materialism, and cunning. On the other hand, medieval Jews like Levi embody the best of what Spain once was—a society anachronistically idealized as multicultural avant la lettre, culturally sophisticated, noble, and tolerant. In between these two polarities, present-day, living Sephardi Jews rarely enter the Spanish imagination except when they can be imagined as fitting the stereotype of descendants of medieval Iberian Jews who continue, after five centuries, speaking Spanish out of love and nostalgia for Spain (Díaz-Mas, *Sephardim* 153, 168). In this imaginary construct, the Jewishness of Sephardi Jews, with its negative connotations, is "compensated for" by their Spanishness. As we will see in chapter 1, this binary construction—present-day Jews bad, past Sephardi Jews good—has a long history that helps us understand how "offensive amnesia" shares space in Spain's cultural imaginary with discourses of antisemitism and philosephardism, all operating simultaneously and, frequently, in paradoxical combinations.[3]

In a qualitative sociological study undertaken with discussion groups across a variety of social, ideological, and age segments in 2009, Alejandro Baer found that people in Spain hold a prejudiced, deep-seated suspicion and conspiratorial view of Jews.[4] These findings confirmed the quantitative data gathered in a 2008 survey by the Pew Research Center, in which 46 percent of people in Spain admitted to having negative views of Jews. This percentage was the highest of any nation in Europe, a full 10 percent higher than that of the second country, Poland (36 percent). While unfavorable views of Jews—and Muslims—have been on the rise in all European countries surveyed, Spain surpassed them all by a wide margin. The survey concluded that Spain was the country with the most negative view of Jews among non-Muslim countries ("Unfavorable Views"). As Baer explains, what these statistics show is that "Spain lacks a taboo on expressing openly antisemitic opinions (and they may not even be considered as such)" ("Between Old and New" 107). Since most people in Spain know no Jews personally and are still installed in a widespread, willful amnesia about the country's Jewish past, their view of Jews is highly filtered by their negative views of Israel and the Israeli-Palestinian conflict (A. Baer "Tanques" 30–31).[5] Notwithstanding processes of secularization and modernization, Baer contends, Spain's antisemitism in the relative absence of Jews is still based in Spaniards' identification with Catholicism in a broad cultural sense (A. Baer, "Between Old and New" 108–10; Baer and López, "Blind Spots").[6]

And yet, Spain's relationship to Jews and Jewishness is filled with contradictions. We must wonder whether the results would have looked different if the survey had replaced the term *Jews* with *Sephardis*. Sephardi Jews reentered Spain's cultural imaginary with full force in the late 1980s, as Spain prepared for the Fifth Centenary of 1492 (the date Jews were formally expelled from the Spanish kingdoms). In connection with this anniversary, cultural and political initiatives sought to officially reconnect Spain with the Jewish world in general and with its own Sephardi heritage in particular. The Spanish central government and several autonomous communities began to sponsor an increasing number of educational courses, exhibitions, and conferences on Sephardi themes. They undertook the publication of books, periodicals, and brochures to disseminate accounts of Spain's Jewish past; opened Jewish-themed museums; organized film festivals; allocated funds to carry out archaeological research and excavations of Jewish sites; and showcased "Sephardi routes" throughout Spain's territory through the Red de Juderías de España / Caminos de Sefarad [Network of Jewish Quarters of Spain / Paths of Sepharad], a publicly funded organization that promotes Jewish tourism in Spain.

This new interest in reconnecting with Hispano-Jewish culture acquired the highest political visibility through the actions of the Spanish royal family, who, since the death of Francisco Franco in late 1975, have demonstrated interest in normalizing Spain's relations with the Jewish people (Rein 321–22; Álvarez Chillida, *El antisemitismo* 461). In 1990, the Prince of Asturias Award for Concord (Princess of Asturias Award since 2015) was given to the Sephardi Communities, and in 1992, King Juan Carlos symbolically welcomed the descendants of the once expelled Jews back "home" in a landmark speech at the Beth Yaacov Synagogue in Madrid. Several other official gestures and initiatives have followed: In 1999, Spain joined in the celebration of the "European

Day of Jewish Culture," a project sponsored by the Council of Europe. In 2004, the Spanish government instituted January 27 as the official day of "Remembrance of the Holocaust and the Prevention of Crimes against Humanity." In 2006, the Cervantes Institute opened a Ladino department to promote the preservation of this language and of the culture of Sephardi Jews, and several universities and research institutes throughout Spain now have Sephardi studies departments or study groups. In 2007, the Prince of Asturias Award for Concord was given to Yad Vashem, the Holocaust Museum in Jerusalem. That same year, the Ministry of Foreign Affairs and Cooperation opened the Centro Sefarad-Israel (initially known as Casa Sefarad-Israel) in Madrid, a center that promotes the understanding of Sephardi and Jewish culture in general and fosters Spanish-Israeli relations (Flesler, Linhard, and Pérez Melgosa 2).

Every Sunday morning since 2008, Spanish national television (TVE) has broadcast *Shalom*, a program dedicated to news and information about Jewish life in Spain. In 2009, the Spanish National Radio (RNE) started weekly broadcasts of two Jewish-themed programs, *Luz de Sefarad* and *La voz de la Torá*. This is also the year in which the Federation of Jewish Communities of Spain founded Radio Sefarad, a mostly web-based broadcasting service that also collaborates closely with and at times produces the audiovisual programs for TVE aforementioned. The much-publicized 2015 law granting Spanish nationality to the descendants of Jews expelled in 1492 is the latest example of this widespread phenomenon in contemporary Spain, the "rediscovery" of its Jewish heritage. This book examines the implications of Spain's current efforts to reclaim the memory of Sepharad through the analysis of a comprehensive range of cultural practices, political initiatives, and institutions.

The Sepharad evoked in these initiatives points to both a place and a time. It is the traditional name used by Iberian Jews to refer to the Iberian Peninsula and the Hebrew word for Spain. It also, and perhaps more powerfully, refers to a constructed imaginary geography in which the Iberian Peninsula stands, among other things, for the often idealized era when Jews inhabited Iberia prior to 1492.[7] To many people in Spain today, the name *Sepharad* projects an aura of mystery and desirability over the territory they inhabit. In a spirit that goes hand in hand with the centrality of tourism in the country's economy, *Sepharad* allows Spain to see itself as the land desired by others and also to re-present itself to the world as a country with a long, esteemed tradition of religious tolerance. Since the death of Franco, whose long dictatorship (1939–75) had promoted an idea of Spain based on the values of unity, homogeneity, Catholicism, and empire, the repurposing of the memory of Sepharad has played a pivotal role in the process of rehabilitating Spain's international image. Post-Francoist democratic Spain has sought to reconstruct an identity for the nation based on the principles of multiculturalism, respect for difference, and religious tolerance.[8] Communities throughout the country, as well as the nation as a whole, reclaim their status as heirs to Sepharad in an effort to showcase their full belonging to modernity and western Europe.

Today, all things Sepharad are marketed throughout Spain, from cultural festivals, museums, historical synagogues, and Jewish Quarters to novels, music, pastries, and cookbooks. Offensive amnesia has given way to a variety of memory practices that are complex, frequently contradictory, and often resulting in unforeseen resignifications. At the local, regional, and national levels, the deployment and celebration of the concept of medieval *convivencia*, the idealized understanding of the "living together" of "the three [Abrahamic] cultures" (Christians, Muslims, and Jews) in the Iberian Peninsula, have especially served the purpose of presenting different localities and the country as a whole as heirs to an exemplary tradition of tolerance and as experienced players in global political and religious conflicts. In conjunction with important transformations in the religious and ethnic makeup of the population due to immigration from Latin America, Africa, and Asia; bitter disagreements about the memory of the Spanish Civil War and the Francoist repression; ongoing arguments about the independence of Catalonia; and in the context of enduring religious conflicts in the Middle East, convivencia serves as an all-purpose symbolic currency (Martin-Márquez 303, Flesler, Linhard and Pérez Melgosa 4). This evocation of convivencia not only avoids confronting the complex and often conflictive history of the three cultures' interaction in medieval Iberia but also avoids acknowledging the specific political use of the legacy of Arab and Jewish Spain before and during the Franco era as a justification and legitimization of Spanish colonialism in Morocco (see Martin-Márquez; Ojeda Mata, "'Spanish' but 'Jewish'"; and Calderwood).[9]

SPAIN'S JEWISH SPACES

The sudden surge of interest in the organization of Jewish-themed activities and initiatives partakes in what Diana Pinto has characterized as the reinscription of a European "Jewish space"—that is, the gradual reemergence of Jewish culture in European political and social discourses, including in areas where Jews have not lived since World War II.[10] From a more critical perspective, Y. Michal Bodemann calls attention to the centrality of non-Jewish actors in the circulation of Jewish cultural motifs and practices across Germany and eastern Europe. He refers to them and their cultural practices as part of a "Judaisierendes milieu" (Judaizing terrain or environment), implicitly marking the constructed nature of space and the important role culture plays in shaping it (Bodemann, "Reemergence" 57–58). Ruth Ellen Gruber analyzes similar phenomena, looking at the promotion of Jewish heritage precisely in locations where Jews and Jewish culture had been completely annihilated, and where, in the present, there are very small and nearly invisible Jewish populations and widespread ignorance of and prejudice against Jews (*Virtually* 5, 13). Spain's initiatives share many of the political, social, and cultural characteristics described by Pinto, Bodemann, and Gruber. But they also embody a very distinct set of cultural tensions and contradictions, as we will see throughout this book.

One could dismiss these initiatives and developments as originating mostly from official governments at the national, regional, and local levels that see them as advantageous for tourism or political and diplomatic purposes. Indeed, one could argue that many of these rapprochements with Jews and Spain's Jewish history are highly self-interested gestures that began during the Francoist dictatorship and, thus, do not necessarily convey real inclusion or a tolerant attitude. In themselves, these initiatives neither imply a truthful attempt to confront Spain's antisemitic past nor signify a desire to establish a meaningful relationship with "real" Jews. In Spain, it is easy to come across shallow, opportunistic, and antisemitic Jewish-themed commentary, activities, and displays. This fact was best encapsulated for us in an anecdote from a former councilman in one of the towns we visited while researching for this book when he told us that he cared about his town's past Jewish heritage but only insofar as it was good for the economy of his town; he could not care less about present-day Jews and only "wanted their money."

This is an opinion echoed in more or less subtle ways in many other voices across Spain. But after traveling extensively in Spain while researching this topic for the last fifteen years, we consider this point of view to be only part of the story. Jewish-related phenomena in Spain today form a much more complex ecosystem, as we hope to show in the chapters that follow. It is one in which even the apparent frankness with which self-serving arguments are expressed function as a shortcut for more complex reasons that participants find more difficult to voice. At the same time, once set in motion, the renewed, broad public attention to Spain's Jewish heritage by a variety of social actors has also brought to the fore personal and community stories, affects, and aspirations, unleashing a series of unexpected consequences. While in Spain Jews have been seen for centuries as doubly remote and foreign (belonging to the past and living in other countries), the wide public circulation of new narratives that place Spain's Jews at their center and the collective and personal discoveries these narratives have initiated have brought forth a far more unsettling possibility to those who come in contact with this information: "What if the Jews had never left? What if we are the Jews?"

At the national level, official initiatives use the memory of Jewish Spain as a tool for diplomatic relations with the United States and Israel by linking Spain with Sephardi Jewish communities seen as the descendants of "those who left." But when activated at the local level in cities and towns, these same initiatives have brought to the fore the issue of conversos and thus the link of current inhabitants of Spain to "those who stayed." While analyzing cultural and political initiatives around the memory of Jewish Spain, we attempt to describe the "landscapes of memory" in which these initiatives emerge and, most crucially, to grapple with these "consequences of memory" (Young, *Texture* ix, 13; *Memory's Edge* 11): the multiple manifestations and developments, at both the local and individual levels, that these initiatives have produced.

One of the most explicit embodiments of this unsettling of identity and direct questioning of the traditional understanding of Jews as foreigners to Spain is found among a small yet significant group of people who have begun to connect with or "return" to Judaism either out of personal interest or because they claim descendance from Jews forced to convert to Christianity. In the Iberian context, conversos were those Jews who converted to Christianity in the fourteenth and fifteenth centuries. There had been cases of voluntary conversions in Spain beginning in the thirteenth century, in a climate of mounting Christian evangelization pressures. But the large number of conversions that occurred at the end of the fourteenth century, as a result of the massacres of 1391, and then again in the wake of 1492 were unprecedented among Jewish communities in Europe. As Jonathan Ray has explained, the phenomenon of the conversos, as well as the blurring of the lines between Christianity and Judaism it produced, "represents one of the most important and enduring legacies of the Jewish presence in medieval Iberia" (*After Expulsion* 160).[11]

As Stuart Hall reminds us, identity, like memory, is not something that can be "discovered" or "recovered," but something that is continually in production and practiced in particular social and cultural contexts (222). The stories communities tell about their pasts are of utmost importance in this process, especially in terms of how these stories affect people belonging to particular groups and communities. As Hall puts it, "far from being grounded in a mere 'recovery' of the past, which is waiting to be found . . . identities are the names we give to the different ways we are positioned by, and position ourselves within, the narratives of the past" (225). It is in this sense of an intervention in a much larger process of reevaluation of cultural identity that we see current identifications and claims of Jewish identity and several other interrelated phenomena in Spain. Claiming this identity takes many forms, from educating themselves about Jewish culture and history to converting to Judaism.[12] As a variety of communities engage in their specific forms of reconnection with Jewish Spain, they find in this local past a means of repositioning themselves within the present identitary map of the Iberian Peninsula. In doing so, they also find that they must position themselves within the narratives of a past that, although initially invoked as benign and glorious, soon proves to be plagued with difficult memories of violence, victimization, and suffering.

Maurice Halbwachs has famously argued that memory is constituted through social frameworks. Andreas Huyssen reminds us that "the act of remembering is always in and of the present" (*Present Pasts* 3). Jan Assmann speaks of memory as "the ongoing work of reconstructive imagination" (14). The "family memories" of those who suspect they have converso ancestry have emerged as part of this memory landscape of public rediscovery, reevaluation, and reconstruction of Spain's Jewish heritage. The Jewish/Christian identity of the conversos has become one of the means by which different communities in Spain can interpret—or appropriate, in a process of "imaginative rediscovery" (Hall 224)—the material Jewish legacy of Spain as their own and Sepharad as their new inheritance.

In the last twenty-five years, cities and towns throughout Spain have excavated and rediscovered their medieval Jewish quarters and cemeteries as part of a process of urban revitalization often driven by the hope of increasing a town's tourism appeal and value. These sites are now part of the urban space in towns and cities that are recognizing and rendering visible their long-disregarded Jewish history in the form of monuments, street signs, and commemorations. The process of making these spaces visible has subsequently triggered a new awareness of these local populations' histories. Suddenly, familiar spaces are seen in a new light.

For the last fifteen years, we have traveled extensively in Spain documenting the ways various cities and towns have facilitated, or not, the production of a Jewish space in their midst. We have visited Lucena, Córdoba, Sevilla, Cáceres, Béjar, Hervás, Ávila, Madrid, Toledo, Segovia, Alcalá de Henares, Burgos, Castrillo Mota de Judíos (formerly Castrillo Matajudíos), Zaragoza, Tarazona, Tudela, Ribadavia, Barcelona, Lérida, Tárrega, and Girona. We were part of the increasing number of visitors looking for the traces of Jewish history in these cities and towns. We often wondered, and joked about, the potential influence of our own visits on the data and numbers that these cities' tourist offices were gathering about international visitors "looking for Jewish stuff." In several cases, we witnessed significant changes in the way these cities have come to see and present themselves. For example, when we visited Lucena in 2004 and asked in the tourist office about Jewish sites or traces of the history of the city's important medieval Jewish community, we were told that there was nothing to see. In 2016, visiting the city again, we took a tour of the medieval Jewish cemetery "discovered" in 2006 and opened to the public in 2013 after 346 tombs were excavated and human remains were reburied in a ceremony officiated by Jewish authorities. Ubiquitous signs now point out the Jewish heritage of the city, and many social actors have brought back into circulation the city's Hebrew name, Eliossana.

As we describe in chapter 2, our guide in Lucena told us that she frequently brought lucentinos to visit the cemetery. The cemetery has been incorporated into the city landscape as part of a popular walk up the hill that people often take, especially on weekends. The guide talked about how she had learned much about the city's Jewish history through the stories Jewish international visitors had told her. Some people, she explained, visit Lucena because their ancestors came from here. She commented on how incredible it was that someone coming from another country to visit the city for the first time would know more about her city's history than she did. She also relayed many stories of Lucena's inhabitants' reevaluating what this new knowledge meant to them personally.

This reevaluation, or process of seeing again, differently, their own city, is the basis of the project Benjamín de Sefarad, sponsored by the Red de Juderías and spearheaded by Lucena. Named in honor of Benjamín de Tudela, the famed twelfth-century traveler and geographer, this initiative consists of exchanges between high school students from member cities in the Red de Juderías who visit each other's cities. Through interactive activities, the host students introduce those visiting to their own city's Jewish heritage and history. In the process, the local students make their town's Jewish history theirs. One participating student explained the effect of talking about the historic Jewish quarter in Seville: "Antes de este proyecto para mí no era tan famoso el barrio de Santacruz; se nos está proporcionando la oportunidad de conocer más sobre nuestra propia capital y saber cosas que nosotros antes ni siquiera pensábamos" [Before this project I didn't know much about the Santa Cruz neighborhood; we are being given the opportunity to know more about our own capital city and learning things that we didn't even think about before] (in M. González).

These are some of the subtle ways in which these cities' inhabitants are experiencing familiar spaces in novel ways and thus contributing to a shift in the understanding of what these spaces signify. In their introduction to the book

Jewish Topographies, Julia Brauch, Anna Lipphardt, and Alexandra Nocke characterize Jewish spaces as Other spaces. They explain, "Jewish spaces are 'Other' spaces. 'Other' spaces challenge conventional conventions of place and space, which, to a large extent . . . still rest on the paradigm of a homogeneous nation-state. . . . Exploring Jewish topographies thus also allows for new, subversive perspectives on the places and spaces of the majority society and for rethinking spatial assumptions that have been taken for granted" (3). In *The Production of Space*, Henri Lefebvre develops the concept of "lived space" as shifting networks of relationships across and with geographic and urban places which overlay physical space: space, he says, is a social product, and a spatial code "is a means of living in that space, of understanding it, and of producing it" (47–48). Similarly, Michel de Certeau speaks of space as created by users: "the act of walking . . . is a process of appropriation of the topographical system on the part of the pedestrian" (97).

As a growing number of cities across Spain incorporate new signage identifying current spaces as locations where Jewish life once existed, the people walking through them find themselves having to re-create their relation to these very spaces and to position themselves in relation to the identities newly evoked by them. As Huyssen explains, urban spaces can be read "as lived spaces that shape collective imaginaries" (*Present Pasts* 7). These interventions are also performing a reconfiguration of the images and symbols through which current inhabitants of Spain "live" those spaces. Edward Soja redefined Lefebvre's "lived space" as a "Thirdspace" that is both abstract and concrete, real and imagined (Soja 11). Thirdspace contains the potentiality of a contestation and renegotiation of boundaries. If Jewish spaces are "environments where Jewish things happen, where Jewish activities are performed" and Jewish places are "locations identified by their connections (historic, performative, legal) to Jewish communities across the globe" (Baruch, Lipphardt, and Nocke 4), newer ways of imagining and living space and place in these cities and towns have the potentiality of opening up a Thirdspace challenging traditional understandings of local and national identity.

An anecdote from our visit to Ávila in 2014 illustrates the challenge that these Other spaces pose to conventional, customary understandings of national and local identity. Ávila is popularly known as the birthplace of the sixteenth-century Carmelite nun Saint Teresa and for its impressive medieval city walls. After the local medieval cemetery was "discovered" in 2012, much as in Lucena, the city began a process of excavation and rehabilitation of this space. We traveled to Ávila with the purpose of exploring how this space, now called "Garden of Sepharad," figured in the life of the city. When we asked how to get there, the tourist office employee told us that we should not bother, that there was really "nothing to see there," and that we should visit the city's cathedral and the many beautiful churches instead. We couldn't help but laugh thinking of what the city's mayor would think about this particular answer, after the city allocated considerable municipal resources and efforts to the restoration project. In September 2013, during a high-profile inauguration ceremony, Spanish and European Jewish authorities lauded the rehabilitation of this space as a reparation for centuries of injustice.[13]

Official, public, and vernacular forms of memory converge in such sites and celebrations. Daniel Levy, Michael Heinlein, and Lars Breuer explain how official forms of memory entail state-centered discourses and commemorative events, public forms of memory are constructed and reproduced by representations in the media and in cultural texts in general and vernacular forms of memory provide a perspective "from below," showing how particular groups react to official and public discourses. Our book attempts to show the interplay between these three distinct, interrelated, and at times competing levels. In the process, we try to locate the possible effects of these initiatives on a population with various degrees of information about and engagement with its Jewish heritage, on Jewish tourists who participate in them, and on the larger discussion about the place of Jews and Jewish culture in post-Holocaust Europe. In this way, this book attempts to articulate the complexities and richness of Spain's memory landscape in relation to Sepharad.

SPAIN'S MEMORY LANDSCAPE

While initially invoked as a shortcut to repositioning Spain as a central player in the global arenas of multiculturalism and modernity, or even as an opportunistic ploy to bring tourists to cities of Spain's interior that had not previously benefited from the sun-and-beach-based tourist boom, the initiatives surrounding the memory of Jewish Spain are in fact functioning as part of an ongoing collective memory work. Jeffrey Olick has explained collective memory as "publicly available symbols and meanings about the past" (*Politics* 6). In the 1990s in Spain there was a temporal coincidence in the development of different discourses of memory: the reengagement with the memory of Jewish Spain, the arrival of a discourse of Holocaust remembrance, and the emergence of a critical reevaluation of the democratic transition and subsequent activism about the previously unrecognized victims of the Civil War and the Francoist repression. This last process of reevaluation of the transition and Francoist victims is what people in Spain refer to when they speak today about "the recuperation of historical memory."

Michael Rothberg developed the concept of *multidirectional memory* to refer to "the dynamic transfers between diverse places and times in the process of remembrance," to the fact that memory is "subject to ongoing negotiation, cross-referencing, and borrowing" (11, 3). What we see in the case of these initiatives that engage with Spain's Jewish past is proof of the paradoxical nature of this multidirectionality: each initiative models itself on and serves as a model for other initiatives to be organized and put forth in the public arena, but together with their stated goal to recognize and honor these communities' Jewish past, each initiative resonates with long histories of antisemitism and philosephardism, with various attempts to bring Jews back and with reiterated fears of Jewish return.[14]

As Sepharad has become an element of symbolic exchange across Spain, initiatives connected to it have become disputed arenas in which nationalist and essentialist notions of identity clash with a desire to partake in ongoing global celebrations of cultural diversity and a recognition of new European imperatives. Even when guided by self-interest, in exploring these memories these communities participate in the processes of circulation and negotiation of what Daniel Levy and Natan Sznaider have called "cosmopolitan memories." In these processes, memories not only travel across national borders but "are also negotiated with reference to narratives generated outside the nation" (Levy and Sznaider, *Human Rights* 134). Multidirectionality, thus, becomes not only a path toward the opening up and channeling of past grievances and silenced memories but also a process that once set in motion produces paradoxical, multivocal, and frequently contradictory effects.

As a mnemonic transnational symbol, the Holocaust was pivotal in the development of transitional political processes, international law, and politics of memory during the 1990s. Levy and Sznaider explain how "memories of the Holocaust have evolved into a universal code that is now synonymous with an imperative to address past injustices (both legally as well as in commemorative terms)" (*Human Rights* 4). These globalized norms demand a confrontation with difficult pasts, rejection of impunity, state accountability, and public inclusion of past regime victims (Golob 127). This code not only prescribes what should be done during a society's transition from an authoritarian to a democratic government but, most importantly for post-transition societies like Spain's, also encompasses "what should not be left undone and must be corrected over time" (Golob 130). This moral mandate to correct over time something left undone, even in the case of a significant temporal gap, is a factor of utmost importance not only in the case of Spain's reevaluation of the late 1970s transition to democracy but also in the case of a pivotal event for this book: the public remembrance and reevaluation of an event much further removed in time, the 1492 expulsion of the Jews.

The belated nature of Spain's memory culture in relation to the recognition of the victims of the Republican side of the Spanish Civil War (1936–39) and the Francoist dictatorship (1939–75) emerged from the fact that these deaths were not publicly recognized either during the dictatorship or in the transition to democracy. This memory was "forced to remain a private matter until very recently" (Labanyi, "Politics" 120). The transition was based on a political pact of future-oriented consensus, in discourses of "shared blame," and a 1977 amnesty law for both anti-Francoist political prisoners and Francoist perpetrators. Its objective, articulated in the 1978 constitution, was the consolidation of a peaceful transition. But the price of peace was that Francoism would not be put on trial. Stability, not justice, was privileged (Aguilar Fernández; Ruiz Torres), so the result was "a transition *without* transitional justice" (Golob 127, italics in original).

This consensus began to be questioned in the mid-1990s in books like Paloma Aguilar Fernández's *Memoria y olvido de la Guerra Civil española* (1996). When, in 1998, Spanish judge Baltasar Garzón indicted the Chilean dictator Augusto Pinochet for human rights violations, the public opinion impact of this news was enormous. Many people began to publicly compare the crimes committed by Pinochet with those committed in Spain by Franco. Seeing the irony of a nation that was righteous enough to bring foreign dictators to justice but had given amnesty to the leaders responsible for or were complicit in Francoist crimes, the descendants of Republican victims found a new way to express their demands. Emilio Silva, who would become a leader in the movement protesting the impunity of Francoism, explicitly connected the two cases in an article entitled "Mi abuelo también fue un desaparecido" [My grandfather was also a disappeared] published in 2000 (Baer and Sznaider, "Ghosts" 337; Ferrándiz, "De las fosas" 171; Labanyi, "Languages" 27). The Pinochet case became famous worldwide for its transnational nature, showing an incipient globalization of justice. But as Golob remarks, the case not only demonstrated the capacity of the law to transcend space through the principle of universal jurisdiction for crimes against humanity but also transcended time by superseding the Chilean 1978 amnesty and 1980 constitution. The Pinochet case was key to Spain's own political process because it judged not an ongoing transition but "the damage done over time by impunity" (Golob 131).

In the year 2000, Emilio Silva led the first public excavation of a wartime mass grave with the help of an archaeologist and a forensic anthropologist. He was looking for the remains of his grandfather, killed by Falangists (those belonging to Falange Española, Spain's fascist party) in October 1936, at the beginning of the Civil War, in Priaranza del Bierzo, in the province of León. That same year, Silva created with Santiago Macías the Association for the Recovery of Historical Memory (ARHM), an association that seeks support to fund exhumations and facilitate the recovery and reburial of the human remains of Civil War and Francoist victims executed and left in mass graves.[15] As part of the process of drawing attention to and reconceptualizing the memory of the victims of Francoism, the ARHM has relied on this transnational language of human rights, especially as it has been shaped in Chile and Argentina.[16] When in 2008 judge Baltazar Garzón attempted to indict Francoism on the basis of this international human rights frame, his case foregrounded the concept of forced disappearances and the systematic stealing of babies belonging to Republican mothers.[17] Both of these issues had gained international recognition after they were articulated in relation to the Argentine Dirty War (Ferrándiz, "De las fosas" 168, 183). The use of images of the disappeared in Spain's public protests against impunity also trace their roots to the efforts of the Mothers of May in Argentina to recover their sons and daughters.

The discourse of human rights in Argentina, which has been permeated by the legal and symbolic modes of addressing the atrocities of the Holocaust, provided a point of entry for the Holocaust in Spain's memory landscape.[18] Thus, explain Baer and Sznaider, "through Argentina as well as through Spain's Europeanization, the Holocaust has found its way to the mass graves of Francoism" (Baer and Sznaider, "Ghosts" 330). Associations like the ARHM, as well as Francoist victims and their supporters, many historians, and writers, refer to the Holocaust in order to describe the magnitude and systematic nature of Francoist repression and to bolster their claims to deserve public recognition.

Thus, since the late 1990s, both knowledge about the Holocaust and a reevaluation of the Francoist past have become linked in a wider public discussion about the process of recuperation of historical memory in Spain.[19] Simultaneously, as we saw, a variety of efforts to recover Spain's Jewish past were being articulated at the national level. Although frequently seen as unrelated events, the celebration of a tolerant past championed by Jewish-themed initiatives should be considered part and parcel of this memory landscape (see Linhard 189–90).[20]

In the year 2000, the same year that the ARHM was founded, Spain joined the Stockholm International Forum on the Holocaust and signed a commitment, together with other European nations, to develop appropriate forms of remembrance of and education about the Holocaust. Since then, the Autonomous Community of Madrid began hosting a commemorative ceremony annually. Following the Socialist Party's victory in 2004, the ceremonies became officially sponsored by the central government through the Ministry of Foreign Affairs. It is not a coincidence that, as Baer explains, the name given to the ceremony is the Official Day of the Memory of the Holocaust and Prevention of Crimes against Humanity ("The Voids" 100–101). It is through this universalizing frame of human rights that the ceremony has been held as a forum open to different groups of victims—namely, not only Jews, but also Romani people and Republicans.[21]

As Baer notes, the memory of the Holocaust in Spain is necessarily conditioned by "the forgotten traces of Sepharad." Evoking Walter Benjamin's proposition that "every document of civilization is also a document of barbarism," Baer ponders on the still unuttered Benjaminian "illuminations" that may surface if Spain were to commemorate the Holocaust on March 31, the date of the 1492 Edict of Expulsion of the Jews from Spain, instead of the internationally agreed-on date of January 27, the date of the liberation of Auschwitz. The voids and burdens of Sepharad, concludes Baer, constitute "a specifically Spanish memory of the Holocaust" ("The Voids" 114).[22] This book attempts to contribute to the discussion of contemporary Spain's memory landscape by examining the presence of those voids and burdens through a sustained look at how different social actors and institutions throughout Spain engage with the memory of Jewish Spain.

SEPHARAD AND SPAIN, 1992–2015

In 1992, Spain commemorated the Fifth Centenary of the expulsion of the Jews in 1492. In 2015, the Spanish government approved the law of nationality for the descendants of Spanish Jews who were forced into exile. Both events drew considerable international media attention and interest, and they stand as milestones marking key transformations in the way Spain has responded to the unsolved cultural and social legacies of the 1492 expulsion.

In 1992, seventeen years after Franco's death, Spain presented itself to the world as a fully democratic, modern society actively participating in international partnerships. The stage for the reintroduction of this new and improved Spain was provided by three major international events: the Olympic Games in Barcelona, the World's Fair in Seville, and the yearlong tenure of Madrid as a "European City of Culture." The year 1992 also marked the Fifth Centenary of 1492, celebrated in multiple ways. The common thread centered on an uncritical marking of the anniversary of Columbus's voyage to the Americas and, secondarily, of the Fall of Muslim Granada and the Expulsion of the Jews. The official events of 1992 were characterized by the glorification of the present and the neglect of any critical discussion about the past (Graham and Sánchez 406).[23] Yet the celebrations of 1492 could not help placing back into national discourse many unresolved issues related to the historic emergence of Spain as an empire during the early modern period. An examination of the ceremony in commemoration of the expulsion reveals how the transition's emphasis on avoiding conflict and looking toward the future had become the main strategy for dealing with Spain's difficult pasts. If the transition relied on a pact of consensus and political amnesty, the events of 1992 were defined as a "reencounter with the Jews" along the lines of a conciliatory convivencia, neglecting to express any sense of collective responsibility for the intolerance that resulted in their expulsion.

The strategy of focusing on reencounter and convivencia attempted to forestall international efforts to bring attention to the expulsion and its aftermath from the perspective of those forced into exile. In 1986, the same year that Spain and Israel established diplomatic relations, Spain's Ministry of Foreign Affairs received information from Tel Aviv and New York about the preparations for 1992 that were being planned by international Jewish organizations. Spain quickly decided to intervene and become an active participant in these projects in order to make sure that they aligned with its interests. Thus, in March 1987, the government created the commission Sepharad '92: The Re-Discovery of Jewish Spain. The choice of the word *discovery*, with its association with Columbus's trip, already declared the official intention to revisit Spain's Jewish past and the present of Sephardi communities as one more element in the celebration of early imperial Spain (Lisbona 350–52).

According to diplomatic records examined by José Antonio Lisbona, Spain wanted to make sure that "the Jewish centers of power in the US" did not "atizar los elementos negativos como el recuerdo de la expulsión, de la persecución inquisitorial, de la intolerancia, de los aspectos negativos del pasado colonial" [stir up negative elements like the memory of the expulsion, Inquisitorial persecution, intolerance, and negative aspects of the colonial past] (351). It was in this context that King Juan Carlos visited a synagogue for the first time, the Tifereth Sephardi Synagogue in Los Angeles, on a visit with the queen to the US West Coast in October 1987 (Lisbona 354–55).[24] A few months later, Jewish community leaders organized a visit of prominent US Jewish authorities to Spain, in order to plan for 1992. Spain was hoping for, and expecting, a substantial monetary contribution from the US in order to undertake a variety of projects, from the rehabilitation of Jewish Quarters and the construction of public monuments to the organizing of exhibitions and the publication of books. But the US contribution did not materialize (Lisbona 355–56).

In 1990, the Prince of Asturias Award for Concord was given to the Sephardi Communities. At the ceremony, Prince Felipe addressed a delegation of Sephardi Jews and described how "desde el espíritu de concordia de la España de hoy, y como heredero de quienes hace 500 años firmaron el decreto de expulsión, yo los recibo con los brazos abiertos y con una gran emoción" [in the spirit of reconciliation of today's Spain, and as heir of those who signed the expulsion decree 500 years ago, I receive you with open arms and great emotion] (Cuartas, "Felipe"). In his open mention of his personal filiation with the perpetrators of the expulsion and in his explicit use of the word *expulsion,* Felipe went further in the direction of acknowledging a wrong committed by Spain than his father would ever go.

The highest-profile act of 1992, presented as "the reencounter of the King with Spanish Jews," took place on March 31, the date of the proclamation of the Decree of Expulsion five hundred years earlier, at the Beth Yaacov Synagogue in Madrid. Presided over by Juan Carlos, it was the first time the king visited a synagogue in Spain. It was also the first state visit of the Israeli president Haim Herzog to Spain. The carefully orchestrated ceremony was preceded by long negotiations involving Spain's Jewish representatives and the Spanish and Israeli governments. At the center of these negotiations stood a profound disagreement about how to deal with the difficult past. Jewish voices outside Spain, including Nobel Prize winner Elie Wiesel, had requested that the ceremony include a formal, official abrogation of the 1492 Decree of Expulsion. Spain's government had responded that the decree had been de facto repealed by the establishment of freedom of religion in the constitution of 1869 and that no further action was required. This was the same answer that the Francoist government had offered in 1968 (Rozenberg 210).

The Spaniards saw the ceremony as a "reencounter" while the Israelis saw it as a "reconciliation" (Rozenberg 325). Spanish diplomats resented the Israeli characterization, rejecting the idea that Spain, five hundred years after 1492, had "something to repair or amend" (Lisbona 362).[25] In consequence, no apology for the expulsion was offered. The king in fact did not mention the word *expulsion* in his speech. He said the present *encuentro* [encounter] was commemorating a past *desencuentro* [failed encounter, disagreement]. The Jews "had to leave Spain," he explained, "como consecuencia de una razón de Estado que veía el fundamento de su unidad en la uniformidad religiosa" [in consequence of a reason of state that saw religious uniformity as the basis of its unity] (Lisbona 369).[26]

The most-quoted part of the king's speech was his phrase "Sefarad no es ya una nostalgia, sino un hogar en el que no debe decirse que los judíos se sientan como en su propia casa, porque los hispano-judíos están en su propia casa" [Sefarad is not a nostalgia anymore, but a home in which it should not be said that Jews can feel as if they were in their own house, because Hispano-Jews are in their own house] (Cembrero). The phrase's double negation (we should not allude to nostalgia in reference to Sepharad, we should not say that Sephardis feel as if they were in their house) reveals Spanish authorities' anxiety about controlling the terms of this highly symbolic ceremony. In effect, the discourse was an attempt to establish the limits of what could and could not be said in the newly democratic Spain about Sepharad and about the king's and the country's relation to its legacy. As Olick has explained, political speech about the past shapes and is shaped by the symbols and cultural frameworks available at specific times and places (*Politics* 7).

These limits are not exclusively set by the Spanish government. In these commemoration ceremonies, Sephardi representatives and the Federation of Jewish Communities of Spain have had a crucial role. Bodemann has argued that acts of remembrance "take place first and foremost in theatrical settings: there is an audience, a stage, there are actors, there is a stage set, and the play, the drama itself" ("Reconstructions" 181). Writing about German commemorations as "theaters of memory," he explains that these events "need Jewish actors; not lead actors, however, but extras" (Bodemann, "Reconstructions" 196). In the commemorations' representation of collective memory, Jewish actors, by their participation and acceptance of their role as secondary, become good citizens. They provide the state with what Bodemann calls "ideological labor," that is, by performing a specific ideological function on behalf of the state ("Reconstructions" 209, 212; "State" 37). In the case of postwar Germany, "the mere physical presence of Jews in Germany could be seen as proof that West Germany was different from Nazi Germany" (Bodemann, "State" 44).

In a similar fashion, the mere presence of Sephardi representatives in the commemoration ceremonies of 1990 and 1992 lent the acts considerable legitimacy as proof that Spain had left its intolerance far behind. This intolerance implicitly referred not only to the persecution of Jews and Muslims in the medieval and early modern period but also to the Francoist dictatorship. The fact that the authority presiding over the 1992 ceremony was the king instead of the president actually reinforced the historical connection of present and past Spain through the monarchy's own family genealogy. This was precisely the point that Prince Felipe had explicitly remarked on two years earlier. In 1990, the Sephardi representatives who received the award expressed through the poem in Judeo-Spanish "A Espania" their unending love for Spain and their lack of resentment for Spain's past actions against them. The poem, read in

Judeo-Spanish by Rabbi Salomón Gaón, head of the World Sephardi Federation, served as a powerful exculpation of Spanish guilt, even when no official apology for the expulsion was extended.

In 1992, an overwhelmingly conciliatory tone dominated the speeches of the representatives of Spain's Jewish communities, a gesture that went along with the wishes of the Spanish government. None of the speeches asked for the official abrogation of the Edict of Expulsion, nor did they explore the possibility that Spain had a debt to pay—even a moral one—to the descendants of those expelled or to the Jewish community in general. Each speech was screened and approved by Spanish diplomats in advance (Lisbona 365). All speeches echoed the official message of celebrating a modern and democratic Spain which should look at the future instead of the past (Lisbona 367–68). If there was a lesson to be learned from the past, it was the mythical idea of convivencia, now put to ideological use as an aspirational goal for the future.[27]

Twenty years later, the discourses surrounding the announcement of a law of nationality for Sephardi Jews in 2012 and its eventual approval in 2015 show certain continuities with but also major differences from the narratives disseminated during the events of 1992. If one of the messages of the 1992 celebrations was that Spain had nothing to repair in regard to the expulsion, when the law of nationality was announced, both Spanish officials and the leaders of the Federation of Jewish Communities of Spain emphasized its restorative nature and its intention to bring closure to a five-hundred-year-long situation of injustice.

What changed in the intervening years? Between these two events, as we saw in the previous section, Spain's memory culture became incorporated into the "cosmopolitan memory" phenomenon, a transnational understanding of memory as the imperative to address past injustices in legal and commemorative terms (Levy and Sznaider). The development of this new memory landscape led Spain to embrace its own version of a strategic "politics of regret" (Olick), in which the law of nationality would be seen as simultaneously offering Spain an added layer of international political legitimacy, an opportunity for economic gain, and a diplomatic advantage.

On November 22, 2012, in an event reported around the world, José Manuel García-Margallo and Alberto Ruiz Gallardón, at the time Spain's ministers of foreign affairs and justice, respectively, announced the Spanish government's decision to grant citizenship to the descendants of Sephardi Jews expelled in 1492. The announcement took place at the Centro Sefarad-Israel in Madrid, an institution created in 2007 as part of Spain's diplomatic efforts toward Israel and the Jewish world.[28] Ostensibly, the intended law would bring closure to a five-hundred-year-long situation of injustice by "reinstituting" rightful Spanish nationality, if not to the actual victims of the expulsion, to their descendants. The project for the law was extensively debated, contested, and amended from its announcement in 2012 until its final approval in 2015.

In their declarations, government officials consistently chose to describe this restitution of nationality as unprecedented, overdue, and restorative. In fact, the law was not unprecedented. The 1982 civil code already allowed Sephardi Jews to apply for Spanish nationality after two years of residency in Spain—just like citizens of territories historically associated with Spain like Latin American nations, Andorra, the Philippines, Equatorial Guinea, and Portugal—instead of the ten years required for other foreigners.[29] The new elements in the 2015 law were the waiver of the two-year residency requirement and the legality of applicants' keeping their current nationality. Other obstacles, however, were inserted in the process. The beneficiaries have to produce documents that "justify their condition of Sephardi Jews with origin in Spain" and demonstrate "their special connection with Spain." Many of these new provisions have drawn scrutiny and criticism: the high cost of the application process, the need to travel to Spain twice, the requirement of exams in modern Spanish language and culture, and the fact that nothing similar to this law is being offered to the current descendants of *moriscos* expelled in 1609, to name a few points.[30]

The Spanish press also remarked on the political considerations surrounding the law's timing and roll out. Vera Gutiérrez Calvo and Miguel González pointed out in an article in *El País*, Spain's main newspaper, that the law's announcement had taken place exactly one week before a scheduled vote at the UN General Assembly on awarding Palestine nonmember Observer State status. Spain intended to, and eventually did, vote in favor of the proposition. The announcement of the reparation gesture would have been timed as an attempt at neutralizing the expected anger that Spain's vote would stir up in Israel and the United States (Gutiérrez Calvo and González). That this law aimed at achieving something more than the resolution of a historic offense seemed also clear by the way it was introduced to the international community. The largest numbers of Sephardi Jews potentially interested in the law live in Israel, Turkey, Venezuela, Argentina, Colombia, and Morocco. However, in March 2014, after the government's approval of a draft of the law in February, the place where Ruiz Gallardón traveled first to present it to the international community was not one of these countries but New York.

The Spanish government also seems to have taken into consideration an economic rationale. In line with timeworn stereotypes about the wealth and business knowledge of Sephardi Jews, many people seem to assume that the return of a sizeable number of Jews as tourists, investors, or residents would help bolster Spain's economy. In an op-ed in the *New York Times*, Ilan Stavans describes the law as "just another chapter in Spain's ambivalent relationship with its Jewish past." The difference between 2012, when the law was announced, and 1992, he argues, is that in 1992, Spain was not immersed in an economic crisis. "Inviting Jews to settle in times of economic trouble is a strategy employed before" (Stavans). Similarly, in an article for *The Guardian*, Susan McGee asks whether the real intention of the law was attempting to draw new investment into a struggling economy, at a time when Spain's unemployment rate was 23 percent (McGee).

As we argue in chapter 1, both political and economic opportunism and self-interest have historically been pivotal parts of the discussions about Spain's rapprochement with the international Jewish community. McGee's article also mentions the fact that this welcoming has happened at the same time that Spain "has been challenged with separatist movements." Indeed, the cliché of the Sephardi Jews' centuries-old attachment to the homeland that rejected them may act as an antidote to the nationalist and independentist desires alive to varying degrees in communities across Spain, which became especially conspicuous in the declaration of independence sponsored by the Autonomous Government of Catalonia in November 2017.[31] As McDonald observes, "We might think of the Law of Return not as conferring Spanish citizenship on Sephardic descendants, but as confirming the Spanishness of Sephardic Jews. Viewed in this light, Spain wasn't offering a homecoming to Jews and their descendants; it was renegotiating the terms of inclusion to claim them as Spaniards, shoring up an explicitly Castilian national identity against the backdrop of renewed assertions of Catalan and Basque nationalism" (McDonald 111).

Central as they are, political strategy, economic opportunism, and self-interest do not tell the whole story of what fuels these initiatives. Frequently, the self-evident expediency of these reasons is only the most visible layer veiling many other less evident, conflicted, and conflicting threads of memory work. For the purposes of our discussion about Spain's current memory landscape, we will focus on the analysis of the law of nationality in contrast to King Juan Carlos's landmark 1992 speech. In November 2012, during the press conference announcing the project for the law, García-Margallo explained how it was meant to "recover the memory of a long-silenced Spain," while Ruiz Gallardón celebrated it as a "reencounter with all those that had been unjustly deprived of their nationality, who, from now on, can claim Spain as theirs" ("Los sefardíes podrán"). Two years later, when presenting the law to Congress, Rafael Catalá, the successor of García-Margallo as minister of justice, characterized it as "histórica porque cierra un capítulo doloroso de nuestra historia" [historic because it closes a painful chapter in our history]. Upon the law's approval on June 11, 2015, the Federation of Jewish Communities of Spain approved the government's characterization of the law, calling it a "long-awaited historical reparation" and a fulfillment of Juan Carlos's 1992 words (FCJE, "Aprobada la ley").

The preamble to the law's text provides a long historical context describing Sephardi Jews as the descendants of the Jews who lived in Iberia in the Middle Ages and reviewing the historical milestones that marked their gradual return to Spain beginning in the nineteenth century. Echoing the tone and language of the 1990 Prince of Asturias Award ceremony, the preamble repeats common clichés about Sephardi Jews—their nostalgia for Sepharad, the preservation of their language as proof of their fidelity to and love for Spain, their "acceptance without rancor" of Spain's history of exclusion and silence about them. Echoing King Juan Carlos's 1992 discourse, it mentions the 1990 award as the beginning of "un proceso de concordia que convoca a las comunidades sefardíes al reencuentro con sus orígenes, abriéndoles para siempre las puertas de su antigua patria" [a process of concord that invites Sephardi communities to reencounter their origins, forever opening the doors of their old homeland for them] ("Ley 12/2015").[32] Also like the 1992 ceremony, the preamble focuses on the present and the future and concludes by stressing "la común determinación de construir juntos, frente a la intolerancia de tiempos pasados, un nuevo espacio de convivencia y concordia" [the common determination of building together, in contrast to the intolerance of past times, a new space of peaceful coexistence and concord] ("Ley 12/2015").

Upon the approval of the law in November 2015, King Felipe delivered a speech that again echoed that of his father Juan Carlos in 1992. In this case, however, it inflated into the realm of the unbelievable the sentimental rhetoric which in 1992 had served the purpose of glossing over the difficult past. "¡Cuánto os hemos echado de menos!" [How we have missed you!], said King Felipe to representatives of Sephardi communities while offering the law as "una nueva y definitiva apertura de las puertas de España a los hijos de Sefarad" [a new and definite opening of Spain's doors to the sons of Sepharad]. To conclude, Felipe reiterated the same hospitality tropes his father had in 1992: "Quiero deciros que ya estáis de nuevo en vuestra propia casa, que ya habéis vuelto para siempre a vuestro hogar" [I want to tell you that you are already in your own house again, that you have finally returned to your own home] (Alberola).

These echoes and continuities illustrate Olick's argument about how collective memory and commemoration operate as the memory of memory. Memory, explains Olick, "is not a thing but a practice, the variety of practices that comprise remembering." What exists is not one memory but a series of multiple mnemonic practices (Olick, *Politics* 10). The temporal nature of memory makes memory "not just a relationship between past and present" but one in which "commemoration—and by extension all mnemonic practices—are continuing processes of utterance and response" (Olick, *Politics* 12). In King Felipe's speech, the commemoration of the Hispano Jewish past appears mediated by the memory of his father's speech, which, in turn, was strongly influenced by the rhetoric and political conditions of the Spanish transition to democracy. Each repetition of this "return home" metaphor, and the recurrent emphasis on its finality, ends up raising doubt about the words' actual signification.

There is a key aspect, however, in which the representation of the past written into the 2015 law differs from that which the king found possible to state in 1992. That year, the king spoke of Sephardi Jews' "having to leave Spain" due to a "reason of State." The text of the 2015 law's preamble explicitly mentions how they left Spain unwillingly "tras los Edictos de 1492 que compelían a la conversión forzosa o al expulsión tomaron esta drástica vía" [faced with the 1492 Edicts, which compelled them to choose between forced conversion or expulsion, they took this last drastic path] ("Ley 12/2015"). The text not only names these reasons but also goes on to condemn them by stating how they "fueron injustamente expulsados" [were unjustly expelled] ("Ley 12/2015"). Further, the law reaches back to pre-1492 anti-Jewish violence lamenting the "persecuciones y padecimientos que inicuamente sufrieron sus antepasados" [persecutions and afflictions that, as a grave injustice, their ancestors suffered] ("Ley 12/2015").[33]

The 2015 law of nationality states, thus, that there were persecutions and injustice and that present-day democratic Spain has responsibility for that historical wrong. Why does a law whose objective is the reform of an article of the civil code regulating the conditions required for naturalization need to judge and characterize actions taken by the monarchs of Castile and Aragon five hundred years earlier? In a 2008 essay about the marketing of the concept of convivencia for Jewish tourism in Spain, we spoke of King Juan Carlos's 1992 speech in terms of the contrast between the official rhetoric of hospitality that presented Spain as the home of Sephardi Jews and the reality of the unsuccessful efforts by Sephardi organizations to negotiate Spanish citizenship for those who actually wanted to "return home" (Flesler and Pérez Melgosa, "Marketing" 75–76). It is in this sense that the Federation of Jewish Communities of Spain connected the approval of the law in June 2015 to the events of 1992, stating that with it "se hacen por fin realidad las palabras que S. M. el Rey Don Juan Carlos

I pronunció en la sinagoga de Madrid el día 31 de marzo de 1992" [the words that His Majesty King Juan Carlos I pronounced at the Madrid Synagogue on March 31, 1992, have *finally* come true] (italics added, FCJE, "Aprobada la ley").

The preamble of the law also offers an answer to the question about what made this new language, not present in 1992, possible in 2015. It states how, among Sephardi communities all over the world,

> Palpita en todo caso el amor a una España consciente al fin del bagaje histórico y sentimental de los sefardíes. Se antoja justo que semejante reconocimiento se nutra de los oportunos recursos jurídicos para facilitar la condición de españoles a quienes se resistieron, celosa y prodigiosamente, a dejar de serlo a pesar de las persecuciones y padecimientos que inicuamente sufrieron sus antepasados
>
> [Love in every case beats for a Spain finally conscious of the historical and emotional experience of Sephardis. It seems just that such recognition would use the available juridical tools to facilitate the condition of Spaniards of those who, consciously and prodigiously, resisted the loss of their Spanishness, notwithstanding the persecutions and afflictions that, as a grave injustice, their ancestors suffered] ("Ley 12/2015")

Beyond the first part of the first sentence, repeating the cliché of Sephardi Jews' love for Spain, what this passage underlines is the fact of Spain's becoming "finally conscious" not only of the "love" of Sephardi Jews but also of the historical injustices they endured. Sephardi Jews here represent the link between a past and present seen as closely interconnected. The belief that a legal instrument may be used to intervene in the effects of a past injustice, no matter how removed in time, reveals the influence, as Golob would put it, of transitional justice culture.

In her analysis of the 2007 law known as the Law of Historical Memory, Golob explains how, although the law falls short of transitional justice cultural norms, certain aspects of it nonetheless contribute to reinforcing the validity of those norms "by normalizing the public return to the past as part and parcel of the ongoing construction of democratic identity" (Golob 128). Something similar occurs with the intention of the 2015 law of nationality. Notwithstanding its shortcomings, and without downplaying the many obstacles aforementioned, this law also normalizes the need to look critically at the past and assume the redress of earlier injustices committed by the nation as a moral responsibility in the present. In the speeches of Kings Juan Carlos and Felipe, Sephardi Jews usefully provided a glorious past of convivencia with which to articulate the nation as a project of hospitality and welcoming of difference.

In the 2015 law, the critical evaluation of the past provides the Spain of the present with cosmopolitan democratic credentials.

Together with the critical confrontation with the past, an important component of transitional justice culture is the inclusion into the fold of the nation of groups previously targeted for exclusion or annihilation. This is one of the objectives of groups like the ARHM, since Francoism justified the repression of certain groups by othering them, accusing them of belonging to an imaginary "anti-Spain" (Golob 135). The 2015 law of nationality participates in this context of an ongoing discussion about articulating a more encompassing idea of who belongs in the nation.[34] By presenting itself as an instrument of intervention in a past injustice that consisted of Sephardi Jews' losing their status as members of Iberian territories, the law presents itself, at a symbolic level, as a reparation for the expulsion.

In his reflections about the significance of the 2015 law, Santiago Kovadloff explains that, in providing a path for the descendants of expelled Sephardi Jews to become Spaniards, Spain is not explicitly asking them for forgiveness, "pero se reconoce en ellos y los nombra como expresión de su propia identidad nacional" [but recognizes itself in them and identifies them as expression of its own national identity]. Kovadloff argues that what the law does do is "modificar la incidencia simbólica de ese pasado sobre su presente al declarar españoles reconocidos a quienes provienen de aquellos judíos que fueron desconocidos como españoles" [declare as recognized Spaniards those who descend from the Jews that were not acknowledged as Spaniards and modify that past's symbolic effect on Spain's present] (Kovadloff).

The aforementioned quote from the preamble of the law reads, "A Spain finally conscious of the historical and emotional experience of Sephardi Jews." This acknowledgment raises the question of how Spain is walking the symbolic path from the "offensive amnesia" identified by Cansinos Assens to the empathic consciousness articulated in the law. This book attempts to tell the story of this "becoming conscious." It is a story full of paradoxes—advances and challenges, ambiguity and rightfulness—that accompany the newly regained visibility of Jewish cultural heritage and presence in Spain's public sphere, the growing contact of current inhabitants of Spain with their Jewish "inheritance," the ongoing memory work of Jewish Spain.

CHAPTER DESCRIPTIONS

Chapter 1, "The Long Journey of Sephardi Myths," explores the long genealogy of myths about Sephardi Jews that has informed Spain's relation to them and to the country's Jewish past. Beginning with the 1797 unsuccessful proposal by Pedro Varela, King Carlos IV's finance minister, to abrogate the 1492 Edict of Expulsion and welcome the Jews back to Spain, the chapter describes the complex and mixed motivations underlying past and present attempts to reconnect with "Sepharad" and Sephardi Jews. In these attempts, assumptions about political expediency and economic advantage for Spain stand side by side with understated desires for reparation. The historical arc traced by this chapter concludes with an analysis of the Francoist post–World War II gestures of rapprochement with Jews.

Chapter 2, "Embracing Spain's Jewish Legacy," discusses the central role that Arab and Jewish material remains have played in the development of Spain's tourist industry, a leading sector of Spain's economy. Key to the inception of Spain as a desirable tourist destination, this legacy has proven to be a steady source of enduring fascination for visitors both foreign and domestic. The chapter examines the 1995 creation and subsequent development of the national tourist route "Paths of Sepharad: Network of Jewish Quarters of Spain," which has triggered a countrywide showcasing of old city neighborhoods as newly conceived Jewish Quarters. The analysis of several case studies illustrates the paradoxes involved in the celebration and marketing of medieval convivencia in spaces marked by destruction and absence.

Chapter 3, "Loss, Redemption, and Converso Dissonances at the Sephardi Museum of Toledo," analyzes Spain's national Jewish museum, created in 1964 by Franco. The chapter discusses the converso history of the Synagogue of the Transit, where the museum is housed, its transformations and political instrumentalizations, and the narratives articulated by the museum through its holdings and exhibition practices. This national museum focalizes a complex manifestation of Spain's desire to memorialize its Jewish past in terms of its present concerns. An in-depth examination of the museum's building and the history of its uses after 1492 finds a persistent presence of what we term *converso dissonances*, traces that are simultaneously concealed and revealed in the museum's space and exhibitions.

Chapter 4, "Exhibiting Jewish Heritage at the Local and Regional Levels," analyzes the mushrooming of museums and exhibition spaces that display the particular ways regions and cities in Spain embrace their Sephardi legacy. Through their depiction of local exceptionality, these museums have become additional elements in the current struggle of different communities to define their regional/national identities within the new political map drawn by the 1978 constitution. The chapter focuses on five regional/local museums: Girona's Museum of Jewish History (Catalonia); Jewish Information

Center of Galicia in Ribadavia, province of Ourense (Galicia); Jewish Museum David Melul in Béjar, province of Salamanca (Castile and Leon); Casa de Sefarad in the city of Córdoba (Andalucía); and the permanent exhibition *Tragèdia al call-Tàrrega 1348* at the Museo de l'Urgell in the province of Lleida (Catalonia). The analysis of this last exhibit, based on an archaeological excavation of human remains connected to the 1348 massacre of Jews in Tàrrega, includes a discussion of the controversies that followed the recent discoveries of Jewish cemeteries in several cities in Spain.

Chapter 5, "Memory Entanglements: Hervás's Jewish Inheritance and the Francoist Repression," looks at the popular Los Conversos festival, celebrated in Hervás, during which the town's inhabitants dress up as "Jews" and stage a play about the local Jewish past. The chapter traces the significant transformations of the festival, from its origin in the play *Los conversos* (1985) by Argentine Jewish playwright Solly Wolodarsky, to the increased reliance on antisemitic traditional legends in subsequent plays written specifically to be performed in the festival by local playwright Miguel Murillo. The chapter addresses the multiple contradictions that arise as Hervás engages in the performance and public dramatization of its local memory work. From the perspective of multidirectional memory, the analysis shows how conflicts related to Hervás's Jewish past become entangled with the more recent memory of local Francoist repression. Hervás's collective memories of stigmatization and shaming are both performed and concealed, its conflicts both mobilized and contained.

Chapter 6, "Returns to Sepharad," explores some of the recent narratives, discourses, and artistic representations of the "return" to Spain's Jewish past to tease out the identitary, political, and aesthetic work performed by them. We analyze how Esther Bendahan, a Spanish writer of Sephardi-Moroccan descent, conceptualizes the return to Sepharad in her fictional work, followed by the diverse modes of reconnection with Judaism and Jewishness being articulated by people in Spain who self-identify as descendants of conversos. We reflect on contemporary artistic elaborations of the Jewish past in the work *Shoah 1492–1945* by Wolf Vostell, a German-born pioneer of installation art who from the 1950s until the mid-1990s lived intermittently in Malpartida (Cáceres), and in the series *Sephardi Portraits* created in the last twenty-five years by the leading figurative painter Daniel Quintero, which attempts to bridge the distance between Iberian medieval Jews and Spain's inhabitants today.

NOTES

1. See Jacobo Israel Garzón's introductions to *Los judíos de Sefarad* and *Las luminarias de Janucá* for more on the fascinating figure of Cansinos Assens, who

was born in a Spanish Catholic family but came to see himself as a descendant of conversos and was identified as Jewish by many of his contemporaries. See also chapter 6.

2. The episode presents a very positive image of Queen Isabel, who signed the Edict of Expulsion in 1492. See Rueda Laffond and Coronado Ruiz for an analysis of the series' simplified, conservative vision of Spanish history and essentialist view of Spain.

3. One frequently sees in Spanish media the term *sefardí*, carrying positive connotations, to speak about Spain's Jewish heritage matters or present-day Jews. The term *judío* is often avoided, because among Spain's general public it is still understood as a term carrying negative connotations.

4. Spain's Jewish population today is less than 1 per 1,000 of the total population of Spain: about 40,000 in a total population of 47 million. Most live in Barcelona and Madrid, about 1,000 live in Melilla, about 500 in Ceuta, and some hundreds in Seville and Málaga (Álvarez Chillida, *El antisemitismo* 464). The Jewish population of Spain in 1877, forty years after the abolition of the Inquisition, was 406 people, most of whom had emigrated from Gibraltar and North Africa. There were also some Ashkenazi financiers from prominent European families. In terms of comparison, there were 71,000 Jews in France and approximately 37,000 in England (Gold 92). By 1950, there were about 2,500, and by the beginning of the 1970s, the Jewish population had grown to 9,000, having emigrated from Morocco and South America, especially Argentina (Rein 313–14).

5. Numerous frictions have marked Spain's historic relationship with Israel (see Rein). Spain was the last European country to officially recognize the state of Israel and to establish diplomatic relations with it, in 1986; both measures were part of the requirements for its entry into the European Community. Throughout the 1990s and 2000s, surveys about Spaniards' views of foreign countries found that on a scale from 1 to 10, Spaniards placed Israel at an average of 3.8. Between 1991 and 1997, given a list of twenty-two countries, Spaniards placed Israel at twentieth, with only Iraq and Iran receiving fewer points (A. Baer, "Tanques" 27).

6. In an article published in the *Jerusalem Post* in October 2010, Stoller and Baer explained that upon receiving the results of the study confirming the widespread existence of antisemitism in Spain, the Spanish government, which had commissioned the study, decided to shift gears and discard its conclusions, producing instead a questionnaire "that not only [did] not measure antisemitic bias, but contained questions drafted in a way that would elicit positive answers" ("Survey"). The government, thus, decided to deny the problem of antisemitism instead of addressing it. See Martina Weisz for further discussion of antisemitism in Spain today.

7. For a general view of the Jewish presence in the Iberian Peninsula see Ashtor, Y. Baer; Amador de los Ríos; Caro Baroja; Gerber; Ray's *The Sephardic Frontier*; and Nirenberg's *Communities of Violence* and *Neighboring Faiths*.

8. The constitution of 1978 and the Law of Religious Freedom of 1980 regulated freedom of conscience. In 1992, the Spanish state signed a series of cooperation agreements with the Jewish, Muslim, and Evangelical communities in order to secure religious equality and regulate the functioning of non-Catholic religious communities.

9. See Eric Calderwood's book *Colonial al-Andalus* for an analysis of how contemporary Morocco has also, like Spain, aligned itself with the myth of convivencia and with the idea of being heirs to an idealized al-Andalus (Calderwood 8).

10. Pinto locates the origin of this interest at the European level in the early 1980s, as a number of events brought about reconsiderations of the rise to power of Nazism in Germany in the 1930s, and sees these activities peaking in 1995, when a series of commemorations marked the fiftieth anniversary of the liberation of Auschwitz (Pinto 180). We will further discuss Pinto's notion of "Jewish space" and Gruber's "virtual Jews" in relation to Spain in chapter 2.

11. The precise status of the conversos, their degree of "Jewishness," the sincerity of their conversion, and the motivations behind their actions have been the subject of numerous and heated debates. See Yerushalmi; Gitlitz; Hutcheson; Ingram; Amelang; and Nirenberg's *Neighboring Faiths*.

12. This phenomenon is studied in a comparative context by Dalia Kandiyoti in *The Converso's Return*, where she analyzes the cultural contexts and literary production that have emerged from the reawakening of interest in converso history, ancestry, and identity in the Americas, Europe, and Turkey. We will further discuss conversos and the continuing suspicions about them in chapter 1 and the phenomenon of the "rediscovery" of converso ancestry in contemporary Spain in chapter 6.

13. A video of the inauguration ceremony in September 2013 can be seen on YouTube, "Cementerio judío de Ávila o Jardín de Sefarad 5," https://www.youtube.com/watch?v=NmQIiPhp5i4. Accessed August 5, 2015.

14. See Tabea Linhard's book *Jewish Spain. A Mediterranean Memory* for a reflection about Rothberg's concept of multidirectional memory in relation to Spain's Jewish past, the Holocaust, and Republican memory in contemporary Spain.

15. It is estimated that there are forty thousand to sixty thousand bodies in mass graves throughout Spain. See Armengou and Belis; Ferrándiz; Jerez Farrán and Amago.

16. In the article "De las fosas comunes a los derechos humanos," Ferrándiz examines what he calls the "legal download," the translation and popularization of international human rights concepts, especially the figure of the "disappeared," in Spain. In 2002, the ARHM succeeded in including Spain in the

UN Working Group on Enforced or Involuntary Disappearances, created in 1980 to investigate disappearances in Chile. In 2004, it sought out the advice of the premier Argentine forensic team that had developed its expertise in the context of the Argentinean National Commission on the Disappearance of Persons.

17. See Ricard Vinyes, Montse Armengou, and Ricard Belis, *Los niños perdidos del franquismo*.

18. See Baer and Sznaider for a description of the means by which the Holocaust became a crucial source for understanding Argentina's dictatorship and for the critical bibliography that has challenged this use of the Holocaust in both the Argentine and Spanish cases.

19. As Labanyi explains, what this movement attempts to "recover" is not a hidden truth that nobody knew about but a reactivation of demands that were put aside during the transition (Labanyi, "Politics" 122; "Languages" 25). These demands clash today with the discourse of the conservative political right that deems it best not to "open old wounds" and considers the questioning of the transition's consensus as weakening the basis of democracy in Spain.

20. Sara Brenneis and Gina Herrmann's recent book Spain, *World War II, and the Holocaust: History and Representation*, explains Spain's role during World War II and the way the Holocaust has been represented in Spanish historical and political discourse and cultural production. Since the late 1990s, together with historical novels about Spain's Jewish past, there has been an increasing number of literary works about the Holocaust written by Spanish authors. See Linhard, *Jewish Spain* for an analysis of the novels *Sefarad* by Antonio Muñoz Molina and *Velódromo de invierno* by Juana Salabert, both published in 2001. In "With Sepharad as a Void" Stacy Beckwith reads these novels together with *La saga de los malditos* (Chufo Llorens, 2003) and *Lo que esconde tu nombre* (Clara Sánchez, 2010).

21. See Baer for a discussion of how this ceremony "pave[d] the way for the institutional recognition of Republican victims" ("The Voids" 102–3). The direct historical connection of Republican memory to the Holocaust is due to the fact that between ten thousand and fifteen thousand Republican refugees were deported to Nazi concentration camps, mainly Mauthausen in Austria, when Germany occupied France in 1940. More than five thousand of them were killed by the Nazis (Brenneis 5). The remembrance of Republican victims of Nazi Germany was deliberately banned during Franco's regime. In 1962, the association Amical de Mauthausen was founded in secret. It was not legalized until 1978, after Franco's death (A. Baer, "The Voids" 98). See Sara J. Brenneis, *Spaniards in Mauthausen* for a comprehensive analysis of the accounts inspired and created by these prisoners.

22. The symbolic links of Sepharad with the memory of the Holocaust can be seen in the 2007 addition of a monument dedicated to the victims of the

Holocaust in the Garden of the Three Cultures in Juan Carlos I Park in Madrid. The original garden was built in 1992 in homage to the Christian, Arab, and Jewish cultural legacy of Spain (A. Baer, "The Voids" 103, 117).

23. For a more detailed critical reading of these commemorations and events as a whole, see Graham and Sánchez, Kelly, and Morgan.

24. Juan Carlos was proclaimed king after Franco's death in November 1975. The timing of the queen's first visit to a synagogue in Madrid in 1976 also coincided with a diplomatic milestone: it was in preparation for the king and queen's first trip to the United States, in which they were planning to meet a delegation of the American Jewish Committee (Lisbona 305–7).

25. The presence and role of the Israeli president Haim Herzog was also contentious. Israel had wanted Juan Carlos to visit Jerusalem, but the Spanish government rejected the idea and invited Herzog instead, in his first official state visit to Spain. Spanish authorities wanted to make sure Herzog, an Ashkenazi Jew from Ireland, was not the protagonist of the ceremony, but a "guest and witness," as the king called him. Herzog had the intention of being the only Jew to speak at the ceremony, in the name of all Jewish people, but both the Spanish government and Spain's Jewish representatives objected, since they saw the event as the reencounter of the king with *Spanish* Jews. See Lisbona 361–69 and Rozenberg 321–41 for more details about the ceremony and other events connected to Sepharad '92.

26. The actions of Portugal offer an interesting contrast: in 1989, President Mário Soares offered an official apology for the persecutions and expulsion suffered by Portuguese Jews. In 1996, the Portuguese parliament unanimously approved the symbolic abrogation of the Portuguese Expulsion Decree of 1497 (Aliberti, "Volviendo").

27. As we will see in chapter 1, this is not the first time that Jews themselves would use an idealized notion of medieval Iberian convivencia as an argument for their integration and equal treatment. It should be noted that the separate Catalan commemoration of 1492 had elements that made it very different from the one in Madrid: the inauguration in December 1991 included a mention of the six hundredth anniversary of the anti-Jewish persecutions of 1391. In June 1992, the Catalan parliament unanimously approved a motion condemning the physical violence and social hostility suffered by the Jewish population and recognizing their contribution to Catalan culture (Rozenberg 338–39). See Rozenberg for an account of the many initiatives and events connected to the anniversary of 1492 that took place throughout Spain.

28. This center was added to preexisting centers dedicated to cultural relations and public diplomacy with different parts of the world: Casa América, Casa Asia, Casa Árabe, Casa África. The Center Sefarad Israel could not be called *casa* ("house" or "home" in Spanish) because the name had been taken by

the privately owned Casa de Sefarad in Córdoba, an institution we analyze in chapter 4.

29. See Ojeda Mata, *Identidades* 138–42 and Aliberti, *Sefarad* 207–13 for a historical review of Spanish laws related to nationality and citizenship since the 1812 Constitution and the process by which Sephardi Jews began to acquire citizenship through a naturalization mechanism after 1869.

30. See Paloma Cervilla's evaluation of the first year of application of the law for the newspaper *ABC* and Tabea Linhard's *Jewish Spain* 184–88 for a discussion of the law's shortcomings. See "Los moriscos" for an overview of the protests by descendants of moriscos against their exclusion from this law. McDonald analyzes the obstacles applicants face and includes an interview with Ruiz Gallardón in which the former minister attempts to justify why Sephardi Jews deserve Spanish nationality and descendants of moriscos do not. Dalia Kandiyoti and Rina Benmayor are currently undertaking an oral history project gathering testimonies from Sephardi Jews from multiple countries who are applying for Spanish nationality. They explore how the application process has led to a new exploration and resignification of Sephardi identity for many of them.

31. Their purported love and nostalgia for Spain has long been instrumentalized this way. Already in Ángel Pulido's 1905 book *Intereses nacionales: Españoles sin patria y la raza sefardí* [National interests: Spaniards without a homeland and the Sephardi race], he compares the ease with which he can communicate in Castilian with Sephardi inhabitants of Belgrade with the difficulty of communication he and his wife experienced in a recent trip to Cardona, a town in Catalonia (5). We will return to Pulido, a pivotal figure in the philosephardi movement, in chapter 1.

32. Linhard notes the philosephardi rhetoric of the draft of the law (*Jewish Spain*, 185), which will be translated into the preamble, as noted by Aragoneses, Aliberti, and McDonald. See McDonald for an analysis of the specific phrase, repeated over and over in philosephardi discourse, referring to Sephardi Jews's "lack of rancor" vis-à-vis Spain.

33. It is important to note that this reference was not present in the draft bill presented by Ruiz Gallardón in February 2014 but was an amendment introduced by the PNV (the Basque Nationalist Party) (Aragoneses 2–3; Aliberti, "Volviendo"). See McDonald for the transcription of the arguments by PNV's Emilio Olabarría Muñoz, who argues that in addition to this law, there is a need for reparations of other historical injustices committed by the Spanish state against moriscos, Berbers, and Saharawis (McDonald 101–3). See Aliberti, "Volviendo" for a detailed comparison between the draft bill and the final text of the preamble and for a comparison with the Portuguese law of nationality for Sephardi Jews, also approved in 2015.

34. Although it is not readily obvious how or why Jews would have any relationship to the Francoist violence against Republicans, a particular conception of Jews and conversos did in fact play a prominent role in the extreme right's explanation of how Republicans became the treacherous and threatening "anti-Spain," as we will see in chapter 1. These two collectives, Republicans and Sephardi Jews, were commemorated side by side, as "brothers in homeland and in misfortune" in King Felipe's January 27, 2015, speech referring to Republicans deported to concentration camps and to Sephardi Jews murdered by the Nazis in the context of the Holocaust remembrance ceremony of that year (Baer and Sznaider, *Memory* 92).

ONE

THE LONG JOURNEY OF SEPHARDI MYTHS

IN APRIL 2012, UPON RETURNING from Israel, where he had attended a meeting of the mayors of cities belonging to Spain's Network of Jewish Quarters, an institution that fosters tourism related to Spain's Jewish heritage, Ferran Bel, Tortosa's mayor, spoke of the value of welcoming Jews as tourists: "Durante los últimos tres años se ha dado un importante impulso a este mercado. Nos hemos dado cuenta de su potencial y lo tenemos que explotar" [In the last three years, there has been an important push to develop this market. We have discovered its potential, and we have to exploit it]. Emiliano García-Page, the mayor of Toledo, reinforced this economic argument by stressing how Spain's Jewish past should be used to attract "visitantes estadounidenses ya que es un mercado potencial y de alto nivel adquisitivo" [US visitors since they are an untapped market with considerable buying power] ("Page apuesta"). The Catalan newspaper *La Vanguardia,* referring to Israeli and Jewish tourists in general, explained, "Se desviven por descubrir su legado patrimonial. Les gusta ir de compras y comer bien. Tienen un alto poder adquisitivo" [They go out of their way to discover their heritage. They like to shop and eat well. They have high purchasing power] (Julbe and Sans). As these assessments repeat throughout politicians' declarations and newspaper cover stories, they reveal how the fantasy portrait of the affluent Jew craving to reconnect with Sepharad has found a new home in contemporary Spain.

These assumptions about the political and economic expediency of welcoming Sephardi Jews back, whether as tourists, citizens, or both, reveal the implicit desire to declare the Jewish past closed for grievances and open for business. Political representatives and tourist promoters consistently present

Spain's recent diplomatic gestures and cultural initiatives as historically unique. Yet both the attempts to "bring back the Jews" and the rhetoric used to justify these pursuits—deploying Jews as symbols of historic diversity and tolerance, depicting them as harboring an ancestral yearning to return, and assuming that they control wide and powerful financial networks—obey a powerful cyclical pattern with a long history of evolving iterations.

In 1797, a little over three centuries after the 1492 expulsion, Pedro Varela, King Carlos IV's finance minister, advanced a proposal to abrogate the Edict of Expulsion and bring the Jews back to Spain. Anticipating possible objections to his project from the king, the Spanish Church, and even Jews, Varela came up with a series of arguments that still resonate in today's reasons for luring international Jews to visit or settle in Spain. To persuade the king, Varela resorted to a purely economic argument. He proposed that Spain invite a number of Sephardi Jewish businessmen from Holland and other northern European countries to establish their businesses in Cádiz, Málaga, and other ports. Their return would become the formula for saving Spain's economy:

> El segundo arbitrio es la admisión de la nación hebrea en España, que, según la opinión general, posee las mayores riquezas de Europa y Asia . . . la política del presente siglo no puede dejar de ver en este proyecto el Socorro del Estado en el fomento del comercio y de la industria, que jamás por otros medios llegarán a equilibrarse con el extranjero, pues ni la actividad ni la economía son prendas de la mayor parte de los españoles.
>
> [The second consideration is the admission of the Hebrew nation to Spain, which, according to general opinion, possesses the greatest wealth of Europe and Asia . . . the present century's politics cannot fail to see in this project the rescue of the state through the development of commerce and industry, by which it would otherwise never be competitive abroad, since initiative and economic enterprise are not abilities most Spaniards have]. (in Pérez-Prendes 83)

To preempt possible objections from the Church, Varela cited Saint Paul, attributing to him the Augustinian justification of the need for Jewish presence among Christians (we will come back to Saint Augustine's arguments below), thus arguing for theological tolerance:

> Las preocupaciones antiguas ya pasaron: el ejemplo de todas las naciones de Europa, y aún de la misma silla de la religión, nos autoriza; y finalmente, la doctrina del apóstol San Pablo, a favor de este pueblo proscrito, puede convencer a los teólogos más obstinados en sus opiniones y a las conciencias más timoratas, de que su admisión en el Reino es más conforme a las máximas de la religión, que lo fue su expulsión.

> [The old preoccupations are gone: the example of all the nations of Europe, and even of Rome itself, authorizes us; and finally, the doctrine of Saint Paul, in favor of this banned people, can convince the most stubborn theologians and the most God-fearing consciences, that their admission to the Kingdom is more in agreement with the key principles of our religion than was their expulsion]. (in Pérez-Prendes 83)

Finally, to convince the Jews themselves, Varela appealed to the antisemitic notion of Jewish greed but, most importantly here, based his argument on the belief that wealthy European Sephardi Jews harbored a deep nostalgia for their former lives in Sepharad:

> Si al mismo tiempo se les dejase entrever que a la admisión de algunas casas de comercio podría seguirse la de toda la nación, me parece se lograría tentar la avaricia de este abatido pueblo, que nunca ha perdido de vista las ventajas y comodidades que ha gozado en España.
>
> [If at the same time they are allowed to glimpse that the admission of some houses of commerce could lead to their whole nation's acceptance, I think the avarice of this beaten people would be tempted, since they never have forgotten the advantages and conveniences that they had enjoyed in Spain]. (in Pérez-Prendes 84)

The ideas supporting Varela's argument were not his own invention. By 1797, when Varela drafted his proposal, such notions about Jews already had a rich and complex past.[1] The theological case for tolerance of the Jews was pivotal to the social structuring of Christian societies in medieval western Europe, including the Iberian Peninsula. The fantasy of the economic superiority of Sephardi Jews and the potential gain from their supposed nostalgia for Sepharad would have a long future as well. Because of the importance that this view of Sephardi Jews holds in explaining both historical and present developments, this chapter provides an analysis of the origins and strategic uses of these notions.

THE GENEALOGY OF TWO MYTHS: CONVIVENCIA AND SEPHARDI NOSTALGIA

Long before Américo Castro's official coinage of the concept of medieval convivencia in 1948, the idealized notion that Christians, Muslims, and Jews lived together harmoniously on the Iberian Peninsula had already been successfully deployed for a host of political purposes. When Pedro Varela spoke in 1797 of "the advantages and conveniences that [the Jews] had enjoyed in Spain," he was repeating an already widely disseminated narrative. In the period immediately following the 1492 expulsion, for strategic reasons connected to their immediate survival and with the aim of finding welcoming communities in which to settle, many exiled Jews wrote idealized accounts of their past in Iberia, recounting with pride and hyperbole the exceptional life they enjoyed there. Tales of past privilege and outstanding accomplishments became a tool for the new exiles and their descendants to further their assimilation efforts and improve their prospects in their new homes (see Ray, *After Expulsion* 142–43).[2]

In time, these ideas became strategically appropriated by a variety of groups and agendas. Varela introduced them tentatively in his failed proposal to Charles IV. But these arguments would be fully reenergized, ironically enough, by Ashkenazi Jewish intellectuals in late eighteenth- and nineteenth-century Germany. As they struggled to find models to conceptualize and pave the way toward emancipation within largely Christian nations, these thinkers recovered and embraced the myth of a prosperous, tolerant, and enlightened Sepharad in order to redefine their identity as integrated, emancipated Jews (Schorsch 71). Mark R. Cohen explains this paradoxical use of a medieval myth for communities aspiring to gain full access to modernity: "In its nineteenth-century context, the myth of the interfaith utopia was used to attempt to achieve an important political end, to challenge supposedly liberal Christian Europe to make good on its promise of political equality and unfettered professional and cultural opportunities for Jews" (M. Cohen 4).[3]

It is on this notion of a tolerant medieval Iberia (extended to also characterize Christian Spain) that most contemporary political and cultural instrumentalizations of the convivencia myth are based. During the first half of the twentieth century, many political players in Spain, across the full spectrum of ideological positions, deployed the discourse of convivencia as supporting evidence to pursue their own goals. Since the transition to democracy in the late 1970s, convivencia has enjoyed a renewed popularity and legitimacy as a model for democratic Spain to follow. In the global present, it constitutes a cornerstone of Spain's own self-image. As the case studies in *Charting Memory: Recalling Medieval Spain*, edited by Stacy N. Beckwith, and *Sephardism: Spanish Jewish History and the Modern Literary Imagination*, edited by Yael Halevi-Wise, illustrate, the depiction of the status of Jews in medieval Iberia has proven adaptable to a wide variety of players within different political and historical contexts around the globe.[4] Even after many critics have questioned the validity of a concept so infused with romantic idealism, convivencia remains a metaphor of choice among many politicians, writers, tour operators, and religious leaders. As Maya Soifer has explained, "Perhaps it is this very quality of malleability that guarantees its phantom-like presence.... Having appeared under the guises of 'peaceful coexistence,' 'acculturation,' and 'daily interaction,' convivencia has become a byword that one can employ in any number of ways. Convivencia can be anything and everything" (Soifer 21).

One recent, popularized example of this historical period's idealization and explicit instrumentalization for the present is María Rosa Menocal's bestseller *The Ornament of the World: How Muslims, Jews and Christians Created a Culture of Tolerance in Medieval Spain.* In her review of Menocal's book, Mercedes García Arenal demarcates the difference between what we know about the medieval Iberian past and what we desire it to have been in order to posit it as a model for the present: "[Menocal] is drawing a myth, a beautiful myth, which, as myths do, proposes a model. The fact that it is a positive and attractive model (even perhaps a necessary one in these hard times of the 'Clash of Civilizations') should not obscure the fact that al-Andalus and Christian Spain were, like all multiple (multiethnic, multireligious) societies, fraught with tension and conflict, very often violent internal conflict, even warfare, which did not preclude mutual influences" (García Arenal 803).[5] García Arenal points out that these idealized portrayals of medieval interfaith relations usually entail an anachronistic application of modern views of religious tolerance and equal rights. Today this use of convivencia has become prevalent, especially when invoked as a synonym for the respect of differences we aspire to in contemporary multicultural democracies.

Arguments citing convivencia as a political model for the present usually contain instances of this anachronistic thinking. When Haskala (Enlightenment) German Ashkenazi intellectuals praised the rights enjoyed by Jews under medieval Muslim rule in Spain as a model to be imitated in nineteenth-century European societies, they were projecting their modern understanding of assimilation onto medieval Jews. Similarly, in 1948, Américo Castro's (14–16) argument in *España en su historia: Cristianos, moros y judíos*—that Spain's cultural identity arose in the Middle Ages from the combination of Muslim, Jewish, and Christian elements—contained an implicit response to the reshaping of Spain at that time into an inherently and exclusively Catholic country under Franco's authoritarian regime. His depiction of the three religions coexisting without much conflict until the Christian persecution of Jews at the end of the fourteenth century also resonated clearly against the belligerent and repressive notions of Spain and the "anti-Spain" that Franco deployed to eliminate dissent (Castro 203).[6] While his emphasis on the "living together" that produced Spain's identity projected a tolerant alternative to Franco's violent suppression of difference, Castro's depiction of medieval Spain failed to acknowledge the unequal relationships of power that existed between the three groups (Soifer 30; see also Ray, "Whose Golden Age?" 11).[7] This fictitious equality evoked by Castro has become preeminent in current deployments of the convivencia notion in Spain, especially when used for marketing tourism. The pervasive slogan regarding Spain as "the land of the three cultures" can be found everywhere in the country to market a specific locality, as we will explore at length in the next chapter.

Contrary to myth, the status of religious minorities under both Muslim and Christian rule was one of clear legal, social, and economic inferiority. In the theological justification for the protection of Jews by Muslims and Christians that circulated in the Middle Ages, inferiority and tolerance, far from being antithetical, functioned as interrelated concepts. As a result, violence and tolerance were in fact interrelated (Nirenberg, *Communities* 7). In the earliest Christian writings, the epistles of Saint Paul, Saint Paul warned against Jewish Christian believers continuing to observe Jewish rituals. His letter to the Galatians set out a series of dichotomies, opposing Letter to Law and flesh to soul. In order to explain how Christians could slip from truth to error, he employed the verb "to Judaize." This association between Judaism and the realm of the flesh (the material world, the Old Testament, the literal meaning of texts) was amplified in the Gospels, creating a theology that identified danger with proximity to Jewish people, rituals, and beliefs (Nirenberg, *Anti-Judaism* 59–64, 84). "Judaizing" by gentile Christians was deeply threatening to the Christian claim of having superseded Judaism, and this threat translated into fierce anti-Judaism (M. Cohen 19–20, 61). By the end of the fourth century, the *adversus Iudaeos* or *contra Iudaeos* tradition, Christian teachings "against the Jews," had become a defining feature of orthodox theology (Fredriksen xv).

Saint Augustine (354–430) produced alternative readings of foundational Church texts to defend the need for the continuing existence of Jews as Jews in a Christian world. In *Against Faustus*, he attributed to Jews a positive, useful, and unique role performed in service of the Church. Because of their unbelief, Augustine argued, the Jews observed the law without understanding its true meaning and thus received no grace. They were the vessels that transported and embodied God's message and preserved the Old Testament, which bore the prophecies fulfilled in the New Testament, but they remained blind to it. Scattered everywhere in the punishment of exile, they existed as witnesses to the message of Christ (Fredriksen 276–77). In *City of God*, Augustine reformulated these ideas, quoting Psalm 59:12, "Slay them not, lest they forget your Law," to conclude that Jews were vital witnesses to Christ's message and therefore should not be "killed" (made to abandon their Jewish practices). Throughout the Middle Ages this psalm would be used to invoke Augustine's authority in matters relating to the Jews (ushering in, presumably, the principle of "toleration" that Varela in 1797 attributes to Paul). The unarticulated paradox latent in Augustine's doctrine of "exclusion within inclusion," however, manifested both as respect for Jewish lives and justification of violence against them. The "slay them not" admonition was on occasions interpreted in its literal sense, resulting in Jewish lives being saved (Fredriksen 348–52). But an invocation of Augustine's using a slightly altered, longer version of the same psalm ("Slay them not, for God does not wish them to be entirely killed and altogether wiped out, but to be preserved for greater torment and reproach, like the fratricide Cain, in a life worse than death") was also used in the Middle Ages to justify their repression and persecution (Nirenberg, *Anti-Judaism* 132–33).[8]

In a literal understanding of the Augustinian notion of the Jew's special function as a blind "living letter" that exists to attest the truth of Christianity, Christian medieval rulers in Europe considered Jews a special form of chattel property. The extreme subjection of Jews served the purpose of extending sovereign power, especially through allowing Jewish moneylending, from which the princes or kings greatly benefited (Nirenberg, *Anti-Judaism* 191–94). Criticisms of this royal "protection," usually voiced by the nobility and often used as a tool for the mobilization of the popular masses, had intensified by the twelfth century: apocryphal tales of Jews engaging in host desecrations, murdering Christian children, and causing plague and disease were repeated throughout Europe. Kings who protected them were accused of being "Jew lovers," addicted to corrupt materialism, and oppressive of their Christian subjects. Discriminatory measures and persecution of Jews came to signify spiritual purity and gradually every ruler in western Europe adopted these measures and eventually espoused expulsion (Nirenberg, *Anti-Judaism* 197–207).[9]

PURITY OF BLOOD, RACE, AND THE INQUISITION IN CHRISTIAN SPAIN

In 1391, following the sermons of Ferrand Martínez, archdeacon of Ecija (Seville), mobs of people throughout Spain attacked Jews with unprecedented violence, destroying their synagogues and massacring tens of thousands. The riots obeyed the slogan of "conversion or death" and resulted in massive numbers of conversions. There had been cases of voluntary conversions in Spain beginning in the thirteenth century, in a climate of mounting Christian evangelization pressures.[10] But the large number of conversions that occurred at the end of the fourteenth century was something unprecedented among Jewish communities in Europe.[11]

The "success" of the conversions immediately brought a profound crisis of classification and identity, transforming the old boundaries that had kept Christians and Jews apart. Suddenly, Jews vanished from the main cities of Castile and Aragon, to be replaced by a new group, the "New Christians," or conversos. The difference between a Christian and a Jew became blurred, and much anxiety ensued over the difficulty of telling who was who. As a result, segregationist measures were put in place so that those who remained Jewish would be geographically separated in distinct quarters from those who had converted. A renewed effort was undertaken to enforce the use of conspicuous badges and "Jewish hats" by Jews.[12] The enactment of further discriminatory legislation that severely limited Jews' economic activities following the preaching of Saint Vincent Ferrer, imposed as a way of sharpening the boundaries between the two groups, brought a new wave of mass conversions in 1412–15 (Nirenberg, "Mass Conversion" 10–12; Amelang 71–72).

The precise status of the conversos, their degree of "Jewishness," the sincerity of their conversion, and the motivations behind their actions would be the subject of numerous and heated debates in both Jewish and Christian circles and would have fateful consequences for many years to come. One of the many significant developments that followed these conversions was the entry of conversos into offices and positions that had been forbidden to them as Jews. Suddenly unhindered by these laws, New Christians were able to take advantage of many professional and social opportunities. Resenting the new competition for offices and marriage alliances at the highest level, the so-called Old Christians tried to impose limits on this ascension to power. The Pauline Christian doctrine that all baptized Christians be treated as equals became questioned. Ironically, while many Christians rejected Christian officials' position that conversos and their children were truly Christian, many Jews, as the fifteenth century progressed, began to see them as Christian, rejecting rabbinic authorities' view that they were still Jewish (Ray, "Whose Golden Age?" 7).

Heated discussions about the rights of conversos to hold office took place in Toledo in the 1430s. A vocabulary of "race" emerged from these debates: the Castilian words *raza*, *casta*, and *linaje* ("race," "caste," and "lineage," respectively) connected behavior to appearance in a deterministic way and connected both of them to nature and reproduction. By referring to Jews as a raza, conversos and their descendants became represented as heirs to all the immutable negative qualities that had been attributed to their forebears. The role of lineage in determining character became more explicitly biological and began to be applied extensively to conversos. Once the conception of raza was in place, it automatically followed that, if Jews were unfit to hold office, their converso heirs would be equally unqualified. By contrast, Old Christians boasted of a genealogical advantage. The terms *cristianos de natura* (Christians by nature) and *cristianos lindos* (beautiful Christians), which encompassed this exclusionary genealogical reasoning, became common terms of reference for Old Christians (Nirenberg, "Was There?" 247–54).[13]

This racial logic, which saw personal character and morality as a byproduct of biology, became the foundation on which the infamous doctrine of *limpieza de sangre* (purity of blood) would be built. In 1449, as a result of the town's rebellion against the Castilian monarchy, Toledo's head mayor Pedro Sarmiento wrote the first official document outlining the statutes of purity of blood. The document sanctioned social discrimination against conversos and posited that Jews and Muslims were biologically inferior to Christians and inherently predisposed to religious heresy and moral corruption. The statutes, later adopted in many cities and institutions, became "the criterion for membership in the Spanish elite" (Feros 61).

This genealogical mentality permeated the discourses of the day. Although some conversos tried to make the opposite argument, claiming that nobility was found in individuals' deeds more than in ancestry, once the genealogical turn was taken, agreement on its validity quickly became widespread. In an ironic twist, Jews and conversos themselves began to use genealogy in an attempt to counteract the charge of belonging to a corrupt lineage. They produced a series of counter-genealogies in which they tried to show the superior nobility of their origins by stressing their kinship with King David, the Virgin Mary, and Jesus himself (Nirenberg, "Mass Conversion" 27–31).[14] This "noble lineage" argument served exiled Jews and conversos, as it bolstered their social standing in their new homes. But for conversos inside Spain it became a dangerous argument, as they were trying both to make people respect their ancestry as noble and to make them forget it, so as not to become targets of the Inquisition (Nirenberg, "Mass Conversion" 32).

The reiteration of charges that conversos were habitually corrupt in their behavior because of their Jewish blood justified the establishment of the Spanish Inquisition in 1481. This special Inquisition was charged with identifying those Christians who deviated from orthodoxy. Its most common accusation was Judaizing, or "acting Jewish," an old preoccupation (to borrow Varela's expression) of Christian theology, as we saw earlier. Culture and biology were inextricable from each other in the Inquisition's search for suspicious people: "Judaizers were to be identified by their behavior, but that behavior only gained meaning in light of their flesh's genealogy . . . since the effects of genealogy were primarily expressed culturally, the religio-racial classification of cultural practice became an important part of the accusational economy. Virtually any negative cultural trait could be presented as 'Judaizing.' . . . [Jewish characteristics] included heresy, apostasy, love of novelty and dissension, ambition, presumption, and hatred of peace" (Nirenberg, "Was There?" 259–60). Thus, almost any practice or idea could be presented as proof of Judaizing if the accused had Jewish lineage. In Inquisition records, conversos were often accused of the error of glorifying their lineage. Their Jewishness transpired in this pride about lineage, Old Christians claimed. By characterizing the concern with lineage as Jewish, Old Christians thus justified the genealogical discriminations embodied in the Inquisition and the statutes of purity of blood. This accusation was a new iteration of an old tradition that blamed Jews for their own segregation from Christians. Thus, when Saint Vincent Ferrer implemented a host of segregationist measures after the mass conversions of 1391, he attributed the invention to Jews, saying: "This is what your own law desires, since you want to be separate from the Christians in faith, you should also be separate from them in conversation" (Nirenberg, "Mass Conversion" 30–36).[15]

Many long-term, powerful ideas about Jews and their relationship with Christians can be traced back to these disputes over the status of the conversos. It is quite ironic that this post-1391 moment of Christianity's triumph over Judaism, when tens of thousands of Jews converted to Christianity, resulted in such a psychological crisis of Christian identity that some of the worst, most harmful ideas about Jews found a new, more powerful reincarnation. This concern with lineage and purity of blood, with its proto-racist thinking, set an important precedent for modern racial antisemitism. Another influential idea that had its origin in the anti-converso polemics written to justify the statutes of purity of blood was the suspicion of a Jewish and/or converso conspiracy to take over Spain (or the world), as we will see later in this chapter.

THE MYTH OF SEPHARDI ECONOMIC SUPREMACY

During the mid-sixteenth century in Europe, a series of highly successful and widely translated and distributed travel books about the East written by both Christian and Jewish authors widely disseminated what Benjamin Braude calls "the myth of the Sefardi economic superman." These accounts "took the real economic achievements of the [Jewish] merchants and entrepreneurs who settled in . . . the Ottoman Empire and made of them economic supermen"

(Braude 182). Frenchman Pierre Belon, the author of one of the most famous of these travel books, said in 1553: "[Sephardi Jews] have so completely seized hold of all the trade in merchandise in Turkey that the riches and revenue of the Turk are in their hands" (Braude 182).[16] These portraits of opulence became commonly accepted throughout Europe. Echoes of Belon's words can be heard in Pedro Varela's justification for bringing the Jews back to Spain because they possessed "the largest wealth of Europe and Asia."

As Braude argues, the life of real Jews living within the Ottoman Empire was not that of "economic supermen." Iberian Jewish exiles did possess very useful knowledge of western Mediterranean languages, Western trading practices and needs, and the industrial processing of woolen textiles. Thus, they excelled in two areas of economic activity: as cultural and linguistic mediators in Ottoman Mediterranean trade and as entrepreneurs in the textile industry (Braude 184–85). This, however, never placed Jews in a position of dominance within the Ottoman economy, as some Europeans claimed. The Ottoman economy was, unsurprisingly, dominated by Muslims. But precisely because of the linguistic knowledge of exiled Jews, any Europeans traveling or conducting business in the East depended on Jews as intermediaries. This limited experience became the source of two misrepresentations: European visitors believed that their guides, translators, and mediators had more power than they actually had, and they also assumed that commerce with Europe was the Ottoman Empire's most important foreign trade, which was not the case (Braude 186–87).

Jews and conversos themselves also contributed to the myth of Sephardi superiority. The boasting about lineage that had begun as a Jewish response to the statutes of purity of blood continued to appear and evolve in the writings of exiled Jews and in subsequent generations of conversos who decided to leave Spain and Portugal under pressure of the Inquisition. Allusions to these arguments became constituent of the genre of Jewish apologetics, defenses of Judaism against Christian attacks, which flourished in the sixteenth and seventeenth centuries among former Iberian conversos wishing to justify their choice of returning to Judaism and encouraging others to do the same (Yerushalmi 48). Among the most influential of these writers were Menasseh Ben Israel (formerly Manoel Dias Soeiro) and Isaac Cardoso (formerly Don Fernando Cardoso).

Ben Israel, born of converso parents in Portugal in 1604, moved with his parents to the Netherlands in 1610, where he established the first Hebrew printing press in 1626. His book *Esperanza de Israel* (*Hope of Israel*), first published in Spanish and Latin in Amsterdam in 1650 and soon translated into English, Dutch, Yiddish, Hebrew, and French, has been one of the best-known and most influential works of modern Jewish letters, continuously in print in several languages from its first edition (Braude 173–74). Isaac Cardoso was born around 1610 in Portugal into a converso family that moved to Spain, where he attained fame and fortune as a professor at the University of Valladolid and as chief physician at the Madrid royal court. At the very pinnacle of his career, in 1648, he abandoned Spain to live as a Jew in Venice and later Verona. In his renowned book *Las excelencias de los Hebreos*, published in Amsterdam in 1679, he explained Jewish law, emphasized the Jews' superior qualities, and refuted common slanders brought against them (see Yerushalmi).

Although from different perspectives and for different reasons, Ben Israel and Cardoso depicted an exaggerated portrait of Sephardi Jews' worldwide power and influence that was very similar to that described by sixteenth-century gentile travel books such as Pierre Belon's (Braude 172, 179). Ben Israel cultivated the "economic supermen" myth with the immediate and practical goal of preserving or extending the right of Jewish trade and residence in different European nations (Braude 181). He was instrumental in negotiating the return of Jews to England in the mid-seventeenth century (Braude 173–74). At that time, the image of the "economic supermen," which, ironically, would later serve as the basis for one of the most potent antisemitic charges against Jews, strongly benefited Jews' political standing in Europe: "The association of Iberian Jews with this political and economic dominance raised their utility in the eyes of all Europeans. Their repute spread as far as Poland, whose ruler took special steps to attract Sefardi merchants. This image . . . played a potent role in the reopening of Western Europe to Jewish settlement, first in the Italian city-states, and then Holland, and later England" (Braude 182). These are the developments that Varela alludes to in 1797, when he mentions how "the example of all the nations of Europe, and even of Rome itself, authorizes us." Spain, he said, should do what other European nations had done: bring the Jews back to bolster the nation's finances. Varela was not writing about recent events, however. As Jonathan Israel has explained, the last third of the sixteenth century, from 1570 onward, marked a turning point in the relationship between western Europe and the Jews, a reversal of the trend of expulsion and exclusion toward Jewish return and reintegration. At this time, Jews were readmitted in the Czech lands, Italy, Germany, France, and the Netherlands (Israel 29).[17] In his argument, Varela was referring to events that had taken place over two centuries earlier. The following section of this chapter explains the historical context that predated Varela's attempt to bring the Jews back to Spain.

OLIVARES, QUEVEDO, AND JEWISH CONSPIRACIES

About 150 years before Varela's initiative, the Count-Duke of Olivares, prime minister of Felipe IV between 1621 and 1643 and the most powerful man in the kingdom, tried to persuade the king to rethink the relationship between Spain and the Jews. At the time, Spain was entangled in the Thirty Years' War (1618–48), a massive military effort against many of the Protestant states allied with France in locations as diverse as Italy, Germany, the Low Countries, Brazil, and the Caribbean. The war required economic resources and financing at an unprecedented scale, and the Count-Duke of Olivares turned to wealthy Portuguese converso bankers for assistance.

Olivares espoused the pragmatic European mercantilism of his time and sought the state's economic interest at the expense of tradition and religious concerns (Israel 2). Since the 1550s, Genovese bankers had dominated crown finances and had made enormous profits for themselves. In 1626, Olivares ended this monopoly and began to use the services of the Portuguese as a means to hold the Genovese demand for higher interest rates in check.[18] The Portuguese conversos could be paid lower rates, and since they lived under the ubiquitous and arbitrary threat of the Inquisition, they could be offered alternative forms of compensation, such as social concessions and offers of protection. For example, they were granted an edict of grace from the Inquisition and complete freedom of movement and permission to conduct business with the American colonies from Sevilla. These measures resulted in the emigration of an unprecedented number of Portuguese conversos to Spain, where they took charge of about half of Spain's financial contracts or *asientos* (Elliott 299–303; Israel 91; Cabo Aseguinolaza and Fernández Mosquera xxviii–xxix).[19]

Olivares's attitude toward Jews and conversos went further than purely economic mercantilism. He became famous among friends and foes alike for protecting conversos at court. One of his assistants, Manuel López Pereira, member of the council of finance in the 1630s, had brothers occupying prominent positions in the Amsterdam Sephardi community (Israel 92). Olivares's and Fernando Cardoso's paths crossed in fact during Cardoso's medical career in Madrid. The prime minister became a patron of Cardoso, who dedicated two of his medical treatises to him. In his biography of Cardoso, Yosef Yerushalmi speculates that Cardoso was probably seeking not just a patron in Olivares but also a protector, given Olivares's fame (169). Olivares also befriended North African Jews like Jacob Cansino, a leader of the Oran community, who lived in Madrid for several periods as an openly professing Jew under Olivares's protection (Israel 92).[20] In addition, it was widely known that Olivares had converso roots: his grandmother, Francisca de Ribera Niño, was the daughter of the powerful converso Lope Conchillos, who had served the Catholic monarch King Fernando. Ribera Niño had married the first count of Olivares in 1539. As we will see below, famous Spanish poet Francisco de Quevedo would use this fact to great effect in his attacks against the count-duke. Olivares's friendships and genealogy led many of his enemies to accuse him of preferring the company of Jews. They also began to spread rumors about his plans to cancel the 1492 edict of expulsion and bring the Jews back to Spain. Needless to say, these rumors caused great scandal.[21]

Beyond speculation and political attacks, there were concrete actions taken by Olivares that spoke clearly about his position regarding Jews and conversos. One of Olivares's lifelong efforts was the modification of the statutes of purity of blood. As early as 1625, he spoke vehemently against these laws during a meeting of the Council of State, describing them as "unjust and impious, against divine law, natural law, and the law of nations" (Elliott 10–11). He sought to modify the statutes, so that a distinguished record of military or mercantile service might remove the taint of impurity and qualify the deserving for titles of nobility (298). He also espoused the project, debated several times in the Council of State, of bringing Sephardi Jews from Holland, France, and Hamburg, with guarantees of immunity from the Inquisition. As Israel explains in connection to the Portuguese conversos, Olivares's plan was that they "would only be required to conform outwardly to Catholicism, as was the practice in France, so as to veil what would have amounted to a government license to practice Judaism in private" (Israel 92).

Olivares's plan did not succeed, and the highly visible presence of Portuguese conversos in Madrid soon became a source of violent conflict. They became the targets of increasing anti-Portuguese hysteria in the 1630s, a xenophobia tinged with anti-Judaism, since many of them were suspected of being crypto-Jews.[22] Notwithstanding Olivares's protection, several of them were sentenced by the Inquisition (Elliott 303–4, 607). In 1632 a massive auto-da-fé, one of the largest ever held in Madrid, was attended by King Felipe IV and Olivares. A group of poor Portuguese conversos who had been accused, by the shaky testimony of a ten-year-old boy, of flagellating and desecrating an image of Christ were condemned and burned alive.[23] Yerushalmi describes the events as "above all a great show of strength on the part of the Inquisition, alarmed at the recent New Christian influx from Portugal." The Inquisition succeeded in arousing the passions of the people of Madrid, who helped the authorities tear down with their bare hands the house in the Calle de las Infantas where the events had supposedly taken place. Subsequently, a convent in honor of the flagellated

Christ was built on the site, and many books and poems were published about the events, including one by Lope de Vega (Yerushalmi 120).

A year after this auto-da-fé, another incident stirred further anti-converso sentiments. On the morning of July 2, 1633, a series of signs were posted in several central Madrid streets. Written in Portuguese, they said things such as "long live the law of Moses and death to that of Christ." A major scandal ensued, with civil authorities and the Inquisition immediately taking action and offering large rewards for information about the culprits (Cabo Aseguinolaza and Fernández Mosquera xii–xvii). The incident prompted the writing of Quevedo's infamous work *Execración contra los judíos* [Execration of the Jews, 1633], one of the most violent antisemitic attacks ever written in Spain. Quevedo placed these events within the context of Olivares's actions and used his vicious antisemitic propaganda to attack the prime minister, especially his mercantilist policy (Cabo Aseguinolaza and Fernández Mosquera x, xxxiii).[24]

One of the pillars of Quevedo's argument is an idea that would reappear in the turbulent politics of the 1930s, as we will see later in this chapter. Quevedo related Olivares's deal-making with Portuguese converso bankers to the episode known as the "Letter from Constantinople." In sixteenth-century Spain, and in the context of the debates regarding the introduction of the statutes of purity of blood in the Cathedral of Toledo, Archbishop Juan Martínez Silíceo brought forth a series of letters supposedly exchanged between Spanish and Constantinopolitan Jews. Today, there is a critical consensus that the whole episode was a hoax and that Silíceo himself forged these letters. The first letter was said to have been written in 1492 by Spanish Jews seeking advice from their brethren in the Ottoman Empire on whether to convert or go into exile. The "reply," supposedly written by the rabbis of Constantinople, advised Spanish Jews to convert and infiltrate Christian society in order to seek revenge and destroy it from the inside:

> Regarding what you state about the King of Spain compelling you to become Christians, let him do it for there is nothing that you can do to prevent it. Concerning what you write about the fact that they are seizing your goods, well turn your children into merchants so that, bit by bit, they may seize their goods. In connection with what you have said about their murdering you, well turn your sons into doctors and apothecaries, so that they may murder them. As regards what you say about their destroying your synagogues, turn your sons into clergymen and theologians, so that they may destroy their churches. Finally, vis-à-vis what you have to say about the vexations that they make you suffer, strive so that your sons may become lawyers, attorneys, notaries, and counselors and that they should always know how public affairs work so

> that they may dominate them and win lands. Follow these instructions in the same order and this way you will get your revenge and through experience you will witness how you shall be transformed from being social outcasts to being held in considerable esteem. (quoted in Soyer 371–72)[25]

Expanding on this argument, Quevedo's *Execración* argues that conversos control everything in Spain. Even if the letters were proven spurious, says Quevedo, conversos were in fact implementing their designs. The economic policies of Olivares had allowed conversos to infiltrate the highest spheres of government and thus were facilitating the conversos' destruction of Spain. Not even the rabbis of Constantinople could have imagined such success (Quevedo 11–13).

Needless to say, Quevedo was a fervent supporter of the purity of blood statutes. He believed that conversos were, and would always remain, 100 percent Jewish and that Judaism could be found in the blood, with just one drop contaminating a whole body otherwise made up of good Christian blood. The passing of time would not mitigate this blood's contaminating effect (Quevedo 14). Given this fact, he exhorted the king to expel the "Jews" (i.e., conversos), just like his father had done in 1609 with the moriscos (Quevedo 25). He reminded the king that God had rewarded the Catholic monarchs with the expansion of the Spanish Empire for expelling the Jews, and that God was now punishing Spain for tolerating them (Quevedo 14).

A few years later, in 1699, Quevedo returned to the conspiracy theory narrative thread in *La hora de todos y la Fortuna con seso,* a devastating critique of Olivares's domestic and international policies. One of its forty satirical episodes, "La isla de los monopantos" depicted an international Jewish conspiracy to secure wealth and power in order to destroy Christianity. In the story, Jews meet in a conclave in Salonika, to which the governor of the Monopantos island sends six men. This governor's name is Pragas Chincollos, an anagrammatic reference to Gaspar Lope Conchillos, the converso ancestor of Olivares. The Monopantos, led by their governor, offer to collaborate with this Jewish conspiracy in the destruction of the world (Elliott 556).[26] This tale brings together the myth of Sephardi economic superiority and the belief in a Jewish international conspiracy to take over the world.

In his article about the myth of the Sephardi economic superman, Braude explains how those Christian authors like Belon and Nicolas de Nicolay, who chose to focus on and grossly exaggerated Ottoman Jews' power and influence, were at the same time propagating common antisemitic charges of malice, fraud, deceit, and usury (182–83). Braude's assertion that these authors "were often reflecting their own fears and paranoias more vividly than the reality they claimed to represent" (190) is exemplified in a quote from Belon: "Since

I have many times been obliged to use the services of the Jews and to frequent them, I have readily learnt that this nation is the most subtle and the most full of malice" (qtd. in Braude 190–91). The quote encompasses both admiration for and fear of the Jews. Similarly, J. H. Elliott considers Quevedo's paranoia regarding a Jewish conspiracy "symptomatic of the reactions of a society that felt itself under threat" (Elliott 680). In a 1949 article, J. A. Van Praag argued that Quevedo's "La Isla de los Monopantos" provided the basic plot for what would become the most famous antisemitic pamphlet of all times, the *Protocols of the Elders of Zion*. Before following that thread to Spain in the twentieth century, the next section looks at the development of the modern myth of Sephardi racial superiority and the racialized difference between Sephardi and Ashkenazi Jews, a cornerstone of the way Spain would come to think about Jews in the twentieth and twenty-first centuries.

MODERN SEPHARDI RACIAL SUPERIORITY

The initial goal of the exiled Sephardi Jews who overstated their learning, wealth, wisdom, and influence was to help consolidate their group identity within new and not always welcoming surroundings. This embellished portrait gained new strength in the mid-eighteenth century when destitute Polish and German Jews began migrating westward into areas where Sephardi Jews had then been living for over two centuries. Believing that these new arrivals blackened the name of all Jews, Sephardi Jews redeployed the myth of their superiority. They emphasized their refinement and assimilation, all the positive characteristics they perceived lacking in Ashkenazi Jews. In an attempt to set themselves apart from a group they perceived as a direct threat to their status, Amsterdam Sephardi Jews set in place discriminatory measures against other Jews and did not use the same synagogues, mix socially, or marry them (Endelman 26–28; Bodian, *Hebrews* 131–33).

As mentioned earlier, by the nineteenth century, Ashkenazi German intellectuals associated with the Haskalah appropriated and reinforced this myth of Sephardi superiority in order to critique and break away from the elements they disliked in their own tradition (Endelman 28–31). Ismar Schorsch has shown how these intellectuals added another set of highly idealized qualities to the already powerful image of medieval Jewish life on the Iberian Peninsula. They described it as a period of "cultural openness, philosophic thinking, and an appreciation for the aesthetic." This mythic model enabled them to critique Ashkenazi Judaism in order to redefine their identity as emancipated Jews, as citizens with rights equal to those of gentiles in nineteenth-century Germany (Schorsch 71). The attractiveness of Sephardi models did not solely belong to the past: "The far more privileged, prosperous, and assimilated Sephardi Jews of Amsterdam, London, and Bordeaux served as the cutting edge of the campaign for emancipation" (Schorsch 75). Thus, this Ashkenazi contribution to the construction of the convivencia myth incorporated into a single argumentative thread the various discourses Sephardi Jews had built over generations about the cultural superiority and assimilation of Iberian Jews both inside and outside of the Iberian Peninsula.

German Jewish scientists in the nineteenth century further bolstered the myth of Sephardi superiority, adding to it the tools of scientific racism. We have already seen how a protoracial preoccupation with lineage and descent in the political context of the purity of blood statutes lay at the origin of this myth. In response to accusations of Jewish racial degeneracy, Jewish scientists posited Iberian Jews as examples of physically perfect Jews, "noble Jews" that served as role models for all Jews (Schapkow 56, 130). The distinction between Sephardi and Ashkenazi Jews, constructed and "scientifically proven" at this historic juncture by physical anthropologists, followed antisemitic Christian thought in vilifying contemporary Jews (in this case, central and eastern European Jews) and praising ancient Israelites. Sephardi Jews became identified with these biblical Jews and were seen as their direct descendants (Efron 81, 88). According to these theories, Sephardim constituted a nobler human type, more beautiful physically and more dignified and proud in their behavior. This distinction between noble Sephardi and degraded Ashkenazi, connected to the myth of a past Golden Age of Spanish Jewry disseminated by nineteenth-century Ashkenazi intellectuals, would also be appropriated in Spain for nationalistic purposes.

SPAIN'S MODERN REENCOUNTER WITH THE JEWS

After Olivares's attempts, other diplomats and ministers would unsuccessfully propose plans to open the country to the Jews' return.[27] In the late eighteenth and nineteenth centuries, a variety of arguments about the place of Jews in Spain's history brewed in political discussions over the gradual decline of Spain as a world power. As Hazel Gold observes, "Ironically, in the later eighteenth and nineteenth centuries, the figure of 'the Jew' inhabits the principal discourses of Spanish society—theology, philosophy, philology, politics, art, literature, journalism—even though Jews are nowhere to be found within the borders of the nation" (Gold 90). These discussions gained urgency as Spain's progressive loss of its overseas empire culminated in the humiliating 1898 defeat by the United States in the Spanish-American War.

While explanations for Spain's decline coalesced into two distinctive ideological fields, both coincided in resting their arguments on their understanding of the figure of a mythical Jew, "a blank signifier, infinitely malleable and continually rewritten in the service of liberal and conservative agendas alike" (Gold 93). Jews were at the center of heated political debate on the issue of the abolition of the Inquisition, the role of church and state, freedom of conscience, and individual rights. These were, at their core, debates about modernity itself and Spain's place in a modern world order. An emblematic example of the political symbolism of "Jewish issues" at this time can be seen in the back-and-forth decisions regarding the abolition of the Inquisition during the first third of the nineteenth-century. After the French invasion of Spain in 1808, Napoleon eliminated the tribunal of the Inquisition, and in 1813, the Cortes of Cádiz officially voted to abolish it.[28] It was then reestablished by Fernando VII in 1814, again eliminated during the Trienio Liberal in 1820, reestablished by the absolutists in 1823, and finally terminated for good by order of the Regent Queen María Cristina in April 1834 (Rozenberg 73).

Jews resurfaced again in debates about religious freedom and the relation of church and state during the preparation of the 1869 constitution. In general terms, conservatives defended the Inquisition, the expulsion of the Jews, and the religious and political unification of Spain by the Catholic Monarchs as the root of Spanish greatness and blamed the nation's decline on the survival of conversos' heretical beliefs, which they saw as the forebears of liberal and Enlightenment thinkers (Álvarez Chillida, *El antisemitismo* 100–101). For the liberals, by contrast, the medieval era was Spain's true Golden Age, a period founded on respect for municipal and regional autonomy and religious coexistence. The Inquisition and the expulsion of the Jews, they reasoned, brought an economic and cultural catastrophe whose effects compounded over the years to bring about the current deterioration of Spanish power (Gold 102–103; Rozenberg 74–78).

These two radically opposed views of Spanish history have survived well into the twenty-first century, and the effect of the Jewish absence since the expulsion is still viewed as one of the critical elements that determined the historical evolution of the country. From extremely different ideological stances, Jews have been consistently associated in Spain's imaginary with modernity, reason, mercantilism, science, urban life, and industry—all values that were for a long time, for many sectors of Spanish society, considered to be dangerous and contrary to "Spanish" values (Villatoro 340).[29] If at the time of Olivares and Quevedo public opinion was overwhelmingly on the side of Quevedo, greater ambivalence, regarding both identification and disidentification with this Jewish Other, would infuse cultural debates from the late eighteenth century onward. In today's Spain, these discourses are being revisited by a variety of institutional and private actors. Current initiatives in regard to the memory of Jewish Spain both echo this complex history and claim a position of candid innocence toward it.

As Susan Martin-Márquez has explained, the rise in Arabic and Hebrew studies in the second half of the nineteenth century would result in an ambivalent process of "formulation of hegemonic as well as alternative conceptualizations of the nation which recognized an incorporation of the other within the self" (Martin-Márquez 28). While these studies mark the beginning of a reevaluation of the Arab and Jewish past, the way these "others" were incorporated was mainly through their "Hispanization." This theory would include Muslims and Jews in Spanish history but would do so through their differentiation from contemporary Muslims and Jews, seen as inferior. Arabists and Hebraists were interested in Muslim and Jewish history and philology inasmuch as these subjects helped to glorify "their own" Spanish history (Ojeda Mata, *Identidades* 282–84).

José Antonio Conde was among the first modern historians to use Arabic as well as Latin sources for his influential, widely translated, three-volume *Historia de la dominación de los árabes en España* (1820–21). As Alex Novikoff explains, Conde wanted "to vindicate Spanish Muslim culture before the eyes of his European contemporaries," but "he could not help but make the comparison between what he saw as the golden age of the (Spanish) Muslim past and the deplorable state of the (non-Spanish) Muslim present" (Novikoff 13, see also Martin-Márquez 28, 54).[30] In the 1860s, as their writings continued to be consumed by a wide public, Arabists Francisco Fernández y González and Francisco Javier Simonet publicly clashed over the meaning of Spanish Arab history for Spain's identity. Liberal Fernández y González proclaimed the cultural accomplishments of al-Andalus, the superiority of medieval Arabic civilization, and argued that a "Semitic inheritance" was still palpable in Spain. Simonet, a devout Catholic, insisted that the achievements belonged only to Christians and that Arab culture did not have any influence on medieval Christian Spain. Medieval Arab intellectuals of al-Andalus like Ibn Hayyan and Ibn Hazm, he said, were racially Spaniards (Martin-Márquez 31; Novikoff 14).

An early example of this process of Hispanization in terms of Hebrew studies is that of José Rodríguez de Castro, whose volume 1 of the *Biblioteca española* in 1781 was dedicated to "Spanish rabbi writers" (Álvarez Chillida, *El antisemitismo* 55). As Michal Friedman explains, his was "part of a broader project cataloguing authors and works he considered 'Spanish'" (Friedman,

"Reconstructing" 58). Andrew Bush has described how, by the mid-nineteenth century, José María García Blanco's standard text for training Spanish Hebraists spoke of "'el español Aben-Ezra' [the Spaniard (Abraham) Ibn-Ezra] among the 'monumentos de nuestras glorias literarias' [monuments of our literary glory]" (Bush 14). Bush and Friedman argue that it is in the work of José Amador de los Ríos that we find the first fully articulated modern history of the Jews of Spain. *Estudios históricos, políticos y literarios de los judíos de España* was published in 1848, and later revised as *Historia social, política y religiosa de los judíos de España* (1875–76). The book received acclaim, and as a result Amador de los Ríos was made a fellow at the prestigious Royal Academy of History. His work influenced some of the most important political figures of the second half of the nineteenth century in Spain, such as Emilio Castelar (1832–1899) (Ojeda Mata, "Thinking" 59).[31] Like his immediate predecessors, Amador de los Ríos saw medieval Spanish Jews as Spaniards. As Bush explains: "Unlike in Germany, however, where Jewish Studies developed primarily as a separate Jewish history, from the time of Amador de los Ríos and his immediate antecedents, modern Jewish Studies in Spain has been primarily conducted by telling the story of the Spanish nation such that 'our Jews' would be counted among 'our forebears'" (Bush 14). This particular view of Spain's Jewish past would have important consequences for future developments in Spanish tourism, politics, and culture, as we will see in the following pages.[32]

Spain's modern reencounter with the Jews took place in parallel with its reencountering of its Arab past. Both have been traversed by a concern over Spain's image abroad, diplomacy, and the international repercussions of internal political decisions. Martin-Márquez has shown how the process of glorification of Spain's Muslim past and its "marketing" began in the late eighteenth century with Spanish intellectuals who tried to incorporate Spain in the discourses of the European Enlightenment. Spanish Arabists pointed to the development of scientific and technological advances in al-Andalus and proposed theories about the Andalusi origins of Gothic architecture and troubadour poetry to justify Spain's place in Europe (Martin-Márquez 26–27). Amador de los Ríos, who wrote about both the Arab and Jewish presence in Spanish literature, art and architecture, did exactly that in his *Sevilla pintoresca,* in which the recuperation of Spain's Arab heritage "coincide[s] with national interests" (Bush 15).

In terms of foreign relations and diplomacy, a revealing case was the petition initiated by the prominent German rabbi Ludwig Philippson in 1854 asking for the repeal of the 1492 decree of expulsion and the institution of freedom of religious worship. Philippson, a representative figure of the emancipation movement, sent the petition in coordination with the Jewish communities of Marseille and Bayonne. He used Amador de los Ríos's book as evidence of the Jewish contributions to Spanish culture and of the presumed tolerance enjoyed by Jews in medieval Spain. He claimed that "freedom of religious worship served as a measure of 'civilization' and called upon Spain to establish her place among the other 'civilized' and 'humane' European nations who had already instituted this freedom" (Friedman, "Jewish History" 103–4; Avni 8–9; Schapkow 226–33).

In a response to Philippson published in *Revista española de ambos mundos* in 1855, de los Ríos offered a very different reading of his own book. Observing how his account of the history of Spain's Jews proved Jewish incompatibility with Spain, he opposed Philippson's idea of repealing the expulsion decree because, he argued, religious freedom was potentially destructive of Spanish national unity (Friedman, "Jewish History" 105). De los Ríos advanced further refutation of Philippson's claims on the grounds that "only a Catholic Spaniard like himself was qualified for the task of engaging with Spanish history and its contemporary implications. Thus, Philippson, 'a man who does not even bear a Castilian surname' and 'who does not even speak in the name of the descendants of the Jews expelled from Spain in 1492,' was unfit for such an endeavor. Philippson's Jewishness, he noted, was an impediment to a balanced rendering of Spanish history" (Friedman, "Jewish History" 106). Extending his critique to other Jewish historians, de los Ríos concluded that "it would be useless to expect from them either an instance of impartiality, or a grain of justice" (qtd. in Friedman, "Jewish History" 114).

As Bush points out, it is important to keep in mind that, in contrast to the development of the "Science of Judaism" in Germany, Jewish studies began in Spain as the work of non-Jewish scholars (19). Spaniards writing about Spain's Jewish history would in fact state this fact—not being Jews—as the most important contributing factor that made their work objective and impartial (Ojeda Mata, "Thinking" 59). Thus, Adolfo de Castro clarified in the first pages of his *Historia de los judíos en España* (1847): "I write this history dispassionately and impartially—passion and partiality belong not to me. I neither am a Jew, nor a descendent from Judaizers [*sic*]. My sole aim is to stand up for the truth—a rule by which every historian ought to be guided" (quoted in Novikoff 14). As we will see in the following chapters, echoes of this double argument—the history of the Jews in Spain is Spanish history and non-Jews are best qualified to tell it—emerge in current understandings of the medieval Iberian Jewish past as part of the patrimony of the locations (towns, communities, the nation) where it once took place.

In spite of Amador de los Ríos's quick effort to discredit Philippson's petition, it became the center of a heated debate. As a result, the Spanish Cortes voted in February 1855 that no Spaniard or foreigner could be persecuted for his opinions or religious beliefs, although freedom of religion was not formally approved. They also voted for considering only "merit and capacity" as considerations for any position or distinction, de facto making the statutes of purity of blood invalid (Pérez-Prendes 87–88). Catholicism, however, continued being the official religion of the state, and other religions were not allowed to be practiced in public (Avni 9).[33]

The international dimension of Spain's position on the Jews again became clear in the wake of the 1868 liberal revolution, which immediately proclaimed its intention to uphold religious freedom. Haim Guedalla, a prominent member of the Hispano-Portuguese Jewish community in London, cousin of Sir Moses Montefiore, who knew General Prim from the time of Prim's exile in London, exhorted the general to cancel the 1492 expulsion edict. The heads of the consistories of Bordeaux and Bayonne followed suit. In contrast to Philippson, a German Jew who had written his appeal as a member of "world Jewry," connecting himself to fifteenth-century Iberian Jews as "coreligionists," the representatives of Bordeaux and Bayonne presented themselves as the direct descendants of the Jews expelled from Spain. They underlined their ancestors' love for Spain, mentioning how the expelled Jews had brought to France, England, and Holland the culture, language, and literature of Spain. The writers of the appeal, their Sephardi descendants, bore Iberian names and enjoyed a prestige that brought honor to their ancient homeland (Avni 10–11). Their argument closely echoed Varela's 1797 appreciation that "[the Jews] have never forgotten the advantages and conveniences that they enjoyed in Spain." These French and English Sephardi Jews introduced genealogy again into the "return" argument by appealing to Spaniards' "patriotic sympathy" and stressing their own cultural and lineage links with Spain.

At the same time these Sephardi Jews reassured the Spanish government that they sought no personal profit from the revocation of the edict of expulsion. In his 1854 appeal, Philippson had already mentioned this same renunciation. After writing about the large number of properties expelled Jews had been forced to leave behind, he quickly concluded that he was not demanding the return or restoration of the magnificent Spanish synagogues and other Jewish property to the international Jewish community. German Jews, in whose name he spoke, had no intention to move to Spain. They were solely asking that Spain make moral amends by paying a debt of honor to the memory of expelled Jews (Avni 9).[34] Echoing this rhetoric in 1868, French Jews said they had no intention of abandoning France, where they were citizens and had found shelter for hundreds of years. They reassured Spain that their intention was merely to cancel "a debt of honor owed to their forefathers, who were torn by this act [the 1492 expulsion] from their beloved homeland" (Avni 11).

The appeal of French Sephardi Jews received a sympathetic response from General Francisco Serrano, who became prime minister after the 1868 revolution. He wrote back expressing how the commitment of the new regime to religious freedom meant a de facto cancelation of the edict of expulsion and that Jews were free to enter Spain and practice their religion (Avni 11). This assurance became law in the constitution of 1869. After passionate debates that generated much publicity and fervor between the liberal Republican Emilio Castelar and the Carlist conservative Vicente Manterola, the Cortes voted in favor of the liberal position, guaranteeing the free exercise of any religion both in private and public and abrogating all the remaining anti-Jewish legislation.

Opposition to religious freedom, however, was widespread and ended up unifying conservative forces angered by their defeat. In 1875, the monarchy was restored and the new Parliament began drafting a new Constitution. The constitution of 1876 reestablished the supremacy of the Catholic religion, stipulating that Catholicism was the state's official religion, and that other beliefs were to be tolerated, but only practiced in private (Avni 11–14). The Board of Deputies of British Jews again appealed to King Alfonso XII, asking that Jews be allowed to live in Spain and practice their religion as equal citizens. This time the appeal was not heard. In 1881, Haim Guedalla requested clarification from Prime Minister Sagasta about whether the edict of expulsion was indeed canceled. Sagasta replied that any foreigners who settled in Spain had the right to citizenship and thus could practice their religion, as long as they adhered to "Catholic morality." After these developments, both the Board of Deputies of British Jews and Rabbi Philippson concluded that Spain did not offer enough guarantees for Jews (Avni 12–13).

Spain's reencounter with "real" Jews in the second half of the nineteenth century set the framework for Spanish/Jewish international relations for decades to come. Guided by a mercantilist logic of expediency, these rapprochements selectively targeted the economic elites. The first of these reencounters took place in Morocco at the time of the 1859–60 Hispano-Moroccan War. With the excuse of a minor frontier conflict close to the Spanish city of Ceuta in northern Morocco, Spain saw an opportunity to launch an offensive that would serve as nationalist propaganda at home and expand its colonial ambitions in Morocco. Public opinion was inflamed by slogans alluding to the continuation of the Reconquest and the fight against the "Moorish infidel."[35] Commanded by General

O'Donnell, Spanish troops won the battle of Tetuán, and triumphantly entered the city on February 6, 1860. Still recovering from an attack perpetrated a few days earlier by Moroccan Muslims, the Jews of Tetuán received the Spaniards as liberators.

A firsthand account of this reception appears in Pedro Antonio de Alarcón's *Diario de un testigo de la Guerra de Africa* [*Diary of a Witness of the War of Africa*]. Alarcón described how the Jews of Tetuán welcomed the Spanish troops shouting, in Spanish, "Bienvenidos! Viva la reina de España!" [Welcome! Long live the Spanish queen!]. Many articles in the Spanish press commented on the surprise of Spaniards at finding these Jews, descendants of those expelled from the peninsula in 1492, still speaking Spanish. During the twenty-seven months that the troops occupied the city, Jews and Spaniards developed a relationship of mutual interest. The Jews received protection and assistance from the Spaniards and engaged in beneficial commercial exchanges with the peninsula. The Spaniards used the Jews as intermediaries and translators, in anticipation of what eventually became a defining relationship for Spanish political and commercial interests in Morocco (González García, *El retorno* 67–79, Rozenberg 43–45).

The second encounter took place during the antisemitic persecutions that began in Eastern Europe in the 1880s. Spanish diplomats in Russia, Romania, and Turkey informed the Spanish government about the precarious situation of Jews in their territories. Many of these Jews spoke Ladino and asked Spanish authorities for assistance. Although Spain seemed deeply interested in the potential economic and commercial advantages of a relationship with Sephardi Jews of the eastern Mediterranean, the government was unwilling to help them make their way to Spain either financially or logistically (Avni 15–17; Rozenberg 46–52). Nevertheless, fifty-three Jewish families made their way to Spain and, for the first time, the question of whether to "repatriate" Sephardi Jews spilled beyond the high political spheres to become the center of a public debate. In the years 1881–82, the main national newspapers dedicated their editorial pages to this issue (González García, "La cuestión judía" 35).[36] In these debates, liberal thinkers interpreted Spain's foreign policy in relation to international Jews as a barometer of the nation's position toward modernity. It also became clear how much Spain's decisions about Jews seeking refuge were shaped by its perception of how the decision would affect the country's international image. This June 1881 editorial from *El Liberal* newspaper illustrates how interconnected these two issues were:

> España abriendo los brazos para recibir en ellos a una masa de población judía, se presentaría a la vista de Europa, con el testimonio más fehaciente de ser una España transformada, libre de la vergonzosa capa de intransigencia,

> secular, culta, empapada de las influencias benéficas del derecho moderno, cristiana en su concepto más sublime, digna de ser catalogada entre las naciones que basan el progreso humano sobre el respeto a la conciencia. ¿Quién osaría de tacharnos de fanáticos, si pusiéramos dentro de nuestras fronteras una losa de cincuenta mil judíos sobre los restos de nuestro fanatismo que nos ha destruido y envilecido?
>
> [Spain's opening its arms to receive a mass of Jewish population would appear to Europe as the most reliable testimony of being a Spain transformed, free of the shameful layer of intransigence, secular, learned, steeped in the beneficial influences of modern law, Christian in its most sublime sense, worthy of belonging among those nations that see human progress as based on freedom of conscience. Who would dare to accuse us of being fanatics, if we put inside our frontiers the tombstone of fifty thousand Jews on the remains of the fanaticism that has destroyed and tarnished us?] (quoted in González García, "La cuestión judía" 36)

Remarkable continuities exist between this formulation and the way subsequent Spanish governments would evaluate the merits of a positive attitude toward Jews as a contribution to securing Spain's acceptance at the table of modern European nations. This instrumentalization of the Jewish issue to enhance its image abroad would only increase in the twentieth century.

PHILOSEPHARDISM, OPPORTUNISM, AND THE SPANISH RACE

The phenomenon known as philosephardism partakes of these fantasies about the political and economic expediency of establishing relations with the Sephardim. Its main proponent, the senator Ángel Pulido was a friend of Emilio Castelar's and very close politically to the liberal party. He began his career as an anthropologist and was one of the first formulators of modern racial ideas in Spain. As he related it, he "discovered" the Sephardim during a cruise along the Danube in 1880 in which he became fascinated by three Sephardi businessmen who spoke to him in Judeo-Spanish. Returning to the Balkans in 1903 to visit his son, who was studying medicine there, he met Enrique Bejarano, the Romanian director of a school in Bucharest and a great admirer of Spain, who informed him about the two million Sephardi Jews who lived around the world and spoke Judeo-Spanish. As Paloma Díaz-Mas explains, "Bejarano's love for Spain convinced Pulido that all Sephardim felt similarly linked to Spain, that they considered it their homeland, and that, despite their expulsion and the persecution they had faced there, they had retained an almost religious veneration for the land of their ancestors" (*Sephardim* 153). Back in Spain, Pulido began a campaign to promote ties with these communities, writing articles and giving speeches in the Senate. These were collected in his 1904 book *Los israelitas españoles y el idioma castellano* [The Spanish Israelites and the Castilian language] (Díaz-Mas, *Sephardim* 153–55; Garzón, "El Doctor Pulido" xi–xxi; Rohr, *The Spanish Right* 15).[37]

In his 1905 book *Intereses nacionales: Españoles sin patria y la raza sefardí* [National interests: Spaniards without a homeland and the Sephardi race], based on the responses from Sephardi communities around the world to a questionnaire Pulido had sent them, he argued that a number of Sephardi Jews should be repatriated to Spain.[38] To defend this position he resorted both to old and new assumptions about the Sephardim. As Isabelle Rohr explains, philosephardism appeared in the context of the debate about Spain's cultural and racial regenerationism that followed the disaster of 1898 (*The Spanish Right* 15). Informed by positivism and scientific racism, regenerationists saw Spain's loss of empire as material proof of its degeneration. In their view Spain suffered from an illness and needed an immediate intervention (Balfour, "The Loss" 25). Along the lines of Emilio Castelar's ideas defending the social benefits of religious freedom, Pulido saw Spain's degeneration not as a sudden illness, but as a gradual process that started in 1492 with the expulsion of the Jews. Repatriating some of them, he concluded, would restore Spain's health by reintroducing a group that had been needlessly excised from the nation (Goode 183). Selective repatriation would also remedy Spain's decline by contributing to its economic regeneration, opening new commercial markets to boost the economy, and compensating for the loss of Cuba (Rohr, *The Spanish Right* 16).

Pulido's views were steeped in racial and biological language. He explicitly articulated the dualistic conception of race based on both culture and biology that, a few years later, became a cornerstone of Francoist ideology. He interpreted the Sephardim's use of language, the fact that they spoke what he considered an old version of Castilian, as proof of their cultural attachment to Spain and of their status as Spaniards (Rohr, "Spaniards" 63).[39] He characterized Sephardi identity by their will to maintain that attachment:

> Quisieron mantenerse fuera de España como tales españoles y transmitir a sus hijos la herencia de sus aristocracias, encarnada mejor que en ningún otro atributo, en aquella riqueza viva, ardiente y luminosa que no había podido arrebatarles la codicia de sus perseguidores: en el habla castellana
>
> [They wanted to live outside of Spain as Spaniards and pass on to their children their aristocratic inheritance, embodied better than in any other characteristic in that live, ardent and gleaming wealth that the greed of

their persecutors had not been able to take away from them: the Castilian language] (Pulido, *Intereses* 56)

Language, in Pulido's argument, becomes a direct marker of true identity. In both of his books, he included several lyrical passages declaring that "los idiomas no son otra cosa sino la exteriorización del alma de los pueblos" [languages are nothing if not the exteriorization of a people's soul] (Pulido, *Intereses* 83). This linguistic nationalism—assuming that language use revealed the true identity and loyalties of a people—was the founding concept of *hispanismo,* the belief in the existence of a shared cultural identity across Spanish-speaking nations, which Spain promoted in Latin America as a compensatory strategy after the loss of its colonies (Pike, quoted in Rohr, "Spaniards" 63–64; Martin-Márquez 49–50). This is the imperial idea of a "Hispanic race," bound spiritually and culturally, to which Sephardim, like Latin Americans, would belong.

Since Pulido constructed his two books as a mix of his ideas and the correspondence he received from Sephardim, it is possible to glimpse signs of a different position, or even dissent in the quotes he includes from those letters. One of the most interesting contrasts appears in *Los israelitas españoles y el idioma castellano,* where Pulido quotes the manifesto of the "Esperanza" academic society, an organization founded by a group of young and highly educated Viennese Sephardim. Published in 1900, the manifesto defends the use of the Judeo-Spanish language among the Sephardim, but rather than understanding it as an expression of love for Spain, the document sees it as an expression of love for their own particular Jewish identity:

> No por amor de Espana, absolutamente no; sino por amor de nosotros mismos, por amor de nuestra existencia y por amor del judaismo debemos SOSTENER LA LENGUA ESPANOL que nuestros padres hablaban y que nosotros aprendemos desde la más tierna edad como nuestra lengua madre!!
>
> [Not for love of Spain, absolutely not; but for love of ourselves, for love of our existence and for love of Judaism we must MAINTAIN THE SPANISH LANGUAGE that our parents spoke and that we learned from infancy as our mother tongue!!] (Pulido, *Los israelitas* 55)[40]

In the context of this manifesto, "La lengua espanol [*sic*]" referred to here is not a diasporic language that reflects the grandeur of an original—the *castellano* that Pulido had in mind. The Esperanza group saw its "lengua espanol" as the language that gives voice to the experience of a minority within a national and social context, to the specific historic conditions in which Sephardi identity developed. But the self-affirming understanding of their language defended by these Viennese Sephardim ended up being absorbed by Pulido's much more politically expedient Spanish nationalist conception. His view of language as the reflection of the immutable soul of a people and his interpretation of Sephardim's use of "Castilian" as an expression of their attachment to and love for Spain have been invoked repeatedly to justify a variety of political initiatives, from the philosephardi rapprochement Pulido started to the use of Moroccan Jews as intermediaries in Spain's colonial expansion in Morocco to the drafting of the 2015 law of nationality for the Sephardim.[41]

In order to explain Sephardim's closeness to Spain, Pulido also used a more strictly biological conception of race, believing that Spanish Jews "had mixed with the Spaniards during their stay in the Iberian Peninsula and that the two peoples had racially improved each other as a result. . . . In his view, the Sephardi Jews were the most beautiful of all Jewish peoples due to their racial fusion with the Spaniards" (Rohr, "Spaniards" 64).[42] Joshua Goode demonstrates how this conception of the emergence of a Spanish race out of the mixture of many peoples was popular among early Spanish anthropologists, among them Pulido himself. In the case of the Spanish-Jewish mixture, they believed the result had improved both groups. But mixture in itself did not automatically yield an improved outcome. Other European nations, these anthropologists noted, experienced degeneration because of it. Ashkenazi Jews, for example, "were degenerate because of their mixtures" (Goode 194). What distinguished Sephardi and Ashkenazi Jews, thus, was that Sephardi Jews had mixed with Spaniards, and that factor accounted for their prosperity and beautiful appearance. Pulido explained: "Los israelitas españoles siguen siendo todavía, dentro de su raza, como los favorecidos por una selección étnica y social que siempre hubo de reconocérceles" [Spanish Jews continue being, among their race, the favored ones by an ethnic and social selection that has always been recognized] (Pulido, *Los israelitas* 86). Whatever was good in (Sephardi) Jews was owing to Spain; whatever was bad in (Ashkenazi) Jews was owing to themselves and other European nations. As we will see, Franco would happily embrace and expand on this idea.

According to racial theories of the time (and surprisingly not unlike the fifteenth-century protoracial notions of the purity of blood statutes), race manifested itself in both biological and cultural attributes, so exiled Sephardim, according to Pulido, both looked and acted like Spaniards: "Nuestras impresiones personales acerca del físico de los sefarditas es que semejan exactamente el tipo español . . . no se ve, en fin, mirando sus ademanes, vestidos y aspecto personal, nada que pueda inducir a señalarlos como de otra raza distinta de la española" [Our personal impression of the physical appearance of the

Sephardim is that they exactly resemble the Spanish type . . . you cannot see, looking at their gestures, clothes and personal appearance anything that would make you point at them as a race different from Spaniards] (Pulido, *Intereses* 30). Pulido underplayed the role of Sephardim's Jewish identity. Curiously, the same perceived lack of differentiation that had caused so much anxiety among Christian authorities in the fourteenth and fifteenth centuries became, for Pulido, a positive quality proving both Spain's and the Sephardim's racial superiority. Pulido went on to claim that since "Spanishness" predominated in their identity, Sephardim suffered isolation and an inability to adapt to their "new" environments and longed to return to Spain (Goode 195). The title of his most famous book, *Españoles sin patria y la raza sefardí* (Spaniards without a Homeland and the Sephardi Race), clearly conveyed this message.

Once again, testimonial letters from Sephardim included in Pulido's books contradict his arguments. In *Los israelitas españoles*, for example, Moisés dal Medico, an interpreter for the Ottoman Ministry of the Navy in Constantinople, writes to Pulido: "los judíos no son, segun lo pretenden sus enemigos, unos parias, gente sin patria; al contrario ellos idolatran el país que les acorda hospitalidad, tolerancia y egualidad de tratamiento" [Jews are not, as their enemies claim, pariahs, people without homeland; on the contrary they idolize the country that grants them hospitality, tolerance and equality in treatment] (*Los israelitas* 174). Thus, Pulido's books themselves include this dissenting view of Sephardim who do not see themselves as "without a homeland," and who do not privilege Spain as the lost homeland.

Furthermore, as Julia Phillips Cohen explains, it is in fact only in the late nineteenth century that Spain reenters the Sephardi imaginary. Focusing on the Ottoman Empire, home to the largest Judeo-Spanish population in the world by the modern era, she concludes, "it is difficult to find any mention whatsoever of Spain in Ladino sources from the eighteenth and early nineteenth centuries. . . . There is no discussion of the loss of the country or of a traumatic rupture with it" (Phillips Cohen). Phillips Cohen argues that these Jews in fact learned about Spain's Jewish past and their ancestors' role in it through the new modes of education they received in the French schools of the Alliance Israélite Universelle beginning in the later part of the nineteenth century. The myth of the Spanishness of the Sephardim, so useful to Spain's nationalist interests, also became useful to many Sephardim at a particularly fraught time: "As their future in Southeastern Europe and the Levant became increasingly uncertain, and as growing numbers of Jewish communities experienced the end of their familiar existence under Ottoman rule, they increasingly sought refuge in the idea of their lasting connections with Spain. The idea that they had preserved an unbroken chain of memory of this country during the many centuries that had intervened lent a semblance of continuity and rootedness to their swiftly changing worlds" (Phillips Cohen).[43]

In terms of Spain's interests, a "patriotic" purpose was at the base of Pulido's deployment of cultural and biological conceptions of race in his characterization of the Sephardim. The *intereses nacionales* mentioned in the title clearly signal the strategic use of the selective "repatriation" of some Sephardi Jews and the use of international contacts as a means to improve Spain's political, economic, and diplomatic standing. In his speeches calling for an expansion of naturalization laws in order to facilitate paths to citizenship, he emphasized that Spain could not afford the influx of impoverished Jews. He quoted his friend Enrique Bejarano to explain the "obvious" fact that "no se trata de admitir gente pobre y buscona, sino gente rica y emprendedora" [this is not about admitting poor and troublesome people, but people who are rich and entrepreneurial] (Pulido, *Los israelitas* 97). This economic rationale resonated powerfully across the Spanish political spectrum and formed the basis of the philosephardist movement in the 1910s and '20s.[44] We find in this rationale, once again, echoes of the myth of Sephardi economic supremacy. As Pulido put it, "Las Cámaras de Comercio deben advertir la trascendencia que puede tener reconquistar la amistad de la raza más comercial y mejor diseminada que existe en el mundo" [The Chamber of Commerce must note the significance that reconquering the friendship of the most commercial and best disseminated race in the world can have] (*Los israelitas* 113). This explains why while Sephardi elites in territories of colonial interest to Spain beyond Spain's borders were reminded of their Spanish identity and "invited back" to Spain, members of the first Sephardi communities in Spanish territory (especially those without economic means) were not considered true Spaniards, and "were forced to live in anonymity, both as Jewish and Spanish" (Ojeda Mata, "Spanish' but 'Jewish" 68, see also Beckwith, "Facing Sepharad" 186–87).

The philosephardists' campaign brought the issue of Sephardi Jews into the public sphere and produced concrete results.[45] The most important took place during Miguel Primo de Rivera's dictatorship: the granting of Spanish nationality to a number of Sephardi Jews through a royal decree signed by Alfonso XIII in December 1924. The decree was not intended for Jews in general, but only for Sephardim who had enjoyed the protection of Spain's diplomatic agents in the Ottoman Empire. But very few people (between four and five thousand) were able to obtain nationality this way, either for lack of clear information or because the process was arduous and required documents that many did not have (Rohr, *The Spanish Right* 27; Avni 31–33; Ojeda Mata, "Thinking" 66).

Notwithstanding its limitations, the decree was an important precedent for the modern rapprochement of Spain and the Jews.

Philosephardist ideas could be found across the political spectrum. They were central in the writings of Ernesto Giménez Caballero, a Spanish fascist ideologue who tried to translate Italian fascism into Spain. Giménez Caballero visited Sephardi communities in the Balkans during the fall of 1929 on a trip sponsored by the Spanish Ministry of State. As Friedman shows in her analysis of Giménez Caballero's work, protofascist ideas of Sephardi Jews having been purified by contact with Spain, and the philosephardism of the 1920s and '30s, laced with antisemitism, played a central role in the development of hispanism (Friedman, "Reconquering").

Philosephardist initiatives also provoked fierce opposition. Joaquín Girón y Arcas, professor of canonical law at the University of Salamanca, was at the forefront of the campaign against Pulido. In 1906, heavily influenced by the conspiracy theories of French antisemitic writing, he published *La cuestión judaica en la España actual* [The Jewish question in present-day Spain]. He wrote of the danger of repatriating Sephardi Jews, arguing that their coming to Spain would lead to the expropriation of houses and even churches, as the Jews would try to recover the properties that their forebears had left behind in 1492 (Rohr, *The Spanish Right* 34).

The Jewish danger was also seen, in Spanish antisemitic writing, as a danger from within. At the same historical junction that Pulido used the language of biological pathology to speak of Spain's sickness's having been produced by the absence of Jews, openly antisemitic writing used the language of race to blame the descendants of conversos for ruining Spain. In *Arte de conocer a nuestros judíos* [The art of recognizing our Jews] (Barcelona, 1916), César Peiró Menéndez argued that "the ulcer that corrodes Spain, the gangrene that rots it and the cancer that kills it is Jewish" (16). The descendants of conversos, "the Jews by blood," suffered from "racial bastardization" and were responsible for the degeneration of Spain. He blamed them for exploiting and ruining Cuba and provoking the separatist revolt that resulted in the disaster of 1898 (Rohr, *The Spanish Right* 32–33). Echoing the "Letter from Constantinople" and Quevedo's conspiracies, Peiró accused Jews of having falsely converted to Catholicism and of bleeding Spain, for they "not only crucify the innocent but also whole nations" (Peiró Menéndez 13). They prospered, while "true Spaniards" were rendered useless and persecuted (Peiró Menéndez 12). Portrayed as astute, deceitful, and well positioned, conversos, Peiró argued, constituted such a powerful minority that they have made Spain "la nación más judaizada de la tierra" ["the most judaized nation on earth"] (Peiró Menéndez 9).

He disparaged contemporary Spanish Jews disguised as false Catholics for initiating the calls for Moroccan, Balkan, and German Jews to settle in Spain (Peiró Menéndez 10). This line of thought would soon feed into the Spanish right's racial conceptualization of Socialists and Republicans in the 1930s as converso-like enemies of Spain.

FRANCO, JEWS AND RACE

Given Spain's colonial interests in Morocco at the beginning of the twentieth century, it is not surprising that wealthy Moroccan Jews were one of the main targets of the philosephardist campaigns. The campaigns explicitly acknowledged Moroccan Jews' usefulness for the colonial enterprise (Pulido, *Intereses* 39; Rohr, "Spaniards" 65–68; Ojeda Mata, "Spanish' but 'Jewish" 67). The Jewish communities' mercantile elites were bilingual or trilingual and played an important role as intermediaries between the Muslim governments and the outside world, as their predecessors had done throughout the Ottoman Empire. They enjoyed a monopoly over the textile trade and over the production and distribution of jewelry, and many held the status of protégés of the European consulates with the implied diplomatic and commercial advantages this position entailed (Rohr, *The Spanish Right* 20).[46]

As an officer of the colonial army in Morocco, Franco's interest in the local Jewish population betrayed a familiarity with philosephardist positions. In 1926, he published an article entitled "Xauen la triste" ["Xauen the Sad"] in *Revista de Tropas Coloniales* describing how the arrival of the Spanish army in the Moroccan city of Xauén in 1869 had been a particularly joyful event to the city's Jewish inhabitants, while the 1924 evacuation of Spanish troops had been devastating to them. Franco described the Jewish population's shedding tears of joy upon the Spaniards' arrival, cheering soldiers, the Spanish nation, and their queen, since Spaniards had brought "civilization and law" and had become their protectors. This paternalistic portrayal of "defenseless Jews," "barbaric Muslims," and "civilized Spaniards" had the clear political aim of enlisting Moroccan Jews as collaborators in Spain's colonial expansion in Morocco (Rohr, *The Spanish Right* 68). Franco's instrumentalization of Moroccan Jews to advance his own political agenda would continue in the Civil War and the postwar periods.

In 1931, the democratically elected government of the Second Republic drafted a new constitution that guaranteed every citizen equal rights under the law. It legislated religious freedom, declaring that the Spanish state had no official religion, and reduced the time of residence in Spain for those who wished to be naturalized from ten years to two for citizens of Latin America, Portugal, and Morocco. These provisions greatly facilitated the naturalization of Moroccan Jews (Avni 34–35). Like Philippson in 1854 and the representatives of the Bayonne and Bordeaux communities in 1868, in 1931 Sabatay Djaen, the chief rabbi of Romania, wrote a letter to Spain's minister of foreign affairs Alejandro Lerroux, exhorting the government to rescind the 1492 edict. In 1932 the minister of education and fine arts, Fernando de los Ríos, responded that it was not necessary as the new constitution nullified it (Rohr, *The Spanish Right* 41).

The Republic also showed other signs of its sympathetic stance toward Jews. De los Ríos's trip to Spanish Morocco in 1931 showed his goodwill toward the Jewish community there, declaring: "I have the pleasure of feeling at home with you." His friendly words made him a target of antisemitic attacks by the Spanish right, who accused him of being a Jew. In November 1933, President Alcalá Zamora repeated the trip, visiting a synagogue in Tetuán. The chief rabbi of Tetuán asserted the loyalty of Moroccan Jews to Spain and said that Alcalá Zamora was the first head of state to visit a synagogue there (Rohr, *The Spanish Right* 44, 47). In March 1935, the government sponsored a celebration honoring the eight hundredth anniversary of the birth of Maimónides in Córdoba, with lectures from Spanish intellectuals and Jewish guests from abroad and the unveiling of a memorial plaque (Avni 38).[47]

In terms of the Jewish population of Spain, by the turn of the century, the only organized Jewish community was that of Sevilla. Of about twenty families, most had come from Morocco, especially Tetuán. This population increased during World War I, when some Jews from Turkey, Russia, and the Austro-Hungarian Empire sought refuge in Spain. At this time, Madrid's and Barcelona's first synagogues were opened in modest rented apartments, and in 1920, a Spanish Zionist Federation was formed. However, when the war ended, many of these Jewish refugees left Spain, including important community organizers and figures like Yahuda and Max Nordau. It was not until 1933, upon Hitler's rise to power, that noticeable numbers of Jews from Germany and Poland, about three thousand, settled in Spain, mostly in Barcelona. By 1936, the Jewish population in Spain was about six thousand (Avni 41–45).

In the meantime, antisemitism was on the rise. Since the end of the nineteenth century anti-Jewish sentiment had been stirred by the dissemination of works by French antisemitic writers like Edouard Drumont and the repercussions of the Dreyfus affair. *The Protocols of the Elders of Zion* was popularized in the 1920s, with its first Spanish edition in 1927, followed by several new editions thereafter.[48] In the early 1930s, antisemitism became a unifying tool for the various conservative, anti-Republican forces in their attacks against their enemies: Republicans, the Soviets, and the French (Álvarez Chillida, *El antisemitismo* 349; A. Baer, "Between" 74). In 1931, the Carlist newspaper *El Siglo Futuro* declared that three Republican ministers were Jews and that their government's progressive legislation was dictated from abroad (Preston 7). In the elections held in November 1933, antisemitism became a recurring theme among the right-wing parties of the CEDA coalition and in their electoral campaigns (Rohr, *The Spanish Right* 55). Even intellectuals like Pío Baroja, one of the best-known writers of the generation of '98, argued that all Jews either openly or secretly supported communism and were behind Russia's revolution. He further argued that Jews were using the Spanish Republic to spark a similar revolution (Avni 38–39). During these years, Nazi propaganda began arriving in Spain in full force, giving further strength to antisemitic feelings. Early admirers of Hitler in Spain, such as Ramiro de Maeztu and José Permartín, elaborated on the propagandist depiction of Germany as a victim of the Jews by drawing parallels with Spain. In 1932, Maeztu published an article in *ABC,* then the most widely circulated newspaper in the country, in which he established an analogy between Isabel the Catholic monarch and Hitler, stating that just as the Catholic queen had to defend Spain against the Jews, the German leader also had to defend his country against them (Rohr, *The Spanish Right* 56).

These ideas found a particularly fertile ground among the Nationalists during the Spanish Civil War. Not only did Hitler provide crucial material support to the right-wing rebels, but his propaganda apparatus was also a main provider of content for the Nationalist media. As Alejandro Baer has shown in an essay about the reactions to Kristallnacht in Civil War Spain, the right-wing Nationalist press echoed the Nazi version of events. It interpreted these events as part of a longer history of struggle against Jews in which Spain had been at the vanguard. A November 1938 editorial in the *ABC* newspaper celebrated how "today Italy, yesterday Germany; many other countries in Europe and America, too, are adopting, in this second third of the twentieth century, measures for defense against the Jews analogous to those decreed four centuries ago by the Catholic Monarchs" (A. Baer, "Between" 78). This argument also appeared in an editorial in *El Pensamiento Navarro* that praised "the brilliant foresight of the Catholic Kings, who were centuries ahead of their time" (Rohr, *The Spanish Right* 93). Franco himself often repeated this interpretation of history that posited Spain as a model that Germany was following (Rohr, *The Spanish Right* 101; Álvarez Chillida, *El antisemitismo* 398).

Nationalist newspapers insisted that the international condemnation of the Nazis demonstrated the alleged international power of the Jews, who were launching an "ignominious campaign against Germany." No mention was made of the murders and arrests of Jews or the burning of hundreds of synagogues and destruction of their property (Rohr, *The Spanish Right* 93, A. Baer, "Between" 80–81). In sharp contrast, the Republican press described the Kristallnacht riots as barbarous antisemitic attacks that, if allowed to continue, would result in Europe's capitulation to Hitler's will and cause the downfall of the Spanish Republic (A. Baer, "Between" 82). The Republican government joined Great Britain, France, and the United States in their condemnations of the attacks and promised refuge to all those persecuted because of their ancestry, religion, or political views after the conclusion of the Spanish Civil War (A. Baer, "Between" 84–85).

It is at this juncture that the Nationalists brought the racial language of purity of blood back into public discourse. This time the targets were the Republicans. Ideologues on the Spanish extreme right argued that Marxist ideas were foreign ideas of Semitic origin. The same extreme physical analogies César Peiró had used to depict the corrupting effect of conversos' Jewish blood appeared in writings by Nationalists about the Republicans who would destroy the "true" Spain through its "bolshevization." These were not presented as mere analogies but linked together as part of a cause-effect mechanism: the reason communism was able to infiltrate Spain was none other than the conversos themselves, whose descendants had enabled foreign Marxist ideas to penetrate Spain. By this logic, the Republicans became part of an ancestral converso plot to destroy Spain already outlined in the "Letter from Constantinople."

Antonio Vallejo Nájera (1889–1960), chair of psychiatry at the University of Madrid, who joined the nationalist movement and became the chief psychiatrist in Franco's concentration camps, developed a bio-psychiatric theory on the roots of Marxism. Author of many works about eugenics and the regeneration of the Spanish race, Vallejo Nájera wrote in 1938 that while the foreign Marxist was "pure Semite," the "Spanish Marxist racial stock" was Jewish-Moorish, of mixed blood.[49] The amalgamation of Jew, Muslim, and socialist became a common view among right-wing intellectuals, who fanned the flames of racial hatred (Preston, 43–47).

Alejandro Baer quotes a November 1938 editorial from the Catholic daily *El Progreso* that elaborates on the idea of a Marxist-converso conspiracy and explains how "the Jews displaced from the cities of Central Europe were counting on the refuge some Judaizing Spaniards (judaizantes) offered them in our country. But it will be possible to shelter them only briefly, because the thrust of our soldiers is continually decreasing the size of the territory where these Semites have come to seek refuge, gladly volunteering to participate in the Bolshevization of Spain" ("Between" 80). At this time virtually no Jews lived in

Spain, and nearly all descendants of conversos had become mixed with the general population and lost any trace of memory of their pre-Christian ancestry. The "Judaizing Spaniards" of this quote were the embattled Republicans in the government that had allowed about three thousand Jewish refugees to come to Spain. An *ABC* op-ed from October 1938 blamed converts (Republicans) for the "infiltration of Semitic ideas in Spain" (A. Baer, "Between" 80). The reappearance of the word *judaizantes* brings us back to the world of the conversos and the Inquisition that persecuted conversos for "Judaizing," "acting Jewish," or "engaging in Jewish behaviors."

The classification of Republicans as judaizantes by the Catholic right during the 1930s repurposes within the political ideological realm Saint Paul's use of the verb "to Judaize." In the context of early Christianity, Saint Paul used this word to warn communities about the temptations of the flesh and the material world (Nirenberg, *Anti-Judaism* 62). In the ideologically convulsive Spain of the 1930s, both the biologically determined immorality of Jews and their connection with the material world to the detriment of the spiritual served to characterize a single identity of Republicans, Marxists, conversos, and Jews. The identification of Republicans and the working class with Jews, characterized as enemies of Spain, justified the violence committed against them (Preston 47).

The Spanish Protectorate in Morocco, the only area in Spain with a significant Jewish community, was the first territory to fall into Nationalist hands upon the coup d'etat of July 1936. There, the antisemitic views of Nationalists were balanced by their belief that Moroccan Jews controlled much of the protectorate economy and could serve the Nationalist war effort.[50] After the Nationalist victory, Franco continued to regard Moroccan Jews as potential facilitators of Spain's colonial ambitions (Rohr, *The Spanish Right* 88–103). While the Nationalists used a belligerent image of the Reconquista to provide a historical justification for the Civil War, in the Moroccan Protectorate Spanish officials invoked the convivencia narrative of harmony among the three religions of medieval Spain as a historic precedent that legitimized and fostered Spanish colonial interests in Morocco. This analogy was also at play when Franco invoked the "blood brotherhood" of Moroccans and Spaniards to justify the recruitment of Moroccan mercenaries to fight on the Nationalist side of the Civil War.[51]

Driven by a mixture of pragmatism, opportunism, and self-aggrandizing authoritarianism, the Francoist policy in Morocco combined Germanophilia with Africanism and philosephardism. In an attempt to rationalize the inherent ideological contradictions among these ideologies, Franco's regime revived the distinction between the Ashkenazi Jews of German and northern European origin, on whom it pinned all the ills of Judaism, and Sephardi Jews. The argument was that Sephardi Jews had been "cleansed" during their stay in Spain (Rohr, *The Spanish Right* 7, 117). As descendants of Spanish Jews, the Jewish population of the Spanish protectorate was, as a 1941 article in the newspaper *El Mundo* put it, "unconnected to the methods and designs of international Judaism" (Rohr, *The Spanish Right* 118). In the script he wrote for the film *Raza* (José Luis Sáenz de Heredia, 1942), Franco himself explained how Spanish Jews were different from all other Jews.[52] As they walk by the synagogue of Santa María la Blanca in Toledo, the protagonist José Churruca explains to his mother the history of this "Church of the Jews" in terms that embrace a teleological version of the convivencia myth in which all religions are evolving together toward a Catholic converging point: "The synagogues, the mosques and the Churches were passed around. The Jews, the Moors, the Christians lived here and *in contact with Spain they were purified*" (*Raza* script, qtd. in Rohr, *The Spanish Right* 117). In the same dialogue, José explains the exceptional nature of Spanish Jews, who, unlike the rest of their coreligionists, did not take part in the crucifixion but set up the conditions for the Christianization of Spain and their own conversion: "When the Pharisees decided that Jesus had to die they wrote to the most important synagogues to get their approval. Not only did the Spanish Jews refuse to do so, they protested and after Jesus' death they sent ambassadors who asked that St. James come to Spain to preach the Gospels" (*Raza* script, quoted in Rohr, *The Spanish Right* 117–18).[53] In José's dialogue, Spain is simultaneously a converso nation ("Churches were passed around"; Spanish Jews "asked St. James to come to Spain to preach Gospels") and current home to a superior race historically produced in a long process of purification facilitated by the Iberian territory. Implied in this Francoist reevaluation of Spanish and Christian history is an argument that simultaneously combines aspects of the convivencia myth with elements of fascist racial superiority. Both arguments would be deployed by Franco throughout his long hold on power from 1939 until 1975, and both, together with diplomatic considerations, would underwrite philosephardi initiatives throughout the Francoist years.

THE JEWISH QUESTION AND POSTWAR DIPLOMATIC RELATIONS

Although officially neutral in World War II, Spain openly sympathized with the Hitler regime. The country provided raw materials for the German armament industry and sent a division of forty-seven thousand volunteers, known as the Blue Division, to fight alongside the German army on the Soviet front.

Between ten thousand and fifteen thousand Republican refugees were deported to Nazi concentration camps, mainly Mauthausen in Austria, when Germany occupied France in 1940. More than five thousand of them were killed by the Nazis (Brenneis 5). At the end of the war, Franco's Spain sheltered many Nazi criminals and collaborators, who lived openly under the protection of the Francoist elite (Rohr, *The Spanish Right* 155–56; Rozenberg 288–90). Franco's Spain was internationally isolated after the Axis defeat. When Spain became officially excluded in December 1946 from the newly formed United Nations and Israel was recognized as a state in 1948, Franco interpreted these events as patent proof of the international power of the Jews. Out of the public eye, Spain tried to break this international isolation by redeploying the idealized version of the country's shared history with Jews and Muslims in the Middle Ages. Starting in 1949, Spain's Ministry of Foreign Relations began an extensive campaign in Washington and Tel Aviv to try to establish diplomatic relations with Israel. At the same time, Franco also emphasized the inheritance of al-Andalus and cultivated Spain's relationships with Arab nations in order to gather their support for Spain's entry into the United Nations (Martin-Márquez 224).

In May 1949, following a Latin American proposal to restore diplomatic relations with Spain, the issue was again discussed by the General Assembly. Among the fourteen delegates who raised their hands to oppose the cancelation of the diplomatic ban on Francoist Spain was Abba Eban, Israel's representative, who explained that Israel had made this decision because of Spain's having been an "active and sympathetic ally" of Nazi Germany. The vote caused much anger in Spain. Franco's government quickly reacted to what it called "a Jewish attack on Spain" (Avni 1–2). The Falangist daily *Arriba* accused Israel of having "knifed [Spain] in the back with unprecedented rancor and ingratitude unknown in history" (Lisbona 145). Spanish authorities were convinced that Israel's negative vote in the United Nations in 1949 and again in 1950 had sealed the international fate of Spain.

The Francoist regime thought that it was necessary that Spain undertake some gestures of reconciliation with the Jewish people in order to improve its image in the international press, especially in the United States. The Spanish Ministry of Foreign Affairs published a pamphlet entitled *Spain and the Jews* to explain the inappropriateness of Israel's vote. The text rewrote the history of Spain's policies and actions toward Jews during World War II and emphasized "the countless benefits that Jews have been afforded through Spain's protection and assistance." The booklet, published in Spanish, English, and French, claimed that Spanish representatives in Nazi-occupied countries had used their influence to save the lives of thousands of Sephardi Jews and provided shelter to those Jews who had escaped into Spain. The pamphlet depicted these as selfless acts in which "Spain, imbued with its universal Christian spirit of love for all the races on earth, contributed to the rescue of Jews, and acted more for spiritual than for merely legal or political reasons." Reiterating the Francoist version of convivencia as the forerunner of Catholic Spain, the pamphlet connected this protection to "a cordial and general impulse of sympathy and friendliness towards a persecuted race, to which Spaniards feel themselves attached by traditional ties of blood and culture" (Avni 179; Rohr, *The Spanish Right* 2).

This propaganda campaign was quite successful in spreading the notion that Spain had done everything in its power to save Jews. It remained a commonly accepted version until it was fully discredited by professional historians in the 1980s.[54] An August 1949 report commissioned by the Ministry of Foreign Relations had identified the issue of religious intolerance as one of the main obstacles preventing a better relationship with the United States. To remove that obstacle, the report recommended, in regard to Jews and Protestants, "insistir sobre la tolerancia religiosa ampliando o aparentando ampliar ésta" [insisting on the issue of religious tolerance, extending it or pretending to extend it] (qtd. in Lisbona 138).[55] Each of these Francoist "reconciliation gestures" were discussed by the Ministry of Foreign Relations with its ambassador in Washington and were first and foremost publicized in the United States.

During the 1950s and '60s the actions of Franco's government regarding Jewish issues inside and outside of Spain would entail a diplomatic balancing act between its relationship with the United States and its relationship with Arab countries. The Spanish Ministry of Foreign Relations firmly believed in the immense international power of the Jews and in the existence of a "US Jewish lobby" with power to influence public opinion. A March 1967 dispatch from the ministry's director for Africa and the Arab World to the Spanish ambassador in Washington discussing the importance of Jewish public opinion in the United States stated that the world media was "for the greater part controlled by Jewish finances" (qtd. in Lisbona 221). Lisbona provides many examples of this dynamic. As he ironically concludes, "Any occasion is ideal to publicize and present evidence of the good disposition of Franco's government to its Jews" (Lisbona 168).

These "gestures of good will" toward Spain's Jews should be seen, thus, as part and parcel of Francoist relations with the United States. These relations became crucial in ending the regime's international isolation after 1953, when Spain signed the Pact of Madrid. This trade and military agreement with the United States compensated Spain with economic and military aid in exchange for allowing the United States to construct air and naval bases on Spanish territory. The pact was part of US Cold War strategy and became the conduit through which Spain ended its international isolation. Coinciding with the signing of the agreement in 1953, Franco would receive Francois Barukh, president of the Comunidad Israelita de Madrid, in a private audience in the Pardo. Barukh was the first Jewish public figure to be received by Franco. The government also authorized the celebration of Rosh Hashanah in the Castellana Hilton Hotel in Madrid, with representatives of the Ministry of Foreign Relations and the US embassy attending the event (although it would not grant the same permission a year later). In Barcelona, permission to build a Jewish community center, which included two synagogues, was granted that same year (see Lisbona 157–74). In 1955, Spain was finally admitted to the United Nations.

Both Franco and Jewish leaders in Spain and Morocco engaged in this game of influences. Franco required Jewish leaders from Spain and Spanish Morocco to vouch for his government to international Jewish organizations, Israel, and the United States (see Lisbona 133, 143–47, 157). In turn, Jewish communities in Spain soon realized that the threat of an international scandal, mostly in the US press, could go a long way toward helping them in their demands for legal recognition in Spain.

The 1960s witnessed several crucial developments in the rapprochement of Spain and the Jews: Franco's tacit collaboration in the Israeli efforts to rescue Sephardi Jews targeted by nationalist groups in Egypt and Morocco, the creation of the Sephardi Museum in Toledo in 1964, and, crucially, the Law of Religious Freedom of 1967 that soon ushered in official recognition of Spain's Jewish associations. The Second Vatican Council's (1962–65) doctrine on religious freedom became a foremost influence on the regime's modification of its laws concerning non-Catholics and their associations. As on previous occasions, international factors and the regime's preoccupation with its image abroad were pivotal in these developments. The balancing act between the interests of the United States and those of the Arab countries was delicate. In the 1960s, Arab diplomats frequently complained about Spain's organization of cultural events or declarations of friendship toward Sephardi Jews. Fernando María Castiella, minister of foreign relations (1957–69), would hold recurring meetings with Arab diplomats to reassure them that these gestures did not mean a rapprochement with Jewish international organizations or Spain's intentions to recognize Israel (Lisbona 262–64). Spain would not establish diplomatic relations with Israel until more than a decade after Franco's death, in 1986, the last European country to do so. Recognition of Israel was a necessary condition for membership in the European Community, which Spain also joined in 1986.

The interrelated myths of Sephardi superiority and convivencia woven into a long history of attempts to come to terms with the double immediate aftermath of 1492—the absence of Jews from Spain and the presence of a substantial number of conversos—reappeared with renewed strength in the twentieth century as historic justifications of discourses of philosephardism, antisemitism, and nationalism. Since the late eighteenth century, through Francoist times, to the Spain of the Transition and contemporary Spain, these interrelated myths have served a multiplicity of purposes. If they were used by Sephardi and Ashkenazi Jews as defense mechanisms to prove their worth amid antisemitic charges and discrimination policies in different European societies, they would also serve in the twentieth and twenty-first centuries to proclaim Spain's worth in the international arena in a climate in which it was no longer considered an important international player.

In summary, while Jews constructed an idealized portrait of Sephardi Jews as an intellectually superior and economically powerful community, Pulido, at the beginning of the twentieth-century, attributed Sephardi superiority to their having mixed with Spaniards. In the 1930s, Franco would again praise Sephardi superiority, crediting it to their contact with a Spain which had purified them. Haskala intellectuals admired and idealized medieval Iberian Jews because of their ability to productively integrate into Muslim society without losing their Jewish identity. Today's tourism campaigns reinterpret this idealized image not only as proof of Sephardi accomplishment but as an index of a tolerance inherent in a Spain that provided the conditions that nourished a Jewish Golden Age. The focus on Sephardi pride and Sephardi models for general Jewish emancipation would shift in Spain to Spanish nationalistic appropriation. It is in this sense that the Jewish legacy of Spain would be incorporated as national inheritance.

NOTES

1. Varela's proposal was rejected, and in 1802, Carlos IV reiterated the prohibition of Jews from entering Spain, placing the Inquisition in control of inspecting and enforcing this policy at the border. In 1819, facing the immigration pressure of a number of Jews from Gibraltar and Tetuán, another Royal Order reinstated the edict's prohibition (Pérez-Prendes 86).

2. These accounts also emphasized the great tribulations and suffering caused by the expulsion. As David A. Wacks explains in *Double Diaspora in Sephardic Literature*, Iberian Jews' religious and literary culture "expressed a diasporic consciousness . . . [the] two diasporas, from the Holy Land and from Spain, would 'echo back and forth' in the Sephardic imagination" (1–2).

3. They explicitly contrasted a "Golden Age" of Jewish life under Muslim rule with the oppressive conditions and persecutions enacted by Christian Europe (the latter came to be known as "the lachrymose conception of Jewish history") (M. Cohen 3–4). For an in-depth analysis of German Jewish perceptions of Iberian Jews as useful historical examples, see Carsten Schapkow's book *Role Model and Countermodel: The Golden Age of Iberian Jewry and German Jewish Culture during the Era of Emancipation*.

4. As Halevi-Wise explains in her introduction to the volume, the "prism of Sepharad" offers a miriad of possibilities:

> If Spain at the end of the Middle Ages tried to abolish religious pluralism, British novelists in the middle of the nineteenth century could use Sepharad either to promote ethnic diversity or to prove its undesirability; while a Marrano's identity could stand for treacherous falsity in one novel, in another it could symbolize a positive badge of steadfastness pushed to the point of martyrium or a sign of persistent multiculturalism in the face of persecution. (Halevi-Wise, "Introduction" 5)

See Calderwood's similar argument about the malleability of al-Andalus "as an idea that travels across time and performs useful work for writers living in different historical and cultural contexts" (75).

5. See Filios, Doubleday for analyses of Menocal's book and its specific idealization of al-Andalus.

6. Claudio Sánchez Albornoz engaged in a highly polemic dispute with Castro about the meaning of Spanish history. In *España, un enigma histórico* (1956), he rejected the idea of Spanish identity's being the result of interaction and contact with Muslims and Jews and argued for the existence of an eternal, immutable, essential *Hispanidad* centered on Catholicism and the fight against Islam. In *Islamic and Christian Spain in the Early Middle Ages* (1979), Thomas Glick argued that cultural influence and ethnic conflict were not incompatible phenomena and that both occurred in medieval Spain (Novikoff 29–30). See Novikoff for a detailed account of the development of the concepts of tolerance and intolerance as categories of analysis in the historiography of medieval Spain.

7. As Jonathan Ray explains, it also "presupposes the existence of relatively uniform and cohesive religious communities," which was not the case in medieval Iberia ("Whose Golden Age?" 11).

8. According to Fredriksen, when Augustine spoke of their "subjection" to Christians, he meant that Jews, having lost their kingdom, must live as minorities within Christian ones, not that they suffer or should suffer actual servitude. Their metaphorical servitude to Christians and to the Church, in Augustine's vision, solely concerned their role as witnesses to scripture. In the Middle Ages, however, this notion of Jews' "subjection" would be used literally, to justify their persecution.

9. Although Jews had an inferior legal standing under Muslim rule, their status as *dhimmis*, "People of the Book," granted them protection and the right to practice their religion. Their persecution under Islam occurred a lot less frequently than under Christianity (M. Cohen xxiii). In both Muslim and Christian Spain a minority of highly educated Jews reached high office and positions of power. Samuel Halevi Abulafia was royal treasurer and advisor of King Pedro of Castile in the fourteenth century (for more on Halevi, see chapters 2, 3, and 6). At the height of the Caliphate of al-Andalus in the mid-tenth century, Hasdai ibn Shaprut was a distinguished scholar, doctor, diplomat, and advisor to the powerful caliph Abdarrahman III. At the beginning of the eleventh century, Samuel ibn Nagrela (the Nagid) was a highly successful poet, chief vizier, and head of the Muslim kingdom of Granada's army. But the stature and privilege of these courtiers could spark anti-Judaism violence to the wider Jewish community, as happened in 1066, when Granada Muslims revolted against the king's employment of Nagrela's son Joseph, whom they killed along with three or four thousand other Jews (see Ashtor 2:178–89, and Nirenberg, *Anti-Judaism* 180–81, for this episode).

10. In 1215, the Fourth Lateran Council established a legal framework for encouraging conversions throughout Christian Europe. That framework consisted of a variety of physical, economic and social pressures combined with "persuasive" measures such as religious debates (the famous "disputations") and compulsory Christian sermons by mendicant preachers in the synagogues (Gerber 101–5). For more on deteriorating conditions for Jews in Christian Spain and on Christian proselytizing efforts, see Gerber, Y. Baer, and Amelang.

11. Many were killed without being given the choice to convert, and the great majority of those who could not escape converted to Christianity. But a fact not well known is that a significant number of Spanish Jews who were presented with the choice of conversion or death chose martyrdom. The Hebrew "Elegy to the Martyrs of Toledo," written shortly after the massacres of 1391, honors these martyrs (Bodian, *Dying* 5–8). See also Ray, *After Expulsion* 146.

12. Ironically, as argued by Ray, Jewish moralists and religious leaders who condemned what they saw as the excessive social interaction with non-Jews in medieval Spain saw these Christian discriminatory measures as the reestablishment of proper boundaries between the two groups, as an imposition from the outside that returned Jews to their true identity. Such is the argument of Solomon Alami's post-1391 *Epistle on Morality* (Ray, "Beyond" 6).

13. There is a long history of debate over whether we can speak of racial antisemitism in fifteenth-century Spain, related to the broader, more generalized claim that biological racism begins only in the modern era. In *Assimilation and Racial Anti-Semitism: The Iberian and the German Models*, Yosef Haim Yerushalmi compared late medieval Spanish ideologies that saw Jewishness as

carried in the blood with nineteenth-century German antisemitic ideologies and understood both as recognizably racial. On the other side, there is a long tradition of Spanish historiography that has categorically denied the validity of the concept of "race" as a useful theoretical tool to understand the Spanish late medieval case, beginning with Américo Castro's rejection of the term. See Nirenberg, "Was There Race before Modernity?," for a thorough explanation of the debate and the politics at stake in these positions.

14. As Ray explains, this identification with a socially and intellectually superior group had its origin in the High Middle Ages: "Spurred by their Muslim counterparts, who sought to promote their own political and cultural independence from the great Islamic centers of the Middle East and North Africa, Andalusi-Jewish intellectuals began to assert their identity as a people apart. Playing upon a popular Jewish notion associating the Iberian Peninsula with the biblical land of Sepharad, they invoked a verse from the Book of Obadiah to identify themselves as descendants of the elite stratum of ancient Jerusalemite society, the most intellectually accomplished and socially superior community of the Jewish diaspora" (Ray, *After Expulsion* 13).

15. This strategy of blaming the Jews for their own victimization has been rehearsed in different forms and appears in unexpected places. Américo Castro, for example, often thought of as a champion of the inclusion of Jews in Spanish history, wrote of "Semitic characteristics" as stable, essential, and inescapable forms of group identity reproduced across time through genealogy. These characteristics, he argued, were introduced in Spain through the Jews and conversos. They included Inquisitorial fanaticism, slandering informants, frantic greed and plundering, the concern over purity of blood, the concern over public reputation, the desire of everyone to be a nobleman, and the negative view of the world (Nirenberg, "Was There?" 244–47; see also Paul Julian Smith, Menny, "Entre reconocimiento").

16. In his description of Iberian Jews' influence in the Ottoman Empire, and therefore in the political and economic success of the Turks, Belon found a way to blame Spaniards, accusing them of creating the instrument of Europe's and Christianity's most serious challenge since the rise of Islam (Braude 183). See Wacks for a description of the social and cultural dominance of Sephardi Jews within Ottoman Jewry. Sephardi Jews, according to Wacks, were involved in Spanish imperial culture (*Double* 192–6).

17. They had already been sporadically admitted into Italian city-states earlier in the sixteenth-century (Israel 37).

18. These ideas had already begun to be put in place by the Duke of Lerma, Felipe III's favorite, who had issued a papal general pardon for past religious offences in 1605, eased restrictions on immigration from Portugal, and signed government contracts with recently arrived Portuguese New Christian financiers (Israel 47–49).

19. The Portuguese conversos began arriving in Spain in 1580, when Spain annexed Portugal under Felipe II. Their converso history and identity differed from that of the Spanish conversos in that they had not suffered the persecutions and mass conversions of 1391 and the expulsion of 1492. Instead, Portuguese Jews were suddenly converted by force in 1497. The majority of these converts were Spanish Jews who had fled to Portugal in 1492. Three main factors resulted in much higher rates of crypto-Judaism and group cohesion in Portuguese conversos in contrast to the Spanish: the Inquisition was not established in Portugal until 1536, and it wasn't very effective until about 1580, giving conversos ample time to cultivate crypto-Judaic practices; the majority had already decided not to convert in Spain in 1492 and were, thus, as a whole, a group with stronger loyalty to Judaism than those who had decided to stay in Spain; and the fact, underlined by the philosopher Spinoza, that the statutes of purity of blood effectively excluded Portuguese conversos from all honors and offices reinforced the feeling of a separate identity. By contrast, most conversos in Spain, by the time the statutes of purity of blood were officially sanctioned in the 1550s, had already intermarried and assimilated into Christian society (Yerushalmi 4–6; Israel 19–20). Thus, from the 1580s onward, most cases of Judaizing in Spanish Inquisition records concern immigrant Portuguese conversos or their children (Israel 48).

20. Cansino's family was in the Spanish service in Oran. He dedicated to Olivares his transliteration into Roman characters of a Salonikan Rabbi's sixteenth-century Ladino text about the greatness of Constantinople (Elliott 300–301; Yerushalmi 167–8). Rafael Cansinos Assens, the twentieth-century Spanish writer discussed in the Introduction, saw the Jewish origins of the surname Cansinos as evidence for his claim of Jewish ancestry. See *Las luminarias de Janucá*.

21. The endurance of the smears against the count-duke due to his perceived closeness with the Jews can be exemplified by Amador de los Ríos's description of Olivares's actions in his 1875–76 *Historia social, política y religiosa de los judíos de España y Portugal*. According to Amador de los Ríos, Olivares had brought Salonikan Jews to Madrid to help the crown's finances and, defying the Inquisition, had arranged to give them a synagogue. He had even tried to abolish the Inquisition but had been stopped and discharged from his powerful position (de los Ríos, *Historia* 843–44). The condemnatory tone of Amador de los Ríos's description contrasts with the approbatory tone of his description of successive proposals to bring Jews back for economic reasons by Manuel de Lira and Pedro Varela (see note 27).

22. Thus, they were often referred to as Jews, especially by those people, like Quevedo, who abhorred their presence in Spain. According to Israel, many of these Portuguese conversos were sincere Catholics, including one of

the richest, Jorge de Paz de Silveira. Many others seem to have been crypto-Jews: the powerful families of Cortizos, Montezinos, and Passarinho, who had strong links with Sephardi Jewish communities in Holland and Italy (Israel 91).

23. Although the accused belonged to a much lower socioeconomic status than he did, Cardoso lived in the same street, Calle de las Infantas, where the events presumably took place. For more on the circumstances that lead to the accusations and Cardoso's account, see Yerushalmi 105–22.

24. The *Execración* was not published until 1996, when the canon and archivist of the Cathedral of Santiago found the manuscript in the *Biblioteca del Real Consulado de la Coruña*. The manuscript had been considered lost since the seventeenth century. We thank our colleague Víctor Roncero López for calling our attention to this work.

25. For the Spanish version of the letter quoted by Quevedo, see page 11 of the *Execración*. For more on the hoax and its circulation, see Álvarez Chillida, *El antisemitismo* 45–51.

26. In great part as a result of this publication, Quevedo was severely punished, incarcerated from 1639 to 1643 for "vilifying the government and making contact with the enemy" (Elliott 553–54). In 1643, Olivares, whose policies had been long attacked, was dismissed. The hostilities against Portuguese conversos reached a new pitch after the independence of Portugal in 1640, and the Inquisition renewed its efforts at persecuting conversos and rigorously enforcing the purity of blood statutes. In 1648 Cardoso left Spain and settled in Venice, which at the time harbored one of the most important Jewish communities in the world and was considered a safe place for crypto-Jews to openly practice Judaism (Yerushalmi 195–96). Many hundred conversos fled Spain for western Europe in the years between 1645 and 1660, due to the increasing pressure of the Inquisition (Israel 119).

27. Manuel de Lira, minister of Carlos II and diplomat at The Hague between 1671 and 1679, proposed the admission of heretics (Protestants) and Jews to Spain's American possessions. His proposal, like Olivares's and, later, Varela's, would be rejected. See Amador de los Ríos's description of de Lira and Varela in *Historia* 844–47.

28. In the discussions about the abolition of the Inquisition at the Cortes de Cádiz, liberal arguments were inspired by the work of Hebraist Antonio Puigblanch, who had denounced its methods in *La Inquisición sin máscara*, published in 1811 (Álvarez Chillida, *El antisemitismo* 100). See Ojeda-Mata, "Thinking" for a pioneering article on the reevaluation of the place of Spanish Jews in nineteenth-century Spain.

29. In "The Narrative Work of the Jewish Conspirator," Lou Charnon-Deutsch shows how mid-nineteenth-century writers across Europe, including in Spain,

portrayed Jews as the conspirators behind these societies' political unrest and revolutionary movements.

30. As Martin-Márquez explains, this argument would help to justify Spanish colonization of North Africa (Martin-Márquez 53–54). Conde, and many other Arabists, supported Spain's colonial intervention in Morocco in the 1859–60 Spanish-Moroccan War. So did Amador de los Ríos, who wrote an Ode in 1860 in honor of the occupation of Tetuán by Spanish troops. As did many other intellectuals and politicians of the time, he celebrated the war as an extension of the Reconquest and portrayed Queen Isabel II as the descendant of Queen Isabel the Catholic (Friedman, "Jewish History" 108).

31. See Nitai Shinan, "Emilio Castelar" for the evolution of Castelar's views on Jews.

32. For more on the development of Arab and Hebrew studies in Spain, see *Orientalismo y nacionalismo español: Estudios árabes y hebreos en la Universidad de Madrid (1843–1868)* by Aurora Rivière Gómez. Manuela Marín's edited volume *Al-Andalus/España: Historiografías en contraste; Siglos XVII–XXI* describes the profound influence of Spanish Arabists' "hispanization" of al-Andalus. For a pioneering assessment of the place of literature written in Hebrew in the Spanish Middle Ages, see David Wacks's article, "Is Spain's Hebrew Literature 'Spanish'?" See Bush, Friedman, "Jewish History," and Shinan, "Estudio preliminar," for more on the founding figure of Amador de los Ríos, and Anna Menny, "Sepharad—Object of Investigation?" for the founding of the CSIC, the Arias Montano Institute, and the Institute for Sephardi Studies in Francoist Spain.

33. Because of these new laws, a small number of Jewish financiers and merchants who had associations with Spanish government officials began establishing themselves in Madrid from the south of France, mostly from Bayonne. In 1865, the Spanish government granted them permission to purchase land for a cemetery on the condition they would not build a synagogue. No cemetery, however, was built at that time. Some North African Jews of Spanish origin also settled in Spain and acquired Spanish citizenship in the period between 1869 and 1875 (Avni 10, 40).

34. As described by Amador de los Ríos years later, Philippson's petition read:

> No venimos . . . a reclamar las propiedades que arrebataron a nuestros padres, ni los inapreciables bienes que nos quitaron; ni siquiera los templos, que nos fueron sagrados en un tiempo, y cuyas cúpulas divisamos todavía. Venimos solamente a borrar la afrenta de la expatriación y a impetrar la libertad de entrar en España para aquellos de nuestros hermanos que quieran hacer uso de ella. No os cuesta más que un *sí*; pero *sí* preciosísimo, por ser el acento de la caridad y de la humanidad, de la justicia y de la civilización

[We do not come . . . to claim the properties that were grabbed from our fathers, nor the invaluable goods that were taken away from us; not even the temples, that were sacred to us long ago, and whose domes we can still make out. We only come to erase the affront of the expatriation and to ask for the freedom to enter Spain for those of our brothers that might want to make use of it. The only price you need to pay is a *yes*; but an extremely precious yes, for it stands for kindness, humanity, justice and civilization] (de los Ríos, *Historia* 850–51)

35. This exacerbated patriotic sentiment is powerfully conveyed in the deeply ironic opening pages of Benito Pérez Galdós's novel *Aita Tettauen*. See Martin-Márquez's *Disorientations* for an analysis of this novel, the diary of Alarcón, and the Hispano-Moroccan War, and see Calderwood 30–73 for the way the memory of al-Andalus is used by Alarcón to justify Spain's military presence in Morocco.

36. The Dreyfus affair (1894–99) will also occupy the main pages of Spanish newspapers and polarize public opinion in two distinct camps, with the fundamentalist Catholic faction following French antisemitic writing (see González García, "La cuestión judía" 37–41).

37. It is not by chance that this book, with an excellent introduction by Jacobo Israel Garzón, was reedited in 1992.

38. As Rodríguez de Castro and Amador de los Ríos before him, Pulido felt compelled to clarify his religion—the fact of not being a Jew—in the introduction of the book, stating that he was Christian and descended from Old Christians (Pulido, *Intereses nacionales* 17).

39. Already in 1868 José María de Murga y Mugártegui, known as "el Moro Vizcaíno" had sentimentally written about Moroccan Jews' conservation of fifteenth-century Castilian as proof of their loyalty and love for Spain (Macías 55). The Judeo-Spanish language has its origin in old Castilian but it is a living language that has evolved in contact with and influenced by other languages (Hebrew, Arabic, Turkish, Italian, French), not an archaeological remnant of old Castilian (Hassán, "Los sefardíes" 42). See also Paloma Díaz-Mas, *Sephardim* 72–101.

40. Iacob M. Hassán offers the same argument: the Hispanism of Sephardi Jews, expressed in their language, has been an affirmation of their own Jewish identity, a differentiating element that explains why many referred to their Judeo-Spanish language as "judío' or "judesmo" ("Los sefardíes" 45). Spain's main competitors in the Balkans for cultural and linguistic influence were France and the French schools of the *Alliance Israelite Universelle* (AIU), a tool of French cultural expansion among Jews living in Muslim countries. Spain was never able to compete with these schools in terms of cultural and linguistic influence (Rohr, *The Spanish Right* 17). In fact, ironically, Pulido himself points out that many of the letters he received and included in his books from Sephardi

Jews were written in French (*Los israelitas* 47, 49). See Díaz-Mas, *Sephardim*; Garzón, "El Doctor Pulido"; Friedman; Goode; and Rohr for more on Pulido's campaigns.

41. In the eyes of the Spanish government today, this is the main difference between the descendants of exiled Jews and the descendants of moriscos (Muslims who were forced to convert to Christianity after 1499 and who were expelled from Spain in 1609). This difference serves to justify the absence of a corresponding law that would allow descendants of moriscos to apply for Spanish citizenship. Not having maintained the language is seen as proof of the severance of their connection to Spain, in detriment of other factors. See "Los moriscos" for an overview of the protests by descendants of moriscos against their exclusion from this law.

42. As Rohr indicates, this racial discourse echoed the Africanist discourse that used similar biological language to speak of the racial ties or "blood brotherhood" that united Spaniards and Moroccan Muslims. Martin-Márquez shows how this discourse served to justify Spain's colonial ambitions in Morocco. The "blood brotherhood" trope was employed by generations of Africanists (Martin-Márquez 51–60).

43. For narratives written by twentieth- and twenty-first-century Sephardi Jews about their feelings, or lack thereof, for Spain, see Pilar Romeu Ferré's article "Sefarad ¿la 'patria' de los sefardíes?" See also Dalia Kandiyoti's *The Converso's Return* on the reawakening of interest in converso history, ancestry, and identity in the Americas, Europe, and Turkey. The relationship with ancestral Spain as a lost home when experiencing the loss of a more recent home is one of the themes present in the work of Moroccan Sephardi writer Esther Bendahan, especially in her partly autobiographical novel *Déjalo, ya volveremos*, as we will see in Chapter 6.

44. The economic opportunism of philosephardism is evident in the report written by José María Doussinague, Spanish commercial agent to Europe, after his 1930 trip to the Balkans. Sephardi Jews, he said, were an "arm for commercial penetration in the region." Naturalizations should be sped up for those whose "position, commercial credit or financial power" were "useful to Spain's commercial expansion." But care had to be taken in not treating them as Spaniards and preventing them from settling in Spain (Rohr, *The Spanish Right* 30–31). Cansinos Assens openly criticizes this mercantilist aspect of the philosephardi campaign, which he preferred to think of as a "historical reparation" (Garzón, "El Doctor Pulido" xvii).

45. In 1915, the Jerusalem-born Jewish scholar Abraham Shalom Yahuda was appointed to a special Chair for Hebrew Literature and the History of the Jews in Spain in the Middle Ages at the University of Madrid. See Friedman's, Muñoz Solla's, and Allyson González's articles for more on this fascinating figure, who

held the first Jewish studies chairmanship created in the Western Hemisphere in a secular university in the modern era (Friedman, "Abraham Shalom Yahuda"; A. González). Another material result of the movement was *Casa Universal de los Sefardís* [Universal House of Sephardi Jews], an organization established in 1920 in Madrid to promote economic and cultural links. Its periodical, a platform of philosephardism, was called *La Revista de la Raza*. It was financed by Ignacio Bauer, grandson of the representative of the House of Rothschild in Spain and head of the Jewish community (Rohr, *The Spanish Right* 25–26; Avni 26–27). See Garzón, "El Doctor Pulido," for more on the far-reaching consequences of the philosephardi campaign, including the 2015 law of nationality.

46. About nineteen thousand Jews lived in the area of the Spanish Protectorate in northern Morocco and Tangier at the beginning of the twentieth century (Avni 29).

47. See Friedman, "Recovering" 244–58, for an analysis of the organization of the event and its diplomatic and international aspirations and Muñoz Solla for the contribution of figures like Ignacio Bauer to its organization and the way it was seen by intellectuals like Cansinos Assens, Yahuda, and José Manuel Camacho. See also Linhard, "Second Republic" for more on Republican initiatives regarding Jewish issues in this period and their relation to prior philosephardist efforts.

48. Preston describes the role of Catalan priest Juan Tusquets Terrats in disseminating the ideas of *The Protocols of the Elders of Zion* in Spain. Terrats's best-seller *Orígenes de la revolución española* [Origins of the Spanish Revolution] popularized the notion of a Jewish-Masonic conspiracy that, through the Republic, was trying to destroy Spain and Christianity (see Preston 34–37).

49. "Like in Reconquest times, we, the Hispano-Roman-Goths fight against the Jewish-Moorish. The pure racial stock fights against the bastard one . . . the Spanish Marxist racial stock is Jewish-Moorish, of mixed blood, which distinguishes him psychologically from the foreign Marxist, pure Semite" (*Divagaciones intranscendentales*, Valladolid, Talleres Tipográficos Cuesta, 1938, qtd. in Álvarez Chillida, *El antisemitismo* 379; Richards 57).

50. Most Jews were forced to finance the war effort, although a small mercantile elite did so willingly. Chief among them was the Banque Hassan of Tangiers, who financed the rebellion (Rohr, *The Spanish Right* 88).

51. See Martin-Márquez; Manzano Moreno; Balfour, *Deadly Embrace*; Calderwood.

52. In 1939 and 1941, after winning the Civil War, Franco worked on a text that became the protoscript of the movie *Raza* (dir. José Luis Sáenz de Heredia, 1942). He entitled it *Raza: Anecdotario para el guión de una película* and published it under the pseudonym Jaime de Andrade. The text and the film reviewed Spanish history in light of and in order to legitimize the Nationalist victory.

They can be called semiautobiographical, but as observed by Kathleen Vernon, in terms of the contrast between the screenplay and Franco's real family history, "the epic chronicle of the Churruca family told in the novel and screenplay is a study in compensatory fantasies" (28). The figure of the hero, José Churruca, is the result of Franco's "mythic self-projection" and "self-idealization" (29).

53. This argument of Spanish Jews' not being guilty of deicide has its origin in the fifteenth-century countergenealogies constructed by Spanish Jews to defend themselves from the statutes of purity of blood. At the time of the 1449 Toledo riots and anti-converso polemics, a letter surfaced, supposedly written by Toledo Jews at the time of Jesus and translated from Aramaic. The letter "sought to establish that the Toledan Jews had been settled in Spain long before the Diaspora, and had in fact opposed the execution of Jesus by their coreligionists in the Holy Land" (Nirenberg, "Mass Conversion" 28).

54. It was discredited in the books *Spain, the Jews, and Franco* by Haim Avni (1982) and *España y los judíos en el siglo XX* by Antonio Marquina and Gloria Inés Ospina (1987). Both books identified two phases of World War II: In the first, from 1939 to the end of 1942, the Spanish government did not discriminate against Jewish refugees, but it also did not allow them to settle in the country, even when they held Spanish passports. In the second phase, from November 1942 onward, Spain changed its policy, leaving its border with France open. Avni and Marquina and Ospina stress the opportunistic nature of Spanish refugee policy, noting that the change after 1942 was largely a response to the development of the war and the Allies' increasing pressure on Franco's government (Rohr, *The Spanish Right* 2–3).

55. In September 1949, Franco's government invited a group of US congressmen to visit Spain. Abraham Multer, representative from New York, met with the Jewish communities in Barcelona and Madrid and petitioned the Spanish government on their behalf. His insistence paid off, and the legal situation of Spain's Jewish communities markedly improved after his intervention. Multer would later inform President Truman of this improvement, something that, apparently, went a long way toward changing the negative impression Truman had of Franco's Spain (Lisbona 136–39).

TWO

TOURISM AND THE EMBRACING OF SPAIN'S JEWISH LEGACY

TOURISM TO SPAIN EXPERIENCED A dramatic evolution from occupying a marginal position at the onset of European leisure travel in the eighteenth century to becoming a top tourist destination in the 1960s. In 2018, 82.8 million international visitors traveled to Spain, making the country the second-most-popular world destination after France, followed by the United States. In terms of international tourist revenues, Spain, with $68 billion, occupied the second place after the United States in 2017 ("Estadística").[1] Tourism has become vital to Spain's economy, currently constituting 14.6 percent of Spain's GDP and 15.1 percent of all jobs (*Travel* 1). From this perspective, the fact that it is within tourism-related activities that some of the most visible and complex efforts to recover the nation's Jewish past have emerged is not surprising.

The evolution of tourism in Spain has consistently hinged on complex negotiations between a foreign appetite for the presence of "exotic" elements in Spain, especially those connected with the country's Romani population and Arab heritage, and the domestic need to emphasize the country's full belonging to western Europe, Christianity, and modernity. As Barbara Fuchs has explained about Spain's Arab heritage, the relation to "Moorishness" was far from over in 1492, when the Catholic Monarchs conquered Granada, the last Muslim stronghold on the Iberian Peninsula. In the aftermath of 1492, Spain engaged in both the repression of moriscos (Muslims converted to Christianity) and an intense cultural negotiation with its own Arab identity (Fuchs 1). Concerning the Jews, their presence in Spain did not end in 1492. As Fuchs and J. N. Hillgarth have shown, in the sixteenth and seventeenth centuries, while Spain emphasized its distance from Jewishness and Moorishness to establish its Christian identity, foreign travelers visiting from other European states consistently constructed Spain as Oriental and Semitic, a racial and religious Other of Europe (Fuchs 7, 116).[2] Throughout Europe, Spaniards and Portuguese were identified with Jews and Arabs, an identification that would become reaffirmed in the writings of Romantic travelers who began to venture into Spain at the end of the eighteenth century (Hillgarth 160).

A telling example is the French writer and politician Maurice Barrès, who, visiting Toledo around 1892, became fascinated by what he perceived as "Semitic behaviors" in people who presented themselves as Christian: "Se prolonga indefinidamente, en mi imaginación excitada, el interés que me dan esos seres que se creen católicos españoles y que reconozco en sus actos como semitas" [The interest provoked by those creatures who believe themselves to be Spanish Catholics and whom I recognize in their actions as Semites has no end in my excited imagination]. In people's faces, continues Barrès, "distinguía numerosas variedades del tipo semítico: árabes y judíos vestidos a la española" [I distinguished several variations of the Semite type: Arabs and Jews dressed in the Spanish manner] (in García Mercadal 538). Thus, for travelers like Barrès, no matter what Spaniards did (go to mass, "act" Catholic, eat pork, never say "I am Jewish" or "I am Arab"), Spaniards were in fact Jews and Arabs, which he could plainly "see" in their faces and behaviors. Spaniards and Spain were fascinating to him precisely for this reason. When observing women praying in Toledo, Barrès wondered if, in their Latin words, they were not expressing "their Oriental soul" and imagined them probably belonging to one of those Toledo families whose ancestors practiced Judaism in secret (in García Mercadal 539).[3]

During the seventeenth and eighteenth centuries, Spain was left out of the Grand Tour, the first significant wave of tourism that took place in western Europe. While a bourgeois leisure class established a travel circuit through Italy and France in search of both culture and rest, these travelers did not venture into Spain, which they saw as remote, dangerous, uncivilized in customs, backward in infrastructure, and culturally marginal (Barke and Towner, "Exploring" 4–5). These same characteristics, perceived as inconvenient and unappealing by the initial travelers doing the Grand Tour, became enticingly fascinating for Romantic intellectuals who ventured into Spain starting in the late eighteenth century and steadily increased in numbers during the nineteenth. Romantic travelers saw in Spain a reservoir of exotic culture almost unblemished by the damaging hand of industrial modernity. Rejecting the perceptions of their predecessors as narrow-minded, moralistic, and unadventurous, these travelers saw Spain, and especially Andalucía, as "a dream world where time could be slowed, life savored to its fullest, and the disturbances and hypocrisy of the modern, 'civilized' world of large European capitals avoided" (Charnon-Deutsch, *Spanish Gypsy* 59). Spain's cultural diversity, especially its Romani population and Arab heritage, became a major attraction in a time of orientalist taste. Spain thus became a favorite travel destination for Europeans, and Spaniards began a deeply ambivalent relationship with this exotic and Oriental conception of themselves (Charnon-Deutsch, "Exoticism" 251). Spain thus found itself in a particular double bind as a culture that had both repressed the Oriental and Semitic elements of its historical identity, constructing them as its Others, and come to represent the "close-to-home" Orient to other Europeans (Charnon-Deutsch, "Exoticism" 262; Colmeiro 129).[4] As Lou Charnon-Deutsch shows in *The Spanish Gypsy: The History of a European Obsession*, travelers like Richard Ford, George Borrow, Washington Irving, Théophile Gautier, and countless others "discovered" in Spain an exotic land where monumental historical ruins like La Alhambra coexisted with "wild and passionate" Gypsies, who became the object of a long-term European fascination and fueled Spain's international tourist industry.

Less known but also influential in the development of Spain's tourism identity was Romantic travelers' fascination with Toledo and the remnants of Spain's Jewish past. Upon their return to France at the end of the War of 1808–14, in which Napoleon's army invaded Spain, many French soldiers published their impressions of Spain. These narratives became extremely popular in France and elsewhere in Europe and established early nineteenth-century Toledo as a Romantic city par excellence (Muñoz Herrera 85). Throughout the nineteenth century, foreign travelers included Toledo in their European tours and became fascinated with its medieval ruins. These ruins best represented the contrast between the city's glorious past and its devalued present, with remnants of the city's Jewish past among those that particularly captivated travelers' imagination. Their travelogues in turn sparked the interest of Spanish intellectuals, who began projecting on Toledo the same attributes of mystery and ruin to depict the city as exotic and evocative of past grandeur.[5]

Testimonies from early foreign visitors would have a deep impact on the views of later travelers and would help articulate the foundational narratives of Spain's tourist industry. Texts and images circulated by these foreign visitors moved fluidly through several generations of travelogues and into the work of historians, conservationists, and government officials making the case for the development of the tourist industry. In 1844, the Spanish government formed a Monuments Commission, the first official agency charged with classifying and cataloging the buildings and monuments that deserved to be protected by the state. The commission's report on Toledo, written by the architect Blas Crespo, included the city's two standing synagogues in its list of priorities (Muñoz Herrera 171).

The commission's secretary was the prominent historian and literary scholar José Amador de los Ríos, who had a personal interest in both Toledo and in Spain's Jewish past. His *Toledo pintoresca o descripción de sus más célebres monumentos* (1845), which contained a description of the two synagogues as prime examples of Arab architecture, was a highly influential work both among historians and among those seeking to develop the city's potential for tourism (García Martín 83).[6] Amador de los Ríos opens his book by addressing Toledo as a woman dressed in rags:

> ¿Qué haces ahí con el semblante triste, roto el hermoso manto de perlas que te cobijaba, despedazada tu corona, escarnecido el riquísimo solio de tus reyes y lanzando del pecho ayes que nadie escucha y suspiros que nadie recoge? ¿Qué haces ahí, defensa de la patria, legisladora del mundo? ¿En dónde están tus sabios prelados, tus ilustres rabinos, tus celebrados ulemas?
>
> [What are you doing standing over there with your sad countenance, the beautiful cloak of pearls that sheltered you broken, your crown torn to pieces, the lavish throne of your kings scorned, and exhaling from your chest complaints that nobody hears, and sighs that nobody registers? What are you doing over there, defender of the fatherland, legislator of the world? Where are your wise prelates, your illustrious rabbis, your celebrated ulemas?] (Amador de los Ríos, *Toledo* 1)

Interspersed among the scene's imagined ruins, Amador de los Ríos sees traces of former grandiosity connected both to political power and to the wisdom accrued by Christian, Jewish, and Muslim traditions. The first section of his book becomes a kind of epic commentary on the architectural and cultural value of Toledo's Christian monuments: the Cathedral, the monastery of San Juan de los Reyes, the Hospital of Santa Cruz, and the Alcazar. By contrast, the second part, dedicated to the city's Arab influence, becomes a lyrical appreciation of Toledo's Arab art and architecture. He repeatedly exposes the lack of appreciation for this architecture in Spain, since everything related to Arabs is unjustly considered *tosco y grosero* [crude and coarse] and is *anatematizado sin conocerlo* [anathematized without understanding it]. This "systematic aversion," says de los Ríos, stands in sharp contrast to the interest of foreign scholars, who have studied and documented Spain's Arab monuments (Amador de los Ríos, *Toledo* 215–16). Amador de los Ríos's argument anticipated many of the rationales that would later be used to articulate foundational narratives of cultural tourism in Spain. He lamented, "Esta aversión sistemática nos ha arrebatado la gloria de ofrecer a la Europa moderna un cuadro completo de las artes de aquel pueblo, en donde cuando el mundo entero yacía en la más profunda ignorancia, brillaba con todo su esplendor la antorcha del saber humano" [This systematic aversion has robbed us of the glory of offering to modern Europe a complete picture of the arts of that (Arab) culture where human knowledge's torch shone with all its splendor at a time when the whole world laid in the most absolute ignorance] (Amador de los Ríos, *Toledo* 216).

The route through Arab Toledo traced by Amador de los Ríos begins with the city's two medieval synagogues, Santa María la Blanca and El Tránsito, before moving on to the former Mosque del Cristo de la Luz, the Taller del Moro, and the Church of San Román. In his description of the Jewish Quarter, he repeats his initial trope about the stark contrast between the glory of the past and the ruin of the present, adding his condemnation of the human violence responsible for the destruction:

> Aquel pueblo . . . ha desaparecido enteramente con sus artes y sus ciencias, con su comercio y con sus pintorescas costumbres. Montones de escombros son ahora las ricas tiendas del alcaná y apenas quedan ligeras huellas de sus famosas escuelas: casas de mezquino aspecto denegridas por el tiempo, trozos informes de murallas . . . he aquí lo que nos ha legado el furor de los hombres, más terrible que la destructora mano de los siglos, cuando tiene por móvil el odio inspirado por la religión y las costumbres.
>
> [That people . . . with their art and their sciences, with their commerce and their picturesque customs, have completely disappeared. The market's rich shops are now piles of rubble and hardly any traces are left of their famous schools: miserly houses darkened by time, misshapen wall fragments . . . this is the legacy of the furor of men, more terrible than the destructive hand of the centuries, when its motive is religious and cultural hate]. (Amador de los Ríos, *Toledo* 232)

The work of Amador de los Ríos, among others, became pivotal in changing the mind-set of Spaniards about the patrimonial riches to be found in their Arab monuments.[7] As tourism developed in Spain, this "glory" of exhibiting Spain's Arab heritage to modern Europe and then to the world would remain a central goal of tourism initiatives. But to Amador de los Ríos, what characterized this heritage was the enormous gap between what was and what is, the overwhelming sense of absence and void that resonated through the empty, devalued, forgotten, and dilapidated spaces.

This theme of human absence and cultural abandonment would be picked up again by foreign travelers like Hans Christian Andersen, who, during his visit to Toledo in 1862, also reflected on the Jewish Quarter as haunted by an overwhelming sense of absence. The image he conjured to capture his impressions echoed Amador de los Ríos's ragged woman:

> Entre los montones de ruinas vimos una columna de granito derribada; sobre ella estaba sentado, en medio de aquel desierto, de aquella soledad, un viejo mendigo ciego, envuelto en andrajos . . . su imagen en aquel lugar me trajo a la memoria un cuadro del profeta Jeremías sobre las ruinas de Jerusalén
>
> [Among the heaps of ruins we saw a fallen granite column; sitting on it, in the midst of that desert, of that solitude, was an old blind beggar covered in rags . . . his image in that place brought to my memory a painting showing the prophet Jeremiah on the ruins of Jerusalem] (in Muñoz Herrera 51)[8]

For Andersen the image encompassed the identity of these ruins and the environments where they stood as indexes of the absence of the peoples they were built by and for: "El templo [la sinagoga Santa María la Blanca] persiste, pero el pueblo de Israel ha desaparecido de aquí; los edificios de alrededor, en otro tiempo tan bien instalados, yacen en ruinas, y casas trasuntos de barracas los han sustituido" [The synagogue persists, but the people of Israel have disappeared from here; the surrounding buildings, in other times so richly built, lie in ruins, and poorly built shacks stand in their place] (in Muñoz Herrera 51). Implicitly, these lines also contain a lament for the degraded present use of buildings that have gone from solidly constructed monuments for prayer and teaching to becoming supporting structures for shacks.

Thus, in a similar vein to Amador de los Ríos, nineteenth-century foreign travelers were both fascinated by Spain's cultural riches and infuriated by what they saw as the domestic neglect of an exotic past's precious legacy. During his visit to Spain in 1846, Richard Ford complained about Spaniards' attitudes: "The Alhambra, the pearl and magnet of Granada, is in their estimation little better than a *casa de ratones* [mouse house] . . . few natives go there, or understand the all-absorbing interest . . . which it excites in the stranger" (qtd. in Barke and Towner, "Exploring" 23). In 1911, three-quarters of a century after the writings of Amador de los Ríos and Ford, the Marquis de la Vega Inclán reworked these ideas to support his petition to undertake the restoration of Toledo's Synagogue of the Transit. In a letter to the Council of Ministers' president, the marquis not only emphasizes the uniqueness of the legacy represented by this building but also aludes to a foreign gaze that looks in contempt at its state of disrepair and delayed restoration. "The world is watching," he warned, and what "the world" sees is shameful: "presenciando a diario el estupor que al mundo entero le causa el estacionamiento y paralización de esta obra durante años y años" [daily witnessing the astonishment that the whole world feels at the years and years of this work's stagnation and neglect] (qtd. in Palomero Plaza 98).

What Amador de los Ríos, Ford, Andersen, and the marquis understood as neglect can also be seen as the result of a prolonged cultural resistance to facing an unresolved conflict that lies at the root of Spain's modern national identity: a conflicted relation to those physical remnants that act as silent evidence and witnesses of Spain's Arab and Jewish past. In a Spain where national identity was predicated on the political, ideological, and physical erasure of Muslim and Jewish differences, to engage in the appreciation, care, and restoration of the material associated with these cultures carried enough conflicted affect that no easy solution could be found. Tourism partly brought an answer to this cultural riddle. Spaniards very quickly understood the usefulness and convenience of paying attention to "the interests of the stranger" both as economically advantageous and as a way to justify caring for a heritage connected to those aspects of Spain's culture that had been banned, persecuted, and expelled from the national body. From these beginnings, foreign and domestic tourist interests engaged in a fraught relationship in which questions of economic growth and material progress were constantly weighed in a complex game of equivalences and justifications against cultural concerns connected to myths of national, regional, and local identity.

During the reign of Alfonso XIII (1886–1931), Spain's government became one of the first in Europe to dedicate effort and funding to the promotion of tourism by creating the *Comisión Nacional de Turismo* [National Tourist Commission] in 1905. During the 1920s and early 1930s, it became even more actively involved in the promotion of tourism by improving infrastructure, accommodations, and transportation (Barke and Towner, "Exploring" 15–16). As Eugenia Afinoguénova and Jaume Martí-Olivella explain, the appropriations of tourism for political and ideological purposes related to nation-building should come as no surprise if we take into account that the state regulation of travel represented the official beginning of tourism in Spain (xiii–xiv). This early intervention represented an attempt to incorporate Spain into European modernity, trying to place the country within the by then classic European Grand Tour.[9] The aforementioned Marquis de la Vega Inclán, a personal friend of the king's, played a pivotal role in these developments. Recognizing how the work and figure of El Greco (1541–1614) stirred significant national and international interest, the marquis financed the creation of a museum dedicated to the painter in Toledo, which he donated to the state in 1907. In 1911, he became the first director of the Royal Commission for Tourism, the precursor of today's State Tourism Office.[10]

Under the marquis's supervision, one of the first projects of the Tourism Royal Commission was the restoration of Toledo's Synagogue of the Transit (Palomero Plaza 111). In this very early conception of the synagogue as an exhibition object, the marquis saw its potential for tourism and fantasized about the attraction it would be for a variety of foreign visitors. The interest of the world's Jewish elite occupied a central place in his reasons for undertaking this expensive restoration. In the aforementioned 1911 letter to the president of the Council of Ministers, in which he encouraged the synagogue's proper restoration and exhibition, he described the ideal visitors he had in mind: "With admiration and respect, a whole intellectual and powerful race would flock there to pay homage to its art, its history and its people, in Toledo, the dramatic and archeological capital of the Semitic race" (qtd. in Palomero Plaza 98). The marquis imagined these Sephardi visitors would come "with great vanity . . . from Salónica's neighborhoods to Argel's melhaks and from the Danube to the boulevards of Paris" (qtd. in Palomero Plaza 111). The two guiding ideas in this letter, the glorification of Spain's cultural heritage and the presence of a foreign gaze, in this case a Sephardi one, eager to reconnect with or discover this heritage, provided the principal guidelines for the work of the marquis. A century later, municipal authorities in cities throughout Spain are still echoing his words and his fantasies.

The first travel guide published by the Royal Commission for Tourism was *Una excursión a Toledo: 14 de abril, 1913* by Manuel Bartolomé Cossío.[11] He conceived the brochure with a foreign audience in mind, as he wrote it to guide a delegation of French teachers in a short trip to Toledo while they attended a conference in Madrid (Jiménez-Landi 516). Once composed, it was distributed all over Spain and had successive editions throughout the 1910s and 1920s, both in Spanish and French. This travel guide was extremely influential in establishing the idea of Toledo as the most representative site in which to experience Spain's history (Camarasa 9–10). Cossío characterized Toledo as "la ciudad que ofrece el conjunto más acabado y característico de todo lo que han sido la tierra y la civilización genuinamente españolas. Es el resumen más perfecto, más brillante y más sugestivo de la historia patria . . . el viajero que disponga de un solo día en España debe gastarlo sin vacilar en ver Toledo" [the city that offers the most complete and characteristic ensemble of what has been genuinely Spanish civilization. It is the most perfect, brilliant and suggestive summary of the fatherland's history . . . the traveler that has only one day in Spain must, without doubt, spend it in seeing Toledo] (Cossío 3).

The success of the marquis's work and the Royal Commission's promotional campaign can be seen in the subsequent spectacular increase of visitors to Toledo: the one thousand annual visits in 1909 increased to four thousand in 1911, twelve thousand in 1912, eighty thousand by 1924, and one hundred thousand by 1925 (Camarasa 17). Cossío saw the city as a perfect example of "la compenetración de los dos elementos capitales de nuestra historia nacional, el cristiano y el árabe" [the symbiosis of the two central elements of our national history, the Christian and the Arab] (Cossío 3). This brochure and his seminal idea of "cultural symbiosis," publicized by the Royal Commission, would influence another frequent visitor to Toledo, Américo Castro, whose theory of the convivencia of Christians, Muslims, and Jews as the defining feature of Spain as a nation was probably conceived there (García Álvarez 199).

Since these early engagements with foreign visitors, tourism has played an increasingly important role in Spain's economy and in Spain's foreign relations policy. During Francoism, tourism stepped onto the center of the economic and political stage. As early as 1938, still in the midst of the Civil War, Franco, de facto leader of the Nationalist side, appointed a head of the Spanish State Tourism Department at cabinet rank (Barke and Towner, "Exploring" 16). In 1951, in a Spain still devastated by the consequences of the war and in economic crisis, Franco created the Ministry of Information and Tourism. Tourism was used to project an image of Spain as politically stable, peaceful, and engaged in postwar reconstruction. It was hoped that foreign visitors would take a positive image away from their vacations in Spain and influence their governments' perceptions of the country. Tourism was organized as a form of propaganda that would lend legitimacy to the regime, viewed with great suspicion by its European neighbors. Its promotion and expansion became, thus, a political tool in the effort to improve foreign relations (Pi-Sunyer 235–36). Tourism became "an increasingly useful auxiliary to the regime's formal diplomacy" (Pack 11), and its development and modernization actually helped Francoism perpetuate itself. It helped make the case that Spain "had finally managed to 'modernize,' 'develop,' and thus 'normalize,' to use the preferred terms of Franco's Minister of Information and Tourism during the 1960s, Manuel Fraga Iribarne" (Crumbaugh 6).

In the eyes of Franco's regime, the political, social, and economic advantages of tourism so outweighed any negative impact that the government was willing "to go to almost any length and pay almost any cost, whether social, human or environmental, to promote the expansion of tourism" (Pi-Sunyer 237). Massive national and foreign investment was poured into Spain's coasts, radically transforming them into vacation destinations (Pack 10). The formula worked, and from the mid-1950s tourism experienced a boom of unprecedented size, rapidity, and duration, turning Spain into one of the world's top tourist destinations. The 4.0 million visitors to Spain in 1959 became 34.0 million by 1973, 40.0 million by the late 1970s, and 54.0 million by 1989 (Pi-Sunyer 237). This upward trend has continued, and in 2018, Spain received a record 82.8 million international tourists ("Estadística").[12] The degree of Spain's dependence on this industry was illustrated in the words of Prime Minister Mariano Rajoy when, in January 2015, he accepted the World Tourism Organization / World Travel and Tourism Council Open Letter on Travel and Tourism.[13] At this ceremony Rajoy characterized tourism as "a strategic sector for both the present and the future of our economy" and "a state policy in Spain." He was not overstating the importance of this sector since, at a time when unemployment reached 25 percent, tourism represented 25 percent of all new jobs created in Spain in 2014 ("Prime Minister").

At the onset of the dramatic expansion of Spain's tourist industry in the 1960s, tourism authorities deployed an exoticist cultural narrative that stressed the peculiarities of Spain's history and culture within the European context as a means to differentiate the country from similar beach-and-sun destinations across the Mediterranean (Pi-Sunyer 237). The famous 1960s slogan "Spain Is Different" tried to emphasize the particular local customs and traditions that, to the regime, defined Spain's national culture and positioned it outside the European norm: popular religious festivals, bullfighting, and flamenco, to name a few. This conception of difference was constructed, ironically, through the silencing and repression of Spain's internal regional, linguistic, and political differences. In its insistence on Spain's differences from modernized Europe, these promotional campaigns repeated a stereotyped image of Spanish folkloric backwardness (Kelly 30; Afinoguénova and Martí-Olivella xii).

The "Spain Is Different" slogan thus partly answered Richard Ford's complaint by embracing that exotic aspect that fascinated foreign visitors. However, the dominant reasons for Spain's success as a destination of mass tourism in the 1960s were not so much tied to a particular vision of national culture but to more prosaic factors. Surveys done in the 1970s and late 1980s found that what attracted foreign visitors to Spain were the country's sun, beaches, and low prices (Williams 124; Pi-Sunyer 237–39). Spain's mass tourism has always been intimately tied to the beach, which still constitutes the main focus of tourist attraction. Despite these clearly stated preferences of foreign and domestic visitors, the development of cultural tourism has been an underlying concern of tourism authorities and a constant theme of official campaigns. The cultural narrative stated by the Marquis de la Vega Inclán at the beginning of the twentieth century has continued as an undercurrent to the official promotion of tourism in Spain. Rather than allowing tourism to be seen as a mere market exchange of money for sun and relaxation, Spain's authorities promote the cultural narrative as providing both distinctiveness and a romantic halo of adventure to the tourist's choice and as a way to promote a perception of tourism as an effect of Spain's national, regional, and local greatness. With the advent of democracy after Franco's death in 1975, changes to tourist promotion aimed to undo the image of a backward, folkloric Spain that was "different" from modern Europe. Yet the cultural narrative of national uniqueness remained at the center of official campaigns, however differently constituted.

The new promotional campaigns, with slogans such as "Everything under the Sun," promoted the image of a modern, Europeanized Spain with a rich and multicultural history and a diversity of attractions (Kelly 31–32; Maiztegui-Oñate and Areitio Bertolín 204). They also tried to undo some of the environmental damage done by decades of unscrupulous construction, commercialization, and overcrowding of the coastal areas (Pi-Sunyer 239) and to overcome the seasonal nature of Spain's tourism, concentrated in the summer months (Maiztegui-Oñate and Areitio Bertolín 204). One of the ways to achieve these changes was the promotion of urban tourism, a main objective of the tourist initiatives of the 1990s (Barke and Towner, "Urban" 346). This promotion, linked to the concept of the historic city and to cultural and heritage tourism, partakes of the current efforts of Spain's Tourism Board, which tries to project an image of Spain that would appeal to a different and more selective clientele: people interested in art, architecture, and cultural heritage (Pi-Sunyer 240).[14] Even the Costa del Sol, an area dominated by mass beach tourism, began to promote itself in the 1990s on the basis of its historical heritage, imitating the cultural campaigns that were put in place to attract people to inland cities (Barke and France 302). These efforts crystallized in the signing of a General Agreement for the Promotion of Cultural Tourism by the Ministry of Commerce and Tourism in 1994 (Maiztegui-Oñate and Areitio Bertolín 197).

Cultural tourism has also served the purposes of autonomous communities wishing to promote their own identities by distancing themselves from the monolithic Francoist tourist policies and narratives that had constructed a monocultural, monolingual, unitary vision of Spain. New tourist policies in these communities were thus tied to the politics of regional or peripheral national identities that found newly free expression post-Franco (Pi-Sunyer 242–43). Following this trend, reclaiming a region's Jewish heritage has figured prominently in these initiatives, a perfect example of the creation of "heritage products for specific markets" (Ashworth, "Heritage" 73).

THE NETWORK OF JEWISH QUARTERS OF SPAIN AND SPAIN'S JEWISH LEGACY

One of the tangible legacies of Sepharad '92, the commission in charge of the 1992 commemorations analyzed in the introduction, was the creation, with the support of the central government, of Caminos de Sefarad: Red de Juderías de España [Routes of Sepharad: Network of Jewish Quarters of Spain] in 1995.[15] The association was funded through the local councils of participating cities, the Offices of Tourism from the respective autonomous communities, and the Spanish Ministry of Industry, Energy, and Tourism. The Network of Jewish Quarters defined itself as "una asociación pública sin ánimo de lucro que tiene como objetivo la defensa del patrimonio urbanístico, arquitectónico, histórico, artístico y cultural del legado judío en España" [a nonprofit public association whose goal is to defend the urban, architectural, historic, artistic, and cultural patrimony of the Jewish legacy in Spain] (Hosta y Rebés 2). This carefully crafted definition approaches Jewish culture as an archaeological object to be explored from historical and ethnographic perspectives. Key in this description is the tension between the terms *patrimonio* [patrimony; property or valued things inherited from an ancestor], a word that establishes a relationship of obligation toward tradition from the point of view of the present, and *legado* [legacy, a transfer of property from one person to his or her heirs], a term that looks at the same action from the point of view of the bequeather and legitimizes a legal relationship of ownership established by the will of a past donor to a recipient. The choice of these two terms to describe what remains of the historic presence of Jews and Jewish culture in Spain attempts to trace a seamless line between a past legal transmission of property and a present obligation to honor that memory.

A drastic interpretation of the past is implicit in the use of these terms to recast the minimal, fragmentary remnants of the history of systematic destruction, pillage, repossession, and vanishing of all things Jewish in post-1492 Spain. From the point of view of the Red de Juderías, these residual elements, once a cursed legacy and an index of shame for those connected to it, have now become a valuable source of material and immaterial property. Ownership has been "legally" bestowed on today's (largely non-Jewish) nation, its communities, towns, and villages. As any legacy, it carries with it an obligation to be preserved and nurtured. Curiously, this same obligation provides a justification for the inability to relinquish ownership. Foreclosing any possible claims from, for example, those who may attempt to claim for present Jewish use one of the historic synagogues now in the hands of the state or the Catholic Church, the words *legacy* and *patrimony* imply that this return is not possible since the current owners are not only legitimate but also have, through accepting this inheritance, engaged in a duty of preservation that would prevent them from altering this covenant. But the fact is that Jewish owners and users of these places did not voluntarily bestow on the Spanish governments these properties.

The word *legado* (from the Latin *legātus*) also carries a diplomatic meaning connected to the concept of representation in both its aesthetic and political meanings, as it refers to an envoy that represents a government or a figure of authority in another land (RAE). The Network of Jewish Quarters has also performed the role of representative of the memory and legacy of Jewish Spain as an envoy from both Spain's national government and the councils of cities and towns in a number of European, Israeli, US, Latin American, and other international forums.[16] Thus, as it attempts to stress the legitimacy of the current owners, the repeated use of the term *legacy* also betrays an underlying anxiety that other people may appear at any moment and claim to be both the rightful heirs and representatives to this heritage. This is precisely what happened upon the "rediscovery" of several Jewish medieval cemeteries in recent years, as we see in chapter 4.

As the official story goes, the idea that originated the Network of Jewish Quarters of Spain emerged in 1994 out of conversations between representatives of Hervás (Cáceres province, Extremadura region) and Girona (Girona province, Catalonia region). A group of representatives from Hervás traveled to Girona to learn from their experiences in the preservation and marketing of their local Jewish heritage for tourism (Hosta y Rebés 2). The idea to collaborate on a heritage project emerged from these conversations. An obvious obstacle for the collaboration was the close to six hundred miles of distance separating the two towns. But there were also many other differences that made these two towns unlikely partners. Hervás is a small town of four thousand inhabitants located in a valley of the Sierra de Gredos in proximity to the border with Portugal. Girona is a provincial capital of one hundred thousand people located on the southern outskirts of the Pyrenees and close to the northeast Mediterranean coast, the shores of the Costa Brava that attract many tourists to Spain. Traditionally, there has been a significant cultural and economic distance separating the two regions where these towns are located. Extremadura is predominantly an agrarian region in the interior of the peninsula that has been on the margins of Spain's tourism routes. Catalonia, by contrast, was one of the first regions to urbanize, industrialize, and develop as a tourist destination.

Since the approval of the 1978 constitution as a key element in Spain's transition to democracy, the process of regional cultural differentiation and identity building undertaken by Spain's autonomous communities has rendered this initial distance even greater. Over the last thirty years, Extremadura and Catalonia have represented opposite poles in an increasingly heated political discussion about the fiscal responsibility of richer regions to contribute to the development of the least economically developed ones (Ross, Richardson, and Sangrado-Vegas 87–88). What bridged the distance between these two places was the shared conviction that by "rescuing" the history and remains of a historic Jewish presence, making it their own and developing strategies to market it, these towns and cities could become more visible on the maps of cultural tourism in Spain, Europe, and the world. In other words, their Jewish legacy could serve as an envoy that would allow them to enter into the international routes of Jewish-themed tourism.

Once the cultural distance had been bridged through the convergence of the towns' Jewish past and determination to become tourist destinations, the geographical distance was addressed by establishing a nodal structure. The initial network was conceived to link Girona and Hervás through a series of intermediate stops. Thus, Tudela (Navarra), Toledo (Castilla la Mancha), Cáceres (Extremadura), and Ribadavia (Galicia) were also invited to join the project (Hosta y Rebés 2). Tourists could visit each of these towns on a five-day tour by traveling about two hundred miles each day.[17] From the very beginning of the project, a variety of considerations were taken into account to decide which cities or towns would partake in the network. Ostensibly Hervás had one of the best architecturally preserved Jewish Quarters in Spain (the case of Hervás is analyzed in detail in chapter 5). Girona had been actively researching its pre-1492 Jewish history and restoring its Jewish Quarter since at least 1992, when the city created the Patronat del Call de Girona. Toledo, situated almost at a middle point between Hervás and Girona, is the city with the most significant material remnants of the pre-1492 Jewish presence in Spain, and thus, its inclusion was obvious (although, per Hostà y Rebés, the fact of its geographical location in the middle of the route from Girona to Hervás was taken into consideration as a contributing factor). Tudela was at the time carrying out substantive archival research of its Jewish history, while Ribadavia had been consulting and collaborating with Girona about local Jewish history through the cultural association Centro de Estudios Medievais (Medieval Studies Center). The often arbitrary criteria for inclusion in the network is exemplified by Assumpció Hosta y Rebés's explanation that the early inclusion of the city of Cáceres was due to the fact that the entity in charge of funding Hervás's Jewish heritage preservation project was Cáceres's provincial government. Thus, Cáceres acted as economic support for Hervás (Hosta y Rebés 2). The city of

Córdoba, which has a medieval synagogue in addition to its famous mosque, and Segovia, a popular destination for a day trip from Madrid, also joined the initiative.

The Network of Jewish Quarters of Spain was officially launched with a ceremony in January 1995 in Girona, with the participation of the initial eight cities' mayors. By 2008, the group of cities had grown to twenty-one, including larger ones like Barcelona, what Gregory J. Ashworth and J. E. Tunbridge would call "big league tourist-historic cities" together with smaller ones like León and Jaén and towns like Tarazona (Zaragoza province, Aragón) and Besalú (Girona province, Catalonia). Only in 2011 and 2012 were the cities of Sevilla and Lucena incorporated into the network, which now expanded to twenty-four member-cities. This development again confirmed that a city's significant medieval Jewish history was not the main criteria for membership in the network, since Sevilla and Lucena could boast of a much more significant Jewish history than many of the cities and towns that had become members years earlier. Cities with a significant and well-documented Jewish history like Burgos still do not belong to the network. As it grew, the association continued exhibiting a mix of smaller towns on the margins of the main tourist destinations, midsize interior provincial capitals, and large urban centers with extensive tourism experience that wanted to add one more layer to their possible cultural attractions. The member-cities all saw in their Jewish connection a point of entry into the tourism industry and a path of access to an audience that may, once interested, end up visiting their town's other monuments and attractions.[18]

The first promotional steps undertaken by the association demonstrate the ongoing close interrelationship established in Spain between tourism and international relations. The focus of the network's diplomatic and marketing efforts has clearly been the United States and Israel (as had been the case for Sepharad '92). The first publicity trips consisted of visits to these two countries. In Israel, the network participated in the international tourism fair in Tel Aviv, and a delegation of mayors and journalists was consequently invited by the Israeli Tourism Office to a multicity trip through Israel in June 1996. The group visited several cities, met with the authorities in each, and participated in the celebrations of the tenth anniversary of the establishment of diplomatic relations between the two countries ("Red 1995–2005" 15–16).

The towns and cities belonging to the network see their "Jewish connections" as direct links to Europe, Israel, and the United States that have the potential of bypassing official national channels. At the national level, the network and its international connections become a sign of a shared transnational history and evidence of the successful post-Franco transformation of the country into a modern democracy. By contrast, at the regional level, this narrative of cosmopolitan connections is frequently read as evidence of a historic difference from the rest of Spain. As we will see, it is surprising and revealing that these advances toward the affirmation of local, regional, and national identities are articulated through Jewish memory in a country where anti-Jewish sentiment has been part of the basis for the construction of national identity for over five hundred years. Spain's tourist industry has played a crucial role in framing the articulation and justification of these narratives.

The Network of Jewish Quarters of Spain project connects local, regional, and national interests with international ones through its participation in European Union initiatives to improve knowledge of Europe's Jewish history and to educate the public about the contributions of Jewish people to European culture. Since 1999, the network has joined the annual European Day of Jewish Culture, a project currently funded as part of the "Europe, a Common Heritage" campaign, sponsored by the Council of Europe. While thirty-one European nations, all members of the Council of Europe, currently participate in the celebrations, it began in 1996 as a more modest local initiative in the French region of Alsace as an open-door day in which the community was invited to visit local historic synagogues and Jewish heritage sites and to attend conferences and cultural activities offering an insight into Jewish culture and religion. In 1999, the Network of Jewish Quarters of Spain, together with the tourist agency of Lower Alsace, B'nai B'rith Europe, and the European Council of Jewish Communities, developed the Alsatian initiative as a European event. Spain's network has remained one of the event's main organizers and sponsors.

Interestingly, the Alsatian initiative was a local response to the demand of American tourists looking for traces of their ancestors, as reported in the conference launching the European Route of Jewish Heritage by Claude Bloch, chairperson of the Jewish heritage commission of B'nai B'rith Europe (*Launching* 4). Many of the outstanding contradictions present in the initiatives studied in this book are already visible, even if in an embryonic state, in this origin story: American Jews wanted to see traces of their ancestors' lives, and tourist agencies responded by opening the abandoned synagogues for them but also for the local non-Jewish population to visit (the report explicitly says most visitors were non-Jews). The activities of the Day of Opened Doors included conferences and information about Jewish culture and history since "in order to safeguard a patrimony, it is first necessary to know it" (*Launching* 4). The structuring theme for the first three years of the initiative was "the Discovery of Judaism." In its Spanish iteration, the slogan announcing the First European

Day of Jewish Culture in 1999 became "Descubriendo la cultura judía en Europa" [Discovering Jewish Culture in Europe].

The contradiction arises around the use of the term *discovery* and its relationship with the concept of *patrimony*, inheritance. One does not need to discover something that is already known. The verb *discover* contains an implicit promise of mystery and adventure in being the first to know about an Other. It also contains an explicit symbolic connection to 1492 and Christopher Columbus's "discovery." The slogan "Discovering Jewish Culture in Europe" clearly echoes the concept chosen by the commission organizing the Jewish aspect of the commemorations of 1992, Sepharad '92: The Re-Discovery of Jewish Spain. The problem of this discovery was compounded by the fact that a better part of what this initiative wanted people to discover did not exist anymore. Of course, one can't protect something that has already been destroyed. The synagogues that were opened in the Day of Opened Doors in the Alsace region had to be opened on a specific day dedicated to this purpose because they had long stopped being open on a regular basis. That is, they had long stopped functioning as synagogues in towns where, after World War II, there were no Jews. The discovery, then, more often than not pertained to the past, a discovery of a past life whose traces in the present were faint at best. The present-day management of this Jewish patrimony (abandoned and partially destroyed synagogues and cemeteries, for example) by non-Jewish organizations such as tourist agencies is not exactly the result of a straightforward legacy. Reflecting on the difficulties involved in the protection and conservation of Europe's Jewish remnants, Max Polonovski argues that we must ask "why and for whom the Jewish heritage has to be protected" (*Launching* 25).

In 2004, as a follow-up to the European Day of Jewish Culture, the Network of Jewish Quarters of Spain, B'nai B'rith Europe, and the European Council of Jewish Communities created the European Route of Jewish Heritage. The development of cultural itineraries in Europe has been guided by the idea that these routes would facilitate understanding and cooperation between countries or regions that might have experienced political conflict, highlighting "their common heritage" (*Launching* 7). Finding transnational common ground that might contribute to a cultural and social sense of European unity has been a priority of the European Union, and envisioning and promoting a newly conceived European heritage beyond that of the nation-state appeared as an obvious way to achieve a sense of European identity (Ashworth 69–70). The objectives of the itineraries, according to the European Institute of Cultural Routes' official website, reflect "the principles which underlie all the work and values of the Council of Europe: human rights, cultural democracy, cultural diversity, mutual understanding and exchanges across boundaries" ("Cultural Routes"). Few of these European routes—which include the Viking Route, the Phoenicians Route, and the Cistercian Abbeys Route, among others—group as many countries and sites, and accomplish as many of their objectives, as the Jewish Heritage Route does.

For most of the countries involved in this initiative, their Jewish sites are mostly Holocaust sites and both the route and the Day of Jewish Culture serve as a means to address the memory of the Holocaust. Indeed, in terms of the Council of Europe's principles delineated in the previous paragraph, the memory of the Holocaust has become one of the most important elements of the European Union's unifying narrative. In his essay "From the House of the Dead: An Essay on Modern European Memory" Tony Judt has famously argued that "Holocaust recognition is our contemporary European entry ticket" (803). He explains: "Hitler's 'final solution to the Jewish problem' in Europe is not only the source of crucial areas of post-war international jurisprudence—genocide or 'crimes against humanity.' It also adjudicates the moral (and in certain European countries the legal) standing of those who pronounce upon it . . . the recovered memory of Europe's dead Jews has become the very definition and guarantee of the continent's restored humanity" (Judt 804). In Spain, as in other nations, these European dynamics and international allegiances become part of local, regional, and national competing discourses of identity. The Network of Jewish Quarters of Spain's unlikely leading role in these European initiatives contains the hope that the recovery of local Jewish heritage will serve as a means to strengthen the connection between the two ideas of community that have the greatest prestige in contemporary Spain, the regional homeland and Europe. These three axes—tourism, Europeanism, and regionalism—have become determining factors in the current negotiations that cities and regions in Spain undergo as it brings its Jewish legacy to the fore.

Emblematic of the symbolic power of this layering of tourism, memory, and political identities in Spain is the design of the official promotional logo of the Network of Jewish Quarters of Spain (see fig. 2.1). The symbol draws a schematic map of the Iberian Peninsula using the Hebrew letters ספרד. Transliterated, these letters spell the word *Sepharad,* the traditional Jewish name for Spain. By juxtaposing and identifying the Hebrew letters and the map, the logo is in fact suggesting a tight identification between the Jewish culture invoked by the letters and the territory suggested by their design. In the apparently coincidental design of the four letters, there is a clear territorial separation between Spain, represented by the three first letters ספר (sfr), and Portugal, represented by the last letter ד (d).

Figure 2.1. Official logo of the Network of Spanish Jewish Quarters on a street wall, Córdoba. ©Darío Contreras.

If we extrapolate this territorial division to the rest of the letters, the logo is, de facto, suggesting a new imaginary geography for Spain, one that would run through the eastern seaboard encompassed by the letter ס, a central strip running north–south suggested by the letter פ, and a third, running along Portugal and reaching into Galicia, represented by the letter ד. To a viewer not familiar with Hebrew, this logo implicitly conveys an intention to transcend the current map of Spain and Portugal by suggesting, first, that Jewish culture sees the whole Iberian territory as a unit; second, that, like letters in a word, the individual identity of different regions acquires full meaning only when combined into a larger unit—a word provides meaning for letters; a nation, for regions—and third, that alternative territorial configurations to the current autonomous communities are possible, and even desirable, when searching for ways to attract different tourist markets from around the world.

To Hebrew readers, as pointed out to us by Professor Stacy Beckwith, the merging of letters and map carries additional meaning. If the letters ספר create the map of Spain and ד, tiny by comparison, is off to the lower side in Portugal, then even more importance accrues to Spain. The letters ספר spell *sefer* (book) and are also the root letters for "to count," "to recount," "to narrate," and for the noun *story*. Since *sefer* is such a familiar word throughout Jewish liturgy, ceremony, and religious cultures, American and other Jewish tourists, in addition to Israelis, are likely, in a glance, to pick up on the age-old "book" or "story" being both in Spain and forming Spain itself when they see the logo. The letter reserved for Portugal both participates in the logo, completing the word *Sepharad*, and is excluded from the important connotations of *sefer* for Jewish culture and tradition.[19]

This apparently new map of the Iberian Peninsula, in which distinct regions have become unified through a common Sephardi heritage and its materialization in the cooperation and common values that the Network and the European Route of Jewish Heritage seemed to encompass, came crashing down in an announcement in May 2016. That month, Girona's recently elected mayor Marta Madrenas announced that the five Catalan cities belonging to the network—Girona, the network's co-founder, plus Barcelona, Tortosa, Besalú, and Castelló d'Empúries—were leaving the network in order to form their own association. As reported in the *New York Times*, the mayor declared, "We think we can do better in terms of showcasing our Jewish patrimony. . . . We want to do it in a more serious manner, with more cultural and scientific rigor . . . it must be about culture and can't be all about tourism and tour operators" (Minder). The announcement by Girona's mayor thus disparaged Spanish cities of the network for their commercialization, commodification, and attention to tourism, claiming for Catalan cities the value of "cultural and scientific rigor." The highlighting of cultural aspirations while attempting to distance themselves from tourist-driven goals is not new, as we will see. What was new was the sudden decision to use it as a justification for the separation of Catalan cities from the network. At the root of the decision, concluded the *New York Times*, lay Catalonia's recently intensified political efforts to separate from the rest of Spain and to create an independent Catalan state (Minder). The Catalan press also used the "culture versus tourism" justification to explain the cities' decision, adding that the underlying reason was an effort by the Spanish government to recentralize the network at the expense of the Catalan cities that had been the network's founders (Carrera). As of August 2019, Girona, Tortosa, Besalú, and Castelló d'Empúries have left the network, but Barcelona is still a member. Palma de Mallorca left the network in 2017, citing the steep increase in membership fees and the added cost derived from the city being on an island ("Palma"). In the meantime, a host of other towns from Utrera (Sevilla) to Aranda de Duero (Burgos) have expressed their desire to join.

JEWISH TOURISM'S ECONOMIC AND CULTURAL RATIONALES

While tourism is not highlighted in the official definition of the Network of Jewish Quarters of Spain, it provides the generative push for the association and continues to catalyze its member cities' efforts. The association's board is made up almost exclusively of the heads of the tourism offices connected to each participating city. Furthermore, from the very beginning of the project, the promise to attract international tourism provided an internal justification for the dedication of local, regional, and national resources to the recovery and preservation of Jewish heritage. In forums connected to Spain's tourism industry, Hosta y Rebés, the network's general secretary since its foundation, stated that its aim is "ofrecer un producto turístico singular de calidad y exportable a los mercados nacional e internacional" [to offer a unique high-quality tourist product that may be exported to national and international markets] (6).[20]

Thus, network officials have strategically deployed the two rationales through which the network justifies its existence. The cultural rationale is the rescuing of a silenced or forgotten heritage. The economic rationale, promising access to the bounties associated with national and international cultural tourism, emerges in domestic and internal justifications for participating in and financing network membership. The cities and towns that decide to invest money in the network's membership fees hope to benefit from the attractiveness of the global tourism trend that Ashworth and Tunbridge have called "the tourist-historic city." As they explain, "history has become heritage, heritage has become an urban resource, and this resource supplies a major 'history/heritage industry,' which shapes not merely the form but the functioning and purpose of the 'commodified' city" (2). Thus, tourism becomes "a means of supporting the maintenance of the artifacts of the past and justifying attention to the historicity of cities" (Ashworth and Tunbridge 3). As explained by Barbara Kirshenblatt-Gimblett, "heritage and tourism are collaborative industries, heritage converting locations into destinations and tourism making them economically viable as exhibits of themselves" (*Destination* 151). These two axes—heritage and tourism—have become inextricably linked.

They appear side by side in the explicitly stated goals of the European Route of Jewish Heritage:

(1) To preserve and promote Jewish heritage as European Heritage.
(2) To make Europeans aware of the cultural richness brought by Jews across Europe during their stay in so many different regions [. . .]
(3) To promote tourism around these sites. (*Launching* 34)

When, in the summer of 2012, the city of Toledo held an official ceremony to unveil a set of five hundred Jewish-themed ceramic tiles embedded in the pavement of the city streets, Ana Isabel Fernández Samper, the president of Toledo's tourism board, described the tile initiative as part of the city's plan to "showcase" its Jewish Quarter, a space she defined as "una de las joyas de la ciudad, aunque quizá no ha estado siempre 'lo suficientemente explotada,' en el buen sentido, claro" [one of the jewels of the city, although perhaps it has not always been 'sufficiently exploited,' in the good sense of the word, of course]. Fernández Samper went on to explain what a "good exploitation" would consist of: echoing the mayor, she declared that the plaques would contribute to transforming the quarter into a "specialty [tourism] product," to strengthen the identification of Toledo with Sephardi culture, to promote the value of Toledo's handicrafts and "showcase the patrimonial wealth of the Jewish Quarter" ("La judería estrena").

Unlike other promotional materials, in which cultural preservation motives are foregrounded, this statement forthrightly engages the language of marketing. Network members frequently make such economically centered declarations when addressing their local constituencies and the media. They are articulated throughout two dominant discourses in Spain: one connected to the economic crisis and another to the perception that pure economic gain is in itself immoral. Thus, as in Fernández Samper's declarations, as soon as the argument of economic gain is uttered, the speaker qualifies it by reaching for the less morally suspect rationales of cultural preservation, job creation, or increased appreciation for other local non-Jewish traditions. The resulting narrative echos the hopes that the Sepharad '92 commission had for the funding and riches it would receive from US Jewish donors.

The case of Tarazona, a small Aragonese city that began reexamining its Jewish past in the late 1990s, is symptomatic of the questions that arise in Spain at the confluence of Jewish heritage and cultural tourism. The city boasts significantly rich Celtiberian, Roman, Muslim, and Jewish cultural legacies. Nestled in the heart of the Moncayo Mountains, Tarazona is far from Spain's coastline and from the increased wealth that tourism has brought to the coastal areas.

Like many towns in the interior, the city has seen its population drop over the last fifty years. Through this period, Tarazona's economy suffered dramatic transformations from being a regional industrial center manufacturing textiles, safety matches, and paper to losing many of its industries and becoming a service-based economy. Since the 1960s, Tarazona has very actively sought to market its cultural assets as a way to increase its tourism revenue. Those efforts resulted in its inclusion in the cluster of Aragonese cities whose Mudéjar architecture was declared a World Heritage Site by UNESCO in 1966 and 2001 resolutions.[21] The town's reclaiming of its Jewish heritage has to be contemplated within these larger efforts. But that which is said to make Tarazona unique turns out to be a trait common to a vast number of cities. In Aragon alone, towns like Zaragoza, Ruesta, Uncastillo, Biel, Sos, Luna, Tauste, Ejea, El Frago, Luesia, Calatayud, La Almunia de Doña Godina, Épila, Borja, Ariza, and about a dozen others are also marketing their Jewish heritage as a tourist attraction, although outside of the Network of Jewish Quarters ("Cinco propuestas" 24–25).

In November 2002, the magazine *Viajar por Aragón* [Travel in Aragon] published a long report on the origins and development of the project to restore Tarazona's Jewish Quarter and create the Moshe de Portella Interpretation Center, a space of information about the town's Jewish history named after a prominent thirteenth-century judge and representative of the crown of Aragon. The report's narrative is divided into two accounts, one cultural-historic and the other economic, which appear strictly compartmentalized in the text by a change in layout and font. The cultural text emphasizes the fortuitous nature of the project's first steps: in the late 1990s, while searching for Roman ruins in Tarazona, local archaeologist Javier Bona and his work group found the Jewish Quarter "by chance" ("Tarazona" 11–12). This narrative of coincidences continues as the text explains how Barbara Goldman, an American scientist "of Jewish descent," who at the time of Bona's discovery was visiting Zaragoza to give a talk, was offered a guided tour of the area and was delighted by what she saw there. The description of Goldman's reaction is particularly detailed and emphatic, explaining how she found herself "overwhelmed with the archeological legacy that [Bona] showed her" and promised that Tarazona could raise "extraordinary interest in the international Jewish community" ("Tarazona" 12).[22]

These declarations are then credited with triggering the involvement of both the regional and local governments to finance a more comprehensive archaeological exploration. As a result, the Association of Friends of Jewish Culture Moshe Portella was born, and the project to build an interpretive center began. The article includes a short explanation of the historical origins of Tarazona's Jewish population, stressing how it was unique among the medieval towns where Muslim, Christian, and Jewish populations lived because there "la cultura sefardita, conviviendo en pacífico mestizaje con la islámica y la cristiana, alcanzó un mayor grado de esplendor" [Sephardi culture, coexisting in peaceful hybridization with Islam and Christianity, reached a maximum degree of splendor] ("Tarazona" 11).

Separated from the report and inside a text box titled "On the margin," we find the alternative account of this same discovery from an economic point of view, entitled "Un filón para el turismo aragonés" [A gold mine for Aragonese tourism]. In case the reader thought that too much attention was being granted to the cultural importance of Jewish heritage, the author rushes to clear up any doubts by claiming that behind official declarations stressing cultural, ethical, historical, and solidarity reasons, "la motivación económica es uno de los principales motores de este plan" [the economic motivation is one of the main engines of this plan], explicitly pointing out, in English, that "business is business" ("Tarazona" 21). This section further stresses the economic rationale of a project that follows the models of Córdoba, Toledo, and Girona, cities that receive planes full of "nutridos grupos de judíos estadounidenses, bien dispuestos a dejarse sus dólares en los comercios y establecimientos de hostelería de la ciudad" [sizeable groups of American Jews, eager to leave their dollars in the city's shops, restaurants and hotels] ("Tarazona" 21). The dramatic split between these two narratives leaves the reader wondering what exactly is being explained here in the midst of so much apparent clarity.

This dual story narrating Tarazona's development of its Jewish quarter as a destination for cultural tourism follows the pattern of other cities so closely that these accounts create a literary genre of their own. This genre is structured on a simultaneous reliance on two discourses that, if taken at face value, could be seen as undermining one another. One is a cultural narrative that emphasizes chance, mystery, and external encouragement as originating forces, while the other one, strictly economic, reveals a programmatic study of tourism trends in larger cities designed to please the perceived interest of a foreign Jewish population constructed along stereotypical antisemitic lines as highly affluent. The simultaneous presence of the cultural memory and the business/tourism narratives across the Network of Jewish Quarters' project is symptomatic of the underlying ambivalence of the enterprise of marketing Spain's Jewish heritage.

DEPLOYING CONVIVENCIA, SUTURING ABSENCE

In Spain, tourism has a long history of being deployed as the quasi-magical element that could amalgamate the conflicting strands of Spain's reality into a common purpose. During the 1960s, the visibility of the tourist image of

Spain as a place for fun and enjoyment in the sun sharply contrasted with the real lives of the people who suffered severe political repression and economic hardship under that same sun. A similar divide currently exists between the heavily promoted notion of convivencia that cheerfully appropriates multiculturalism as an autochthonous solution and several less superficially optimistic trends: the growth of conflict between Catalonia and the central government; the unease over the increasing presence of foreign immigrants; the rise in the polls of a new far-right party that targets Muslim immigrants, gender equality, and regional autonomy; the unsolved debts of historical memory in relation to Francoist victims; and Spain's participation in international conflicts involving cultural, ethnic, and religious clashes.

The deployment of the concept of convivencia is especially widespread in Spain's tourist industry. Myriad cities and towns advertise themselves as sites where the visitor—from study abroad students to domestic and international travelers—can experience "the Spain of the three cultures." At the center of these marketing efforts, however, rests a silence about the historical failures at implementing that convivencia at home. In the praise this concept receives from politicians, tour operators, and cultural events' organizers, there is no discussion of the reasons why this phenomenon has to be marketed today as an archaeological attraction. These initiatives' celebration of convivencia often precludes a true exploration of the much more complex and nuanced reality of past and present Christian-Jewish relations (see similar argument in Gruber, *Virtually Jewish* 9). There is a certain lack of interest in attempting to represent the less pleasant story of how the happy medieval coexistence invoked was brought to an end, or how, perhaps, it was never that happy to begin with. The stories told are often out of step with contemporary historical research about medieval and early modern Spain and with contemporary debates about the complex relations that cultural tourism establishes with sites that celebrate the history of a minority ethnic group while commemorating—or not, as is often the case in Spain—the atrocities committed against them.

Most of these towns and so-called Jewish Quarters embody a wishful cultural fantasy of visibility, one in which traces of Jewishness can be experienced by the visitor when, in fact, no traces of Jewishness are visible or likely to be experienced. These traces have all been systematically transformed or destroyed, while the Jews who inhabited them were killed, expelled, or assimilated after their conversion to Christianity. As they proceed on the path toward recovering and marketing their Jewish heritage, an unavoidable set of questions accompany these cities, their citizens and representatives, as well as the tourists visiting them: Why did their once significant Jewish population disappear?

How do you celebrate a heritage that has all but been made to disappear? How does one present convivencia as having, at the same time, to justify its absence?

Juan García Atienza's 1978 *Guía judía de España* was reedited in 1994 as *Caminos de Sefarad: Guía judía de España*. The book, which describes itineraries through several cities based on their Jewish traces has to constantly face up to the reality of these remnants' absence. He concludes his introductory remarks by stating, "De todos modos, creo necesario avanzar la evidencia—triste, si queremos verlo así—de que en España hay una fundamental carencia de restos judíos" [In any case, it is necessary to present the evidence—sad, if we want to see it this way—that in Spain there is a fundamental lack of Jewish remnants] (74). The sentence, with its curious caveat signaling the fact that some may disagree with the desirability of the country having Jewish remains, warns the reader that there might not be a Jewish Spain to visit after all. In his Aragón itinerary alone, García Atienza says (about Monzón), "Se ha perdido toda huella del lugar donde pudo estar emplazada la aljama judía" [We have lost trace of the site where the Jewish *aljama* could have been situated] (162); (about Zaragoza), "Zaragoza es, reconozcámoslo, mal que nos pese, la gran aljama perdida de España" [Zaragoza is, let's recognize it, even if it weighs on us, Spain's great lost aljama] (168); (about Huesca), "En esa calle—aunque no sabemos su exacto emplazamiento—se encontraba la sinagoga mayor" [On this street—even though we do not know its exact location—used to be the main synagogue] (170); (about Tarazona), "La huella de estos establecimientos (sinagogas y tiendas regentadas por judíos) es hoy prácticamente irreconocible" [The trace of these establishments (synagogues and Jewish stores) is today practically impossible to recognize] (172); (about Teruel), "No queda ningún resto judío en el interior de la ciudad" [There are no Jewish remnants in the interior of the city] (177). Similar statements can be used to describe virtually all towns and cities in Spain. Most were destroyed in or soon after the major anti-Jewish persecutions of 1391.

But García Atienza's guide makes explicit his intention to focus on "the life and legacy of Spanish Jews" and not on their "suffering and persecution." Like Rodríguez de Castro, Amador de los Ríos, and Pulido before him, García Atienza thought it pertinent to clarify that he was not Jewish and that this fact gave him "una objetividad de la que carecen demasiado a menudo los investigadores de origen hebreo" [an objectivity too often absent in the researchers of Hebrew origin] (García Atienza 10). His text is filled with stereotypical generalizations and contempt for contemporary Jews and admiration for medieval Jews. Contemporary Jews, whom he identifies primarily with the state of Israel but also includes among them his former Argentine Jewish editor and the president of Madrid's Jewish community, relish a morbid and exclusive remembrance of persecution and death instead of focusing on what Jews have contributed to "culture and knowledge" (García Atienza 13).[23]

Regarding the 1492 expulsion, he says that among Jews there is "un afán por hinchar hasta lo inverosímil el número de expulsados" [a desire to inflate the number of those expelled to an unimaginable extent] as well as to interpret as "racial hate" what was only "obedience to the approved laws of that time." To these and several more examples of Jewish purposeful "misinterpretation" of historical facts, García Atienza offers in contrast his "effort to put things back in their right place" (11–12), consisting, mainly, of an account of what he calls "the other side of the coin." He summarizes his intentions with the extremely unfortunate phrase "que el aroma de un pastelillo cocido en el horno de una aljama pueda con el hedor de la carne chamuscada" [that the scent of a hot pastry out of an aljama's oven might overcome the stench of scorched flesh] (16).

The first tourist guide published by the Network of Jewish Quarters in 1996, *Caminos de Sefarad / Routes of Sepharad*, attempts to strike a different tone in its introductory pages, summarizing the intentions and hopes of the network's project.[24] Dedicated to the eight cities that founded the network (Cáceres, Córdoba, Girona, Hervás, Ribadavia, Segovia, Toledo, and Tudela), the guide is the result of the collaboration between an "edition committee" composed of these cities' mayors, a "technical team" of tourism representatives, and members of the University of Extremadura, coordinated by the Tourism Board of Cáceres. The prologue, written by Javier Gómez-Navarro, secretary of commerce and tourism, speaks of Spain as a place where there have been "many cultures that, after centuries, have mixed." Echoing the aforementioned assumptions of a long tradition of Arabists and Hebraists, he declares "those cultures have become our own." He also conveys the network's interpretation of the nature of the "legacy" of Sepharad when he writes of "that culture which, many centuries ago, the Jewish people *gave* to us" (*Routes* 5, italics added). Following the secretary's remarks, the one-page "Presentation" also embraces Spain's Jewish legacy as Spanish, explaining that this legacy "is physically and spiritually rooted in us" and that without it "we have accepted to live with an important part of our history mutilated" (*Routes* 7). It also reveals the network's hopes of finding in this legacy both an internal agglutinating factor ("a common heritage, a collective treasure for many Spanish cities and towns") and an external platform for transnational relations in Europe and beyond ("the integrating, universalizing, globalizing will of many local institutions has led us to a deep conviction about the necessity of incorporating this piece of our past history to our global history") (*Routes* 7).

This presentation is followed by a five-page historical overview of Jewish life under Visigothic, Muslim, and Christian rule. This summary speaks about peaceful coexistence but also mentions Visigothic persecution of Jews, how anti-Judaism was used as a political tool in the Trastámara brothers' fraternal conflict for the throne in the fourteenth century, the massacres of 1391, and the expulsion without attempting to justify or gloss over these events. It is after this summary, in the individual descriptions of each city that compose most of the guide, that we encounter the blissful celebration of convivencia and the consistent downplaying of persecutions noted by Jeffrey Juris in his article about the guide (265). In Segovia, the guide says, "co-existence among these three cultures was especially tolerant and peaceful" (*Routes* 77, qtd. in Juris 266). On the persecutions in Córdoba, it notes, "This Jewish area was assaulted in 1391, although the motive was just theft and not the slaughtering of Jews, as some used to believe" (*Routes* 28, qtd. in Juris 267). In Girona, before the fourteenth century, relations were peaceful "but for the minor incidents predictable in a situation of coexistence between a minoritary [*sic*] Jewish community and a dominant Christian one." After that, Jewish persecutions are vaguely attributed to "changes of mentality," fanaticism, and intolerance (*Routes* 43).

If Amador de los Ríos remarked on the overwhelming sense of absence that resonated through the empty and forgotten streets of former Jewish Quarters, the destruction that was "the legacy of the furor of men," this guide's descriptions of those same places try to assure the visitor that there is, in fact, something tangible to see. Having to grapple with the paradox of promoting a Jewish legacy that is all but absent, these narratives argue that it is not possible that nothing would be left to be seen, that some traces must remain. Old streets and buildings, thus, are charged with the weight of carrying memory. The guide says, about Segovia, "This city, which received with great hospitality all the cultures that arrived in it, cannot possibly lack the testimony of Jewish presence in its streets. . . . [They] are the testimonies of a co-existence that, although it is true that on several occasions it was conditioned by intolerance and lack of understanding, lasted for many centuries and left an important mark on the very city's structure" (*Routes* 75).

About Girona the guide says, "Although the Inquisition tried to delete anything that might remind [people] of their presence there, the Jews' presence persisted in the city. Even today, more than five hundred years later, the streets in the *call* [the Catalan term for Jewish Quarter] retain the memories of that community that lived in Girona for more than seven centuries" (*Routes* 43). Tabea Linhard shows how in fact this memory has to be literally "produced" in order to be "found" in the streets of Girona's call. She analyzes

Figure 2.2. "Jewish Quarter Street," Tarazona. ©Daniela Flesler.

a 2004 tour script to Girona's call entitled *Les set portes del Call* [The Call's seven doors] in which convivencia is foregrounded, historical conflict is defused, and the impact of antisemitism in Spain concealed (Linhard, *Jewish Spain* 167).

Together with performed tours such as the one described by Linhard, cities belonging to the Network of Jewish Quarters have striven to fill the material void of premodern Jewish traces with visual markings that proclaim their presence. The extensive display of newly manufactured and erected signs and symbols in these cities is an excellent example of the way circulating images and texts are used to frame a tourist site and construct a desired tourist gaze (see Rojek; Urry and Larsen). These ubiquitous signs speaking of "Jewish Quarters" and "Jewish Quarter Streets" (see figs. 2.2 and 2.3) point to a place where there once might have been something that we can no longer see and convey how, as explained by Michel de Certeau, "the places people live in are like the presences of diverse absences. What can be seen designates what is no longer there. . . . Demonstratives indicate the invisible identities of the visible" (108).[25] Many of these signs are in Hebrew, sometimes without translation (see figs. 2.4, 2.5, 2.6).

Figure 2.3. "Old Jewish Quarter Street" sign, Segovia. ©Daniela Flesler.

Figure 2.4. "Jewish Quarter" signs in Spanish, English, and Hebrew in street pavement, Toledo. ©Daniela Flesler.

Figure 2.5. "Door of Granada" sign in Hebrew and Spanish, Lucena. ©Daniela Flesler.

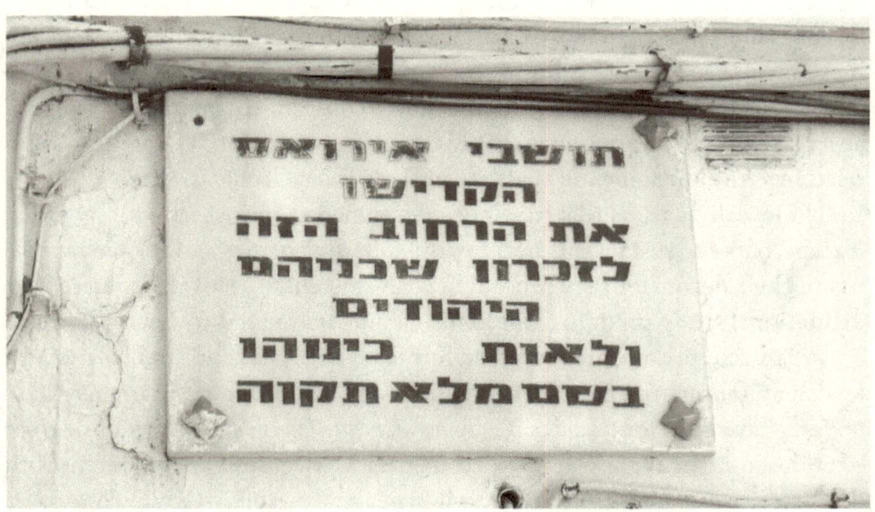

Figure 2.6. Commemorative plaque reading, in Hebrew, "In memory of the past Jewish inhabitants of Hervás." ©Daniela Flesler.

Restaurants, bars, hotels, and other commercial establishments display names like "El Fogón sefardí" (Segovia), "Restaurante La judería" (Segovia, Lucena, Sevilla), "Restaurante Patio de la Judería" (Córdoba), "Bar El Judío" (Ribadavia), and "Centro Comercial La Judería" (Jaén). Icons like the Star of David and the menorah appear on promotional signs for taverns, restaurants, hotels, and inns, wrought within the iron grilles that protect windows and doors and in shops that sell them in the form of badges as souvenirs of these cities' rediscovered Jewish heritage (see fig. 2.7).

In some cases, the Star of David also appears as decoration on a city's or town's landmarks, whether or not these landmarks are related to the city's Jewish "roots." In Hervás, for example, it appears not only on the sign explaining facts about the Jewish Quarter but also on the sign for the city council and even in Catholic churches and convents that have never had any Jewish connection. Churches, cathedrals, and other landmarks with no connection to local Jewish history also figure prominently in the "sites of interest" recommendations in the *Routes of Sepharad* guide. The signs clearly mark which areas tourists should see. In their efforts to capitalize on any tourism attention a city or town gets, local authorities wish to guide tourists to any and all monuments in that town, and the way to signal this is to connect these monuments with the network's signage. As a result, these signs turn just about everything designated for tourist consumption Jewish by association, even when the identification does not make much historical or cultural sense.

Both hosts and visitors must constantly confront this paradox of Jewish absence exhibited as presence. In this way, Spain's initiatives can be seen in relation to the phenomenon analyzed by Ruth Ellen Gruber in *Virtually Jewish*. In Old Jewish quarters that have been developed as tourist attractions across Europe, bars and restaurants bear Jewish-sounding names and use Jewish motifs in their décor; tourists can buy Jewish souvenirs; festivals, conferences, exhibitions, study programs, and music concerts related to Jewish heritage are organized; plaques are placed on former synagogues and streets; and new Jewish museums are opened, often with government support, in towns where no Jews have lived for decades (Gruber, *Virtually Jewish* 5–6). Various degrees of philosemitism are at play here, as are various degrees of engagement with the historical record. As Gruber puts it in her analysis of eastern European examples, "sincere attempts to study or reintegrate what has been lost, destroyed, or forgotten coexist with superficiality, slogans, lip service, and show" (*Virtually Jewish* 9).[26]

In Spain, with the desire to showcase the cultural capital of religious and ethnic tolerance and, thus, the past moments of convivencia, these narratives

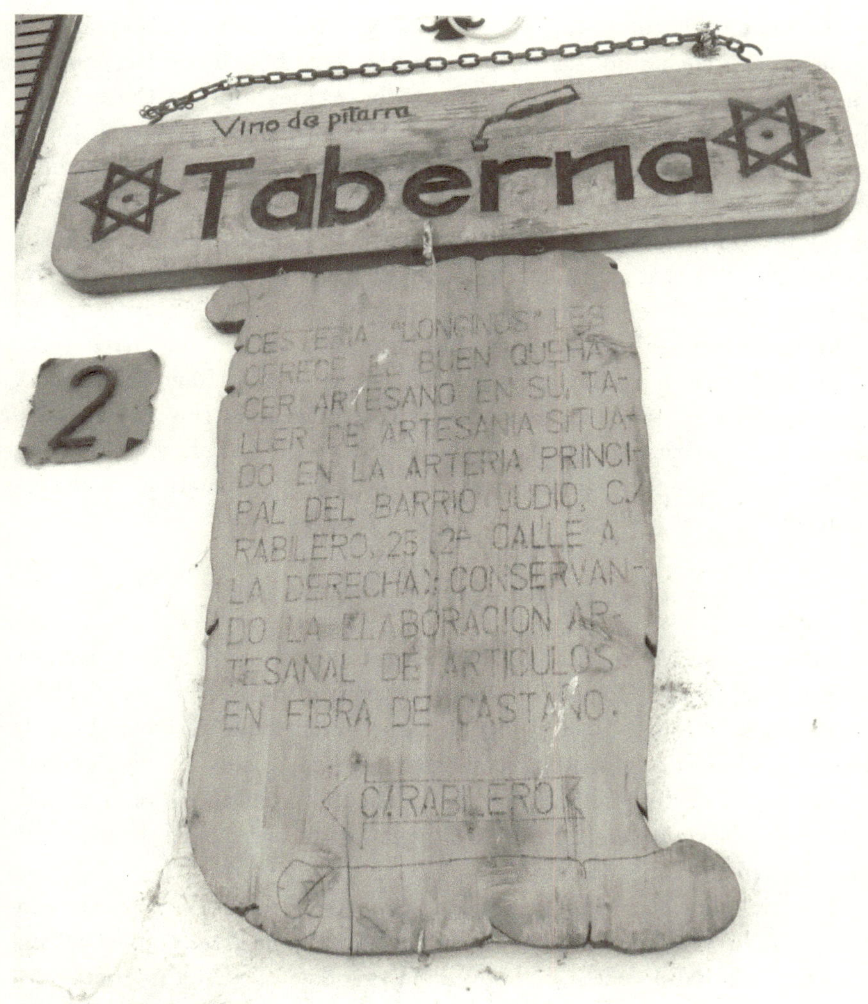

Figure 2.7. Tavern sign, Hervás. ©Adrián Pérez Melgosa.

and tourist framings run the risk of alienating at least some of the purposeful visitors they seek to attract. For many Jewish visitors, absence becomes these sites' most significant feature, as it connects with the many historical instances of Jewish persecution. As a Jewish tourist said to us after visiting Sevilla, Córdoba, and Ribadavia, "The absence is overwhelming; it is as if the Jews had never existed." Mark Meyerson explains it by stating that in these Jewish Quarters, a "healthy dose of imagination" is necessary to conjure up past Jewish life (*Jewish Renaissance* 1).

Different groups of visitors see tourist sites in ways that are different from those intended by authorities or tour organizers. Although nothing could be further from the celebratory intentions of these cities' officials, these Jewish Quarters without Jews can be visited as places for mourning, similar to the eastern European sites that have become popular destinations for Jewish heritage tours and, especially, in relation to Holocaust tourism. After all, horrifying massacres took place in them, most virulently in 1391. Ironically, many of the Jewish Quarters that are today exhibited as spaces of convivencia were created, together with renewed impositions of special clothing for Jews, in order to police the frontier between Jews and Christians, a frontier that had become blurry after the 1391 mass conversions (Nirenberg, "Mass Conversion" 9–12). These spaces constitute examples of what Tunbridge and Ashworth call "dissonant heritage," sites that evoke great sensitivity within a collective memory, and whose meaning, ownership, interpretation, and representation are socially contested.

THE PRODUCTION OF JEWISH SPACE

One of the initiatives through which the network has sought to give visibility to designated Jewish Quarters has been the embedding of small bronze plates displaying the Sepharad/Iberia logo in the pavement along designated streets and on the doors of commercial establishments (see fig. 2.8). The plates aim to serve as signs alerting tourists that the streets they are walking on, although they may look no different from the streets nearby, were once the everyday spaces where Jewish people lived.

The symbols are a marketing tool, but they also recall the very reason why Jewish Quarters were created in the first place: to assuage the anxiety arising from the lack of differentiation between Jews and gentiles. In this contemporary iteration, the anxiety is that, unless marked by these embedded plates, the Jewishness of the streets, the restaurants, and buildings frequented by the tourist may look, feel, and taste exactly like any other in that city. The plaques are necessary because the specifically Jewish memory of these streets is not there, accessible for people to see. The guide *Caminos de Sefarad* wishes this was not the case when it says of Segovia that "this city . . . cannot possibly lack the testimony of Jewish presence in its streets" (*Routes* 75). Memory is not simply there to be seen; it needs help to be seen. The past "is not simply there in memory, but it must be articulated to become memory" (Huyssen, *Twilight Memories* 3). As James E. Young explains, a site's memory is dependent on the historical consciousness of visitors.[27]

Figure 2.8. Symbol of Network of Spanish Jewish Quarters in street pavement, Córdoba. ©Darío Contreras.

Figure 2.9. New ceramic tiles in the streets of Toledo's Jewish Quarter. ©Adrián Pérez Melgosa.

A paradigmatic example of the effort at making this memory easily graspable and visible are the handmade ceramic tiles embedded on the street pavement and house walls of Toledo's Jewish Quarter. Toledo is a very popular tourist destination as a day trip from Madrid that receives 2.5 million tourists annually. In comparison to most other cities in the network, which have virtually no material remains to show, Toledo boasts the physical presence of two medieval synagogues. One of them, the Synagogue of the Transit, houses the state-owned Sephardi Museum, Spain's main Jewish museum. Both building and museum are emblematic of Spain's complex relationship with Jewish culture, and we dedicate the next chapter to them. Despite these magnificent historical structures, there is no contemporary Jewish life in the city and no living Jewish community there.

These tiles and their Jewish-themed decorations tell as many stories as those of the people who walk on them as they visit, stroll, or go about their day on these re-marked streets of Toledo's historic Jewish Quarter. Since this Jewish Quarter has been emptied of its Jewishness, these newly layered tiles and their designs painted by Toledo's current artisans end up pointing back at themselves and at the present rather than to Jewish history. They are their own referent.[28] They also become multilayered signs of a series of wistful narratives of cultural misencounters, of yearnings for magical formulas of reconciliation, of desires for attention from the Jewish Other, and of fears of what this attention might bring.

The ceramic tiles' design combines indigo and white colors, the signature colors of the city. Fernández Samper, the president of Toledo's tourism board, described them as having "allegorical motifs from Hebrew culture." On their faces, the tiles display four different designs: a menorah, a Star of David, the Iberia/Sepharad symbol of the Network of Jewish Quarters, and the Hebrew word חי, *chai* (see fig. 2.9).

Fernández Samper explained the Hebrew word *chai* as signifying "life." The word is in fact a powerful symbol in modern Judaism, with important historical resonances intimately connected to the Holocaust. The technical translation is "alive," as in "to be alive," and is often said in reference to the against-all-odds survival of Jewish people and the people of Israel: it appears in the slogan "*'Am yisra'el hay!*" (עַם יִשְׂרָאֵל חַי, The people of Israel are alive!). The word has become a popular symbol of pride and defiance, frequently worn as an amulet on necklaces in today's Israeli culture. It functions as an important sign of self-affirmation, community resilience, and even religious or patriotic commitment.

A case in point is the frequent appearance of this word in the comments written by Israeli tourists in the visitors' book of the Sephardi Museum of Toledo. For example, a comment from July 2014, reads: "The People of Israel are alive. Even here when a Jewish person arrives in their heart there will always be the inspiration that our people have survived thousands of years despite others having tried to destroy us."[29] The appropriation of this word by Toledo's tourist promoters is thus poignantly ironic. The ones displaying this symbol of survival are not Jews but city authorities in an overwhelming Christian city trying to attract Jewish visitors or to make this quarter look "Jewish." The tiles adorn the streets of a Jewish Quarter devoid of Jews, in which most traces of its Jewish identity have been purposefully destroyed. There is no Jewish survival in Toledo, nothing alive in terms of lived Judaism or Jewish culture. This seems a good example of an instance in which we can interpret the eagerness to produce the Jewish Quarter for tourism as cynical appropriation.

And yet, there is an interesting dissonance produced by the presence of symbols that once were anathema in Spain occupying such a public space. It is not necessarily negative that restaurants and other commercial venues would want to associate themselves with Jewish symbols and that people, both tourists and nontourists, would visit them. The "aspirational convivencia" that is staged in public celebrations of Hanukkah in public spaces of many cities throughout Spain—a relatively new occurrence—can produce subtle shifts in the way people perceive these spaces and cities. It is remarkable to see this celebration, for example, in the same Toledo streets that historically saw the erasure of all visible signs of Jewishness. In December 2015, on a visit to Toledo, we were struck by the menorah hanging from a telephone wire above a street in the Jewish Quarter. It was easy to interpret it as another sign of commercialization and consumer culture, of authorities' willingness to do anything to attract tourists. But what moved us was its location in such a meaningful corner: not across from either of the synagogues, but across from the Monastery of San

Figure 2.10. Ornamental menorah from public celebration of Hanukkah in the streets of Toledo's Jewish Quarter, December 2015, across from San Juan de los Reyes (seen on the left). ©Daniela Flesler.

Juan de los Reyes. This monumental building, constructed between 1477 and 1504 by the Catholic Monarchs, best exemplifies the historical process of Christian occupation of Toledo's Jewish Quarter at the end of the fifteenth century. According to chronicler Hernando del Pulgar, it was built on the grounds that used to belong to the houses of prominent converso Don Alonso Álvarez de Toledo, which were bought and demolished by order of Queen Isabel (Pérez Higuera 11) (figs. 2.10 and 2.11).

Instances such as this public celebration of Hannukah are examples of what Diana Pinto has called the construction of a new "Jewish space" in Europe. This is a space, literally and metaphorically, where non-Jews acknowledge Jewishness as part of their own European legacy and identity (Pinto 179–82). Observing this very trend in Spain, Germany, and Poland, three countries with a historically powerful and numerically large Jewish presence that came to a tragic end, Pinto remarks on its dialectical nature. As they remember and celebrate a lost Jewish past, these nations are praising their present pluralist democracies (Pinto 181–82).[30] At their best, these spaces "link Jews and non-Jews

Figure 2.11. Publicity poster for public celebration of Hanukkah in the streets of Toledo's Jewish Quarter, December 2015. ©Daniela Flesler.

in generative cultural engagements and interactions that rework notions of Jewish (and majority) culture and identity" (Lehrer, *Jewish Poland* 2).

Layers of different commemorative moments, diverse mnemonic signifiers that attempt to memorialize the same person or event, coexist in Toledo. Samuel Halevi (1320–60), one of medieval Spain's most famous Jews, chief royal treasurer and adviser to King Pedro of Castile, and owner of the Synagogue of the Transit (today Sephardi Museum), has had the street he lived on named after him. Two plaques can be seen on this street: An older plaque, from 2001, reads, "Legends of Toledo. 'The Treasure of Samuel Leví.' Samuel Leví, Royal

Figure 2.12. A 2001 plaque about Samuel Halevi reflecting the antisemitic legend in the street bearing his name, Toledo. ©Roy Lindman, under Creative Commons License.

Treasurer, who chose to die by torture rather than confess where he hid his riches" (see fig. 2.12). A newer plaque's message (which we photographed in July 2015) can be seen as overriding the one conveyed in the earlier plaque, telling a more historically precise and neutral narrative and staying away from "legend": "He was the royal treasurer of the king Pedro I. He went to prison and he was subjected to torture and as a consequence he died. He was the one who ordered the construction of the current synagogue of El Tránsito that was built between the years 1355 and 1357" (see fig. 2.13).[31] As we will see later in this chapter in the case of another "medieval legend" from Segovia, city officials are becoming increasingly aware of the fact that these "legends," as reflected in the older plaque, are far from inoffensive or innocuous. As visitors aware of medieval

Figure 2.13. Newer plaque about Samuel Halevi reflecting different memorialization moment, Toledo, July 2015. ©Adrián Pérez Melgosa.

Jewish history would note, they reflect and perpetuate the very ideas about Jews that justified and led to their persecution and eventual expulsion from Spain.

Many visitors notice these discordant juxtapositions. A Sephardi woman from Australia who went to Spain in a "roots tourism" personal journey told us how upset she was to find promotional posters for the "Exhibición de Antiguos Instrumentos de Tortura" [Exhibition of ancient instruments of torture] prominently displayed all over Toledo. This popular, privately owned exhibition opened in 2008. Located in the historic Jewish Quarter, close to the Sephardi Museum, it shows a collection of replicas and some historical torture instruments used by the Inquisition throughout Europe.

A few years ago, Toledo actually had a Jewish institution, a bookstore and Judaica store in the Calle del Ángel, 15, called Casa de Jacob. The store functioned from 2000 to 2010 as an informal Jewish information center in Toledo, a place where visitors could find scholarly books about Jewish history and culture, kosher food, and Judaica objects. The well-intentioned aim of its owners was stated on the website Toledo Sefarad: "Nuestro deseo es acoger al Pueblo Judío, contribuir a la reparación de la memoria histórica de España en relación con el Pueblo Judío, divulgar la cultura judía con especial atención a la cultura hispano-hebrea y sefardí, y hacer de Casa de Jacob un lugar para la memoria y la reconciliación, un lugar de encuentro" [Our wish is to welcome the Jewish people, to contribute to the repair of Spain's historical memory in relation to the Jewish people, to divulge Jewish culture with special attention to Sephardi, Hispano-Hebrew culture, and to make Casa de Jacob a place for memory and reconciliation, a place of encounter] ("Librería judaica").

In 2007, its owner, María Teresa Llurba, explained to us that by opening the bookstore, she and her husband wanted to normalize a Jewish presence in Spain, to contribute to the visibility of Jewishness as something belonging not just to the past but to the present. The bookstore suffered many attacks and was repeatedly vandalized with antisemitic graffiti (see fig. 2.14). In 2007, it suffered an arson attack with diesel oil. At the time, it was reported that the bookstore "had been the target of neo-Nazi groups since its opening" (Moreno). The bookstore closed in 2010, and its owners relocated to Barcelona.

The importance that this institution had for Jewish visitors is explained in the travel account of Beverly Gray, a tourist from the United States. Describing her trip to Toledo, she explains that she enjoyed the two synagogues and the Sephardi Museum, noticing "heartwarming video footage of modern Jews celebrating holidays and life-cycle events: proof for Spanish visitors that Judaism lives on." She also comments that, at the museum, "the guards on the premises have little sense of exactly what they're guarding. When I asked in my best

Figure 2.14. Bookstore and Judaica Store Casa de Jacob in Toledo with antisemitic graffiti in its walls, July 2007. ©Adrián Pérez Melgosa.

schoolgirl Spanish if there were any modern synagogues in Spain, all I got was a shrug." She then describes finding Casa de Jacob, where she and her husband spoke at length with David, a member of the family who owned the bookstore. David told them his family believed they were Anusim, descendants of Jews forced to accept baptism. Gray concludes, "Our chat with David allowed us, as we moved on to Toledo's magnificent cathedral, to feel a little more at home in this very Catholic place" (Gray).[32]

Since Gray's profile is exactly that of the tourist that Toledo and the other cities of the Network of Jewish Quarters of Spain are trying to attract, it is worth noting what she saw and how she felt in Toledo. Although impressed by the medieval synagogues and the museum, Gray was interested in finding a Jewish connection between past and present. We see her desire to find these connections in the experiences she singles out for her account: the video showing modern-day Jewish celebrations, her questioning the guard about the existence of a modern synagogue, and her conversation with David at Casa de Jacob. Gray was disappointed at the guard's apparent lack of interest in answering her question, yet her disappointment would have probably been even greater if she had found out that there were no synagogues in use and no Jewish community in Toledo. By contrast, her conversation with David and the video at the museum gave her the sense of continuity that she was looking for, the proof that "Judaism lives on." This continuity is what is encompassed in the meaning of the word חי, "alive," for Jewish visitors.

As we have noted, the efforts to make Jewish traces visible coexist with previous signs that belong to different memorialization moments. In Segovia, the sign announcing one of the city's churches, the Church of Corpus Christi, now also notes, "Antigua Sinagoga Mayor de Segovia" [Old main synagogue of Segovia]. The building now houses the convent of the Franciscan nuns of Santa Clara de Asís. One of our favorite anecdotes from our visits to different Jewish Quarters came from what happened there in the summer of 2007 when we rang the bell of the convent and asked whether it was possible to visit the church. The nun who answered the door, a smiling and no-nonsense diminutive old lady dressed in a black habit, said that it was closed but that she could give us a postcard of the interior instead. We insisted, explaining that we were in Segovia only for a day and that "the real thing" would be so much nicer to see than a postcard. Her response was, "Actually it looks much better in the postcard; the church does not look as nice as it does in the picture." In their apparently candid assessment of the building, her words indicated a resistance to the very message the Network of Jewish Quarters promotes, which depicts remaining objects and sites, no matter how transformed, as precious material links to Spain's Jewish past.

When we returned to Segovia the following year, we found the Corpus Christi Church open and were able to see the interior. Reconstructed according to the original after a fire destroyed it in 1899, the Mudéjar capitals, columns, and arches bore a striking resemblance to those in the synagogue of Santa María la Blanca in Toledo. Entering the church, we were surprised—as many visitors are—to find across the main entry door a large oil painting depicting the antisemitic legend that justified the confiscation of the synagogue from Segovia's Jewish community in 1410. Painted in 1902 by Vicente Cutanda, and entitled *El milagro de la Eucaristía* [The miracle of the Eucharist], the painting depicts a group of Jews running away in horror at the vision of a consecrated Host floating in the air above the cooking pot where they had intended to boil and desecrate it. According to the legend, explained on the flier we received with the ticket, the episode took place in this building. After hovering over the boiling water, the Host broke through the synagogue's wall, leaving a crack behind as evidence.

Domestic visitors from Spain, in their Tripadvisor comments, have many positive things to say about the synagogue/church but do not like having to pay to get in and find the price of one euro too expensive. Some comments by English-speaking visitors note the dissonant elements in the building: "Nothing Jewish to be seen at all in this small church. A question of shamefully misleading advertising," says one. "I found it offensive that an extremely large painting involving an antisemitic episode is displayed on one wall," says another. The episode, in fact, is not just commemorated in this painting. Each September, the city of Segovia celebrates a popular religious procession in honor of the Eucharist, the Catorcena. The procession begins at a different church every year and ends at the Church of Corpus Christi, the physical place of the miracle. The legend of the hovering Host, which served as the excuse to seize the synagogue, is thus commemorated annually and remembered in practice. Through the embodied performance of the procession accompanying a Host through the streets of Segovia, the city reactivates this antisemitic legend every September as a foundational moment of its history and identity.

As we saw in Toledo, mnemonic signifiers belonging to different historical moments and interpreting the past in radically different ways are collapsed in the visitor's experience. The visitor encounters these contending symbols side by side and sometimes simultaneously in the public space of Spain's Jewish Quarters. This juxtaposition of old and new signs, images, and practices is a perfect example of the plural and dynamic quality of memory, of its entangledness in synchronic and diachronic terms (Feindt 35, 43). Similar jarring juxtapositions occur in other cities as well. In Zaragoza, initiatives that attempt to educate people about and recognize the city's Jewish heritage coexist with the surviving commemoration of its most famous saint, Dominguito del Val, patron of altar boys and the child protagonist of Spain's first blood libel. He is commemorated as having been, "according to tradition," tortured and ritually murdered by Jews in 1250 in a chapel dedicated to him in the Zaragoza Cathedral, in a street in the city center that still bears his name and in a church built in the 1960s also bearing his name and containing a large, Christ-like statue of his martyrdom.[33]

The reidentification of these quarters as part of a Jewish past, the reemergence of narratives about the Jews who once lived there, and the re-marking of their streets with a variety of symbols closely associated with Jewish culture carry the paradoxical effect of reinvigorating the historic silencing of the events that led to the creation, abandonment, and destruction of these spaces in medieval Spain. We may draw a point of comparison from Gabrielle Schwab's reflection about the role of Holocaust commemoration plaques in modern-day Germany. She speaks of the silences that exist in the "talking" that these plaques are charged with performing. Writing about Tiengen, her hometown in Germany, she recounts how, as an adult, she found a book about Tiengen's prewar Jewish inhabitants. Somehow, she had never thought that there could have been Jews there. The book contained information about where Jews lived, where their shops were, and what happened to them and to the physical spaces they inhabited: who took whose house, whose shop, how they were deported, where they lived. Suddenly the book made a different town appear in front of her eyes, superimposed onto the familiar space of her childhood hometown. She concludes:

> I was never able to see Tiengen with the same eyes again and never will. It has become a haunted city, and the erasure of all traces of Jewish life is now but a material manifestation of the German denial of the Shoah. There is a material denial of lived experience and affect even where people are willing to acknowledge the historical facts. . . . Today some of Tiengen's houses wear commemorative plates that identify their Jewish history. But these speak without speaking, empty signs that point to the denial of history rather than its endurance. . . . To look at the commemorative plates that encrypt the town's Jewish presence is not to see. (Schwab 91)

Something similar happens in many cities in Spain that seek to commemorate their Jewish legacy. The Jewish street signs demarcate zones for tourists to see but, in the same gesture, silence and mask the history of destruction behind those signs. In fact, as we have seen, in many cases this history gets completely taken over by the celebration of the motif of convivencia or by a boisterous pride in the depth of local singularity. What the signs point to is not there to see, but there is no explanation for why. Along with this silencing, however, and in a manner similar to Schwab's experience, some local citizens and visitors may change their previous impressions of these sites and turn to see them as haunted by the violence, forced conversions, and appropriations that took place to result in cities where Jewish life once thrived now being as empty of Jewish presence as they are today.

Local authorities tend to greet the discovery of a forgotten Jewish cemetery, a finding of a possible former synagogue, or a water depot that could have been a mikveh as a treasure trove, material proof of the town's important historical status as a Jewish enclave. This is the case of the city of Lucena, which in the tenth and eleventh centuries became a very important center of Jewish life, teaching, and learning. Its splendorous Jewish past remained mostly invisible and virtually unacknowledged by the local population for over five hundred years. But in 2006, a large Jewish cemetery was "discovered" on the outskirts of the city during construction of a beltway. The finding was followed by a promotional campaign advertising the town as a place with Jewish heritage and later by the preparation of Lucena's candidacy for the Network of Jewish Quarters, which it joined in 2012. That same year, during his visit to Lucena in connection with the discovery of the town's Jewish cemetery, the French Israeli rabbi

Meir Gabay evaluated the importance of the town for the history of Judaism in medieval Spain by stating, according to the account of the local press, "Primero Lucena, después Lucena, y muy detrás Toledo y el resto de ciudades" [First Lucena, then Lucena, and far behind it are Toledo and other cities] ("El rabino").

Gabay, who created Agudas Ohalei Tzadikim, an association devoted to properly restoring and preserving Jewish cemeteries, may have articulated this hyperbole in order to provide a referent against which to measure the magnitude of the loss caused by the disappearance of Lucena's Jewish population. But rather than considering Gabay's words as markers of a haunted legacy, the local press interpreted them as an unequivocal expression of the value of their city and a sign of a bright tourism future. Consider the expressive, long title with which the local newspaper, *Lucena Digital*, summarized Gabay's visit and the laying of a commemorative plate at the graveyard: "El rabino Meir Gabay destaca la relevancia de la necrópolis judía, que puede atraer a miles de visitantes de esta religión, y considera que Lucena es más importante en la historia del judaísmo que Toledo y otras ciudades españolas" [The rabbi Meir Gabay emphasizes the importance of the Jewish cemetery, that can attract thousands of visitors of this religion, and considers that Lucena is more important in the history of Judaism than Toledo and other Spanish cities]. What better way to describe a city's desires in the competitive map of today's Network of Jewish Quarters?[34]

Indeed, the cities in the network both collaborate with each other in shaping the marketing of themselves and engage in competition for visitors' attention. As Ashworth explains, this is one of the paradoxes of tourism: "Tourism tends to both standardize and differentiate. It exploits and thus encourages the propagation of the unique character of places as differentiated products, while also tending to standardize many aspects of the product on offer" ("Heritage" 77). In these cities' negotiations of homogeneity and rivalry, their Jewish Quarters not only place on display the very absence of Jewish evidence that is promised but also establish a competition with other cities over the importance of that which is now absent.

And yet, again, not everything is absence. Lucena has no Jewish inhabitants, but it has a Jewish cemetery. Today, when the neighbors of Lucena go on a walk around their city, they encounter a once familiar place that has become newly resignified as a Jewish space. It is at the edge of their city and part of their city and themselves. Our guide in Lucena told us that she frequently brought *lucentinos* to visit the excavated cemetery. It has been incorporated in the city landscape, located at the end of a popular walk that locals take frequently, especially on weekends (see figs. 2.15 and 2.16). The process of making these sites visible again after archaeological excavations, of naming them as Jewish, produces

Figures 2.15 and 2.16. Lucena's newly discovered Jewish cemetery at the edge of the city, January 2016. ©Daniela Flesler.

for people a new awareness of their own city and their own history. Local reactions vary, occupying a whole spectrum, as can be seen in the online commentaries to the announcement of new signs marking Lucena's historic Jewish sites. These range from suspicion and anger about the city's decision to invest public money in projects that they do not think would result in material gain in a time of economic crisis to intense curiosity, interest, and pride in a virtually unknown aspect of their city's history that might attract tourist attention.

The example of Lucena also illustrates another important aspect of the dynamics at play in the recovery of Spain's Jewish past, which is the role played by Jewish visitors in general and Sephardi Jews in particular. These visitors validate and give legitimacy to the project of looking for, investing money in, and identifying with a city's Jewish heritage. As we have seen in this chapter, the recovery and gradual embracing of Spain's Arab and Jewish heritages have taken place with an acute awareness of a foreign gaze that, at different historical periods, both despised and valued Spain because of its Jewish and Arab connections. The Marquis de la Vega Inclán deployed this awareness of the foreign gaze as part of his wish to attract Sephardi Jews to Spain. The highly consequential nature of their visit, or "return," together with the parallel effort of reconnecting with and showcasing a national and local Jewish heritage, is analyzed in the following chapters.

NOTES

1. By the end of the 1990s, Spain occupied the second position after France. In 2008 the United States surpassed Spain in second place, and in 2010 China took third place, leaving Spain fourth. In 2013, however, Spain regained the third position, maintaining it in 2014 and 2015 ("International"). The impact of these international tourists' presence is felt more acutely in Spain, with a population of 47 million, than in France and the United States, with populations of 67 and 328 million, respectively.

2. Spain's othering was magnified and demonized in the discourse of the Black Legend, in which English, Dutch, Italian, German, and French writers, beginning in the mid-sixteenth century, characterized Spaniards as racially Moorish, of mixed race, black, and Islamic, and attributed to them characteristics that were seen as going hand in hand with this racial makeup, like cruelty and barbarism (Fuchs 20, 122–26). Spain, in this representation, "served as the negative image of modernity" (Schmidt-Nowara 158). This discourse sought to morally disqualify Spain's conquest of the Americas in order to serve the colonial ambitions of rival European nations. See Hillgarth and Greer, Mignolo, and Quilligan's edited volume *Rereading the Black Legend*.

3. We thank Lou Charnon-Deutsch for introducing us to Barrés's text.

4. As observed by many critics, this paradoxical situation of Spain complicates Edward Said's concept of Orientalism, narrowly focused on the British and French cases as representatives of a "European mentality." See Charnon-Deutsch, Colmeiro, and Martin-Márquez for critical explorations of the Spanish case.

5. See J. Pedro Muñoz Herrera's book *Imágenes de la melancolía: Toledo (1772–1858)*, in which he analyzes the construction of Toledo as a Romantic city by both foreign and domestic visitors.

6. *Toledo pintoresca* followed his successful *Sevilla pintoresca*, in which he analyzed the city in terms of its patrimonial value and heritage, relating its art and architecture to national history, especially in reference to Spain's Arab heritage. Some years later, he published the foundational texts of modern Jewish studies in Spain: *Estudios históricos, políticos y literarios sobre los judíos de España* (1845–1848) and *Historia social, política y religiosa de los judíos de España* (1875–1876). For more on his crucial role in the development of Jewish studies in Spain and on the modern reevaluation of Spain's Jewish heritage, see Friedman, "Jewish History" and Bush.

7. Charnon-Deutsch quotes from one of Richard Ford's letters to the Spanish Arabist Pascual Gayangos, in which Ford congratulates himself for selling so many copies of his travel guide to Spain, *Handbook for Spain* (1845), which, in his view, would "send a large supply of ricos ingleses [rich Englishmen] into Spain" (in Charnon-Deutsch, *Spanish Gypsy* 104).

8. Many other Romantic travelers saw in Toledo the physical remnants of Spain's intolerance toward Jews. Among them, Sebastian Blaze, one of the Napoleonic military men who wrote about his sojourn in Spain during the war of 1808–14, recounted his sight, in Toledo, of the Inquisition's pyre at la Vega as "a monument to the victims of intolerance" in *Memoires d'un apothicaire*, published in 1828 (Muñoz Herrera 79).

9. Although by the nineteenth century Spain was firmly established as a popular destination on the Grand Tour, Italy, France, and Switzerland continued to draw significantly more visitors (Barke and Towner, "Exploring" 8–9).

10. In a 1925 article, Santiago Camarasa, a Toledo businessman, journalist, and entrepreneur, explained how Spaniards had still to realize Spain's great tourism potential. He posited that tourism could provide Spain the kind of revenue that countries like Italy or France enjoyed and celebrated the creation of the *Comisaría Regia de Turismo* and the work of the marquis (Camarasa 3–8). For more on the work of the commission under the marquis's leadership, see Cabanillas García.

11. Cossío (1857–1935) was director of the Institución Libre de Enseñanza and had written an authoritative book about El Greco a few years earlier, in 1908, in

which he analyzed how the city of Toledo had had a defining influence on the painter (García Álvarez 200).

12. As summarized by Sasha D. Pack (2), "By 1968, Spain surpassed all rivals in tourism revenue per capita, and only Italy and the United States grossed more income from tourism . . . between 1959 and 1969, revenue from foreign tourism covered two-thirds of Spain's trade deficit." This spectacular growth mirrored the one experienced in international tourism worldwide, from 25 million international tourists in 1950 to 1.4 billion in 2018, according to the World Tourism Organization ("International").

13. The open letter "calls on Heads of State to acknowledge tourism's key role in delivering more sustained and balanced socio-economic growth and to prioritize the sector higher in national policies in order to maximize its potential" ("Prime Minister").

14. Tourism demand worldwide has been changing in this direction, distancing itself from the summer/seaside holiday mainly due to a wide range of environmental and climatic reasons (Buhalis 80). Cultural tourism has grown from a small niche market to a firmly established, mainstream, mass-tourism activity (McKercher and du Cros 135).

15. As we note in the introduction, another tangible result of Sepharad '92 has been an increased interest in Spain's medieval Jewish past by writers and readers of fiction. In many novels written since 1992, the main plot has centered on the expulsion or the Inquisition or important Jewish or converso characters. Paloma Díaz-Mas ("Judíos y conversos" 170) has analyzed how in a number of these texts, often published with funding provided by local and regional cultural institutions, the Jewish plot is part and parcel of an effort to recognize the local or regional past. See also Stacy Beckwith, "Transitions" for the intimate relationship between historical novels and the cities they depict and promote.

16. Among the most prominent examples of this representational role are the network's trips to Israel, Latin America, and the United States; the central role this organization took as one of three coordinators of the European Day of Jewish Culture (together with the European Association for the Preservation and Promotion of Jewish Culture [AEPJ], and the European Council of Jewish Communities, B'nai B'rith Europe); and its participation in the *Erensya* (meaning both "inheritance" and "legacy" in Ladino, *herencia* in Spanish) meetings of Centro Sefarad-Israel with Sephardi communities around the world.

17. Ironically, the model for the network may have originated in the tourist promotion of the Route of Santiago de Compostela, based on medieval Catholic pilgrimages, and in the initiatives undertaken to celebrate and take advantage of the Holy Compostelan Year in 1993: "Taking advantage of the celebration of the Holy Compostela Year, the autonomous regions involved, especially Galicia, made important investments in order to improve the

resources and infrastructures of the route as well as developing an important marketing campaign. Especially interesting were unique events related to the route such as the celebration of medieval markets in ten cities along the route. These markets recreated the life and atmosphere of Medieval times in order to regain the value of the culture, the artistic and monumental wealth, the gastronomy and the crafts of those towns" (Maiztegui-Oñate and Areitio Bertolín 201).

18. As Assumpció Hosta y Rebés put it to us in an interview conducted in Girona in June 2008, "We have small towns for which the Jewish legacy is their only tourist attraction and big cities like Barcelona that do not need it to promote themselves. Who cares about a Jewish legacy if you have Gaudí? But still, it is a good addition for them. Besides, they have a present-day Jewish community" (our translation).

19. We thank Stacy Beckwith for this analysis and for her guidance regarding Hebrew terms.

20. The equilibrium between the agendas of cultural preservation and tourism has been addressed through the creation of a third arm of this organization, the RASGO program. An acronym of the Spanish words for restaurants, lodging, signage, guides, and cultural offerings, this program attempts to coordinate the activities of private restaurants, hotels, and tourist services that want to associate themselves with the network. It sets a series of standards connected to quality of service and certain awareness about some Jewish cultural traditions.

21. The "Convention Concerning the Protection of the World Cultural and Natural Heritage" was adopted by UNESCO in 1972. Of the 754 properties that the committee has inscribed on the World Heritage List (582 cultural, 149 natural, and 23 mixed properties in 129 States Parties), 37 are in Spain. Mudéjar is Arab-style architecture commissioned by Christian rulers.

22. Targeting exactly this Jewish "purposeful cultural tourist" audience, Heritage Tours, a US company that specializes in private, upscale cultural tours, now offers, under its Jewish Heritage section, an option called "Off the Beaten Path: A Secret Jewish Heritage in Tarazona, Spain."

23. He recounts his impressions of the Diaspora Museum in Israel and characterizes the rooms dedicated to the Jewish experience in Spain as "un cuadro patético de las persecuciones, marginaciones y vejaciones que sufrieron los hebreos hispánicos" [a pathetic picture of persecutions, marginalizations and humiliations suffered by Hispano-Hebrews]. The museum had a "regusto por lo macabro y lo trágico" [relish for the morbid and tragic] and revealed "ese espíritu decididamente victimista . . . que caracteriza demasiado a menudo a buena parte del pueblo judío" [that spirit of victimization . . . which too often characterizes a good part of the Jewish people] (10).

24. The guide was published in Spanish and English. We are quoting from the English 1996 edition.

25. In regard to figure 2.5, an anonymous reader's comment to the Lucena newspaper article announcing the placement of the plaques explains: "The most hilarious and absurd aspect of this story . . . is that the plaques signal monuments and places that have not existed for centuries . . . or maybe they are invisible . . . for example, the picture that illustrates the article: 'Door of Granada.' Can someone tell me where it is? This is the place, OK [where the door was located], but where is the gate? Wouldn't you think that a visitor to Lucena will leave disappointed?" ("Comienzan").

26. A thoughtful critique of the concept "virtually Jewish" can be found in Lehrer, "Virtual, Virtuous, Vicarious, Vacuous? Toward a Vigilant Use of Labels." Lehrer contends that *virtual* has come to signify in this context "inauthentic," as if "an essential Jewishness, a 'real thing' that can be held up as a unitary standard" existed (384). As she explains, these sites are much more complex than that. In this chapter, we attempt to explain these sites' absence but also, as Lehrer suggests, "the possibility of new fruit growing in the spaces that were emptied" (387).

27. Young explains this in his consideration of the 1991–96 installations of Shimon Attie, in which the artist projected photographic images of the historic Jewish past on specific streets and houses of Berlin. Attie sought to intervene in this public space projecting his own mediated memory of it at the same time that he "makes as his object of memory the distance between then and now, the ways that even his own acts of remembrance cannot but gesture indirectly to what was lost and how we now recall it" (Young, *At Memory's Edge* 62–67).

28. Urry and Larsen explain this mechanism as one in which "there is the seeing of particular signs that indicate that a certain other object is indeed extraordinary, even though it does not seem to be so. . . . The attraction is not the object itself but the sign referring to it that marks it out as distinctive. Thus the marker becomes the distinctive sight" (Urry and Larsen 16).

29. We thank Santiago Palomero, the museum's director, for giving us access to the books containing visitor's comments and Shirley Wagner for the translation from the original Hebrew.

30. See Lustig and Leveson, and Linhard, "Europe's Jewish Spaces," for a critique of Pinto's concept given the persistance of antisemitism in Europe.

31. For more on the figure of Halevi, see chapters 3 and 6 of this book.

32. This bookstore can be compared with the Jarden Jewish Bookshop in Krakow's Kazimierz, in some ways the protagonist of Lehrer's book *Jewish Poland Revisited*. The Polish bookstore encompassed for Lehrer those commercial establishments that provided tourists and locals a "balance of Jewish and non-Jewish identification" and whose success "has lain in part with their willingness to engage with the messy variety of claims on, concerns about, and desires for Jewish life, culture, and space" (Lehrer, *Jewish Poland* 137).

In contrast to what Lehrer describes about Kazimierz, Casa de Jacob was the only establishment in Toledo that provided such a space, and it did not last. But a new Judaica bookstore, in proximity of the Sephardi Museum, opened in 2014. It is possible that, with time, it could provide a "home" similar to that which Casa de Jacob offered. In chapter 6, we analyze the story of the owners of Casa de Jacob in the context of a discussion of Spain's "new Jews."

33. In 2002, a study of the martyr that takes the legend as historical truth was awarded a prize cosponsored by Spain's and Aragón's governments (Alvarez Chillida, "Presencia" 153).

34. Other recent cultural initiatives in Lucena are also directly related to the objective of distinguishing the city for tourist purposes. For example, a chorus that performs Sephardi music is called Elí Hoshaná: Ciudad de Lucena. On their website, they explain that their performances in several cities of the Network of Jewish Quarters were instrumental in supporting the candidacy and eventual membership of Lucena in the network and in promoting Lucena as a tourist attraction (Coro Elí Hoshaná).

THREE

LOSS, RESCUE, AND CONVERSO DISSONANCES AT THE SEPHARDI MUSEUM OF TOLEDO

IN 1964, IN A SPAIN beginning to experience its first period of economic growth after the Civil War and deeply submerged in a prolonged authoritarian regime, Francisco Franco, the country's dictator, issued a decree that called for the creation of the Sephardi Museum in Toledo. Owned and funded by the Spanish state, the museum is housed in the building known as Sinagoga del Tránsito [Synagogue of the Transit], one of only three standing buildings that had once been used as synagogues preserved in Spain since the Middle Ages.[1] Its founding document from March 18, 1964, describes the museum as a materialization of Spain's desire to strengthen its links with Sephardi Jewish communities around the world. Franco's gesture was part of a post–World War II concerted strategy that, as we saw in chapter 1, sought to improve Spain's image abroad by dispelling lingering doubts about its sympathy with Nazism.

Apart from these initial declarations of intention, the museum received minimal governmental support and remained closed until 1971. Its scant initial collection grew slowly, mostly from private donations. In the late 1980s, the socialist government of Felipe González turned again to the Sephardi Museum of Toledo as a powerful political symbol. By this time, the process of democratic transition begun after Franco's death had redrawn Spain's political landscape, and the socialist government had embarked on a dynamic process of economic and political modernization. In 1982 Spain became part of the NATO alliance and in 1986, the same year in which Spain normalized its diplomatic relationship with Israel, the country secured admission to the European Economic Community. In this context, the development and renovation of the museum and its emblematic potential became of utmost priority for the socialist government as a way to internationally disseminate the idea of a Spain that had parted ways with authoritarianism and embraced modernity and democratic values.

These instances of governmental instrumentalization are part of a long history of interventions in the museum's physical building and exhibits by political authorities at the highest national level. As we will see below, the history and meaning of the museum begin with that of the building itself, a magnificent Mudéjar structure that not only provides the backdrop for the collection but also stands as the museum's main exhibition piece, a fact highlighted in every official guidebook (López Alvarez et al., *Guía* 2006, 16; *Guía* 2011, 18). The many reappropriations of the building through its complex history—a synagogue for about 130 years, a church for about 400, archive, hospice, cemetery, army barracks, and, since 1964, a museum—have contributed a series of both material and conceptual layers to its structure. Each reappropriation can be seen as "wrapping" the building with new historical layers of meaning. This complex history is today "wrapped" by the museum in exhibits that simultaneously reveal, contain, and conceal its superimposed layers.

By all accounts, the post-1492 synagogue was completely severed from the Jewish community in which it originated. Its use was subsequently guided by the needs of the Spanish monarchy, the military-religious Order of Calatrava, the Catholic Church, and the Spanish state. In this, its history seems to reflect a simplified history of the formation of Spain as a nation: the Arab, Jewish, and Christian coexistence of the Middle Ages gives way to a monolithic, monocultural Catholic Spain. And yet, the Jewish connections of the building have never completely disappeared, in the same way that Jews and Muslims did not disappear from Spain after 1492. Conversos and their descendants participated in the life of the building as a church and influenced its development in a way parallel to their participation in post-1492 Iberian society. In the twentieth and twenty-first centuries, Sephardi Jewish benefactors were instrumental in the transformation of the building into a museum, and more recently, Spain's small Jewish community has also been instrumental in the growth of the museum and its collection as well as in its role as participants in the construction of its narratives.

This chapter analyzes the Sephardi Museum, its building and exhibits, as complex spaces of negotiation of the dissonances between Spain's past and present identities, between the desires of official narratives and the traces of silenced memories. The complex histories of both the museum and its building have become not only emblematic of but also key players in the multifaceted relationship between Jewishness and Spain. Its most poignant exhibits are composed of the few material fragments that have been rescued from the widespread violence and destruction that decimated Iberia's medieval Jewish communities. These "salvaged" objects, which include the building itself, are mixed throughout the permanent collection with artifacts used or produced within the Sephardi communities of North Africa and the Mediterranean at large. Through the selection and display of these objects, the museum aims to show the history of Jewish presence in Spain while emphasizing a narrative of Sephardi survival, continuity, and return. As it displays this narrative of restoration and rescue, the museum also has to account for the building's post-1492 transformations. Out of view is the history of resilience, renunciation, and self-erasure of the conversos, those Jews who converted to Christianity and stayed in Spain after 1492. This silenced memory permeates the building and the fact of its survival. Reading the converso dissonances of the building allows for a reinterpretation of the museographic project itself.

A CONVERSO BUILDING AND ITS TRANSFORMATIONS

As we will see, through its transformations, the building where the museum is housed contains a material record of the complexity of the social, cultural, and political relations between the Jewish and converso communities and the Spanish state over the centuries. Thus, the history of the building's appropriations and reappropriations is pivotal to understanding the museum itself and for gaining a sense of the history of Spain's Jewish communities. This history also becomes emblematic of the important yet veiled roles that converso communities, their culture, and experiences have played in the building and in the history of Jewish life in Spain from the fourteenth century to the present.

The synagogue was built around 1359–61 by Samuel Halevi Abulafia (1320–60), chief royal treasurer and advisor to King Pedro of Castile and member of a prominent Jewish family that had served the Castilian kings for several generations. Constructed by Arab architects from Granada, it was an exceptional building from its inception, since it was built at a time when strict limits had been imposed on constructing new non-Christian temples across Castile.[2] Toledo was at the time embarking on a process of urban "Christian occupation" through the strategic construction of numerous new convents and churches (Palomero Plaza 78). Halevi's residential palace was located next door to the synagogue, on the site that today serves as the El Greco Museum. In contrast with its austere brick exterior, the temple once had a lavish and colorful interior. Under an elaborately designed wooden coffered ceiling, the walls were profusely decorated with polychrome stuccowork depicting intricate geometric and calligraphic motifs. Sunlight filtered to the interior through a series of lobed horseshoe windows covered with latticework. Along each of the walls, ornamental calligraphic bands surrounded the interior space with biblical and historical inscriptions in Hebrew and Arabic. The historical inscriptions gave information about the construction of the building and offered praise and tribute to both Samuel Halevi and King Pedro, testifying to the King's patronage. Today, a good deal of the decorative stuccowork, including some of the bands with calligraphic inscriptions, still exists. Most of the original walls' colors have been lost, but shades of richly saturated greens, blues, reds, oranges, whites, and blacks are still visible in some fragments.

By 1359, when the synagogue's construction began, Halevi had risen to a position of great prominence and wealth by successfully managing King Pedro's finances and overseeing his tax collection. He also served as the king's confidential advisor, taking part in many important political and economic decisions. In some instances, such as his 1358 trip to Portugal, he acted as the king's diplomat, negotiating a political treaty. An engraved inscription in the synagogue attests to Halevi's high standing in King Pedro's court. The Hebrew inscription reads: "the king exalted him and set him on high, above all his princes . . . into his hands he entrusted all that he had . . . and since the day of our Exile no son of Israel has attained to such exalted estate" (qtd. in Y. Baer 1: 363). Halevi amassed a fortune for the king, at the expense of rebellious nobles, whose estates he confiscated. His relatives and other Jews served under him as administrative officials (Y. Baer 1: 363). Even so, in 1360 or 1361, shortly after the synagogue's completion, he and his kinsmen throughout Castile were arrested in Toledo for reasons that were never clearly stated and still remain uncertain today. As Yitzhak Baer describes it, "he was taken from Toledo to Seville; and, after an attempt had been made to extort a large sum of money from him, he died in prison under torture, like other Jews before him" (1: 364).

Halevi served Pedro at an especially difficult time for Iberian Jews. The spread of the Black Death since 1348, for which Jews were blamed, produced general religious and social unrest and violent attacks on Jewish communities throughout Castile and Aragon. The civil war that ensued in 1366–69 between Pedro and his half-brother Enrique of Trastámara had devastating consequences and intensified the already increasing wave of anti-Judaism. Enrique, seeing an opportunity to use Pedro's political and economic reliance on Jews such as Halevi as a propaganda tool, began calling his brother "King of the Jews."[3] As a result, Jews were further persecuted and, in the case of several communities in northern Castile, massacred upon Enrique's victory. Years after this civil war, representations of Halevi as the archetype of the hated Jew who takes advantage of Christians were still widely disseminated in Toledo and Castile.

In 1378, shortly after the end of the Trastámara civil war, Ferrand Martínez, archdeacon of Écija, began his vehement sermons in Seville inciting violence against Jews. His preaching resulted in the unprecedented massacres that destroyed most Jewish communities and their material culture in Spain throughout 1391 (Y. Baer 1: 362–69). Rather than providing physical evidence of the power and stability of Toledo's thriving Jewish community, as it is still frequently characterized, the fact of the synagogue's construction represents the determination of exceptional Jewish leaders like Halevi to find a space for Jews and Judaism within Christian Spain at a time when hostile actions against them were on the rise. And yet, the very fact that Halevi met his violent death as the synagogue was being completed testifies to the frailty of his purpose.

In the Hebrew "Elegy on the Martyrs of Toledo," written shortly after the massacres of 1391 by Jacob Albeneh, Halevi's synagogue is mentioned as one of nine desecrated in that city during the attacks (Roth 129–33). We do not know exactly what happened to the synagogue then or in the following years. There is an abundance of written documentation about the post-1492 building but not much about its use as a synagogue before 1492 (Álvarez Delgado 342). What is obvious is that, together with the Synagogue Santa María la Blanca—and in contrast to all the other Jewish buildings in the city, and in the rest of Spain too—it did survive.

The history of Halevi exemplifies how easily privileged Jews in Christian Spain could go, in a few years, from occupying positions of great power to becoming prime scapegoats and targets of violence. The history of Halevi's synagogue becomes emblematic of the sweeping erasure of Jewish life that took place in the late fourteenth and fifteenth centuries in Spain. The museum and its official guidebook, however, do not explore these parallels between the building and the history of Iberian Jews. They focus their narratives on the different ways in which Jews settled in Spain but have difficulty narrating the complexity of the history of violence toward this community, as well as its banishing, a problem shared by Jewish-themed tourist/cultural initiatives in general. We see an example of this disengagement from the narrative of conflict in the official website of the museum, in which, under the heading "The Museum," we find three sections providing further information about each of these areas: "History of the Museum," "History of the Synagogue," and "Areas of Operation." The one dedicated to the history of the synagogue summarily states: "La sinagoga fue mandada erigir a mediados del siglo XIV por Samuel ha Leví, diplomático y tesorero real del rey Pedro I. *Las diversas vicisitudes históricas* han hecho que fuera iglesia, archivo de órdenes militares, ermita, barracón militar y, finalmente, Museo Sefardí" ["The synagogue was commissioned in the mid-fourteenth century by Samuel ha Levi, diplomat and royal treasurer of King Pedro I. *Diverse historical vicissitudes* resulted in its being a church, military orders' archive, shrine, barracks, and, finally, a Sephardi Museum"] (italics added). By depicting the history of the building's changing ownership as a succession of "vicissitudes," of unexpected, random changes, this historical summary refuses to acknowledge any agency or responsibility behind the events it describes.

This rhetorical gesture, the recourse to impersonal grammatical constructions, is a common feature of the way many contemporary narratives aimed at a general public narrate the persecution of Jews and conversos in Christian Spain. In these accounts, events take place for no clear reason, and no one is particularly responsible or accountable for the consequences. Events are also carefully circumscribed to a long-gone past with no repercussions in the present. By referring to the forced appropriations and transformations of the synagogue as "historical vicissitudes," this short narrative both silences this history and naturalizes it, making it seem the product of an inevitable and inexorable destiny. It also presents the building's current form, the museum, as the natural and happy end result ("finally") of this historical process of appropriations of the building and transformation of its uses.[4] In this self-promoting narrative, the museum has rescued the synagogue, which now exists as a legacy for all inhabitants of Spain.

The history of these transformations deserves further analysis. The official guidebook of the museum (*Guía del Museo Sefardí*) unambiguously states that the synagogue "is, without a doubt, the most significant piece of all the museum" (López Alvarez et al., *Guía* 2006, 16; *Guía* 2011, 18). The guide carefully analyzes the architectural and artistic features of the building that belong to its pre-1492 identity as synagogue, describing its structure, decoration, and Arabic and Hebrew inscriptions (16–21). In the section "A Museum in a Monument," the guide describes the building's Jewish origins and the presence of the Islamic and Christian traditions in its construction and decoration as testimony and result of the tolerant coexistence of Christianity, Islam, and Judaism in Toledo. To explain the post-1492 Christian transformations of the building, the guide resorts to a poignant biological analogy, "un edificio hijo de varias sangres que hace virtud de la inteligente conjunción de lo diverso" ["a building born of several blood lines that makes a virtue of the intelligent combination of that which is diverse"] (López Alvarez et al., *Guía* 2006, 143–45; *Guía* 2011, 39–40). The vocabulary reminds us, though ironically, of the discourses of "purity of blood" that would make the lives of conversos extremely difficult in fifteenth- and sixteenth-century Spain. While the analogy praises diversity and mixing, there is no mention made here of those groups, such as the conversos, that transcended and problematized both the Catholic unity of post-1492 Spain and the concept of clean-cut divisions in three self-contained religious groups: Muslims, Christians, and Jews. Interestingly, the building itself may be better understood if we consider it a converso structure that, as we will see, not only experienced a number of religious and secular transformations throughout its history but also possibly survived thanks to the existence of conversos.

Analyzing the case of German synagogues transformed into museums, Sabine Offe (82) explains that in post–World War II Germany, "former synagogues were rendered invisible through 'rededication' of their function"; "no building, street, or site was permitted to preserve the memory of the Jews who once lived there, their former function and significance forgotten. The memory of a history shared by Jews and Gentiles was hidden from the visual and physical consciousness of post-war Germans" (83). The case of post-1492 Spain is more complex, as exemplified by the history of the Sephardi Museum's building. Although the synagogue was rededicated to other functions, its original Jewish identity managed to resist complete erasure.

Two years after the 1492 expulsion of the Jews from Spain, the Catholic Monarchs Isabel and Fernando transferred the synagogue to the Military Order of Calatrava, the first military order founded in Castile in the twelfth century. The synagogue was renamed Church of San Benito and became an archive, hospice, and burial place for the order's knights. In 1500, the Calatravan prior visited the synagogue for the first time and was appalled by the visible Hebrew inscriptions. Upon seeing the inscriptions within the building, he ordered their destruction: "todos los letreos que están en la dicha yglesya asy en lo alto conmo en lo baxo que son de letra judiega los hagares rapar e quitar y tornar a blanquear y lo cual por que paresce cosa muy necesaria e sera servisio de dios" [all the words that are in this church both high above and down below that are in Jewish letters you must remove them and repaint white, which seems something very necessary and which will be a service to God] (in López Alvarez et al., "Nuevos datos" 480–81).

At the time of his visit, everything in the building, architecturally and decoratively, as well as the fresh memory of its still recent Jewish religious use, spoke of its identity as a synagogue. In this document, the prior repeatedly refers to the building as a church, a gesture that condenses his desire to reshape it to fulfill its new function. The "necessary" step of removing its "Jewish letters" and covering them with white paint reflected his larger intention to remove those elements that pointed toward the building's origin as a synagogue. The inscriptions, however, were not removed and neither were most of the other elements that identified the building as Jewish. The added Catholic elements, such as the altar, choir, and sacristy were, for the most part, built over as superimposed layers upon the otherwise original structure. The Hebrew inscriptions, however, carrying with them the connection of the building to its original use, have always remained visible, coexisting with the Catholic elements and surviving most of them.

Even more remarkably, exterior Hebrew inscriptions also persisted on the building's façade for hundreds of years after its "conversion" to Catholicism. The 1752 drawing by the renowned calligrapher, royal notary, and member of the Royal Academy of History Francisco Javier de Santiago y Palomares (Toledo 1728–96) shows the facade as it stood in the mid-eighteenth century.[5] In this drawing, the original Hebrew inscriptions on two beams above the larger front windows and on a beam above the entrance door can still be seen. These exterior inscriptions disappeared at some unknown time after 1752. The current physical building of the synagogue, after its many transformations, still attests to this converso condition. As we approach its main entrance, we see a steeple holding two bells. A small wrought-iron cross crowns the structure. The presence and privileged position of the steeple presides over the access into a museum dedicated to Sephardi Jews and housed in a synagogue, reframing the building as an entry into a Catholic church (see fig. 3.1). This prominent steeple, one of the most visible elements of the Christianization of the building, is actually a fairly recent addition. We do not know exactly when it was built, but we know that it was sometime after the mid-eighteenth century, since the bell tower is not visible in Palomares's 1752 drawing.

The Halevi synagogue's converso status is also captured in its most commonly used name today, Sinagoga del Tránsito. At some point between 1547 and 1552 the Calatravan knight Íñigo de Ayala y Rojas commissioned a painting, *The Transit of the Virgin*, to artist Juan Correa de Vivar to be hung in a lateral chapel (López Alvarez et al., *Guía* 2006, 13–14). The oil painting represents the Virgin Mary on her deathbed, surrounded by the apostles and, in the upper part of the composition, her ascent into heaven. In the seventeenth century, the painting lent its name to the church, which began to be popularly known as Church of the Transit. By the eighteenth century, this name would completely displace the official name of Church of San Benito. The "transit" part of the name has survived until today, even though it has reverted to being called a synagogue. This popular name speaks literally of the converso identity the building has acquired through its history of transformations, an identity emerging from

Figure 3.1. Exterior of the Sephardi Museum in Toledo. ©Antonio Vélez, Creative Commons License.

experiences of radical change. The word *transit* refers to the moment of the Virgin Mary's death, her assumption or bodily resurrection to heaven, as portrayed in Correa de Vivar's painting. The name, however, cannot avoid evoking the other *tránsitos* experienced by those who once prayed in it: the transits of exile, conversion, death, and, in a few cases, quiet, or even hidden, return. The paradoxical pairing of "synagogue" and "Virgin Mary," in which acts of erasure coexist with the tenacious ability of physical memory to persist in unexpected places, finds parallels in the experiences of the many converso individuals who lived close to the synagogue/church.

CONVERSO CONNECTIONS

The possible influence of well-positioned conversos and their descendants in the fate of the synagogue after the building was transferred to the Military Order of Calatrava adds intriguing possibilities to the unanswered question of why the visibly Jewish elements of the temple were not destroyed. We are not suggesting that these conversos were all crypto-Jews and thus that because of their heritage they would have wanted to protect the synagogue. As Gitlitz explains, conversos were a highly diverse group in terms of socioeconomic status, occupation, and religious belief, ranging from wholly crypto-Jewish to completely Christian and all the possible combinations in between (Gitlitz 84).[6] But the fact of the closeness of conversos to the authorities in charge of the building after 1492 and their participation in the building's life and evolution after 1492—a fact never acknowledged in the synagogue's museography—complicates the official narrative of loss and rescue offered by the museum.

Conversos became a numerically significant group after 1391, as a result of the violent, organized persecutions during which thousands of Jews were killed and many others converted in order to save their lives. In 1492, conversos seem to have composed between 2.8 and 4.0 percent of the total population of Spain. In Toledo, however, a city historically inhabited by numerous Jews, they composed between 15.0 and 19.0 percent (Martz 66).

The mass post-1391 conversions facilitated the possibility of holding city and church offices that had been prohibited to them as Jews. In Toledo, conversos began to occupy prestigious and influential posts in the city, as canon priests and chaplains in the cathedral, members and officers of the confraternities, and *jurados, regidores, alcaldes,* and notaries in the city government (Martz 23). This success led to their scapegoating in the popular uprising of 1449, in which they were forced out of their posts, robbed of their possessions, and, in some cases, killed. The infamous statutes of purity of blood, which prohibited conversos from holding public office, were promulgated in Toledo at that time (Martz 23–24). According to the exclusionary genealogical logic of this doctrine, the possession of any amount of Jewish or Muslim blood barred individuals from public office. However, these attempts to limit conversos' access to posts of power "appear to have been but temporary setbacks, and *conversos* continued to exercise great influence in high places" (Martz 37). Wealthy Toledo converso families usually intermarried among themselves, but they also married and formed alliances with the two leading, noble, Old Christian families of Toledo, the Ayala and the Silva. They also entered into the royal service of the Catholic Monarchs, sometimes occupying very high positions.

The high level of access and influence that some of these converso families achieved in both the royal court and Toledo's most important institutions of government may be exemplified by the cases of Hernán Álvarez de Toledo and Lope Conchillos. Álvarez de Toledo held the positions of royal treasurer, secretary and councilor of the Catholic Monarchs. Among his many diplomatic missions, he accompanied Isabel in the 1492 Granada campaign, carrying on political negotiations with King Boabdil (Martz 48).[7] Lope Conchillos, a converso of Aragonese origin, was one of Fernando's most trusted ambassadors, fulfilling duties more closely related to what today we would call a spy, eventually becoming a member of the king's council and his preferred secretary (Martz 84–5). In having access to the queen and king and their trust, both Álvarez de Toledo and Conchillos also had access to the main decision-maker of the Order of Calatrava, since, in 1487, King Fernando had become grand master of the order.

At the time of the synagogue's transfer to the Calatravan order, these two individuals and their families had strong links to Toledo as well as to several military orders, among them, Calatrava. Hernán Álvarez de Toledo was both a regidor in Toledo (1471) and commander of the Military Orders of Alcántara and Santiago. Two of his sons were also commanders of the Orders of Alcántara and Santiago (Martz 48–50). Lope Conchillos was regidor of Toledo in 1510, treasurer of the Toledo royal mint, and secretary of the Orders of Calatrava and Alcántara. With King Fernando's blessing, he married María Niño de Ribera, the daughter of one of Toledo's most powerful and wealthy families (Martz 84–85). His youngest son, Fernando, became friar in the Order of Calatrava; his eldest son, Pedro Niño de Rivera, who married Isabel de Silva, the daughter of a marquis, inherited the family's fortune, titles, offices, and privileges. He was regidor of Toledo between 1540 and 1562, chief controller of the Council of Finance, a commander of Calatrava, chief recorder of the Indies, and lord of two villages (Martz 106).[8]

Conversos were regularly in attendance at Catholic religious services. The former Jewish quarter, in the Santo Tomé parish, where the Halevi Synagogue was located, was renamed Barrio Nuevo (New Quarter) after 1492. As in other cities throughout Spain, in Toledo most Jews continued to live in the same geographical areas after converting to Christianity. Although they lived throughout the city, Santo Tomé and its neighboring parishes held the highest numbers of converso families (Martz 68; Amelang 88). Three hundred ten conversos from Santo Tomé were reconciled with the Inquisition in 1495–97. Since there are no figures for the total population of each parish in this period, it is not possible to determine the percentage of conversos in each parish (Martz 70).[9] It is, however, extremely likely that at least some of these converso parishioners of the former Jewish Quarter, now practicing Christians, attended religious services in the new Church of San Benito. The memory of its recent use as a synagogue would have been alive for many of them.

María Elena Díez Jorge, in her book *El arte Mudéjar: Expresión estética de una convivencia* explains how the transformations of mosques and synagogues into churches, as opposed to their destruction, and the construction of churches in

Mudéjar, or Arab-style, served a proselytizing function: the presence of Muslim and Jewish visual and decorative elements, mixed with those of Christianity, would "invite" new converts into these churches, making them feel more comfortable. The Mudéjar style would, thus, serve to suggest a conciliatory tone, making the goal of Christian conversion and consolidation more palatable (qtd. in Palomero 78). In this sense, we can think of the survival of the synagogue's structure as codependent with the presence of conversos willing to pray, as Christians, within its walls.

Converso connections actively influencing the transformations of the synagogue can be seen in the circumstances surrounding the placing of the painting *The Transit of the Virgin* in the synagogue/church. In 1547, a Calatravan knight, Don Íñigo de Ayala y Rojas, had obtained Emperor Carlos V's permission to build a small private chapel in the church. The chapel was conceived as a delicately decorated plateresque arcosolium, a niche opened in the south wall containing an altar. Ayala y Rojas provided that two masses a week would be given in this chapel in perpetuity and obtained the pope's permission to be buried at its base (Cadiñanos Bardeci 9).[10] He also commissioned Juan Correa de Vivar to paint a scene of the transit of the Virgin Mary to be placed inside the arcosolium atop his grave. The canvas's measurements were designed to fit this space ("El Tránsito"). One other condition was that his portrait be incorporated into the composition among the apostles and other characters surrounding the Virgin's deathbed.[11]

Íñigo de Ayala y Rojas's family had suffered a major scandal of defamation in 1538, just nine years before he obtained the king's permission to donate both the altar and Correa de Vivar's painting to the Church of San Benito. At that time, Alonso de Rojas, Iñigo's brother, was archdeacon of Segovia and the canon of Toledo's cathedral. A powerful and overbearing man, he seems to have had many enemies. Íñigo, Alonso, and all the Rojas brothers lived together in a mansion in the Santo Tomé Parish (Gonzálvez 60–63). One night, the statue of a lion with Alonso's coat of arms disappeared from the front of that mansion. It was later found in the public square on a stage that the Inquisition used for its autos-da-fé with a sanbenito, the penitential garment worn by those punished by the Inquisition, hanging from its neck. A sign said that the lion should be burned with "firewood of Romero," referring to the last name Romero, that of Alonso and Íñigo's grandmother. The meaning of the action was clear to everyone in Toledo: Alonso was being accused of belonging to a family of conversos (Gonzálvez 65). This was essentially true: Aldonza Núñez, his great-grandmother, belonged to a converso family.[12] According to some documents, and to popular accounts widely disseminated at that time in Toledo, the Inquisition had condemned her as a Judaizer after her death, and her bones were disinterred from the family crypt and burned (Martz 40).[13]

In a city like Toledo, where, for many centuries, Christians, Muslims, and Jews had shared the urban space, had close daily contact, experienced conversions, and witnessed ups and downs in the fortunes of each religious faith, the implicit obsession of the statutes of purity of blood with clearly demarcated religious identities resulted in placing a large part of the population under constant scrutiny and suspicion. The "stain" of having an ancestor punished by the Inquisition was felt acutely and had real consequences for generations: the descendants were not only socially shamed but also banned from many professions (Martz 62–65).

This climate of denigration, public innuendo, and doubt about a respected and powerful public figure in the city forced the authorities to start an inquiry into who could have been behind the accusation and whether it was founded. Íñigo de Ayala y Rojas's gesture of building his arcosolium soon after the incident can be interpreted as a gesture paralleling the legal process initiated for his brother's benefit. His conspicuous public request for royal permission to build the side chapel, his donation of the painting of the Transit of the Virgin with his likeness kneeling and praying inserted in the painting among the Virgin and Apostles, his desire to rest in that niche after his death, all seem designed to provide a strong and visible statement of commitment to the Catholic faith, and, by extension, an attempt to fend off all the negative repercussions that could fall on him and his family if the converso condition of any of his ancestors was proven. Íñigo's intervention in the building would become the most permanent element, both architecturally and symbolically, of the building's Christian period: the arcosolium today stands out, highly visible, in the south wall of the Great Prayer Room of the synagogue.

Inside this private arch that used to serve as an altar and as a tomb's niche, the museum today tells the history of the building's Christian period by means of a text and a series of images on a small wall panel (see fig. 3.2). This was not always the case; what is shown in this space has changed dramatically over the last several years, a fact that speaks of the dissonance this arch produces in the narrative of the synagogue as a recovered Jewish space. In the photograph on the cover of the 1997 guide, the niche's walls are empty and a menorah stands on the table that served as the altar, on the very space where Íñigo's remains once rested. In the photos used in the museum website's virtual visit, taken sometime before 2014, the menorah is gone and in its place a painting hangs on the wall. The image reproduces the appearance of the niche itself and the sacristy's door next to it at some unknown point in the building's Catholic history.

Figure 3.2. Arcosolium and altar of Don Iñigo de Ayala y Rojas at the Sephardi Museum July 2014. ©Daniela Flesler.

Today, this same painting is accompanied by two more framed reproductions of nineteenth-century paintings showing the synagogue's interior when it was a church. The explanatory text accompanying these images, entitled "The Synagogue after the Expulsion: From the Church of San Benito to the Chapel of the Transit," describes the transformations experienced by the synagogue in becoming a church, including the construction of the arcosolium itself. It shows a small image of Correa de Vivar's painting *Transit of the Virgin* and identifies the painting once exhibited in this space as the origin of the name *Tránsito*. The text also explains how the painting was commissioned and donated by a Calatravan knight who is probably the one that used to be buried in the niche's base. It, however, mistakenly identifies the knight as Francisco de Rojas, Íñigo de Ayala y Rojas's brother.[14]

Thus, the arcosolium today stands as a symbol and remnant of the building's Christian period but devoid of its converso connections: it stands empty of the painting that gave its name and new identity to the synagogue, emptied of Íñigo de Ayala y Rojas's grave and of the converso history of his family. Therefore, it is silent about the centrality of the purity of blood statutes to the negotiation of identity in early modern Toledo and the cultural anxiety they produced. The irony of the placement of the narrative of the Christian period inside this arcosolium is the converso background that frames and haunts this niche, as it haunted its owner and the church itself.

THE CREATION OF THE SEPHARDI MUSEUM

In her analysis of the creation of German Jewish museums since the mid-twentieth century, Inka Bertz explains that they were "the product of non-Jewish concerns and were directed primarily toward the non-Jewish public" (81). She further explains: "In the Jewish Museums, Germans have created a 'Jewish space'; yet that space is predominantly occupied by their own needs. To date, Jewish museums in Germany, unlike those in the United States or other European countries, have less to do with the 'construction of Jewish identity' than with the 'reconstruction of German identity.' They are *German* Jewish museums—which is not the same as being 'German-Jewish' museums" (Bertz 107). Is this the case of the Sephardi Museum as well? Yes and no. On the one hand, the museum was created to address Spanish political and economic needs. And yet, Jewish benefactors, especially Moroccan Sephardi Jews and other members of Spain's current Jewish community have been instrumental in its development, in the decisions made by its board of trustees and in the programming of its activities. In terms of its relation to the public, the museum aims to educate a domestic gentile audience, but it also explicitly addresses and operates under the assumption of an international gaze that includes foreign tourists in general and Sephardi Jews in particular.[15] As detailed in our analysis of Jewish-themed tourist initiatives in chapter 2, the awareness of this gaze, the synagogue's potential to attract international attention, became the prime engine at the center of the restoration of the site as a high-profile national project. The origins and response to this "external gaze" have generated two narratives about the building that, despite being mutually contradictory, have been simultaneously at work throughout the process of building, curating, and marketing the museum.

On the one hand, it was the gaze of nineteenth-century European Romantic travelers that first spurred international interest in the synagogue. This gaze, fascinated by ruins, mystery, and the remote past, was more interested in the original identity of the building as a synagogue than in its subsequent transformations. Jewish (and Arab) material culture from Spain was alluring as a trace from a long-forgotten past. On the other hand, this external gaze also spurred a drive for modernization within Spain, for restoring the building to a state in which Spain's highest authorities could be proud to show it to potential high-profile international visitors. These narratives of romanticism and modernization, with their paradoxical relation of mutual competition, are two underlying drives that the museum attempts to reconcile while striving not to fully resolve them. The museum wants to be both the Romantic space where we can experience the medieval synagogue as it was and a modern museum with innovative exhibition technologies and curatorial practices.

Thus, a central part of the building's modern transformation into an exhibition space has been the reclamation of its historic Jewish identity and the removal of most of the elements associated with its life as a church.[16] This transformation began at the end of the nineteenth century, when the building lay abandoned after a process of deterioration that had begun in the eighteenth century. Its decline was accelerated early in the nineteenth century, when it was used as a barracks during Napoleon's invasion of Spain. While Francisco Pérez Bayer's work in 1752 had established the reasons for considering the synagogue a historical building of great artistic value, it was not until the publication of the first illustrated travel guides in the first half of the nineteenth century and the arrival of the railroad in 1858 that this interest became widespread. Subsequent descriptions and studies of the Halevi synagogue, especially those popularized in travel narratives and guides, began producing public awareness about its patrimonial value and, on May 1, 1877, King Alfonso XII declared the building a national monument (Palomero Plaza 88–89). From 1910 to 1964, it became part of the Patronato del Museo del Greco, directed by the Marquis de la Vega Inclán, who took a special interest in restoring and transforming it into an object for public exhibition. His vision for the building has been the basis of what is today the Sephardi Museum (Palomero Plaza 112).

The marquis's plans included the exhibition of the building, the creation of a center of Hebraic studies, and the possibility of using the space to show the world "a refined manifestation of the incipient national culture" (qtd. in Palomero Plaza 98). In his 1911 letter to the Council of Ministers encouraging the synagogue's proper restoration analyzed in chapter 2, the marquis's argument managed to turn a foreign interest that stemmed from a Romantic infatuation with ruins into a rationale for reconstruction and modernization. The marquis's words persuaded the ministers; immediately, permissions were granted, restorations took place, and the building became ready for exhibition. By 1913, King Alfonso XIII and Queen Victoria Eugenia's official visit served to confirm the high profile and regard that the newly conceived space had attained at a national level—a recognition of Spain's Jewish past that overlapped with the country's acquiring of its protectorate in Morocco in the fall of 1912 and Spain's broader Orientalist cultural and political project in North Africa. Soon, the building became a visit de rigueur for foreign heads of state: the French president in 1913, the prince of Monaco in 1918, the king and queen of Belgium in 1921, and the shah of Persia in 1922 (Palomero Plaza 112).

The activities of the synagogue as an exhibition space continued during the 1920s and '30s. After the Spanish Civil War, in 1941, the Instituto Benito Arias Montano de Estudios Hebraicos y de Oriente Próximo and the journal *Sefarad* were created as part of the Consejo Superior de Investigaciones Científicas (CSIC) in Madrid. The creation of the Arias Montano Institute was soon followed by the Center of Hebraic Studies in Toledo. Both of these academic initiatives were the direct antecedents of the Sephardi Museum. After Franco's decision to create the museum in 1964, its first directors were the eminent Hebraists Francisco Cantera Burgos and Federico Pérez Castro, who were also directors of the Arias Montano Institute.[17]

The creation of these institutions was part of the concerted Francoist strategy to improve Spain's image abroad, especially in the United States. As described in chapter 1, several conciliatory gestures, which culminated in the Law of Religious Freedom of 1967 and the official recognition of Spain's Jewish communities shortly after, took place in these years. Among these gestures was Franco's secret collaboration with the Israeli Mossad to help many Moroccan Jews formerly inhabiting the Spanish protectorate relocate to Spain after Morocco's independence in 1956. Creating the museum was a powerful gesture aimed at fostering the links with these returning Jews. Some of them, like the Pinto-Coriat family, would become important benefactors of the museum. It can be argued that the museum might not have been created if it weren't for them.

In 1965, as Franco's government announced the approval of the statutes by which the Jewish community of Madrid would be officially recognized, César Kahon, a Sephardi industrialist living in Madrid, donated a check in the amount of 1 million pesetas to Franco, who promised to use the money to promote the link between Sephardi Jews and Spain. The money was, indeed, used to buy art objects for the recently created Sephardi Museum (Lisbona 227–28).[18] Jacques Pinto Coriat, a renowned businessman from Tangier, was involved in the creation of the museum from the very beginning. In 1965, he was named cochair of the museum's board of trustees, together with other eminent Sephardi Jews Jacques Bentata and Elías Nahmías. For the inauguration of the museum, Pinto Coriat gifted the costly silk tapestries that hung on the walls of the Great Prayer Room until 2015. In 1979, together with his wife, Lunita Toledano, he donated the land adjacent to the museum where the museum's administrative offices were built.

As published in the BOE (Official State Bulletin), the Decree 874/1964, which legalized the creation of the museum, justified and explained its establishment as a way to maintain and strengthen Spain's links with Sephardi Jewish communities around the world, who were represented in the document as descendants of the Jews expelled from Spain in 1492. The decree recognized Hispano-Jews as part of Spanish history but presented the Francoist idea that Sephardi Jews were worthy of this consideration because of their extended contact with Spanish soil from which they incorporated the grandeur of the "Hispanic character." As explained in chapter 1, according to Francoist propaganda, the contact of Sephardi Jews with the Hispanic "temperament and mind" had resulted in their physical and cultural improvement. Implicit was Franco's belief that contact with these immaterial and indefinable purported virtues of Spain had "purified" Sephardi Jews (unlike Ashkenazi Jews, who, in his view, had been contaminated by all the vices of materialistic Europe). As reprinted in the museum's guide, the decree for the museum's inception says:

> El interés que ofrece la historia de los judíos en nuestra Patria es doble, pues si por una parte, su estudio es conveniente para un buen conocimiento de lo español, dada la presencia secular en España del pueblo judío, también es esencial a la entidad cultural e histórica de este pueblo la asimilación que una parte de sus linajes hizo del genio y la mente hispanas a través de una larga convivencia.

> [The history of the Jews in our homeland is of twofold interest: if, on the one hand, its study is beneficial to a good understanding of that which is Spanish, given the centuries-long presence of the Jewish people in Spain, it is also essential for the cultural and historical identity of Jews, the assimilation undertaken by part of its kin of the Hispanic temperament and mind, which was carried out through a long period of coexistence]. (BOE April 11 I, Decree 874/1964, reprinted in López Alvarez et al., *Guía* 2011, 29)

In spite of these initial steps, the museum remained an unfulfilled promise for several years. Since 1970, it has belonged to the Spanish state and has been managed by the Spanish Ministry of Culture. Its inauguration in 1971 was a much-publicized political event attended by Francoist national and local authorities and by national and international Jewish authorities and benefactors, among them Salomón Gaón, president of Madrid's Jewish Community, and Elías Nahmías, president of the World Sephardi Federation. Among the objects that the museum exhibited at this point, as reported in a 1971 article in the newspaper *ABC*, were several Jewish gravestones, the Tarragona marble basin and ritual objects such as a Torah scroll donated by Madrid's Jewish community ("Se inaugura"). However, as Selma Holo explains, in 1971, "[the museum] remained disorganized and without professional guidance. The museum had no scholarly underpinnings, educational programming, library, archives, acquisition policy, or security system. And, it had no objects [*sic*]. Visitors had no means of understanding where they were or why the synagogue had a Christian name. Only after 1981 . . . did it receive any attention and begin to advance, in several stages, to its present status as a fully modern museum" (67).

Only at the beginning of the socialist government of Felipe González in 1982, after democracy had been reestablished in Spain, did the museum begin to truly function as such. The museum became an absolute priority (Holo 56–57).[19] It was seen as a privileged space in which to showcase Spain's new democracy and modernity, the material proof of the reemergence of Spain as a country respectful of diversity and pluralism ready to partner with Western democracies as a player on the world scene. After the extensive restorations carried out between 1985 and 1994, King Juan Carlos inaugurated the renovated space in 1994. Closely linked in its timing and intention to Sefarad '92, this inauguration was considered the true opening of the museum, newly conceived as a democratic project. In 2003, attesting to the museum's continuously high political profile, it was reinaugurated by Prince Felipe. Like Pedro I, Fernando I, Carlos V, Alfonso XIII, and Franco had before them, the direct personal interest that Felipe González, Juan Carlos I, and Prince Felipe took in this building reflects an effort to capitalize on its symbolism as a material vestige of a past of idealized religious coexistence. Yet the building manages, as does Spain's Jewish legacy, to resist being fully instrumentalized by any particular ideology. Its symbolism escapes attempts to relegate it to the past and continues to activate new meanings that transcend political attempts to tame them.

MODERN REFORMS

In the aftermath of the Holocaust, European politicians and curators faced a series of dilemmas in their efforts to properly restore and utilize the many damaged or partially destroyed synagogues and Jewish institutions that stood in cities where a Jewish presence had been all but erased. Structural reforms, repairs, and reconstructions carry deep symbolic meaning. Ruth Ellen Gruber has described this dilemma in Germany: synagogues constituted "sites of glory," magnificent buildings that attested to the past prosperity and the cultural and aesthetic achievements of local Jewish communities, while they also represented "sites of shame," "physical reminders of the deliberate destruction of a people, which may have been carried out, supported, or witnessed by the local population" (Gruber, *Virtually Jewish* 104). How much and what to repair and reconstruct as proofs of past splendor and what to leave intact to provide material traces and memorials for the remembrance of destruction is very much still an open discussion.[20]

Reflecting on these dilemmas, Gruber asks, "For whom, then, are the synagogues and ghettos being renovated? What should be the function of a restored synagogue, ritual bath, or Jewish quarter in towns where no Jews live?" (Gruber, *Virtually Jewish* 104). These dilemmas, although less publicly, have also become part of the discussion about the proper way to reconstruct and use the Synagogue of the Transit. The tension between these two identities, the "site of glory" and the "site of shame," is further complicated by the Romantic and modernizing narratives that, as we have seen, have driven the creation of the museum. These are further compounded by the double purpose outlined in Franco's edict: to exhibit the ways in which Jewish culture has been important to Spain and how Spain has been an influential and improving factor in the development of Sephardi Jews. The contradictions emerging from the deployment of these conflicting narratives across the Sephardi Museum account for many of its dissonances.

The evolving significance of the rationale guiding the museum's reconstruction can be illustrated by surveying succeeding editions of the museum's official guide. The guide has progressively highlighted as important information the restorations undertaken in 1985–94 and 2001–3, during the country's democratic era, while quickly passing over the Francoist reforms. With every new edition, the sections dedicated to the democratic-era reforms have progressively taken more space and a more central location in the text. For example, in the 1997 guide these modern restorations were not given their own section, only appearing sketched in a few sentences. But the 2006 guide dedicated two full sections to them at the end ("A Museum in a Monument [1986–2003])" and ("Restoration of the Synagogue of the Transit [1988–2003]"). The 2011 edition moved these sections to the very beginning of the text. The descriptions of the restorations fully embrace the modernization and "site of glory" narratives in an effort parallel to the democratization and international ambitions of Spain's democratic transition. Along with this celebration of democracy, the guide explains the reconstruction efforts as attempts to restore that which had been damaged, to heal past wounds, and to bring the synagogue, and Spanish/Jewish relations, back to life.

Unstated, but fully operative in these rationales, is the principle that every modification should serve as a means of highlighting the building's initial historic use as a synagogue at the expense of not displaying the post-1492 history of the building, the messiness of its in-betweenness, or the violence that attended the post-expulsion period. The most recent restorations are described in the guide as aiming to "paliar la diversidad de actuaciones sufridas por el edificio a lo largo del tiempo y permitir que la sinagoga forme parte del nuevo Museo como la principal pieza de su colección" [mitigate the various interventions suffered by the building through time and allow the synagogue to be part of the new Museum as the main piece of its collection] (López Álvarez et al., *Guía* 2006, 15). Modern renovations have repaired the general damage to the building's structure and removed the Catholic additions to its interior: the choir, the Calatravan knights' tombstones, the altarpiece, and the altar. As Carlos Baztán, one of the architects involved in the 1990s renovations, explained it: "nuestro trabajo ha consistido, sobre todo, en retirar las capas superpuestas" [our job has consisted of, above all, peeling off the layers] (Botín). Although this aim is understandable given the museum's goal to recuperate the original synagogue, this peeling off of the post-1492 layers would result in the erasing of the history written on the building by each of the successive groups to claim and make use of it. Completely peeling off this post-1492 history is, in fact, impossible. The post-1492 experiences of expropriation, violence, conversion, accommodation, and survival have left indelible physical traces on the museum's building and constitute an intrinsic part of Sephardi Jews' experience in Spain.

The concept of "wrapping," as developed by Herman Lebovics, is useful to explain the relationship of incorporation, appropriation, and resemanticization of Jewish remains in contemporary Spain. Lebovics reads Fredric Jameson's analysis of Frank Gehry's house in California, in which Gehry wrapped a 1920s bungalow with modern industrial materials and designs, as an apt metaphor to think about the colonial incorporation of native cultures into the high culture of metropolitan France (Lebovics, *True France* 57). The Francoist point of view regarding Jewish remnants, as we have seen, is that they are "improved," legitimized, because of their belonging to Spain. In the relationship between the one doing the wrapping and the wrapped, there is an obvious hierarchy; what is wrapped is subordinated, incorporated. But the wrapped is not eliminated: "what is wrapped can also be used as the wrapper; the wrapper can also be wrapped in its turn" (Jameson 102). Thus, Halevi's synagogue became wrapped by the Church of San Benito and this by the Chapel of the Transit. The different stages of the building from national monument, to the Franco era, through the socialist government and on to the present accumulated their nation-building wrappings on those initial religious transformations. At each point, the wrapped (whether the Jewish, Christian, Francoist, or democratic layer) may become dominant to certain visitors.

The current name of the building, Synagogue of the Transit, exemplifies the reemergence of the past Jewish and Christian wrappings over today's modern museum. A more complex example of the instability of these wrappings appears when one of the intended audiences of the building, Jewish tourists, reappropriate the site as evidence of the historical magnificence and resilience of their culture. Along with and in most cases replacing the museum's official narrative of respect for the diverse historical heritage of today's Spain, Jewish visitors, especially those from the Sephardi diaspora, find in the building a part of their own cultural heritage. In an Ashkenazi-centric Jewish present, the synagogue becomes material evidence of the sophistication and endurance of the Sephardi tradition.

What links the different wrappings or presentations of the building is the interest in seeing it as a site of glory, be it for Franco's Spain, subsequent democratic governments or for various groups of visitors. In between each wrapping, however, there is a space of instability where questions remain open and unanswered because their answers may awaken a variety of "site of shame" stories. Why is this building a museum today? What happened to the community it served? Why is there no Jewish community in today's Toledo? How is it possible that Toledo's neighboring Synagogue of Santa María la Blanca still belongs to the Catholic Church? It is in these spaces of interaction remaining between the layers that the relationships between wrapping and wrapped acquire meaning, even if they are not explicitly addressed.

These spaces of interaction are made of what we have called the converso identity of the building. Traces of these converso in-between spaces appear throughout the museum for visitors to see, although they are not explicitly underlined in its museography: no explanatory panel describes them or points them out. The exterior bell tower provides a conspicuous example: given that it distorts the general structure of the synagogue, it has minor artistic value (it is a narrow rectangular shape, built in rustic brick and crowned by a simple neoclassical triangular roof rendered in stucco) and no structural value (it does not support any other structural element); it seems unusual that none of the restorations of the building have touched it. These restorations removed even more cumbersome Catholic elements of the building's interior—altarpieces, Calatravan knights' tombstones, priests' living quarters—yet the bell tower remained. Santiago Palomero Plaza, the museum's late director, explained to us the decision to keep this very visible bell tower and cross as an element bearing witness to the history of diverse ownership and uses for the building. The museum, argued Palomero Plaza, does not want to erase that history.[21]

Similarly, writing about the deterioration still visible today on some of the wall's stuccowork and on some Hebrew inscriptions, Palomero Plaza states that beyond the intrinsic technical difficulty of reverting to the original polychromies hidden under multiple layers of paint, there lies the intention to allow "the history of the building's deterioration to be 'read'" (Palomero Plaza 168). It is telling that the word *deterioration,* and therefore the connection to the "site of glory" narrative, appears linked in Palomero Plaza's explanation. However, in the transformation of the synagogue into a church, parts of the building suffered much more than time-inflicted, natural deterioration. In the eighteenth century, when the church became a chapel, the stuccowork of the walls was completely destroyed on the west side, and partially destroyed on the south and east sides in order to convert the Women's Gallery into a dwelling for the priest. Today, small fragments of stuccowork recovered during the building's restoration are sparsely attached to the modern whitewashed walls of the Women's Gallery like scattered pieces of an unresolvable puzzle (see fig. 3.3).

The sight of these recovered fragments on the large expanse of the white walls gives us a sense of the vastness of the destruction suffered by this room, emblematic of the devastation experienced by Iberian Jewish culture in general. But as in the case with the stucco and inscriptions on the Great Prayer Room, nothing is explicitly said about this destruction or the context in which it took place. Informed visitors can draw their own conclusions, if they carefully read the historical section of the museum's guide. This is one of the many instances in which visitors with different levels of information would see different things

Figure 3.3. Pieces of original stuccowork on wall of Women's Gallery, July 2014. ©Adrián Pérez Melgoa.

or be able to read differently the meanings created in between these interacting layers. As it throws a veil of impersonality over the history of destruction and neglect, this deterioration story also manages to silence an alternative history, the one connected to the surprising survival of the building in the midst of the almost complete eradication of Jewish material culture in Toledo and in Spain in general.

THE EXHIBITION OF OBJECTS AND THE SEPHARDI MUSEUM NARRATIVES

"Exhibitions," Barbara Kirshenblatt-Gimblett reminds us, "are also exhibits of those who make them" (*Destination* 2, 78). The Sephardi Museum of Toledo contains a variety of museologic practices in its exhibits. It is a cultural history museum that explains the history of Jews in general and of Sephardi Jews in particular from antiquity to the present; it is also an archaeological museum containing rescued Jewish artifacts and remains, an ethnographic museum of the customs and rituals of Sephardi Jews and a museum of art exhibiting significant works by contemporary artists. The wide curatorial spectrum covered by these practices reveals the museum as a very ambitious institution, much more complex (and well-funded) than the local and regional museums and interpretive centers we study in the next chapter.

In her book *Double Exposures*, Mieke Bal analyzes several museum exhibitions using the metaphor of narrative fiction. Narrative, as defined by Bal, is "an account of a sequence of events, made up or not, presented from a particular perspective and suggesting that the reader endorse that perspective" (*Double* 136). Exposition, as it takes place in museums, is narrative, according to Bal, at two levels. The first level emanates from the presence of an object itself: "the very fact of exposing the object—presenting it while informing about it—impels the subject to connect the 'present' of the objects to the 'past' of their making, functioning, and meaning" (Bal, *Double* 4). A second level occurs through the sequential nature of the visit: "the 'walking tour' links the elements of the exposition for the 'second person.' Walking through a museum is like reading a book. The two narratives overlap but are not identical" (Bal, *Double* 4).[22] Following Bal, we see these two narrative levels at work in a walking tour of the museum.

As we enter the building, we encounter a security check and above it, a wooden beam fragment from the synagogue's façade found during the museum's restorations. The beam fragment, engraved with the Hebrew word meaning *faithful*, was part of the series of Hebrew inscriptions that decorated the original entrance to the temple around the front windows and above the entrance door seen in the drawing by Palomares. The inscriptions come from Psalms 118:20 and Isaiah 26:2, and they read, "This is the gate of the Lord; the righteous will enter through it" and "Open the gates, that the righteous nation may enter, the one that remains faithful." These verses were traditionally placed by many Sephardi communities over the entry doors of their temples. Today, a lighter-toned piece of wood has been placed next to the fragment, engraved with the remaining characters of Isaiah 26:2 in Hebrew.[23]

The beam literally welcomes the visitors to the museum and attempts to address some of the difficult questions entailed by its history: Whose building is this? Whose history does it represent? Whose voices speak through it? Kirshenblatt-Gimblett summarizes the conflicts at work in Jewish museums in Europe today by asking "Who is telling whose history to whom and why?" ("Why" 2). In their present relocation and recontextualization, the beam's expressions, "righteous nation" and "the one that remains faithful," point as much to the original addressees of the poem, medieval Jews, as to the newly democratic Spanish nation that in the early 1990s had just completed a tránsito of its own, a transition from a long dictatorship associated with European fascism to a parliamentary democracy respectful of diversity and human rights. The museum's authorities invite visitors to contemplate this contemporary reading of the beam by beginning the prologue to the museum's guide with the psalm, "This is the gate of the Lord; the righteous will enter through it" and by explaining its current presence in the museum's entrance as "un saludo y una invitación al conocimiento de una cultura cuyas raíces se hunden en el Próximo Oriente Antiguo y de cuyo sustrato se conforman nuestras tradiciones culturales" ["a welcome and an invitation to the knowledge of a culture rooted in the Old Middle East, one of the threads from which our cultural traditions are constituted"] (López Álvarez et al., *Guía* 2006, 11).

Thus, the reinscription of the two verses onto the museum reinterprets the actors in the sentence, the "faithful" who enter this space today, those for whom the doors are open, as the interested visitors, the ones who want to learn. This reinterpretation of the beam's message substitutes, not without rhetorical violence, visitors entering a museum for Jewish worshipers entering a synagogue and again posits the museum as the logical end result of the historical process of transformations experienced by the building. The "invitation to know" inscribed on the wall assumes not only that visitors might not know about this culture, that they are alien to it, but also—and here lies part of the effort the museum has recently embarked on—that this culture is an integral part of Spain's national roots. The museum thus invites its visitors to expand their understanding of national culture to include a previously unknown part of it. In the particular case of visitors from Spain, it invites them to contemplate this culture as their own heritage, as part of themselves.

As we enter the museum's main hall, the Great Prayer Room of the original synagogue, we find a series of panels that explain what a synagogue is, describe the structures that existed at this site before the synagogue's construction, and provide a brief history of the synagogue before and after the expulsion. The fourth panel, entitled "Spanish Synagogues," describes the fate of the hundreds of synagogues that existed in Spain before 1492: their destruction or "transformations" into churches, monasteries, hermitages, barns, infirmaries, hospitals, schools, private houses, and pharmacies. It explains that only three complete synagogues have survived: two in Toledo and one in Córdoba. A list follows, detailing the small and fragmentary material traces of some of these buildings in different cities and towns. Finally, the panel's narrative ends with a sobering list of ninety-seven cities and towns from which there are written documents mentioning the existence of one or more synagogues of which no material traces remain. In Seville, the panel says, it is believed there were twenty-three synagogues. The listing of each town, name by name, has something of an elegiac tone to it; it contains an homage and also a troubling reminder of the extent to which anti-Jewish violence and forced absence after 1492 were followed by the systematic work of cultural erasure.[24] The extraordinary nature of the building one enters is thus put into context. From the vast destruction and absence the list enumerates, this synagogue has survived. The main narrative the museum tries to communicate is precisely this story of survival and endurance in the midst of destruction and loss.

Both at the beginning and end of the visit, we see the Great Prayer Room of the synagogue, the main space and object of the museum. Upon our first contact with it, at floor level, we can see the original east wall, where the *hekhal*, or "Torah ark," was situated, with its intricate geometric decorations and Hebrew inscriptions. As we pause to sit on either of the two sixteenth-century mosaic seats constructed for the Calatravan knights, we may contemplate a worn fragment of the original floor, where the Catholic altar used to be (although no reference to the altar, and thus to the post-1492 interventions, is made here). On the south wall on our right, inside Íñigo López de Ayala's arcosolium, we find the brief illustrated history of the transformations experienced by the synagogue. But a richer contextualization of what this main room signifies within the museum's narrative appears only at the end of our visit, as we see at the end of this chapter.

The museum's permanent exhibition occupies five rooms, two patios, and the stairwell that connects the first and second floors. Room 1 is titled "Traditions of the Jewish People and Their Origins"; Room 2, "The Jews' Arrival in Hispania"; Room 3, "The Jews in the Christian Kingdoms"; and Rooms 4 and 5, "Sephardi Jews." The North Patio, or Garden of Memory, exhibits the remains of medieval gravestones originally found in Spain's Jewish cemeteries and the East Patio displays part of an archaeological excavation and sculptures made by contemporary Jewish artists. As we will see, each patio frames our understanding of the rooms associated with it, inviting and guiding the visitor's reading of the exhibition rooms connected to them. The exhibition space of the stairs carries a pivotal weight in what Bal terms the "meaning-producing sequentiality" of the visit ("Exhibition" 15).

DIFFERENCE AND LOSS

In Room 1, a glass case with the caption "Traditions and Origins of the Jewish People" features a series of ancient objects (jugs, bowls, plates, coins, religious idols) from archaeological sites in the Middle East on loan from the Israel

Antiquities Authority. On the opposite wall, we find a series of glass cases captioned "Judaism as a Way of Life." The cases display a series of religious ritual objects from a variety of origins in time and place: in the center stands a large bronze menorah ("Holland, seventeenth century") and to its left, a wool tallit, or prayer shawl ("Morocco, twentieth century"); a silver-and-ivory perfumer ("Central Europe, nineteenth or twentieth century"); a glass-and-silver perfumer ("Morocco, nineteenth–twentieth century"); and a brass-and-glass Hanukkah lamp ("Tunisia, nineteenth century"). The two sacred books exhibited are labeled as originating in Vienna, 1815, and Buenos Aires, 1965. On the right-hand side, we can see silver circumcision instruments ("Morocco, twentieth century"), silver cabalistic amulets ("Persia, twentieth century"), and a contemporary sculpture, a clay bust entitled *Junto al muro* [Against the wall], by Elias Nir Shalom, that consists of a mostly featureless model of a bearded male head with a prominent aquiline nose, wearing a kippah and leaning his forehead against a wooden cube engraved with the Star of David.

This kind of exhibit of sacred objects is a common feature of all Jewish museums in Spain. It is a manifestation of the paradox Kirshenblatt-Gimblett shows as entailed in displaying things that were never meant to be displayed by constructing them as ethnographic objects (*Destination* 2–3). By grouping together these objects from diverse origins, practices, and traditions, the exhibit suggests an irreducible commonality among the people who produced and used those objects, a commonality that transcends time and space. A well-meaning attempt to educate the public about a subject called Judaism, this exhibit shows the inherent dangers of such a task. The mere fact of having to show who Jews are and what Judaism is implicitly differentiates "them" from a Spanish "us" that needs no explanation.

The exhibit materializes a reductionist conception of Jewish identity as equivalent to a normative understanding of Jewish religion. The museum's guide restates this view: "La religión es el signo más significativo del judío a lo largo de la historia. Es el nexo de unión entre los distintos grupos y el motor que impulsa su vida diaria, sus costumbres y sus celebraciones" ["Religion is the most significant feature of the Jew (*sic*) throughout history. It is the nexus that unites diverse groups and the engine that fuels their daily life, their customs and celebrations"] (López Alvarez et al., *Guía* 2011, 82). The exhibit, therefore, implicitly compels us to look at these objects from a cultural distance, from an outside perspective that implicitly states that Jews are "them," not "us," and that "their customs" and "their celebrations" are not only distinct from ours but essentially homogeneous throughout history, regardless of cultural origin.

Exhibited as ethnographic pieces of information, rather than as a spotty and fairly arbitrary set of Judaica, the ritual objects become artifacts. Reflecting on the distinction between artifacts and works of art, Bal explains that the artifact "is first and foremost considered to be a representative of the larger context of the culture from which it derives. Hence, it is read . . . as synecdoche," a small part that comes to signify the whole (*Double* 78). Implicit in this way of presenting objects is the perception of cultural difference and fetishistic disavowal. We read an object as synecdoche by assuming the unity and homogeneity of that culture. The object becomes information about that culture and acquires the status of proof. When a museum exhibits objects as artifacts, it discourages the visitor from perceiving the work's aesthetic qualities and its status as representation. The objects are perceived as not "our own," separating them and severing them from us (Bal, *Double* 78–81).

The Sephardi Museum, as we have seen, aims at reincorporating Jewish identity into Spanish identity, but by implicitly defining Jewish identity through objects associated with a normative understanding of Jewish religion, the exhibit sets a distancing mechanism into motion. These exhibits do not normalize Jewish life but rather exoticize it, giving the impression that the people portrayed are far removed from present-day reality, strange people with strange customs (see a similar point in Gruber, *Virtually Jewish* 162). Bertz explains how these unknown or unrecognizable objects produce "a sense of alienation or a feeling that such objects (and those making use of them) were themselves alien or 'exotic'" (87). Offe observes, "Jewish life located solely in Jewish museums . . . seems remote, cut off from current developments. Its exhibition in glass cases creates the impression of something outside normal life" (88). This impression is magnified in this exhibit by the fact that not a single one of the objects displayed in the "Judaism as a way of life" case comes from Spain.

This estrangement is further reinforced in the *Celebrations Cycle* exhibit in the Women's Gallery on the building's second floor. There, several glass cases explain Jewish holidays and celebrations through a series of objects and photographs. One of these items is identified as a Sephardi Chair of Elijah, or circumcision chair. Next to it, an explanatory panel tells us the chair comes from Jerusalem, dates from the nineteenth century, is made of wood and ivory details, is decorated with a Star of David, and contains a biblical inscription in Hebrew.

On the upper section of this explanatory panel, we find a reproduction of the eighteenth-century print *La circoncisione–La circoncision* by Antonio Baratti. The image appears with no information about its provenance: without date, title, or author, it is there as if neutrally illustrating a circumcision ceremony that ends up standing for all circumcision ceremonies, as if no mediation existed between reality and this very specific and historically bound print's representation of it.[25] Baratti composed this engraving from a sketch by Pietro Antonio Novelli, a Venetian artist fully involved in the then burgeoning publishing industry. Novelli's main clients were the nobility and the Catholic Church. The intended audience for this circumcision scene was probably curious Catholic nobles for whom Novelli acted as a popular anthropologist. This exhibition exemplifies Bal's definition of exposition as "gestures that point to things and seem to say: 'Look!'—often implying: 'that's how it is'" (*Double* 2). Exposing, says Bal, "works much like a third-person, realistic narrative, as in the tradition of the great realist fiction of the nineteenth century . . . although every visitor knows at an intuitive level that an exposition is a representation, the presence of the object provides an undeniable urge to recognize its 'truth'" (*Double* 5).

Why is there a copy, a photograph, of this print, and not the original, which the museum actually owns?[26] It would have been feasible to display Baratti's engraving with an indication of its status as representation (title, artist's name, date), as the museum does with other artworks. However, this sketch, reproduced industrially as an engraving and now reduced to a photograph on a narrative panel, hides its history of production and circulation to become an "objective" illustration of a ritual. This rhetorical gesture is repeated in the other photographs exhibited in the Women's Gallery. We are shown contemporary photographs of Jews performing religious rituals, like a young man at his bar mitzvah. Ritual objects made into artifacts, prints made into photographs, and photographs made into truth all contribute to an exhibit that objectifies and makes strange the people and practices it portrays.

The effect of estrangement is compounded throughout in a series of mini-installations that aim to explain Judaism and Jewish practice by simulating scenes of Jewish life, a practice that Gruber also finds in other European Jewish museums (Gruber, *Virtually Jewish* 161). As these installations and virtual reconstructions attempt to render Jewish cultural practices hypervisible and "accessible," they intensify the distancing effect. An example in the Women's Gallery is the Shabbat table set with plates, glasses, eating utensils, candleholders, bread, and wine that no one will ever eat or drink. In the same section, we also find objects in positions that would only make sense if a person were holding them, like the scene of an open prayer book with an open tallit above it, suspended in the air, in the shape that it would have if a person were wearing it (see fig. 3.4). Like the table set as if an invisible family were sitting at it, these ritual clothes stand in front of us as if worn by a ghost. The tallit that appeared folded in the glass case of Room 1 is here worn by an absent

Figure 3.4. Shabbat table, Women's Gallery, Sephardi Museum. ©Adrián Pérez Melgosa.

man. As occurs in the Jewish Quarters analyzed in the previous chapter, by attempting to make a Jewish religious practice visible and accessible, the scene cannot avoid showing its practitioner's literal invisibility and erasure, this person's absence.[27]

Continuing our itinerary, Rooms 2 and 3 are dedicated to Jewish life in Spain during the Roman, Visigoth, and Arab periods.[28] The most outstanding characteristic here is that three small cases can accommodate remnants from a period that spans seventeen centuries. The cases contain a few unmarked lamps and jugs, Latin and Arab coins, and stone inscriptions with tenuous Jewish connections. The one object that stands out, exhibited in a separate glass case, is the fifth-century marble basin inscribed in Hebrew, Latin, and Greek and decorated with peacocks, which the museum uses as its symbol. The label explains that the basin was probably used in a synagogue for ritual washing or ablutions and later repurposed as a sink, but it also notes that historians like Cantera Burgos believe it might be a child's ossuary used in cemeteries to place the bones of the dead. This possibility, of the basin's not being a washbowl but an ossuary, connects the few objects exhibited in the room to the following space of the museum, the North Patio, or Garden of Memory, which we enter from a door in the middle of Room 2.

Bertz observes that in the case of Germany, the establishment of Jewish museums was prompted less by preserved collections than by preserved buildings, most often synagogues (89). As we have seen, this is also the case for the Sephardi Museum. In the national museum of Spanish Jewish life, there is a dearth of Spanish Jewish objects shown. Not only are most objects not from Spain, but among those that actually are, the most numerous, visible, and massive are mortuary objects: the gravestones that compose the Garden of Memory, and, perhaps the ossuary/sink. The gravestones on the North Patio have been among the objects on exhibit since the museum's opening in 1971. Before the reforms of 1985–94, they were situated in the middle of each room of the museum, without any kind of explanatory plaque. As we will see, much thinking has taken place since then to carefully historicize and contextualize them.

As we enter the patio, we find the large granite and marble gravestones on the floor, each labeled with a description of its shape and material and a short narrative identifying where it was discovered, to whom they were dedicated, and the dates of their crafting. A different panel contains a reproduction of the Hebrew inscriptions from every gravestone followed by their Spanish translations. The inscriptions honor the dead to whom they were dedicated, praising them and describing their lives and accomplishments. Most of the gravestones date from the fourteenth century and were originally placed in Jewish cemeteries, but after the Jews were expelled in 1492 and these cemeteries became property of the Catholic Monarchs, the stones were used for a variety of purposes. Most of those exhibited in the museum were found in the nineteenth or early twentieth centuries in private homes or convents, where they had been used as watering troughs or laundry sinks for centuries. In them, we see clear signs of damage and traces of their post-1492 uses: some are chiseled down, their inscriptions partly erased and several contain drain holes that were carved in them to drain water when used as sinks. Ironically, this transition from gravestone to sink resounds with the ambivalence attached to the identity of the child's ossuary/basin that the museum has chosen as its symbol (see fig. 3.5).

Presiding over the stones, we see a wall with a poem by the Jewish medieval philosopher, linguist, poet, and rabbi from Granada, Moses ibn Ezra (1055–1136), engraved in large metallic Hebrew characters and, next to it, a small plaque with the Spanish translation. Exhibiting the poem in this space, its staging among the tombstones, serves the purpose of aligning the poem's message with that of the museum. The poem reads:

Figure 3.5. Garden of Memory: Jewish gravestones framed by poem of Ibn Ezra, North Patio, July 2014. ©Daniela Flesler.

> Son tumbas viejas, de tiempos antiguos,
> en las que unos hombres duermen el sueño eterno.
> No hay en su interior ni odio ni envidia,
> ni tampoco amor o enemistad de vecinos.
> Al verlas, mi mente no es capaz de distinguir
> entre esclavos y señores.
>
> [Ancient graves weathered by time,
> where people now are sleeping forever:
> they have neither hate nor envy within them;
> they know no love or fear of their neighbor.
> And seeing them so, I couldn't discern
> The difference between a slave and his master].[29]

Ibn Ezra's ubi sunt–themed poem speaks of the equalization, equanimity, and absence of feeling brought by the finality of death. The poem begins by explaining its setting: the poet is looking at old graves, from old times. The placement of this particular poem here thus invites us to identify with the poet's perspective and to take the poem's words as indicative both of what we are looking at and of the feelings we should experience. So by exhibiting the poem stating that in the graves' interior there is no hate, envy, love, or enmity and that, looking at these graves, we cannot distinguish among slaves and masters, the museum is inviting us to contemplate *these* gravestones, the ones *we*, as visitors to the museum, are looking at, through the equalizing perspective of the poet's eyes. The highly visible location of the poem is intended to inscribe and control our reading of the gravestones (especially those who read Hebrew). But the very presence of these gravestones emptied of the human remains they were made to protect, so far away from the cemetery where they were originally placed, along with the traces of mutilations performed in order to force them into new uses, tells a story very different from that of the poet's gaze.

On the door that opens onto the patio a panel—in Spanish only—provides historical context to the stones exhibited. It tells us that the stones were originally situated in Jewish cemeteries all over Spain: those of Toledo, Barcelona, Gerona, León, Palencia, La Palloza (Galicia), Béjar (Salamanca), and Sevilla. Underneath this explanation, a reproduction of a document signed by Queen Isabel in December 1492 and written for the Catholic Church authorities in Toledo adds to the story. It is, we realize, the document through which Queen Isabel I grants "permission" to the Church of Toledo to take the gravestones of Toledo's Jewish cemetery and use them as they see fit:

> Por la presente vos fago merced e gracia donación pura e perfecta e non reuocable que es dicha entre biuos, para agora e en todo tienpo e syenpre jamas, de toda la piedra que ouiere i me pertenesciere en el honsario de los judíos desa dicha cibdad para los hedificios i lauores de la dicha yglesia quedando la dicha tierra i suelo del dicho honsario para común de la dicha cibdad de Tolledo para que la dicha piedra i suelo del dicho honsario podades hazer e fagades todo lo que quisyeredes i por bien touieredes commo de cosa vuestra propia. I por esta dicha mi carta vos do licencia i facultad i auctorida para tomar e apprehender e aver la posesión real i actual vel quasi i sennorio e propiedad i dominio vtille i directo de las dichas piedras del dicho honsario

> [Through this letter I confer upon you the mercy and grace of the pure and perfect and irrevocable donation as is stated among the living, for now and forever, of all the stones that may exist and may belong to me in the cemetery of the Jews of this said city for the buildings and construction of the said church relegating the said land and soil of said cemetery for the common use of the said city of Toledo so that the said stone and land of said cemetery

> you can and may do anything you might want and that you may consider it and own it as if it were your own. And by this my said letter I give you license and faculty and authority to take and apprehend and take real and actual possession of this estate and property and useful and direct control of said stones of said cemetery]

Queen Isabel's letter contains a speech act—a performative speech that enacts the message of its words. Through this letter she is in fact both taking possession and bequeathing the stones she just seized to the Church of Toledo. In a reiterative manner, the words emphasize that the donation is irrevocable; that since the stones belong to her, the church's authorities can do whatever they want with them; that they should act as if the stones were their own; that it gives them license, faculty, and authority to take the stones and have total and actual possession of them. This is the justification of the back-conversion of a memorial object into a commodity that may be used as building material. What is not explicitly said, but subsists as a tacit understanding behind her words, is that the stones belonged, until very recently, to someone else; that the queen has in fact been in possession of them for less than a year; that the stones are, in fact, "de los judíos." The "pure and perfect and irrevocable" nature of the transaction is undermined by the fact that its legitimacy needs to be so acutely emphasized and repeated throughout the document.

The ownership of these and other Jewish gravestones and remains taken from cemeteries all over Spain has in fact been highly contested and has become a matter of recent bitter controversy, as we see in the next chapter. In their current use as part of the Garden of Memory exhibition, the gravestones are returned to their function as memorial objects but also put to new use as museum pieces. They are thus converted, like the synagogue itself, into a cultural commodity that serves the current purposes of the museum.

The gravestones' connection to the museum, the advisability of exhibiting them there and the question of which is their proper home have also been subjects of debate. Contradictory decisions in this regard throughout the twentieth century have resulted in the gravestones' being moved back and forth between Toledo's Archeological Museum (today Museo de Santa Cruz [Museum of the Holy Cross]) and the Sephardi Museum. As Palomero Plaza explains, in 1916 eight gravestones with Hebrew inscriptions were moved from the Archeological Museum to the synagogue, obeying an order issued by the Ministry of Public Instruction and Fine Arts. In the 1920s, a different order resulted in the transference of the gravestones to the Archeological Museum. Between the years 1964 and 1969, upon the official creation of the Sephardi Museum in the synagogue, the Museum of the Holy Cross gave them in deposit to the Sephardi Museum. In exchange, the Sephardi Museum gave the Museum of the Holy Cross the Calatravan knights' tombstones (Palomero Plaza 112–14).

As we saw in terms of the building's modern reforms, these exchanges reveal an anxiety over the precise demarcation of the borders between Christian and Jewish identities. The Jewish gravestones, no matter their geographical provenance, would now belong in this museum of "Jewish things" and the Christian gravestones, no matter that they had been at the synagogue for four hundred years, would be moved to an "all Christian" museum, empty of Jewish remains. Only Jewish objects would be exhibited at the Sephardi Museum. The ironies of these decisions are multiple: the classification of the gravestones as either Jewish or Christian in order to be located in their proper place seems to obey purity of blood statutes. As we have shown, the synagogue's converso status appears unremarked on in the museum's curatorial decisions. At the same time, the building has been characterized by the museum's authorities as "a child of mixed blood."

Selma Holo describes how these gravestones exemplify the difficulty of some of the decisions that the museum's directors have had to make: "At the opening reception of the museum some knowledgeable Jewish guests remarked that the presence of these stones immediately adjacent to the synagogue was markedly un-Jewish. They pointed out that according to Jewish law a cemetery had to be located outside the precincts of the town—never on the grounds of a synagogue" (73). The answer to the Jewish guests was that this was not a synagogue but a museum and not a cemetery but a "garden of memory" (Holo 73). They had, however, said in different contexts that this space was conceived as an "open-air cemetery" (Palomero Plaza 169; López Alvarez et al., *Guía* 2011, 119). The question of whether these gravestones are today next to a synagogue is a slippery one too, related to the question of what exactly is the nature of this building. There were also requests by the Jewish community to occasionally use the synagogue for religious services that were denied on the grounds that the building was now a secular museum, not a religious site.

This disagreement between Jewish guests and non-Jewish museum authorities over the identity of the space, together with the back-and-forth decisions about where to house these gravestones, emanates from Queen Isabel's so-called donation and subsequent use of the stones. Implicit in the history of these gravestones is an unresolved violence that stands in contrast to the message of peace and reconciliation that the museum intends to project. The actual graves containing human remains that the poetic voice of ibn Ezra's poem spoke of used to rest in a Jewish cemetery located, we presume, as Jewish law prescribes, on the outskirts of a city. The Garden of Memory, thoughtful and well-intentioned as it is, cannot avoid the fact that these stones are now disconnected from the remains of the people they speak about. They belong neither in a cemetery nor to the community that made them, and they exhibit the physical traces of a subsequent use that scorned the sacred function for which they were intended.

Their placement in this quasi-cemetery next to a quasi-synagogue in fact mimics the Catholic practice of placing cemeteries next to churches and reminds us of the Christian, or shall we say converso, post-expulsion period of the history of the building, when the Calatravan knights were literally buried under the Great Prayer Room of the synagogue. More than remnants of medieval Jewish life in Spain, these gravestones are indices of the interruption and transformation of that life and its memory.[30] Through their dual identity as gravestones and washbasins, these objects convey a double drive for the museum as a whole: to memorialize the Spanish Jewish past and also to wash it away, to cleanse and mask the violence and excesses suggested by the near absence of Spanish Jewish remains and material culture and the history of the Jews who remained in Spain after 1492. In themselves, these out-of-place mortuary monuments become one more reminder of the loss that marks this and other Spanish Jewish museums, a loss redefined by the gravestones as irreversible given that it is marked by death.

From the patio, we reenter the building at Room 3, dedicated to the Jewish communities in Christian Spain from the twelfth through the fifteenth centuries. The few objects salvaged and exhibited in this room embody in their histories of displacement and decontextualization described in their labels the material destruction of Jewish life in Spain. Thus, these exhibits continue the narrative thread of death, expropriation, and dispossession that the Garden of Memory both shows and conceals. The cases contain a capital from a column dating back to the twelfth or thirteenth century found in the convent of San Juan de los Reyes and thought to have belonged to one of the Toledo synagogues destroyed in 1391. Next to it, we see a group of stucco fragments showing traces of intricate geometric decorations and Hebrew letters. These were part of the Halevi synagogue and were found buried in the building's well during the 2002 archaeological excavation. Here, we also find copies of a famous set of fifteenth-century dishes, the so-called Tesorillo de Briviesca (Briviesca's Little Treasure). This "treasure" provides a good example of the difficulty of assigning a Jewish identity to medieval artifacts found across Spain.[31] The pieces associated with them also become emblematic of museums' drive to construct a formulaic version of Jewish identity and to dismiss the complex mixture of attachments, cultural forms and social strategies that characterized medieval Jewish culture. In fact, apart from specific design features in ceremonial and ritual objects, Jewish material culture in Iberia—clothes, architecture, furniture, housewares—was very similar to that of the Jews' Christian and Muslim neighbors. Medieval Iberian Jews shared the aesthetic taste of the societies in which they lived. Differences were dictated more by economic status than by religious identity.

In 1938, a group of construction workers found a clay vessel buried below the foundation of a house in Bivriesca (Burgos). Hidden inside were coins, several silver plates, silver and gold horse ornaments, rings, earrings, and other jewelry. In an official archaeological study from 1938, the original owners of the objects are described as a noble local family (because of several coats of arms found), probably of warrior linage (as implied by the quality of the horse ornaments), and of distinguished taste (visible in the careful detail of the Arabic engravings on the silver plates) (Monteverde 4, 5, 9). The *tesorillo,* concluded the report, was probably hidden by this noble family in 1367 as a precaution against the predatory behavior of the troops sent to Castile by the Prince of Wales against King Don Pedro (Monteverde 11). Yet when two more of these buried treasures appeared later, one in 1985 and another in 1988, they were identified as possibly Jewish.

By 2002, when some of the findings unearthed in Briviesca were shown in Toledo as part of a special exhibit entitled *Memory of Sepharad,* this new Jewish identity had been established: they became the "tesorillos judíos de Briviesca." For the exhibit, one of the foremost specialists on this site, Belén Castillo Iglesias, provided a new interpretation of the evidence and reimagined the owners of the hidden treasures as a Jewish community rather than a single family. The new narrative paid attention to the location of the findings (all on the same street and in the area of the medieval Jewish Quarter of Briviesca) and the accumulation of portable wealth in money and family heirlooms found (so many that it seems probable that they came from several families). This new interpretation identified a new historical framework to justify the hiding of these objects: in 1366, after Enrique II defeated his half brother Pedro I for the crown of Castile, the victorious troops pillaged many Jewish communities that had been supporters of the defeated party (Castillo Iglesias 99, 100). Castillo Iglesias's discussion moves between affirming and questioning the treasure's provenance. After affirming that these circumstances "unambiguously demonstrate" the objects' Jewish filiation, she cites as puzzling the presence of heraldic objects and symbols of nobility, since their use remains undocumented among Jews in this period (102). The tesorillos, concluded Castillo Iglesias, were hidden by their Jewish owners. Yet most of these objects (all except the plates to which she assigned a ritual function for the Passover dinner) may not be indicative of medieval Jewish material culture in Castile (102).

Another conclusion may be derived from this frustrated search for Jewish material culture: dishes, coins, spoons, rings, and earrings could have been "Jewish" during the Iberian Middle Ages as long as they belonged to Jews or were used in Jewish contexts. Away from that relationship, the object itself might have originated from and would easily become part of other communities and other cultural practices. In this sense, we can reread the exhibition cases in Room 1, which, in addition to ritual objects, contain quotidian objects that do not have any visible Jewish markers: glasses, plates, and jars that could have belonged to a Christian or Muslim family as well. These everyday utensils present a competing narrative to that of difference and otherness, rendering their owners indistinguishable from their neighbors.

Through the exhibition of Jewish objects, the museum participates in what Sabine Offe (86) terms "the discourse of salvage and rescue," by which objects and buildings "are salvaged and dug out, rediscovered and restored." Offe meditates on the ultimate irony contained in this act of restoration: "a fictitious, symbolic gesture of attention, respect, and shelter that the museum bestows on the object and that was never granted to its owner" (87). A profound ambivalence becomes palpable again. As the museum proudly exhibits the beautiful objects that have been reincorporated into Spain's national identity narrative, the objects themselves become the traces of an absence, of those who were systematically excluded from Spain's national project. As Offe puts it, "the buildings symbolizing memory, the synagogues transformed into museums, testify to the absence of those who once dwelt in them; the objects displayed and turned into symbols of salvage refer to the murder of those who once cherished them" (87).

RETURN AND RESCUE

This narrative of destruction and loss, which the museum ambivalently, reluctantly, displays in its three first rooms, coexists with the redeeming story of return and renewal that the museum wants to highlight. This narrative begins at the East Patio, conceived as a rest area, and a gathering space for concerts, lectures, and other educational activities the museum frequently offers. This patio gestures toward the past of the synagogue but also toward the present and its future. It exhibits the results of the archaeological excavations undertaken in 1987–90 and a gravestone from one of the Calatravan knights who used to be buried inside the synagogue, a token of the use of the building as Calatravan church, archive, and burial ground.[32]

But the objects that are the clear protagonists of the patio's exhibition are five metal sculptures by contemporary Jewish artists. Three of them, the bronze *Warrior II, Baruch Espinosa,* and *Teacher with Disciples,* are works by David Aronson. Born in Lithuania in 1923, Aronson immigrated to Boston with his Orthodox Jewish parents as a child. He is known for his expression of what art critics have called the "in-between cultures" condition of the immigrant experience. The two other sculptures are abstract works by Martina Lasry, the artist who emigrated from Tangiers to Madrid in 1961. *Genesis* and *Messianic Era,* both from 2002, are part of her work on the symbolism of Hebrew letters, inspired by the book of Zohar and the Cabala. These five sculptures are the first elements of the museum to represent Judaism as a living culture. They capture histories of displacement and immigration from the twentieth century and connect them both with their artists' histories and with contemporary global concerns. Thus, these artworks become connected to present Jewish life and aim to connect and implicate the museum's visitors. Through the work and life of Lasry, present-day Spain at least begins to make an appearance as an active destination in this global map of movement and circulation of Jewish people and objects. Palomero Plaza saw these works as "showing the vitality and creativity of present-day Judaism" (Palomero Plaza 160). These sculptures thus introduce a new narrative to the visit: that of Jewish return to Spain and Spain's implied desire for redemption.

Reentering the main building, we find two set of stairs leading both up to the Women's Gallery on the second floor and down to Room 4, which connects with the museum's Great Prayer Room again, the bookstore, and the exit. On the walls of the stairs leading up to the second floor, we encounter several paintings by contemporary Jewish artists: the abstract painting *Door of Jerusalem* by Anna Lentsch and two expressionist portraits, *Maimónides* by David Aronson and *Sephardi Woman or Mourning Woman* by Benjamin Levy. On the upper landing, next to the door of the Women's Gallery, we see a realistic oil portrait with some naïf traces entitled *Alegrina Pinto Coriat.* Painted by Andrés Parladé y Heredia between 1910 and 1930, the portrait is intrinsically connected to the recent history of the museum since Pinto Coriat is the mother of Jacques M. Pinto, the Moroccan Jewish businessman who, having relocated to Spain in the 1960s, became one of the museum's main benefactors. The presence of these contemporary works of art continues and enhances the message of the East Patio: Jewish culture is not dead and does not belong to the distant past. It has a dynamic present and a modern history. After the stories and evidence of death, absence, and destruction experienced in the previous spaces of the museum, these contemporary works of art speak of life and survival.

Continuing with the thematic thread of Jewish life in the present, and the individualization of the people represented by the objects in the exhibits, we arrive at the Women's Gallery, which occupies the entire second floor. This room is now dedicated to the cycle of Jewish celebrations, to their modern and contemporary history and, in connection with Room 4, at the bottom of the stairs, to Sephardi Jews. Some of the objects exhibited in this room were donated by Sephardi families who, like Lasry, moved from Morocco to Spain in the twentieth century. Among them, we find a manuscript containing the circumcision registry of Rabbi Isaac Vidal Ha-Serfaty from Tetuán, with data entries between 1880 and 1941, very possibly belonging to the set of objects the museum acquired from Raquel Ha-Serfaty Chocrón (López Alvarez et al., *Guía* 2006, 29), who appears in a 1975 BOE registry as having taken Spanish nationality that year. We also find the marriage contract between Massod Abecassis and Rachel Ben Assayag, from Morocco, 1904, donated by Ruben Benaim of Ceuta and reproduced in full color as cover image of the 2011 edition of the museum guide. Other objects represent Sephardi communities established in other parts of Europe and North Africa: Italy, France, the Balkans, and Tunisia. We also find here a panel explaining the history of Jewish return to Spain in the modern era, beginning with the reencounter with Sephardi Jews during the Hispano-Moroccan War in 1859–60 and describing present-day Jewish communities in Spain.

The highlight of this room is not an object, however, but the magnificent view of the Great Prayer Room from its five open balconies. The experience of looking at the Prayer Room from the synagogue's second floor constitutes the climax of the museum's walk-through. We see the Great Prayer Room from this new perspective, both spatially, from above, and from the perspective of the knowledge we have acquired by having walked through the museum. Bal explains, "As in reading a novel, where the reader accumulates an understanding and affective relationship with the events and characters, walking through an exhibition creates, in the experience of the visitor, an accumulative relationship with the art on display." This accumulative relationship has, as its outcome, an effect (Bal, "Exhibition" 20). Viewing the Great Prayer Room for the second time, from the high-angle panoramic view of the balcony, produces a strong impression. The view becomes a culminating and simultaneous experience of the building's stories as survivor, testimony, example, and exception. As survivor, testimony, and example of a past period of splendor, the building inspires us with the awe associated with an object of glory. Yet its being an exception to the widespread destruction of Jewish material culture also brings the viewer in contact with its status as a survivor, testimony, and example of an act of shame.

At the far western end of the room and next to a balcony, a small mock-up provides a view of what the Great Prayer Room might have originally looked like. In the model, the intricate stucco decorations of the walls appear painted in bright white, red, and green colors. An intense light filters through the windows, giving the room a lively and luminous appearance.

From the balcony, visitors also have a commanding panoramic perspective of the Great Prayer Room in all its magnificence (see fig. 3.6). We can see the length of the room from west to east and also view more closely the Hebrew inscriptions that now stand closer to our eye level and to the ceiling with its elaborate woodwork designs.

As our eyes go back and forth between the miniature model of the synagogue's past and the grandeur of its present reconstruction, we become more patently aware of the careful restorations that the museum has undertaken. The lively colors of the mock-up reveal their simplicity in comparison to the faded patches of painting on the walls and the fragmented or cracked stucco decorations of the real building. The unavoidable comparison implies that the history of the building, its endurance against all odds and its rescue have endowed it with a magnificence and gravity that surpasses the original's.

Thus, the synagogue's transformation into a museum, a transformation that the museum identifies with democratic Spain, becomes resignified. The juxtaposition of the imagined original to the restored present form emphasizes once again, this time as knowledge born out of the visitor's experience of the space, the underlying narrative expressed throughout the visit; the museum wants to be read as a restorative gesture whose function is to undo the historic wrong to a Jewish culture that was persecuted and destroyed in the past and to revive the convivencia ideal as a myth useful to the present. The restoration of the synagogue becomes a stand-in for the restoration of Jewish heritage to Spain's national memory. Offe argues that Jewish museums make visible the memory of a shared past and its loss: "By being there, geographically, physically, and by being listed on maps, in telephone books, in guidebooks, in tourist offices, and in subway stations, their physical presence can be seen as a reintegration into a memory, which reconstitutes symbolically in buildings what those to be remembered were denied, their *droit de cité*" (84–85). This *droit de cité* goes in a double direction here: first toward the past, to the reconstitution of the rights that Jews were denied after 1492 in Spain, but also toward the present, to the legitimization of the current model of Spanish democracy.

Figure 3.6. Great Prayer Room from Women's Gallery balcony, July 2015. ©Adrián Pérez Melgosa.

As we proceed down the stairs to the last exhibition room in the museum, we encounter the contemporary oil portrait *Samuel Halevi* by Daniel Quintero. We analyze this painting in the context of Quintero's work on Spain's Sephardi memory in chapter 6. In Room 4, dedicated to Sephardi Jews, we encounter an emblematic exhibit contributing to this narrative movement away from destruction and willful effacement of this destruction into restoration and redemption. At first sight, the objects seem simple enough, starting with one more iteration of previous exhibits in the Women's Gallery: a studio photograph shows a couple dressed festively. Next to them, two mannequins, one male and one female, stand dressed in similar clothes. The people in the photograph are identified as R. Yishaq Ha-Serfaty and Rahel Obadia. The garments, a label indicates, are part of the traditional Moroccan Sephardi wedding attire. The juxtaposition of photograph and mannequins introduces a reality effect to the exhibit that is further reinforced by the presence, between the two mannequins, of a marriage contract signed on July 2, 1919, by Moisés J. Emergui and Esther J. Moryusef in Larache, Morocco. We also see their paper wedding invitations. In a way similar to the sculptures by Lasry, these objects are resignified through their identifying label. In this case, the caption says that the whole ensemble is on loan from the Emergui family from Alcázar and Larache (Marruecos) and Madrid (see fig. 3.7).

Again, individual identity is foregrounded here. These mannequins are not mere placeholders standing for whole groups of people. The caption transforms the wedding garment exhibit into a story of survival, continuity, and return. The Emergui family wedding garments are thus evidence of a peculiar *longue durée* narrative, one that, starting at the home of a Sephardi family in Larache in 1919, points both to the past of 1492, when their ancestors left Spain, and to the present, when their descendants live in Madrid. A similar story emerges from the background of the texts that accompany the exhibit. They were written by Jacob Hassán, one of the foremost specialists in Sephardi language, literature, and culture in Spain. Hassán, who died in 2006, was a founding member of the Association of Friends of the Sephardi Museum and member of the museum's Consejo Asesor Científico. Like Lasry's, the Pinto-Coriats', and the Emerguis', Hassán's personal story exemplifies this pattern of return to contemporary Spain.[33] Together with the works of art, regalia, and narratives connected to present-day Sephardi Jews, these exhibits display something perhaps more important for the museum, the willingness of these returned Sephardi Jews to collaborate with it. This not only serves to legitimate the project of the museum as a whole but also allows the museum's narrative to culminate in a tale of redemption.

Figure 3.7. "Sephardi Jews" Room, July 2014. ©Daniela Flesler.

As we have seen, relocated Moroccan Jews played a pivotal role in the creation and development of the museum. As members of the museum's Association of Friends, they have helped with the restoration of the building, made key donations, placed important pieces in deposit and helped in the programming of its activities. The first cultural event at the museum was the 1982 ceremony honoring Jacques Pinto. The mayor of Toledo presided over it and placed a commemorative plaque in his honor (López Álvarez et al., *Guía* 2006, 29–30). In 1993, King Juan Carlos I and Queen Sofía gave the annual Royal Toledo Foundation Award (a prize awarded to people or institutions who have performed outstanding work on behalf of the historical patrimony) to the Pinto family for their substantial contributions of property, artifacts, and funds to the museum (Holo 74).

The museum's connection to Jews living in today's Spain, to their lives and culture, has increased over the years. This relationship is a central objective of the current museum administration. Since 2004, the museum has significantly increased its educational and cultural activities, which include exhibitions of contemporary art, music concerts, lectures, courses offered in conjunction with the University of Castilla–La Mancha, book presentations, theater and dance performances, film festivals, and community outreach to schools and families. These activities show the vibrancy and contemporaneity of Jewish life and culture, thus offsetting the impression that Jews and their culture are things of the past, only accessible through fragments rescued through careful archaeological work—an impression that visitors might be left with by the ethnographic/historical sections of the museum.

By reconnecting the past and the present, the museum reinforces the message of tolerance and inclusiveness it wants to promote. In reference to controversy caused by contemporary art exhibits, Palomero Plaza has explained that contemporary work by Jewish artists shows Hispanic-Jewish culture as something belonging to the present, not confined to the past, and has explained that the museum wants to make this statement about Jewish culture's being alive (Palomero Plaza 217–22).[34] Indeed, these contemporary artists, together with the supporters and donors aforementioned, embody in their work and life stories the currency, wide pluralism, and diversity that characterize Jewishness, a fact not at the forefront of the permanent exhibit in the ethnographic/historical rooms.

This linkage between past and present also serves the museum's mission in a different way, rescuing medieval Toledo as a city that can model tolerance and convivencia for the present. Palomero Plaza posits that the museum's building itself is the epitome of "the lesson of medieval tolerance and cultural intermixing that Toledo gave the world in the Middle Ages" and that it is essential that this lesson should not remain a mere reference from a mythical past, but be reactivated today.[35] To develop this vision of tolerance and respect for diversity, the museum has set forth several initiatives that closely connect with its cultural and outreach activities.[36] This vision is also highlighted in the museum's shop and bookstore. The books about Jewish and Sephardi cooking, the history of Sephardi Jews in Spain, Jews in Latin America, the Jewish quarter of Toledo, and Judaism explained to non-Jews seem to address that ideal, "just" visitor welcomed by the beam fragment at the entrance, the one who "wants to know." Many souvenirs also address the museum's objective of transmitting a message of peace and respect for difference, like the 2014 calendar "Tiempos para la convivencia" produced by Fundación Pluralismo y

Convivencia, a state-owned foundation created in 2004 that seeks to promote religious freedom and cooperation with religious minorities in Spain (Pluralismo). The calendar, whose title, like many elements of the museum, tries to bring about a connection between the medieval past and the present, includes various Jewish, Muslim, Buddhist, and Christian religious holidays.

CONCLUSION

Many critics have explained how state museums serve as sites where national narratives are created as privileged arenas for the articulation of identity (Karp 14–15; Zolberg 70; Lebovics, *Bringing* 143). The roots of the ambiguities of the Sephardi Museum lie in the paradoxical fact that it attempts to create a national narrative of tolerance and pluralism through the reincorporation of Jewish culture in Spain, yet it cannot avoid evoking in its exhibits the complexities of that history. In the same way that Jewish museums in other parts of Europe cannot avoid speaking about the Holocaust and the issue of looted art (see Heimann-Jelinek; Purin), museums in Spain cannot avoid the facts and consequences of the attacks against Jews, the appropriations of their material culture, the Inquisition, their expulsion, and their concomitant five-century near absence.

Since its inception, the Sephardi Museum has been asked to perform two key tasks at the national level: provide a valuable instrument of education to help shape that "new Spanish" citizen who embodies democratic sensibility and establish itself as proof that the transformation, modernization, and internationalization of Spain have been achieved. As we have seen, the exhibits provide a portrait of Spain as a nation that has learned to value the historic presence of Jewish people among its citizens, a country that is sensitive to the achievements of Jewish people and their history of victimization. Yet the exhibits also point toward a society that remains highly resistant to acknowledging the full extent of the implications of its Jewish past in its present and the Spanishness of its current Jewish communities. Indeed, as described by Jacob Hassán, many people in the Jewish community in Spain do not see the Sephardi Museum as a "Jewish" institution that represents them and are thus reluctant to collaborate with it (Hassán, "De tolerado" 71–72).

This national museum dramatizes how Spanish society at large remains profoundly hesitant to fully explore the duplicities that haunt its relationship with Jewishness. The synagogue, its magnificent reconstruction and the care devoted to transforming it in the center of the museum attest to the bright side of this relationship, even if embedded in this care lies a self-serving purpose. Yet the history of damage and appropriations sustained by the synagogue itself and the great spaces of silence and loss that resound in the fragmentary nature and scattered origins of the exhibits speak of the deep shadows haunting Spain's relationship with its Jewish past and present. In spite of the museum's intention to make the most out of these fragments, it is impossible to escape the questions raised by the dearth of remnants of a group of people who populated the Iberian Peninsula for more than one thousand years.

Presence and absence, survival and destruction overlap among the museum's displays, composing a narrative steeped in ambivalence and contradiction. In this sense, we can interpret some of the characteristics of the Sephardi Museum as moves to preempt accusation or as strategies to work through guilt. As Sabine Offe argues in the case of German Jewish museums, "museums are not just places that exhibit objects but places that institutionalize a ritual space . . . a place to deal with guilt in a highly ritualized way" (85). Borrowing Carol Duncan's concept of art museums as spaces for "rituals of citizenship," Offe speaks of the tragic irony stemming from the "symbolic gesture of attention, respect, and shelter that the museum bestows on the object and that was never granted its owner." This gesture serves as an "imaginative act of restoration" (Offe 87; see also Purin 143). Like most post-1945 Jewish museums in Europe, Spain's Sephardi museum repeats this poignant gesture.

Yet the converso narrative that we have attempted to rescue adds another layer of complexity to this observation. What most seems to stir the museum's and the nation's unease is not on display and concerns that group of people of Jewish origin who never left Spain but continued living in the same streets and praying in some of the same buildings. The very fact of their presence introduced a set of disturbances to the officially preferred narrative of mutual incompatibility and contradistinction between Jewish and Catholic Spain. These disturbances or dissonances can be read in the Sephardi Museum's building and exhibitions: the surviving Hebrew inscriptions presiding throughout centuries of masses, the chapel of a Calatravan monk fearful of his family's converso connections who still chooses to rest eternally within the former synagogue's walls, the external cross and bell tower topping the main facade of a synagogue become Jewish museum, the tombstones removed from Jewish cemeteries and repurposed as water basins first and as emblems of democracy later, the engraved words that once welcomed Jewish worshippers transformed into a salute to tourists, and the museum itself as both site of memory and symbol of convivencia in a city that historically has been emblematic of Catholic and Francoist Spain.

Jacob Hassán has described how the negotiations of identity vis-à-vis Jewish heritage and Catholicism carried out by both New and Old Christians produced the cultural substratum for the emergence of the cultural identity of modern Spain (Hassán, "Realidad" 357). The underplaying of the converso memory of the building that houses the Sephardi Museum amounts to a resistance to research into the very origins of the modern relationship of Spain and Jewishness. The Synagogue of the Transit is also, in spite of the silence about this issue in its current official use and narratives, a museum of converso Spain. As the exhibits continue to emphasize narratives of rescue of Sephardi culture as imaginative acts of restoration and the return of Sephardi Jews as proof of national redemption, the space of the museum continues to be haunted by the memory of the conversos.

NOTES

1. Currently only three medieval synagogues' buildings remain in Spain: two in Toledo (Sinagoga del Tránsito and Sinagoga de Santa María la Blanca) and one in Córdoba. Segovia's former Sinagoga Mayor, today Corpus Christi Church, was rebuilt in close architectural resemblance to the original temple after it burned in the nineteenth century. In 2003, ruins of the foundation and wall fragments of what archaeologists think might have been a medieval synagogue were discovered in Lorca (Murcia).

2. Art historian Juan Carlos Ruiz Souza has revised the dates of 1357–59 posited by traditional historiography, arguing that the synagogue was built between 1359 and 1361, after the construction of the Palace of Santa Clara of Tordesillas, in Valladolid, with which it shares architectonic and decorative characteristics. Pedro I had an excellent relationship with Muhamad V of Granada, and Ruiz Souza argues that the Granada emir's artists traveled to Tordesillas first and Toledo later to work for Pedro I during the intervening years of 1359 and 1362, after which the emir suffered a coup d'état (Palomero Plaza 80–81; Ruiz Souza 235–37). The mid-thirteenth-century Siete Partidas, the Council of Zamora in 1312, and the Ordenamiento de Alcalá of 1348 all prohibited building new non-Christian temples, although many of the regulations established by these laws were not enforced (Estow 168–69).

3. Clara Estow explains that the accusation that Pedro showed special favor to Jews was completely false, but it has had a "persistent lure, power and effectiveness" (173). For more on Halevi's relationship to King Pedro, see Estow's book *Pedro the Cruel of Castille, 1350–69*. In a chapter about Jews and power in medieval Europe from his book *Anti-Judaism*, David Nirenberg explains how "the love of Jews" was a common, powerful form of criticism labeled against Christian kings and frequently arose around debates over the limits of royal power. The accusations against King Pedro are a perfect example of this phenomenon (Nirenberg, *Anti-Judaism* 197–200).

4. The museum's official guide reproduces this language of "vicissitudes," of historical accident, utilizing the same word: "Las vicisitudes que atravesó la judería toledana, incluida la destrucción de parte del barrio judío en 1391, no afectaron a la sinagoga" [The vicissitudes that the Jews of Toledo went through, including the destruction of part of the Jewish quarter in 1391, did not affect the synagogue] (López Alvarez et al., *Guía* 13).

5. The drawing is included in the manuscript *De Toletano Hebraeorum Templo* written in Latin in 1752 by Francisco Pérez Bayer (Valencia 1711–94), librarian, theologian, Hebraist at the University of Salamanca, jurist, and important personality of his time. The manuscript constitutes the first monographic study of the synagogue and is a crucial historical source of information due to its detailed transcription of the Hebrew inscriptions found on the synagogue's walls and the inclusion of the exterior drawing by Palomares (Palomero Plaza 85). For a study of the medieval aspect of the synagogue's exterior, see architect Antonio Miranda Sánchez's book, *Reconstrucción de la portada medieval de la sinagoga del Tránsito*.

6. The relative number of those who were New Christian assimilationists in relation to those who were crypto-Jews is impossible to know, but the most credible recent scholarship believes that the first far outnumbered the second (Gitlitz 76).

7. The Catholic Monarchs' regard for the family can be seen in their actions regarding Álvarez de Toledo's children: the eldest son was made count of Cedillo by the Catholic Monarchs and when one of the daughters, Constanza de Toledo, married into the Ayala family in 1496, King Fernando and Queen Isabel donated part of her dowry (Martz 50–51).

8. The upward mobility of this family can be seen in the marriages of one of the daughters, Francisca Niño de Ribera, who married Pedro López de Ayala, the third count of Fuensalida, in the early 1530s. After his death, she married into the powerful Medina Sidonia house of Andalucía (Martz 104–7). As detailed in chapter 1, these are the ancestors of the powerful Count-Duke of Olivares, who would embark on a (ultimately unsuccessful) rapprochement of Spain and the Jews in the seventeenth century.

9. The numbers of conversos in each parish can be calculated based on Inquisition records of those punished and "pardoned." The Inquisition, established by the Catholic Monarchs in Spain in 1478, arrived in the city of Toledo in 1485. It operated in cycles of punishment and pardons. After punishments, conversos could buy a "rehabilitation," which consisted of penances, prohibitions, and exclusions from certain occupations and the monetary payment of one-fifth of one's estate. Those who relapsed were subject to be burned at the stake (Martz 61–62). "Pardon" phases in Toledo occurred in 1486–87 and in the mid-1490s. Inquisition records of the cash payments

have survived in the document *Judaizantes del arzobispado de Toledo,* which offers parish-by-parish names and professions of those conversos punished in earlier years. The number of those reconciled in Toledo in 1486 was about three thousand people. Linda Martz asserts that an educated guess of the total population of Toledo at the time would have been about twenty thousand, so the reconciled converso population would have been about 12 to 16 percent and the total converso population about 15 to 19 percent of the total population of Toledo (Martz 65–68).

10. Íñigo de Ayala y Rojas's grave, together with those of other Calatravan knights buried in the synagogue/church, would be moved to the Museo de Santa Cruz in the 1960s, upon the creation of the Sephardi Museum.

11. The painting was removed from the synagogue/church upon the ecclesiastical confiscations of Mendizábal in 1836, which resulted in the expropriation of monastic properties. It is today at the Prado Museum in Madrid (Cadiñanos Bardeci 11).

12. She had married Diego Romero, chief controller of Enrique IV, secretary of Juan II, and *alcalde mayor* of Toledo. Their daughter, Mencía Romero, married Iñigo Lopez de Ayala, a nephew of the first count of Fuensalida. Their daughter Aldonza de Ayala, Alonso and Iñigo's mother, married into the Rojas family (Martz 39–40) The family followed the common pattern of wealthy converso families marrying their daughters into Old Christian families of power and prestige (Martz 42).

13. While many people in Toledo were convinced that the woman condemned by the Inquisition was Alonso's great-grandmother Aldonza Núñez, other documents affirm that the woman condemned was Mayor Álvarez de Toledo, mother-in-law of Aldonza, and not Aldonza herself, in which case the "stain" would not directly affect Alonso de Rojas, although both women were buried in the same family crypt (Gonzálvez 67–68). The grave consequences of the accusation against the Rojas family can be seen in the extraordinary measures taken to investigate it: the Emperor Carlos V himself opened an investigation, which continued for 150 years (Gonzálvez 65–67). No "stain" in the family's blood could be proven and many witnesses testified to the family's "cleanness" from impure blood, but there are enough reasons to believe the accusation was true. The authorities in charge of the case in the seventeenth century were people like the general inquisitor and archbishop of Toledo Cardinal Bernardo de Sandoval y Rojas (1546–1618), whose honor and name were compromised in the case, since he had family ties with the Rojases (Gonzálvez 69). Martz (40) sees the exculpation of Aldonza Núñez as a clear case of "the genealogical distortions that occurred in later years as well-placed descendants sought to escape the stigma of an ancestor punished by the Inquisition."

14. As Inocencio Cadiñanos Bardeci explains in his 2006 article about the painting, identifying the donor as Francisco instead of Íñigo was a common mistake made throughout the twentieth century and can be traced back to the catalogs of the Prado Museum, where the painting is housed today (Cadiñanos Bardeci 6). Santiago Palomero Plaza told us that the Sephardi Museum followed the Prado Museum's information and that it would change the identification if the Prado does (personal interview, July 2015).

15. The Sephardi Museum, with about 300,000 annual visitors, ranks consistently as the most visited of the national museums of Spain (this list does not include the Prado and Reina Sofía Museums in Madrid, which receive about 3.0 million annual visitors each and are considered in a special, separate category). Most visitors are university graduates and come from Spain (59.8 percent), although this is one of the national museums most frequently visited by foreign nationals (45.0 percent). These foreign tourists come mainly from Europe and America (France 18.7 percent, United States 19.5 percent). Among the visiting groups, 16.0 percent are schoolchildren, a number that reflects the museum's emphasis on educational activities directed to them ("Conociendo"). The museum is one of the most-visited sites in Toledo. From the 1.5 to 1.7 million visitors Toledo receives annually, 1.0 million visit the cathedral; 600,000 visit the Church of Santo Tomé, which houses the painting *El entierro del conde de Orgaz* by El Greco; and 300,000 visit the Sephardi Museum, the Alcázar, and the monastery of San Juan de los Reyes (Palomero Plaza 232–33). Coinciding with the celebrations of El Greco, the museum received a record 350,000 visitors during 2014.

16. Soon after the synagogue became a national monument, restoration work was undertaken in order to alleviate the significant damage the building had undergone. In a 1900 report by the Academy of History in which this damage is assessed, it was decided that the building should be restored as a synagogue instead of as a church (Cantera Burgos 69).

17. In 1955, Francisco Cantera Burgos wrote *Sinagogas españolas*, a book that became a classic. In the section about the Synagogue of the Transit, he lamented the lack of attention and care suffered by the building at the time of his writing. He lists dust, water leaks, and visitors who steal floor tiles as the destructive agents that "act with ample freedom" against the synagogue (Cantera Burgos 89).

18. The provenance of some objects seems to have been directly linked to the actions of Franco's government in favor of Moroccan and Egyptian Jews during the Six-Day War. Angel Sagaz, Spanish ambassador in Egypt, writes in an August 1967 letter to Fernando María Castiella, minister of external relations: "Me expusieron el deseo de ofrecerme para su conservación en esta Embajada o su eventual traslado a España una serie de pergaminos y libros" [They expressed their desire to offer me a series of parchments and manuscripts

for their preservation in this embassy or, eventually, to be transferred to Spain]. Notwithstanding Sagaz's reluctance, given that these sacred objects were cataloged by the Egyptian government as artistic patrimony, some pieces were given to the Spanish embassy, writes Sagaz, "para que se conserven en la comunidad judía de Madrid. Me añadieron que en el futuro algunas de estas piezas desearían exhibirlas en la Sinagoga de Toledo" [so that they may be preserved within the Jewish Community of Madrid. They added that, in the future, they would like to exhibit some of these pieces in Toledo's Synagogue]. Sagaz concludes in a self-congratulatory and self-exculpatory note: "Creo que es de agradecer por nuestra parte que se confíe en España la custodia de aquellos objetos sagrados pertenecientes a sinagogas cerradas, es el único país que por razones evidentes puede y debe hacerlo" [I believe we must be grateful that the custody of those sacred objects belonging to closed down synagogues be entrusted to Spain, it is the only country which, for obvious reasons, can and must do it] (letter reproduced in González García, *Los judíos* 578).

19. Holo explains how other museums, most notably the Prado in Madrid, were not "useful" politically and were severely neglected in the same years.

20. In the Holocaust context, some synagogues' reconstructions have been criticized for attempting to reproduce the exact way a synagogue looked before the war, since this was seen as an undoing of post-1938 history (Gruber, *Virtually Jewish* 165). Berlin's New Synagogue's restoration is an example of the compromise "to make the history of the building and its builders perceptible through a visible contrast between magnificent architecture and its violent destruction." As Gruber describes the end result, "The ornate halls and exhibit displays end abruptly in a wall of glass overlooking a vast, open plaza, the space where the sanctuary once stood, with its rows of pews and its proudly prosperous congregation. Deliberately left empty, it is a conscious expression of absence that recalls not simply the destruction of the synagogue but the destruction of the Jewish congregation that once worshiped there and, by extension, the destruction of millions of other European Jews and their world as well" (*Virtually Jewish* 105). Architect Daniel Libeskind's famous design of Berlin's Jewish Museum also attempts to "give a void form without filling it in" (Young, *At Memory's Edge* 164).

21. Personal interview, July 11, 2014.

22. In *The Texture of Memory*, James E. Young describes museum exhibitions in similar terms, as aesthetic creations that narrate events for certain purposes, creating meaning and coherence, emplotting them in a narrative sequence (viii–ix).

23. A panel next to the beam shows Palomares's drawing together with the two Hebrew phrases translated into Spanish, indicating that the Spanish translations are taken from the classic 1955 book by Francisco Cantera Burgos, *Sinagogas españolas*.

24. We can see here echoes of the elegiac tradition in Jewish and Arab letters. The aforementioned "Elegy on the Martyrs of Toledo," written after the massacres of 1391, names and describes the martyrs of the city and also Toledo's synagogues, one by one, as part of its honoring of the dead: the Great Synagogue, the New Synagogue, the Synagogue of the Prince Samuel Halevi, Synagogue of the Cordovan, Synagogue of Aben Ziza, the Abidarham Synagogue, the Suloquia Synagogue, Synagogue of Ben Aryeh, and the Alguiada Synagogue (Roth 129–33).

25. The 2011 museum guide reproduces other prints by Baratti but, in this case, identifies them as his, adding that they were made in Berlin: two to illustrate the explanations about the festivals of Sukkot and Pesach, and one to illustrate the burial of the dead in the section about the Garden of Memory. The museum's catalog lists six Baratti prints from Berlin in its collection.

26. The original, together with other prints by Baratti, is located in the section of the building occupied by the museum's offices.

27. The way the Jewish Museum of Vienna exhibits ritual objects offers an interesting counterexample. Most of its objects are exhibited in a "viewable storage area," as a crowded mass of objects, showing them out of context, emphasizing how they were often torn by force from their appropriate settings, since most of these objects were looted by the Nazis (Gruber, *Virtually Jewish* 178). Michael Baxandall explains how the museum visitor "is hard put not to be a voyeur, intrusive and often embarrassed" when being shown these objects "not designed for looking at" (39).

28. Although these historical periods refer to a centuries-long Jewish presence in the Iberian Peninsula, dating from AD 70, at least, to roughly the thirteenth century, the room is called "La llegada de los judíos a Hispania" ["The arrival of Jews in Hispania"].

29. The Spanish version exhibited in the museum is identical to the one provided by Angel Saenz- Badillos and Judit Targarona Borras in their anthology of Hebrew poets of al-Andalus; the English translation can be found in Peter Cole's *The Dream of the Poem*. We thank David Wacks for providing us with these references.

30. We analyze the recent "discovery" and treatment of Jewish cemeteries, including the one in Toledo, in the following chapter.

31. Javier Castaño uses the example of the Tesorillo, among others, to explain the "interpretation problems" presented by Hispano-Jewish material remains. As he explains, many objects and buildings identifed as Jewish might very well not be Jewish. See also Lacave's article, "De cómo se judaízan unos baños: Mallorca."

32. A sign indicates that the tombstone is on loan from the Museum of the Holy Cross.

33. In the 1950s, Hassán emigrated from Morocco to Spain. After Hassán's death in April 2006, the new edition of the museum's guide explicitly honored his memory stating: "Textos escritos por Jacob Hassán, miembro fundador de la Asociación de Amigos del Museo Sefardí e ilustre investigador de la lengua, literatura y cultura sefardí, sirva de homenaje a su memoria" ["Texts written by Jacob Hassán, founding member of the Association of Friends of the Sephardi Museum, and renowned researcher of Sephardi language, literature and culture. May this serve as an homage to his memory" (*Guide* 2011, 168).

34. Palomero Plaza made this argument when addressing visitors' complaints about various temporary exhibitions, like "Jewish-themed Spanish Ceramics" or the work of Cecilia Najles, an Argentine Jewish painter living in Spain. The ceramics were exhibited in the Great Prayer Room and the paintings in the Women's Gallery. Visitors complained that these modern works obstructed the view of the fourteenth-century stuccowork, something they found disconcerting and disrespectful (Palomero Plaza 217–22). We analyze the equally negative responses to a 2015 temporary exhibition of German painter Wolf Vostell in the museum's Great Prayer Room in chapter 6.

35. As he states in the museum's 2012 newsletter,

> La lección de tolerancia medieval y de mudejarismo cultural que dio al mundo Toledo en la Edad Media (cuya máxima representación es el propio edificio que alberga el Museo, la Sinagoga del Tránsito) no debe quedar como simple referencia de un pasado mítico, englobado erróneamente en el mito de las Tres Culturas idílicas, que algunos han pintado para consumo indiscriminado de masas. Muy al contrario, ese fenómeno de aculturación mutua entre una mayoría dominante y dos minorías debe permanecer hoy como una lección hodierna.
>
> [The lesson of medieval tolerance and cultural intermixing that Toledo gave the world in the Middle Ages (whose main representation is the very building in which the Museum is located, the Synagogue of the Transit) should not remain a mere reference from a legendary past, wrongly aligned with the idyllic myth of the City of the Three Cultures, which some have created for indiscriminate mass consumption. On the contrary, the phenomenon of mutual acculturation between a dominant majority and two minorities must remain as a lesson for today]. (*Agenda Octubre 2011–Marzo 2012* 18)

36. One is the Laboratorio Multicultural Francisco Márquez Villanueva, a scholarly platform dedicated to the Harvard University professor of Spanish literature and disciple of Américo Castro. The institute's activities have included the series of conferences "Voices of the Moriscos" (2010–11); "Voices of the

Conversos" (2011–12); and "Voices of the Captives" (2012–13). The Observatorio por la Paz y la Tolerancia Gregorio Marañón, inspired by the life and work of Marañón (Madrid 1887–1960), a scientist and liberal intellectual, is an outreach branch of the museum aiming at disseminating "values of multiculturalism, peace and tolerance." The observatory collaborates with the Social Film Festival of Castilla–La Mancha. Finally, the museum sponsors the Taller de Creación contemporánea Yehuda Halevi, named after the Jewish medieval poet "of understanding and hope" who composed a good part of his work in Toledo (*Agenda Octubre 2011–Marzo 2012* 24). As an example of what he saw as the museum's relevance for the present, Palomero Plaza stated on a number of occasions that the synagogue, as a space that symbolizes the "encounter" between Christians, Muslims, and Jews, would be the ideal place for the signing of a definitive peace agreement between Israelis and Palestinians.

FOUR

EXHIBITING JEWISH HERITAGE AT THE LOCAL AND REGIONAL LEVELS

SINCE 1992, OVER SIXTEEN SMALL museums and interpretive centers dedicated to the local Jewish past have mushroomed across Spain and plans for the construction of several others have been announced. While Toledo's Sephardi Museum was founded as part of a longer process of conservation for the historical medieval synagogue where it is located, these regional and local museums have very few material or preexisting objects to build their exhibitions around. Each aspect of these Jewish museums—their collections, physical settings, promotional materials—attempts to provide an answer to the questions, Why open a Jewish museum in towns without Jews, and why establish an exhibition space when there is so little to show? Consistently, the exhibits answer these questions by providing locally specific narratives of their towns as "sites of glory." They try to demonstrate that their locations were eminently important in relation to Jewish history and culture by explaining that they had a large medieval Jewish community, they were the birthplace of prominent Jewish intellectuals, or they were the sites of key events in Iberian Jewish history. They also coincide in depicting the local medieval past as one in which convivencia flourished, allowing Jewish culture to thrive. Their local iterations of the exceptionalism and convivencia arguments are offered as proof of the essentially righteous character of each town's present society. Medieval Jews become once again instrumentalized as witnesses, this time of the idea that tolerance is an essential quality of these communities.

As we saw in chapter 2, the "Jewish turn" undertaken by many Spanish cities, of which these museums are one of the more visible elements, is intimately woven into local hopes to attract tourism, ameliorate prolonged situations of high unemployment, and respond creatively to an economic crisis. It is also, in many cases, driven by hopes of political gain. In many ways, these museums participate in the larger phenomenon of the emergence of Jewish museums across the globe, from Melbourne (1977) to Cape Town (2000), and from Prague (reestablished in 1994 after the 1906 original) to Alaska (2004). Europe has been an especially active locus of Jewish museum building, with cities from Berlin (2001) to Moscow (2012) and Warsaw (2013) turning to the museum concept as a way to confront—or not—their recent difficult pasts.[1] As Svetlana Boym explains,

> Jewish museums and sites are now emerging all over Europe, from Girona to Prague, representing a strange mix of local and global fashion. They lie on the main tourist route, often in places where there are hardly any Jews left. Ever so slightly these museums rewrite history to portray their region as more tolerant toward Jews and collectively suffering from Big Brother (in the Jewish Museum in Girona, Cataluña, Jews are said to have been supported more by Catalans than by Castilians; in Brandenburg they were supposedly better treated than in the rest of Germany, and so on). The establishment of a Jewish museum is often a symptom of local nostalgia, if not of bad conscience. These museums both document the repressed history and serve as a profitable tourist business, which is supposed to attract global wanderers to the 'progressive' local landmark. (*Future* 203)

Jewish museums in Europe exhibit great variety in terms of size, style, concept, and physical setting (Gruber, *Virtually Jewish* 157–58).[2] Not surprisingly, so do those in Spain. They have opened in large cities like Barcelona, with the Centre d'Interpretació del Call [Jewish Quarter Interpretive Center] (2008), and in midsize provincial capitals like Girona, where the Museu d'Historia dels Jueus [Museum of Jewish History] opened in 2000, and Segovia, where the Centro Didáctico de la Judería de Segovia [Information Center of Segovia's Jewish Quarter] opened in 2004. Many have opened in smaller cities and towns: Tarazona opened the Centro de Interpretación Moshe Portella [Moshe Portella Interpretive Center] (2002), Ribadavia the Centro de Información Xudía de Galicia [Jewish Information Center of Galicia] (2003), Béjar the Museo Judío David Melul [Jewish Museum David Melul] (2005), and Besalú the Centro de Interpretación de la Cultura Judía [Center for the Interpretation of Jewish Culture] (2008).

Some, like Casa de Sefarad in Córdoba (2006) and the Museo de la Judería [Museum of the Jewish Quarter] in the Realejo Quarter of Granada (2013), are privately owned. Others are dedicated extensions of preexisting public museums, as is the case of the Centre d'Interpretació del Call, an extension of the Museu d'Història de Barcelona; the section "Sephardi and Amazigh Cultures" in the Museo Arqueológico de Melilla (2011); and the modest display dedicated to local

Jews at the Museo de las tres Culturas in Puente Castro, León, since 2012. Similarly, in the Museu Comarcal de l'Urgell-Tàrrega in Lleida, the display *Tragèdia al call: Tàrrega 1348* [Tragedy in the Jewish Quarter: Tàrrega 1348] became a permanent exhibit in 2014. Some of the most recent additions are run by for-profit tourism companies like Centro de Interpretación de la Judería de Sevilla [Interpretive Center for the Jewish Quarter of Seville], which opened in 2012, and the Palacio de los Olvidados, Espacio de la Cultura Sefardí [Palace of the Forgotten Ones, Space of Sephardi Culture], which opened in 2014 in Granada.

Several other Jewish museums are being planned across Spain. In Lorca, the discovery of the foundation and parts of the walls of what seems to have been a synagogue has led the city council to undertake the construction of the Centro de Cultura Judía y Sinagoga "Shaarei Yerushalayim" [Jewish Cultural Center and Synagogue, "Doors of Jerusalem"]. While work preparing the vestiges of the synagogue for public visits was completed in 2018, the center still remains in its planning stages as of 2019. The Centro de Interpretación de la Cultura Judía [Interpretive Center for Jewish Culture] in Plasencia was scheduled to start construction in 2014, although no clear signs of material progress were noticeable in 2019. The recently renamed village of Castrillo Mota de Judíos [Mound of the Jews] in the province of Burgos has developed an ambitious plan to build a large local Jewish museum, for which it is actively courting potential Jewish donors. This Centro de Interpretación de la Cultura Sefardí en el Camino de Santiago [Interpretive Center for Sephardi Culture in the Way of Saint James] is part of the village's plan to recover its Jewish heritage. This initiative officially began in 2015, when, as a result of a referendum among its fifty-six inhabitants, the village officially changed its name.[3] It was during a visit to Mota de Judíos that David Hatchwell Altarás, the president of Madrid's Jewish Community, announced his plan to build a Museo Judío de España, a comprehensive exhibition space that will coordinate its activities with, among others, this village's future interpretive center (Escudero Ríos). In March 2017, Lucena's mayor announced plans to open a Jewish museum there in the near future. Also in 2017, the city of Málaga announced that it was planning to build a Sephardi cultural center that would function as a museum of Spanish Jewish thought. In October 2012, the Centro Sefarad-Israel signed an agreement with the Madrid City Council to start work on the Museo Samuel Hayón, which will be dedicated to the history of Spain's Jewish communities.

THE POSSIBILITIES OF IMPERFECT FITS

In her analysis of contemporary Jewish museums from around the world, Barbara Kirshenblatt-Gimblett establishes a distinction between "perfect-fit" and "imperfect-fit" museums, depending on the close alignment, or lack thereof, between the museum's mission, the story it tells, the interests and identity of the stakeholders, and those of their audiences. Perfect-fit museums, such as the Jewish Museum in New York, "are created more or less by, more or less for, and more or less about Jews" (Kirshenblatt-Gimblett, "Why" 1–2). Most European Jewish museums, however, are imperfect fits.

As noted in our study of the Sephardi Museum, most of Spain's Jewish museums are not primarily directed or funded by Jews or a Jewish community. The only existing perfect fit among these museums would be the one-room Museo de Historia de la Comunidad Judía de Madrid (Madrid Jewish Community History Museum), supported and curated by a Jewish community. Opened in 2007 and housed within the Beth Yaakov Synagogue in Madrid, this very small exhibit chronicles the history of the reestablishment of Madrid's Jewish community during the twentieth century. It is officially open to any interested visitor but requires a previous appointment and personal preregistration to access it. In effect, it serves as a quasi-private museum for the very community it chronicles. All the other museums represent varying degrees of imperfect fits. The Sephardi Museum of Toledo has welcomed the collaboration and input of Jewish scholars and experts, but these individuals serve clearly subsidiary roles. The Museum of Jewish History in Girona, while still chiefly financed by Girona's city council and the Spanish and Catalan governments, has proactively developed a network of financial support that includes Jewish foundations, families, and individuals. Among the newly opened museums, the Jewish Museum David Melul in Béjar has the distinction of having been funded by Melul, a Moroccan Jew, and it is officially set up under the guidance of the Federation of Jewish Communities of Spain.

Thus, although most of these museums are not strictly Jewish institutions, Jewish perspectives and voices are slowly being incorporated into them. Berhnard Purin has documented how postwar Jewish museums in Germany and Austria also began as institutions administered by non-Jews, their exhibits staged from a non-Jewish perspective. Over the years, however, they have evolved to include Jews at the administrative and curatorial levels. In some cases, descendants of emigrated Jews have transformed communities around Jewish museums in their ancestral cities and towns (Purin 139). It will be interesting to see whether a similar process occurs in Spain.

Each museum's mission to promote its town or region through the recuperation of the local community's Jewish heritage strongly determines the stories it tells. These stories are closely aligned with the interests of the institutional, entrepreneurial, or private stockholders and are used to enhance their image and promote the town. In turn, the communities frequently find in these celebratory narratives new information to enhance pride in their local identity. From this perspective, the fact that the theme of these museums is "Jewish" may be rendered as purely accidental, one more hook devised to entice tourists to visit a specific town in the hope that they will also visit local monuments like Roman ruins (Segovia), the Mosque (Córdoba), Cathedrals (Seville, Barcelona), taste the local wines (Ribadavia), or even, ironically, the famous regional ham (Hervás, Béjar). Yet many of these smaller museums have their own characteristics and interest which transcend their apparently fortuitous origins. We have chosen for detailed analysis five regional/local museums that represent a variety of geographic locations and approaches. They also stand out for the tight relationship, in terms of objectives and ambitions, they have established with the cities in which they are located. These are Girona's Museum of Jewish History (Catalonia), Ribadavia's Jewish Information Center of Galicia in the province of Ourense (Galicia), Béjar's Jewish Museum David Melul in the province of Salamanca (Castile and Leon), Casa de Sefarad in the city of Córdoba (Andalucía), and the permanent exhibition *Tragèdia al call: Tàrrega 1348* at the Museo de l'Urgell in the province of Lleida (Catalonia).

These institutions are examples of imperfect-fit museums in which the scarce and fragmentary nature of the objects exhibited—and several of the exhibitions themselves—stand in dissonance with the narratives of local Jewish achievement and peaceful convivencia most cities try to convey. This misalignment further includes the non-Jewish background of most stockholders and their hopes for international tourism revenue as well as the controverted nature that anything Jewish acquires in towns and cities from which Jewish people were expelled or in which they were forced to convert centuries ago, where the Holocaust represents a distant concern, and where the most common references to Jews, their culture, and religion occur in the context of news reports about the Israeli-Palestinian conflict. But as Kirshenblatt-Gimblett reminds us, imperfect-fit museums, precisely because of the frictions they awaken, are both full of pitfalls and possibilities ("Why" 5).

GIRONA'S MUSEUM OF JEWISH HISTORY

Girona's museum is the second-most-ambitious exhibition gallery dedicated to the medieval Jewish past in the country, surpassed only by the national Sephardi Museum in Toledo's collection, which is larger and more comprehensive in scope. Girona's museum came to be thanks to the establishment of the Patronat Call de Girona in 1992. The patronat is a municipal board established in coordination with Girona's provincial council and the Generalitat de Catalunya (the Autonomous Government of Catalonia). This organization was born with the mandate to preserve and promote Jewish heritage and the historic Jewish Quarter of Girona as part of the larger effort by Joaquim Nadal, Girona's mayor between 1979 and 2002 and a professor of history, to revitalize the Barri Vell, the Old Quarter. The patronat established the Nahmanides Institute for Jewish Studies in 1997 and the Museum of Jewish History in 2000. Both the institute and museum are today based at the Bonastruc ça Porta Center, the assumed Catalan name of Nahmanides (Moshe Ben Nahman Girondi 1194–1270), the Jewish legal scholar who argued on behalf of the legitimacy of his faith at the Disputation of Barcelona in 1263.[4] The museum occupies the lower, more ancient parts of the building, while the library is in a dedicated wing that has been completely modernized in search of functionality over the desire for preservation of medieval history that led to the museum's renovations.

Initially funded and mostly maintained by the governments of Girona and Catalonia, the museum is also sponsored by Spain's Ministry of Culture and several Catalan banks. Over the years, the board has made an effort to reach out to Spain's and Catalonia's Jewish communities and counts as its benefactors the Rich and Schalit Foundations, a roster of over thirty Spanish Jewish individuals and families, the Israeli Embassy in Spain, the Jewish Community of Barcelona, and the Israel Museum in Jerusalem. Girona's museum is unique in many ways: from its focus on celebrating Girona's and the rest of Catalonia's Jewish history and, thus, being part of the negotiations of and about Catalan nationalism through its diverse roster of public and private sponsors to its seminal role in the articulation of the Network of Jewish Quarters of Spain.

To visit the museum, one must undertake a short walk through a maze of narrow cobblestone streets in Girona's historic city center. Its unassuming entrance appears on the ground floor of a recessed and narrow four-story building with a clean neoclassical facade. The meandering walk and the inconspicuous entrance collaborate in creating a sense of time-travel and secrecy that will later be enhanced inside the museum. Architecturally, the building seems to be the result of joining together a series of smaller disparate constructions set up at uneven heights, each with its own entry point. One of the main interventions carried out in the renovation has been to link these uneven pieces through a complicated circuit of stairs and narrow passageways, connecting them to a central patio where the floor is inlaid with a twelve-foot-wide Star of David made of polished black marble.[5]

The second major architectural intervention has been to strip these old buildings down to their structural components, peeling off the layers of modifications accrued over time.[6] Visitors wind through the twists and turns that link these ancient, narrow, and capriciously laid-out structures. The bare construction, a set of minimalist elements, implicitly suggests immediate material access to the past, as if visitors had unmediated access to the fragile and precarious structural origins of the buildings. Some of these elements are tempered glass floors almost invisible in their transparency, others become hypervisible as highly polished shiny floors, new staircases, and walls that stand in stark contrast to the ruggedness of the old masonry. The juxtaposition of very new elements of glass and steel lends a sense of authenticity to the old structures, and the hypermodern and elegant display techniques help make the old seem more precious. But the suggestion never succumbs to stating itself as a fact. The structures visitors walk through might only contain as many traces of their assumed pre-1492 Jewish owners as of the many people that lived in them over the succeeding five centuries. The intricacy of these architectural negotiations between a precarious and almost silent past that is difficult to access and interpret and a technologically savvy present provide a suitable metaphor for the convoluted negotiations between tourist, academic, economic, and political interests that have coalesced to make these Jewish museums possible (see fig. 4.1).

According to the patronat's website, the buildings date back to the fifteenth century and stand on the site where once was "a synagogue and other communal areas used by Girona's Jewish community." However, no actual material signs of the synagogue, nor of any communal service buildings, have been identified. In the late 1980s, the city government began buying the buildings from local entrepreneur Josep Tarrés i Fontan (see note 5 in this chapter), and during the 1990s extensive renovations were undertaken to transform it into an exhibition center. This recourse to finding a physical setting with enhanced claims of Jewish ownership is a common one across local Jewish museums. Following an archaeological logic that assumes that cultures leave traces on the locations where they lived, most of these museums locate themselves in former Jewish Quarters and seek Jewish traces in the buildings. What they find, however, is the rubble of history, the succession of destructions and transformations, and their repurposing and rebuilding. Hypervisible and added Jewish elements, like the Star of David embedded in the central patio, become emblems of the museum's intention of recovering a Jewish inheritance. Like the signs embedded in the streets and pavement of many newly rediscovered Jewish Quarters throughout Spain, these elements point mostly at themselves; they are their own referents. They become themselves the visible and tangible, and perhaps

Figure 4.1. New and old construction materials are combined in the building of Girona's Museum of Jewish History. ©Adrián Pérez Melgosa.

self-serving, proof of the recovery of a memory the object of which, in this sense, disappears in its representation (see fig. 4.2).

In the words of the patronat, the museum's goal is "to preserve and publicize the history of the Jewish communities of Catalonia, which throughout the entire medieval period formed part of, and made a decisive contribution to, the history of the country and its cultural and scientific development" (Patronat). Here, the attention to "the history of the Jewish communities of Catalonia" becomes a two-way street: it provides a narrative of contradistinction with the rest of the Iberian Jewish communities while also establishing a fluid cosmopolitan claim to validate connecting Girona to the global Jewish community. This focus on regenerating the symbolic value of the city both at the local and cosmopolitan levels stands in direct relation to the promotion of the city for tourist purposes. In fact, the national offices of the Network of Jewish Quarters were housed in the same building as the museum until June 2016, when they moved to Córdoba. That year, as if materializing the museum's particularist narrative, Girona, along with four other Catalan towns, separated from the Network of Jewish Quarters of Spain. As we saw in chapter 2, Marta Madrenas, who became Girona's mayor in 2016, explained the split as a result of the irreconcilable differences between the "touristy ambitions" of the rest of the members and the "cultural and scientific rigor" of the Catalan approach (Minder).

This emphasis on distinguishing Catalonia's presentation of its Jewish heritage from the touristy way this is supposedly done in the rest of Spain is

Figure 4.2. Star of David embedded in the central Patio of Girona's Museum of Jewish History. ©Adrián Pérez Melgosa.

related to the negotiations of present-day Catalan nationalism, but it is also part of a longer process by which the governments of different autonomous communities in Spain have sought to define their regional/national identities within the political map drawn by the 1978 constitution. After decades of cultural repression under the dictatorship of Franco, the Spanish Constitution recognized the diverse cultural and linguistic heritages of the seventeen communities that make up Spain, granting them relative political autonomy. As we saw in chapter 2, cultural tourism served the purposes of autonomous communities wishing to promote their own identities by distancing themselves from the monolithic Francoist tourist policies and narratives that had constructed a monocultural, monolingual, unitary vision of Spain. New tourist policies in these communities were tied to the politics of regional or peripheral national identities that found newly free expression post-Franco, when regional governments gained control over the tourism industry (Pi-Sunyer 242–43).

City governments, such as Girona's under mayor Joaquim Nadal, viewed the preservation and rehabilitation of their old quarters as part of this project of rediscovering regional and local identity and "sought to recuperate Sephardi history and culture as a specific iteration of local Gironan identity" (Nadel 4). Linguistic policy, a pivotal component of Catalan identity affirmation, appears foregrounded in the Bonastruc ça Porta Center's use of Nahmanides's Catalan name, stressing the idea that "Nahmanides was not only a Jew, but rather a Sephardi Catalan" (5). In fact, the original plan for the museum, sent to English-speaking potential donors, envisioned calling it "Catalan Museum of Jewish Culture and Institute of Sephardi and Kabbalistic Studies in the Restored Jewish Quarter of Girona, Spain" (Hosta, quoted in Nadel 5). Apparently, the exclusively regional focus was not attractive enough to find donors, and "Catalan" was dropped from the title. The museum exhibits themselves, however, clearly focus on Catalan Jews' exceptionality to convey the exceptionality of Girona and Catalonia.

In a description of his visit to the museum in the summer of 2014, Joshua Furst, writing for *The Forward*, commented on the intensity of the pull exerted by present Catalan politics on the local reception of the exhibits. Intrigued by the reasons why present-day Girona and Catalonia were so keenly interested in their Jewish history, Furst interviewed the librarian at the Nahmanides Institute. The librarian went on to deliver a short lesson on Spanish and Catalan relations and concluded with the statement, "The Jews are a metaphor for our suffering" (Furst, "Slouching"). A similar anecdote is told by Jeffrey Juris in his article about the first tourist guide published by the Network of Jewish Quarters of Spain. Juris describes his conversation with a research assistant in Girona who told him that, as a Catalan, she identified with the Jews. The Spanish state had repressed both Jewish and Catalan culture. Recovering Jewish heritage was a contribution to the struggle against intolerance and cultural repression, such as that historically directed against Catalan history, language, and identity (Juris 273). Other city officials have echoed these comments (see Nadel). Here, the philosephardist argument for the defense of the Spanishness of Sephardi Jews we analyze in chapter 1 has been repurposed as a defense of the exceptionality of the Catalan experience.[7]

One of the main aims of the museum is to put on display the accomplishments of past Jewish intellectuals and artisans who lived in Girona in the Middle Ages. The exhibits emphasize their intellectual achievement, everyday work, and contributions to the growth of the city. The board's website emphasizes this point when it describes the museum as a space designed "to recall and rehabilitate the history of the city's Jewish inhabitants who, with very high cultural attainments but at the same time often leading anonymous daily lives, contributed to the wealth and success of the city" (Patronat). A circular nationalist reasoning, not uncommon in museological practice, and also found in the Sephardi museum of Toledo, is at work here: Girona was a special city in the Middle Ages, as demonstrated by the "wealth and success" of its Jewish community. In turn, the local Jewish community thrived because it was part of the "wealthy and successful" city of Girona. But *Sepharad*, the most common signifier displayed throughout most Spanish Jewish museums, does not exist as a reference here. The museum instead refers consistently to "Catalan Jews."[8]

Thus, in a room dedicated to "the cultural inheritance of Catalan Judaism" a wall-wide panel lists the names, professions, and occupations of medieval Jews in different cities in Catalonia and the Balearic Islands. These lists are offered as proof that "in medieval times the representative figures of Catalan Judaism were prominent in the production of scientific, literary and philosophical works." The panel "is an homage to these many illustrious names" (Patronat). The panel reads: "The Catalan Jews were distinguished in the study and exercise of mathematics, medicine, astronomy, languages and sciences in general. Outstanding Jewish Catalan figures took part in an important chapter of medieval knowledge." This general characterization highlights those individuals as uniquely "distinguished" and "outstanding" and chooses to note this aspect of their lives as the inheritance that present-day Catalonia has received from medieval Jews. These particular Jews that the museum identifies help to construct today's image of Catalonia as a highly cultured and intellectually advanced society.

The emphasis on the high level of productivity achieved by Catalan Jews continues as the theme of an adjacent room whose name has clear Catholic overtones: "The Daily Bread: Professional Activity." In this room, a series of panels shows reproductions of images from a medieval document depicting "the main occupations of the Jewish inhabitants of Girona: craftsmanship, commerce and moneylending were the most important among them" (Patronat). These occupations, however, do not single out any distinctive quality of *Catalan* Jews. These were the same professions Jews had in the rest of the peninsula.

A special section of the museum is dedicated to the figure of Nahmanides, who was born in Girona. Here we find information about the 1263 Disputation of Barcelona, in which he defended the supremacy of the Jewish faith against the arguments of Dominican friar Pablo Christiani, himself a converso. While today he is invoked as an example of the great scholarly achievements of Jews in medieval Girona, during his life Nahmanides's scholarly achievements and great success at defending Judaism in the disputation led to his being persecuted, accused of blasphemy, and forced into exile in Jerusalem, where he spent the last three years of his life. The disputation intensified the Dominicans' missionary zeal against the Jews (Y. Baer 1: 155–59).

As is the case in other museums dedicated to Jewish history in Spain, the collection is characterized by a dismal lack of objects. The most significant—a bronze belt buckle, silver earrings, and five tombstones with Hebrew inscriptions—were found in the area known as Montjuïc (Hill of the Jews), the location of Barcelona's medieval Jewish cemetery.[9] The room devoted to the Jewish cemetery has its floor completely paneled in white acrylic rectangles onto which images of a bucolic green mountain are projected, and the walls display a large format of Girona's street layout, outlining the path probably followed by medieval Jewish funerary corteges. On the floor, we see the massive tombstones engraved with Hebrew and on the sides, cases with personal objects (see fig. 4.3). The installation's peaceful and beautiful virtual landscape highlights the "out of placeness" of these objects. As is the case of the headstones found at the Sephardi Museum in Toledo, no careful and well-intentioned installation can replace the fact of these headstones' having been removed from their place in a cemetery.

Displaying ancestral objects, Jean Baudrillard argues, allows us to conjure continuity and to dispel the anxiety associated with absence and death (104). As these museums set out to dispel this anxiety of human finality in connection with their town's Jewish past, their exhibits end up summoning echoes of material absence and physical death. Edward Rothstein has put forward the criticism that "a museum of Jewish religious artifacts is partly a Jewish morgue, less a tribute to Judaism's continuity than a memorial to a world of belief left behind—in some cases, forcibly so" (Rothstein, "The Problem"). Rooms such as this one materially suggest "morgues." Spain's Jewish museums add a particular tension to this "problem of Jewish museums," as Rothstein calls it. In them, a silent struggle is constantly being waged between the palpable display of Jewish absence and the symbolic pull of museums as institutions that contribute to community affirmation and identity building.

Girona's museum also resorts to virtual reconstructions in its exhibitions: mock-ups, videos, mannequins, and other newly made objects. Like in Toledo's Sephardi Museum, in their eagerness to provide visibility to Girona's Jewish past, these installations forcefully point to the absence they try to fill. In a room dedicated to the Jewish Quarters of Catalonia, the museum promises a "virtual recreation [*sic*] of life in the Jewish Quarter of Girona in the fourteenth century." The visitor finds a short video projected on a screen, a miniature model of the layout of Girona's Medieval Jewish Quarter, and two mannequins (see fig. 4.4). These life-size faceless mannequins become emblematic of the intricate signification contained in the play between visibility and absence that characterizes these exhibits. Since no explanatory caption introduces them, the visitor must construct an interpretation for their presence in the area devoted to the reconstruction of medieval everyday life in the Jewish Quarter of Girona. We assume the clothes represent the way local Jews dressed in the Middle Ages.

Figure 4.3. "Jewish cemetery." Girona's Museum of Jewish History. ©Adrián Pérez Melgosa.

Figure 4.4. Mannequins at Girona's Museum of Jewish History. ©Daniela Flesler.

But what makes these attires Jewish? Given the unadorned simplicity of the garb, the most remarkable item is the red-and-yellow circular badge attached to one of the articles of clothing. If the badge is what identifies the attire as Jewish, its mere presence renders insignificant the rest of the garments: if the clothes themselves had been distinctive of medieval Aragonese Jewish people, a badge indicating their difference would have been unnecessary. Jews, in fact, dressed in the same way as their gentile neighbors (Lipton 20). We assume this red-and-yellow badge must refer to the distinctive mark prescribed by Pope Innocent III at the Fourth Lateran Council in 1215 to distinguish Jews from others. In medieval Christian thought, the colors red and yellow were associated with evil (Lipton 7). The implementation of laws mandating the wearing of this badge in the Iberian Peninsula was patchy and erratic. Jaume I implemented it in Aragon, but by 1313, the bishops at the Council of Zamora complained of the lack of enforcement of the badge prescription. Thus, this exhibit represents medieval Spanish Jews by a badge, an accessory imposed on the Jews by Christian authorities, placed on clothing worn by two faceless structures that stand as placeholders for an absent human body.

Together, these items attest not so much to a visible Jewish difference but to an "anxiety of sameness." Jews, disturbingly, could not be visually told apart from Christians (Lipton 160). In its search for the distinctive traces of everyday life in medieval Aragonese Jewish culture, this exhibit ends up locating it within the narrow confines of a badge, a gesture that is repeated in other Jewish museums in Spain. Sabine Offe affirms that "museums classify and isolate whatever they put on display" (88). In their very reliance on visuality to represent Iberian Jewish culture and the recurrent focus on displaying difference, museums end up dramatizing the anxieties about the in/visibility of Jewish identity that during the late fourteenth and throughout the fifteenth centuries would result in a series of laws forcing Iberian Jews to move into Jewish Quarters and to wear badged garments in efforts to make their identity visibly distinguishable from that of Christians.

When describing the nature of the work of the Inquisition, Marcelino Menéndez Pelayo, the prominent conservative nineteenth-century historian, explicitly voiced this "anxiety of sameness." The Inquisition, he said, helped to "disipar aquella dolorosa incertidumbre, en la que no podía distinguirse al fiel del infiel, ni al traidor del amigo" [dispel that painful uncertainty by which it wasn't possible to distinguish the faithful from the unfaithful, the traitor from the friend] (Menéndez Pelayo 894). If, during the fourteenth century, proximity and sameness created a crisis of classification between Christians and Jews, exhibits such as this, often with the best intentions, end up resorting to a similar logic of differentiation, using their reconstructions of a makeshift past to neatly create Jewish difference. In their attempt to show what Jewish medieval life consisted of, these exhibits resort to the fetishization of a small collection of objects and the selective editing of the available historical record. Unwittingly, these museums construct and end up separating Jewishness into a newly created virtual Jewish Quarter.

For the visitor paying close attention, an explanation of this badge appears later in the museum visit, in the thematic area titled "A Difficult Relationship: From Coexistence to Marginalization." In that thematic area, a reproduction of a document from Majorca, dated 1394, explains that Jews should sew this round yellow-and-red badge (the *rodella*) onto their clothes and wear it whenever they leave the Jewish Quarter (hence, again, the irony of the mannequins, wearing it in an installation about Jewish Quarters). Both this thematic area, which also features a copy of the Edict of Expulsion, and the following one, "Converso Society and the Inquisition," confront the history of discrimination and persecution suffered by Jews and include objects associated with it—a confrontation that we do not explicitly find in Toledo's Sephardi Museum. For example, an eighteenth-century shield of the Inquisition, made of stone, is exhibited with a reference to its link to a local landmark. The caption reads, "This shield of the Inquisition may have been on Sant Domènec convent, headquarters of the Holy Office in Girona." Through these objects and references, the museum is willing to identify Girona and Catalonia with narratives that go beyond that of convivencia.

As a visible institution that is part of the city's intention of a rapprochement with the Jewish world, this museum also becomes a site where different actors can stage their own stakes in or opinions about that rapprochement. In their study of Jewish space in contemporary Poland, Erica Lehrer and Michael Meng speak about the need to look at "the local meanings and lived experiences" surrounding Jewish sites (3). One of these lived experiences encompasses the interaction of one of the museum's neighbors with this Jewish institution. Since at least 2008 (when we first visited Girona's museum) two Palestinian flags have been hanging from the balconies of a private home facing the museum's entrance. The flags were placed there by Marta Latorre, who lives in the apartment right above the museum's entrance (fig. 4.5).

In a video posted online in 2010, Latorre explained that she hung the flags to show her solidarity with the plight of Palestinian people and as a protest against Zionism. Latorre stated that she had received pressure from the museum authorities to remove the flags. In the video, we see a gathering of about twenty people who came together at the main entrance to the museum to express their

While in Girona information panels are written in Catalan, English, and Castilian, here the panels are exclusively written in Galician. Implicitly, this linguistic choice acknowledges that Ribadavia is located away from the traditional thoroughfares of international tourism. But it is also a decision rooted in the linguistic and identity disputes currently being waged accross Spain's autonomous communities in search of local and regional differentiation from what they see as the encroachment of Castilian language and culture. Ribadavia receives a total of about 17,000 to 20,000 annual tourists. The vast majority are from Spain (in 2014, of a total of 17,295 visitors, 15,669 were from Spain, and 1,626 were foreigners) and about half of those are Galician ("Ribadavia registró"). Most non-Galician-speaking people from Spain can understand enough of it by extrapolating from Castilian or Catalan. But still, the use of the Galician language serves to make visible a larger regional/national difference.

The Information Center addresses a visitor who does not know much about Judaism or about medieval Spanish and Galician history. One of the first panels introduces the question "What is Judaism?" and proceeds to provide a basic answer characterizing it as "the oldest monotheistic religion, from which Christianity and Islam originated." Swiftly, the text moves on to the very specific to highlight Galicia as a beacon of convivencia where Jews who had experienced prolonged periods of persecution lived in "peaceful coexistence with Christian and Muslim peoples in their countries of residence for centuries."

The following panels reinforce this depiction of the exceptionality of Galicia. A panel entitled "The First Jews," which refers to the oldest documented presence of Jews in Galicia, asserts that "the lands of Celanova . . . [a town twenty-five miles southeast of Ribadavia] are the best Peninsular paradigm of rural *convivencia* of the 'three cultures,' Christians, Muslims and Jews, in the High Middle Ages." As in other museums, convivencia lacks surviving material evidence. But rather than resorting to virtual reconstructions, the Ribadavia Center rescues little-known historical events with specific local connections and opens them up to reinterpretation. The next panel, entitled "Jewish-Christian Fraternity," boasts how "in contrast to other places of the Crown of Castile or Aragon, in the Kingdom of Galicia in the Middle Ages there weren't popular antisemitic uprisings." The narrative also highlights how Jews "joined Christians and Moors in rebellions against the abuses of noblemen." This union, known as the "Santa Hermandade" (Holy Brotherhood) existed only between 1467 and 1469, but it is presented as proof that while the rest of Spain's antisemitic uprisings were being waged in Toledo (1467), Sepulveda (1468), and Tolosa (1469), in Galicia "by the end of the Middle Ages, the Jewish-Christian fraternity had become a friendship."

When referring to an attack that led to the destruction of the Ourense synagogue in 1442 the narrative manages to present the event not as a challenge to this "friendship" but rather as its confirmation. The panel emphasizes how both the municipal authorities and the Catholic Church condemned the attack and excommunicated the guilty party, "treating the crime as if it were a sacrilege committed against a Christian church." Even if, after reading about the destruction of the Ourense synagogue, one still manages to cling to the convivencia myth, the next section of the exhibition, larger and better documented, presents an even steeper challenge to the notion. This section refers to an Inquisition case that took place in Ribadavia in 1606. Popularly known as "El malsín" [The informer], the process started when Xerónimo Bautista de Mena, a converso from Ribadavia, accused two hundred people, including some of his own family, of practicing Jewish rituals. The Inquisition detained and condemned many of them in subsequent autos-da-fé, including de Mena himself. The exhibit provides a detailed account of the story. Under the title "Fellow Ribadavia Neighbors Condemned by the Inquisition," a panel lists a series of names and provides their places of origin and their sentence.

Through this exhibit, we have moved away from the compartmentalized groups (Christians, Muslims, Jews) that coexist in the paradigm of convivencia to the much murkier waters of converso identities, with their diverse and conflicting identifications and loyalties. The town has embraced the story of this informant and the tragedy that ensued through annual celebrations of the Festa da Istoria. One of the main events of this festival is the biennial staging of the play *El Malsín*, which tells the story of Xerónimo Bautista de Mena's accusations and their consequences for Ribadavia. Why do Ribadavia's festival and its museum choose to focus on this unflattering story of treason and subsequent violence, which does not fit the convivencia slogan or any sort of idealized portrait of the town? One reason is that the story of the informant legitimizes Ribadavia's place in Jewish matters by showing that the town had a significant population of conversos. The issue of placing itself on the map would thus be covered. But something else is at play here. By honoring and mourning the suffering of their converso neighbors, the exhibit and the play invite Ribadavia's current inhabitants to imagine conversos as part of their own history. What this entails, and the fraught possibilities of performing memory, as it occurs in Hervás's performance of a play about its local past, is explored at length in the following chapter. The very concrete ways in which some towns are constructing the legacies of exiles and conversos as their own inheritance is further explored in the following museum cases.

JEWISH MUSEUM DAVID MELUL IN BÉJAR

Béjar's museum has the distinction of being financed by a Jewish patron and benefactor (in collaboration with the Jewish Communities of Spain and the local government). Born in Melilla to a Sephardi family, David Melul arrived in Béjar in the late 1940s to study at the local Industrial Engineering College. Melul's father, who had important business relationships among the textile manufacturers in Béjar, insisted that David study there (Melul 31). Melul has recounted his very fond memories of the city, at that time a prosperous midsize industrial town, where he felt welcomed and made many friends. He has also pointed out that he was probably the first Jewish person that the people of Béjar had seen and gotten to know since remote times (Melul, "Reencuentro" 33).

As told in the museum's website, after three years, Melul moved to Barcelona to complete his studies and became a successful businessman and active member of the Jewish community, occupying for some time the post of honorary consul of Israel in Spain. In subsequent visits to Béjar, he began to contemplate the idea of creating a museum that would remember Béjar's Jewish past (Museo Judío David Melul). In an interview with Radio Sefarad in March 2004, he explained that it was the mayor of Béjar, Alejo Riñones, who approached him with the idea of helping the town purchase a fifteenth-century historic house, for which it could secure a renovations grant. At this point, it was not clear whether the museum might be dedicated to Béjar's history in general, with a section about the Jewish presence in the town, or to Béjar's Jewish history in particular. It seems clear now that Melul's agreement to help the town with the purchase influenced the decision to dedicate the museum to Béjar's Jewish and converso inhabitants. An article in the local press in February 2004 states that Melul donated an additional €25,000 and ensured the contribution of an equal amount by the Federation of Jewish Communities of Spain toward completion of the building's renovations and the museum's opening. He also nominated Antonio Avilés Amat, a local expert on Sephardi issues, to be the museum director ("David Melul").

Melul himself, in a booklet entitled "Jews and Converts in the History of Béjar," published shortly before the museum's inauguration in 2004, told the (perhaps apocryphal) story of how he came to be aware of and interested in the Jewish past of the city. While a student there, he came into contact with an old gentleman, Don Juan Muñoz, who had been a diplomat in Sofia, Bulgaria. Melul states that he will tell Muñoz's story as Muñoz told it to him: while trying on new clothes in a store in Sofia, his first diplomatic post, Muñoz met the store's owner, a Sephardi Jew with whom he spoke "in the Spanish of Cervantes" (Melul 36). Melul intervenes to remind readers that this encounter took place before Ángel Pulido's "discovery" of Sephardi Jews of the Ottoman Empire and, thus, before there was awareness in Spain that such people existed. Muñoz was greatly surprised to hear the man's story: his family had left Spain in 1492, but they had preserved their language, "the treasure of their lives." One day the Bulgarian Sephardi man showed him a small room in the back of the store filled with old books and, in its center, a "centuries old" chest that contained, among fine cloth, an old key. Muñoz was told this man's family brought the key from Spain; it was the key to the house where they had lived. The climax of the narrative occurs when, upon Muñoz's asking which city the tailor's family had left, the tailor answered, "Béjar" (Melul 38). Melul entitled his story "Reencuentro de dos Bejaranos después de 400 años" ["Reencounter of two Bejaranos after 400 years"].

Given this story, it is not surprising to find the motif of the old key—the literary cliché par excellence of sentimental narratives about Sephardi Jews and a staple in Spanish souvenir shops—playing a central role in the museum. The museum's logo, as explained by director Avilés Amat in the leaflet that serves as museum guide, is "a key that gets transformed into a lush tree . . . symbolic of the exile of the Jews in 1492 through the key of the houses that they abandoned" (Avilés Amat). As we will see below, keys are also pervasive on the second floor of the museum, dedicated to Sephardi Jews who left Spain in 1492.

Central also to Melul's story is the motif of the reunion after centuries of separation. The title "Reencounter of two Bejaranos after 400 years" characterizes the meeting of a Spanish diplomat from Béjar and a Bulgarian Sephardi tailor from Sofia as a "reencounter," embracing the view that, because their ancestors five hundred years before them might perhaps have lived in the same city in Spain, their meeting in the twentieth century constitutes a reencounter. This anachronism sustains a sentimental and localist nationalism—the key is guarded as a treasure, in the story and in the Sephardi imagination, as constructed here by Melul, because Béjar was a beloved, cherished, unique, irreplaceable home, so much so, that a Bulgarian Jew in the twentieth century, who has never been in Spain, should feel himself identified as a *bejarano*. Bejaranos strictly means "people from Béjar," but the choice of bejaranos instead of "from Béjar" in Melul's title implies that their belonging to the city is a main feature of their identity. This characterization is not an obvious one in the case of the character of the Bulgarian Jew, who probably would not characterize himself as a bejarano.

This localist nationalism sustains many initiatives related to the recuperation of the Jewish past in cities and towns across Spain, as we have already seen. Since many towns in Spain's interior are trying to attract tourism, they need to highlight their uniqueness and attractiveness, even if this means wildly stretching the historical record to promote their towns as particularly peaceful, tolerant, and welcoming of Jews and, in this way, make it coincide with the cliché of convivencia. This desire to put Béjar on the map, both of Sephardi sentimental nostalgia for a lost home and of convivencia tourism, is pivotal in the museum's conception. Alejo Riñones, the mayor responsible for the project, has explained that the museum's purpose is to provide information about Béjar's Jewish past and thus "to recuperate, centuries later, the *convivencia* and tolerance that was broken" (Riñones, "Presentación").

Melul also explained, in a 2004 radio interview, that the museum's objective is to promote "the union of peoples, to transmit the message of tolerance in convivencia" ("Entrevista"). This message is also conveyed in the museum's logo, which shows, on top of the key/tree, a dove holding an olive branch in its beak. The museum's director explains these images as symbolic of the "peace and concord with other beliefs and cultures as attitudes that the museum tries to transmit" (Avilés Amat).

The success of these objectives was greatly forwarded in early 2004, when the museum authorities found out about the plan for the "First World Summit of the Bejars," a personal initiative of Iako Behar, a Bulgarian Sephardi Jew living in Mexico, who organized the "reunion" and visit to Béjar of people from around the world whose last names are Behar, Bejar, Vejar, Bejarano, and Becherano. Iako Behar, his son, and two grandsons sent four thousand invitations to people with these last names, most of them Sephardi Jews, out of which sixty-two "Bejars" from the United States, Canada, Chile, Mexico, France, Bulgaria, Israel, and South Africa traveled to Béjar for a September 6–9, 2004 gathering. Melul, Riñones, and José Luis Rodríguez Antúnez, the architect in charge of the renovations and spatial conception of the museum, thus arranged for the museum's opening to coincide with this event. We can imagine that this reunion fulfilled many of their aspirations, as the perfect embodiment of the spirit of Melul's short story—the visiting Bejars were the present-day incarnations of the Bulgarian tailor of his short story, only with the means to actually return to their supposed ancestral home. Hosting this visit at the same time that the city was trying to put itself on the map in terms of Jewish heritage tourism was a marketing opportunity that a city like Béjar could only dream of, impossible to conceive and pay for and all the more valuable because the organizers were the Bejars themselves, instead of the city. The summit was an invaluable vehicle of publicity for Béjar, and it is no wonder the city's authorities welcomed the visitors with open arms and made their visit coincide with the museum's opening.

The museum commemorated the visit of the Bejars with a plaque in its entrance hall that explains that, on September 7, 2004, the museum was inaugurated "in the presence of descendants of those Jews who were forced into exile in 1492, who have preserved in their last names the place name of the city with which they have reunited after five centuries of absence." The plaque thus embraces the reunion motif of Melul's short story, with its sentimental anachronism, and replaces the motif of the house key with that of the last name that has been treasured and preserved for centuries. Melul himself and the Bejars played a pivotal role in the development of the museum's collection and in the conception of its exhibitions. Thus, while the origin of the museum has most of the same ingredients as its counterparts (a town undergoing an economic crisis, a desire to get a slice of the tourism pie, a search for unique identifying traits in their past) the intervention of Melul seems to have been instrumental not only in encouraging the Jewish theme, but also in providing a unique approach to the local Jewish past by placing emphasis on the Sephardi bejaranos. The connection between medieval Jewish Béjar and current Sephardi Jews from around the world makes this space into a peculiar kind of doubly perfect-fit Jewish museum: one that simultaneously caters to the hopes for economic development of a local Spanish community and to many present-day Sephardi Jews' genealogical nostalgia for reconnecting with a material origin in Spain (even if a fabled one).

The museum is housed on three floors. The ground level is dedicated to the history of the Jews in Spain and Béjar, the second floor to the Inquisition and the post-1492 life of the conversos, and the third to Sephardi Jews in the diaspora. Next to the plaque about the Bejars, the entrance hall contains a second plaque dedicated to David Melul, in memoriam, and a map of medieval Jewish settlements in Castile and Leon, where the different towns are marked as having a Jewish population or constituting an aljama, a higher administrative organization that meant that the town had a larger number of people and a range of community services. The plaque literally puts Béjar on the map, stating its importance by showing it had an aljama.

Other elements on the ground floor speak about Jewish life in Spain before the expulsion and about the particularities of Béjar in relation to that history. The Jewish ceremonial objects exhibited are characterized by their connection to David Melul and Jacobo Israel Garzón, a close friend of Melul and president of the Federation of Jewish Communities of Spain between 2003 and 2011.

This connection endows the objects with a special quality: they do not—or do not only—stand synecdochically as ethnographic artifacts for Jewishness. They have an owner—a well-known owner—and, thus, an individual history.

As happens in other Spanish museums, this one also features a sharp contrast between the traditional architecture of the building that houses it and the traces of the highly technical intervention needed to render visible the building's ancient origins. But in Melul's museum the architectural renovation also becomes an exhibit in itself, shaping structural elements into metaphoric renderings of some of the abstract ideas and emotions that the museum wishes to put on display. Thus, at the end of the first-floor itinerary, we find a room called "Sala de los dos destinos" [Room of the two destinies]. A triangular-shaped hole in the wall, as if indicating the opening of different paths, evokes the moment of the edict and its aftermath. The triangle is carefully constructed out of neatly arranged thin bricks and opens onto a hollow space that ends at another brick wall, but this time the exposed surfaces of the bricks are coarse and sharp as if they had been forcibly broken. Sudden rupture is also conveyed by the sharp contrast between the carefully finished brick section of the wall and, next to it, another part of the wall of uncarved stones capriciously placed in what appears an impossible balance. In the same room, a feeling of vertigo and disorientation emerges from the floor, a transparent sheet of tempered glass that allows visitors to look into a deep, round void opening beneath them (see fig. 4.7). While standing over this void, visitors can view a projection of a video showing the words of the Edict of Expulsion while a voiceover reads them aloud. On the opposite wall, we find a transcription of the edict into modern Spanish and Hebrew.

As recounted by Ruth Behar, who participated in the Summit of the Bejars and wrote an ethnographic analysis of the event, the architect José Luis Rodríguez Antúnez, who guided them in their visit, explained the rationale of this room and the museum's organization at that time as follows:

> the plan was for people to enter this room, in the dark, and hear the Edict of Expulsion read to them in the resounding voices of Ferdinand and Isabel as if they were Jews in Spain in 1492. With the appropriate sound effects and the glass floor covering a huge pit, the idea would be for museum visitors to feel the ground quaking under their feet, and find themselves forced to make the decision of whether to stay and convert, or leave Spain and go into exile. He hoped museum visitors would put themselves in the shoes of the person who had to make that decision five hundred years ago and decide what they would do. Those who chose to stay would proceed through the museum and learn about the history of Béjar after the expulsion; those who chose to leave

Figure 4.7. "Room of the Two Destinies." Jewish Museum David Melul, Béjar. ©Rina Benmayor.

> would skip that history and go straight to the top floor, to that room that was still empty, and waiting to be filled with the stories of our Sephardi diaspora. (Behar 134–35)

The converso path of the second floor provides information through a series of wall panels about the overwhelming influence the Inquisition played in conversos' lives and their gradual integration and assimilation into Old Christian society. Special emphasis is placed on the presentation of Don Francés de Zúñiga (1490–1532), a local converso who acquired notoriety first as the court jester of Don Álvaro de Zúñiga, Duke of Béjar, from whom he took his name, and later of Emperor Carlos V.[12] The conference room located on this floor pays homage to him by bearing his name.

On this floor, we also find a large mock-up of the town of Béjar as it may have looked in the fifteenth century. The houses in this model are painted in various shades of ocher and red. Several houses, however, appear uniformly painted in a slate gray color. The legend identifies these houses as those where Jewish families once lived. In case this distinction is not fully clear, a four-inch-tall bearded figurine resembling a Hasidic Jew has been placed next to the larger concentration of these gray buildings. The base of the little statue reads, "Béjar." In 2016, a short documentary by Carmen Comadrán about the life of the local converso population and their relationship with their neighbors and the Inquisition entitled *Conversos* and made expressly for the museum was incorporated into the collection on this floor.

The compound effect of this information can raise the question in visitors about whether this converso lineage is part of their history. The exhibits simultaneously exoticize Judaism and interpellate visitors as possible descendants of conversos. The information panels, the gray color in the map, and the little figurine performatively homogenize and compartmentalize medieval Jews and present them as alien. But these same exhibits also provide grounds for the visitor to identify with conversos by including specific examples of local conversos, placing the name of the village at the feet of the figurine of the imaginary Jew and even by identifying Jewish dwellings in a gray color that more closely matches the actual tones of the slate and stone of most houses in the village.

The third floor is dedicated to those Jews who left Spain and is motivated by the nostalgia, localist pride, and calls for return and reunion that lie at the heart of the museum's project. It begins with an appeal for the visitor to feel virtual nostalgia through the contemplation of an image of Béjar presented as if from the perspective of those who, leaving the city to go into exile, would have seen it for the last time. The hall opens onto a room presided over by two large wall maps showing the destinations of those exiled, while Sephardi music plays in the background. Hanging from the ceiling, an oversized iron key hints at how the maps and music should be interpreted. The symbol of the key both condenses and makes palpable the idea that the post-1492 Sephardi diaspora has always maintained a material link to the life they left behind. A panel entitled "Very large key" explains that the key has inspired the logo of the museum and "aims to evoke the farewell [to], reminiscence [about] and re-encounter with Sephardi culture." The motif of the mythical key repeats on a half-open old wooden chest that lies on the floor. Inside, the visitor finds a cluster of rusty old iron keys. While no claims are made that these are actual examples of keys held by Sephardi families as proof of the homes they left behind in 1492—there is no explanatory panel or caption next to them—the exhibit appeals to their symbolic power.

A panel displaying a carefully chosen part of the poem "La llave en Salónica" [The Key in Salonika] by Argentine writer Jorge Luis Borges completes this room's installation. The museum's installation quotes and modifies the poem's first stanza:

> Abarbanel, Farías o Pinedo,
> arrojados de España por impía
> persecución, conservan todavía
> la llave de una casa de Béjar o Toledo
>
> [Abarvanel, Farias or Pinedo,
> hurled out of Spain in an unholy
> persecution, still possess
> the door key to a house in Béjar or Toledo]

While the original poem alludes to the keys that Salonika's Jewish families held from their former houses *in Toledo,* the quoted poem in the museum adds Béjar as another possible origin for these emblematic keys. This alteration is signaled modestly by a small white arrow and the city's name in bold. Like the map identifying Béjar as an aljama, the gesture provides another literalization of the museum's main intention: to inscribe Béjar into the map of the Sephardi diaspora. The original poem by Borges, however, reflects on the impossibility of returning, which is suppressed by the museum's choice of the stanza displayed. A later line reads, "Hoy su puerta es polvo, el instrumento cifra de la diáspora" [Today its door is dust, the instrumental cipher for the diaspora]. In the poem, the key stands for the impossibility of return—there is no door that it can open—and is a confirmation of the hold that the experience of exile has on Jews.

Thus, despite the museum's push to naturalize this mythical connection, the exhibits also contain a counternarrative. Here and there we find traces that point to the impossibility of return, reparation, and/or redress. One of the most emblematic of these counternarratives appears in Borges's poem and its central metaphor of the key that outlived the door it once opened. The gap separating keys and ancestral home is also embedded in the key that serves as logo to the museum and the many keys in coffers, vitrines, and ceilings. The very fact that they are in the museum points to their mechanical obsolescence. These are orphaned keys; no locks and no doors await them to reveal their secrets.

The climax of the museum's visit is its last room, called the "Room of the Bejars." This room, empty at the time of the First World Summit of the Bejars in 2004, has been filled with the help of the people who participated in the 2004 event. It contains family photos; a variety of testimonial objects; and first-person narratives, family histories, and copies of works written or produced by people bearing any of the surnames that can be connected to the word *Béjar*, such as a copy of anthropologist Ruth Behar's documentary film about the Sephardi Jews of Cuba, *Adio Kerida*. These memorabilia are exhibited as part of an extended family album that contains the history while in exile of the Jewish bejaranos.

This exhibit thus physically and symbolically claims Béjar as a privileged point of origin of the Sephardi diaspora. We see this gesture first in the museum's entrance hall where Béjar is proudly identified as an aljama and repeated in the maps of the diaspora and in the insertion of the town's name next to that of Toledo in Borges's poem. The most remarkable performance of this gesture rests within the family albums of the Bejars, which in effect seem to imply that the Sephardi diaspora carried within it a kernel of Béjar's essence through a group of people that took the village with them in their names as silent witness to their sufferings and achievements. Arguably the reiteration of this gesture of cartographic insertion indicates that the main purpose of the museum is to insert Béjar into the imaginary cartography of the Jewish diaspora and through it into the more material itineraries of Jewish heritage tourism. The museum wants to believe in a kind of sympathetic magic stemming from the phonetic proximity of the town's name and the surnames of many Sephardi Jews. With no other justification but this phonetic resemblance, the museum builds a narrative of how Jews are a constituent part of Béjar's history (that is why so many carry the village name) and how the town is an essential component of the history of Sephardi Jews.

As demonstrated by the "family album" exhibit on the third floor and as explained by Ruth Behar in her ethnographic analysis of the Summit, many Bejars themselves are also invested in this narrative, if only to provide a genealogical and affective sense of origin for themselves, a story of origin that they want to believe in (Behar 139–40).

Mieke Bal describes the self-reflective work of critics who attempt to overcome the intrinsic power relation and "'object status' that 'third personhood' entails for their 'other,' the object of exposition, the one pointed out." She quotes the critic Hubert Damisch speaking of his search for "an analysis which would be less *about* a painting than it would have to reckon *with* it" (Bal, *Double* 169). We can read a similar intent at the Melul museum: the exhibitions are not, or are not primarily, *about* the Jews but, in great part, made *with* them, with Melul, Garzón, and the Bejars. The coincidence of first and third persons, of being spoken about but also being expository subjects, means that the intrinsic power imbalance and objectivization of the "I speak about you" relation does not completely hold here. In his 2004 radio interview, David Melul mentioned Spanish Jews' important presence on the museum's board of trustees (among them, Jacobo Israel Garzón) and emphasized that they should have "important weight" in the museum's decisions, in that this museum was being made for them ("Entrevista a David Melul").

CASA DE SEFARAD/CASA DE LA MEMORIA IN CÓRDOBA, ANDALUCÍA

Inaugurated in 2006, Casa de Sefarad has the peculiarity of being a completely private institution. Its director, historian Sebastián de la Obra, explains that the museum "Es un centro cultural y museístico privado, independiente y libre, sin un solo recurso público" [is a private, independent and free museum and cultural center, without any public funding]. One of its main objectives, as indicated in its second name, "Casa de la memoria" [house of memory] "es un ejercicio de la recuperación de la memoria de los judíos hispanos" [is an exercise in the recuperation of the memory of Hispano-Jews] (R. Castro). In order to describe its location, the Casa de Sefarad uses the very same language we have seen before in locations along the Red de Juderías: "The House of Sepharad is in the street with the oldest original name in the Jewish quarter—Judíos (Jews)—at the very heart of the historical city center, the Jewry of Córdoba . . . the old Jewish quarter is nowadays the best preserved urban collection of buildings of all the Spanish medieval Jewries" (Casa de Sefarad website). However, as we will see, this institution has used its location "at the very heart" of the former

Jewish quarter to disrupt the narrative of convivencia so uncritically embraced by most cities belonging to the Red de Juderías.

While Casa de Sefarad's permanent exhibition contains some of the same features of other museums—explanations about the Jewish life cycle, Jewish holidays, and so on—and presents Córdoba as a "site of glory" for Jewish life, paying attention, for example, to the conservation of its synagogue and to the figure of Maimónides, some of its rooms present a unique perspective, showing Córdoba as also a site of shame. This is especially the case of the room dedicated to the Inquisition and the persecution of conversos, in which we find panels with explanations about its functioning and scope and a copy of a sanbenito from sixteenth-century Córdoba (see fig. 4.8). Instead of speaking about the Inquisition as something imposed from the outside, as we find in Girona and Ribadavia, this museum emphasizes the functioning and consequences of the Inquisition's actions in Córdoba itself. Two of the walls in this room pay homage to victims from Córdoba, listing the names and occupations of conversos burned at the stake or in effigy for Judaizing and the year of their punishment (see fig. 4.9). On the next wall, we find descriptions of the repressive role of the Inquisition in the lives of well-known figures of sixteenth- and seventeenth-century Spain such as Fray Luis de León, Santa Teresa de Ávila, Juan de Ávila, Juan Luis Vives, Juan de la Cruz, Mateo Alemán, and Fernando de Rojas. These are writers and thinkers whom most people in Spain know well from having studied them in school. The descriptions narrate their encounters with the Inquisition, the prohibition of their books, or how they were persecuted because of their converso ancestry.

Casa de Sefarad is also unique in its extensive cultural programming. It is in its educational activities, workshops, concerts, lectures, and active presence in social media where we can best find these institutions' potential for impact on the general public, the kind of effect Kirshenblatt-Gimblett points at when she argues that imperfect-fit museums are full of pitfalls but also full of possibilities ("Why" 5). The museum's interactive activities involving the public offer potential processes of education, discovery, and transformation for both visitors and the local population. Casa de Sefarad has gone further in this respect than any of the government-funded institutions, putting together exhibitions, conferences, and events that are truly critical of the market-driven, easy-to-digest, and idealized convivencia narrative. Instead, its activities have demonstrated constant engagement with the most difficult and conflictive issues surrounding the memory of Jewish Spain and its connections with other difficult memories.

Using the motto "Donde hay atención, no hay olvido" [Where there is attention, there is no forgetting], these activities actualize the memory of Jewish

Figure 4.8. Inquisition Room, Casa de Sefarad, Córdoba, July 2011. ©Daniela Flesler.

Spain by connecting it to the memory of the Holocaust and to other difficult memories with close resonances, especially the memory of the Spanish Civil War and the Francoist repression. Every January since 2007, the Casa de Sefarad has commemorated the Holocaust with events such as a conversation with survivor Haim Vidal Sephiha (2007); an homage to the righteous (2008); a conference by philosopher Reyes Mate on the concepts of memory and victimhood (2011); debates about the disabled, homosexuals, and Jehovah's Witnesses who were victims of the Holocaust (2012); exhibitions on Andalusians in concentration camps (2015); the Roma Holocaust (2016); and Albanian Muslims who saved Jews during the Holocaust (2018).

An exhibition in 2014 and 2017 focused on the many historical instances, across time and space, of book destruction—and also on those who dedicated their lives to saving them. The title, *Donde se queman los libros, al final se quemarán personas,* was based on nineteenth-century German Jewish poet Heinrich Heine's famous admonition, "Where they burn books, they will also ultimately burn people" (R. Castro). It included historical examples ranging from the burning of Aztec codices and sacred books in Tetzoco, Mexico in 1530 by Juan de Zumárraga (1468–1548), the Basque Franciscan inquisitor and first bishop of Mexico, to the destruction of books in different Spanish cities

Figures 4.9. List of victims' names, Inquisition Room, Casa de Sefarad, Córdoba, July 2011. ©Daniela Flesler.

by Falangist followers and Francoist officials during the Spanish Civil War, the burning of books during the Argentine military dictatorship (1976–1983), and the destruction of the Sarajevo library in 1992. Like the exhibit in the Sephardi Museum that we analyze in chapter 6, several of these exhibits have caused controversy and discomfort, since they are pushing the boundaries of the usual, conventional frames of reference—mainly, the convivencia slogan—often used in discussing Jewish issues in Spain today. Casa de Sefarad is also sketching a series of transnational and transhistoric networks that connect the city's Jewish history with other places and other histories of both barbarism and righteousness.

The "Storytelling" sessions/conferences in September 2018 included an homage to the Argentine Sephardi writer Reina Roffé by staging her work *Aves exóticas*, about women who did not follow conventional rules of gendered behavior in their respective times. Roffé is an exiled writer from the Argentine dictatorship who has lived in Spain since 1988. The presence of her work in Casa de Sefarad, like many other activities, was a statement about the liveliness of Spain's Jewish present. The conference "De Diego Lucero a Bruno Ibañez: Historias de los savonarolas cordobeses" [From Diego Lucero to Bruno Ibáñez:

Histories of Cordoban Savonarolas] returned to the echoes and links between Inquisitorial times and the Francoist repression. The focus here, once again, was on local instances of extreme political violence and brutality of two men "of different times and similar behavior," Diego Rodriguez Lucero, named senior inquisitor of Córdoba in 1500 and the Francoist military official Bruno Ibáñez Gálvez.

Another remarkable event sponsored and organized by Casa de Sefarad, entitled "Con nombre propio: Acto de restitución de la memoria, homenaje a los quemados por la Inquisición de Córdoba desde 1483 hasta 1731" [In their own name: Act of memory restitution, homage to those burnt by the Inquisition of Córdoba from 1483 to 1731] took place in 2010. The event, which can be seen in a YouTube video, consisted of painting the exterior white wall of Casa de Sefarad with information about Córdoba Inquisition victims: their first names, last names, occupations, what they were accused of, their punishment, and its date. This information, probably gathered from Inquisition records, echoes that found inside the Inquisition Room of the museum. The act of taking this information from within the museum, to be "aired out" in the street, imprinted over the outside wall by stenciling each individual victim's information with aerosol, has the obvious goal of making it more visible for all eyes of the city to see, as a public performance. As Charles McDonald describes the YouTube video, "Journalists, photographers, local Cordobans, and tourists are assembled in the tiny winding street to watch. Many of them participate, shaking and then spraying the paint cans while Haim [who works in Casa de Sefarad] holds the stencil in place. After each stencil is applied, the name is intoned by a voice off-camera. The moment slips between solemnity and giddy exuberance, with a mix of pensive and smiling faces" (McDonald 55).

The organizers described this commemoration as "an act of poetic justice." Sebastián de la Obra explained that the event itself, with its participants coming from different countries, Jewish, Catholic, Muslim, and agnostic, was a metaphor about the respect for difference and diversity, against the very intolerance of the "project of social, political and cultural engineering" of the Inquisition ("Con nombre propio"). As with all commemorations, this event was made of and for the present and encapsulated, in its mix of irreverence and condemnation, the critical stance from which this museum articulates its exhibits and message. McDonald highlights the uniqueness of this approach, "In a discursive milieu in which cultural heritage is commonly conceptualized as an inert historical legacy, rather than the shifting ground of the present, Casa de Sefarad is a heretical institution" (55). The ultimate aim of this museum's transnational and transhistoric focus extends into the future as well. In an interview for Córdoba television, de la Obra stated that he sees Jewish Spain not as archaeology but as something alive in the present. He regards his work as memory for the future, as sowing seeds that future generations will fully appreciate ("Entrevista Sebastián de la Obra"). In this vision, the obligations of memory work extend both to the silenced past and to the construction and imagination of that future.

TRAGÈDIA AL CALL: TÀRREGA 1348 EXHIBITION AT THE MUSEO DE L'URGELL

A highly explicit exploration of the violent side of Jewish-Christian interaction in the Iberian Middle Ages takes place in the exhibit *Tragèdia al call: Tàrrega 1348* (Tragedy at the Jewish Quarter: Tàrrega 1348). A permanent exhibit in the Museu Comarcal de l'Urgell in the province of Lleida, Catalonia, it was inaugurated in 2014 with funds provided entirely by the Spanish Ministry of Culture. The exhibit documents the local massacre of over three hundred Jewish men, women, and children at the hands of their neighbors during a bout of the Black Death in 1348. This event, long forgotten by the local population, acquired renewed notoriety after six mass graves with human remains were found while digging the foundations for a new housing development in 2007. The mass graves' location was in the vicinity of the area known as Les Roquetes, where the town's medieval Jewish cemetery once stood (Colet et al. 73–74).

The construction story provides an apt metaphor for the crossroads at which these towns and cities across Spain find themselves when they engage in the rediscovery of their Jewish past. It was also by chance and in the course of construction projects that remains from medieval Jewish cemeteries were found in other Spanish cities as well: in Valencia in 1996, in Lucena in 2006, in Toledo in 2008, and in Ávila in 2012. It is, literally, in the effort to lay the foundations for a solid future within the relentless pressure of globalization forces that long-dormant local issues resurface. At first, the findings are met with the same glee with which a treasure hunter contemplates a newly discovered buried chest.[13] But, as the case of Tàrrega so poignantly shows, these findings contain a different kind of treasure. What archaeologists found were 159 individual graves and 6 mass graves with at least 228 bodies. The mass graves, in which most bodies showed signs of violent trauma as the cause of death, were dated to the mid-fourteenth century by the evidence of two sets of coins and by carbon-14 testing. The careful orientation and disposition of the bodies led archaeologists to conclude that the bodies were buried by the surviving members of the Jewish community after the attack had ended (Colet et al. 80). Archaeologists also found a series of small surviving objects: bronze rings (two of them, with Hebrew inscriptions, confirming the archaeologists' suspicion that this was, indeed, the Jewish cemetery), buttons, coral and jet necklace beads, glass-paste bracelets, and, in one of the mass graves, a necklace with ten silver and bone amulets belonging to a child that seemed to have suffered from a slight malformation of the lower limbs (Colet et al. 76; Colet Marcé and Saula Briansó 243–44). These "treasures," rather than providing immediate material wealth, remind the finder of an outstanding debt connected to the past. Their open presence forces these societies to reconfigure the image they have of themselves.

Following the discovery at Les Roquetes, a bitter controversy ensued. As would happen the following year in Toledo, the finding was not immediately communicated to the Federation of Jewish Communities of Spain (FCJE). This led to mounting distrust and suspicion, as later recognized by the principal archaeologists at Tàrrega (Colet Marcé and Saula Briansó 248). Soon, the word spread and representatives from Barcelona's Jewish communities and Jewish organizations contacted the Tàrrega and Catalan governments to demand a stop to the excavations.[14] On July 22, 2007, the FCJE wrote the *Protocolo de actuación para la exhumación de restos humanos en necrópolis judías históricas* (Action protocol for the exhumation of human remains in historic Jewish cemeteries) and sent it as urgent communication to Spain's Department of Justice and the governments of Barcelona, Tárrega, and Lucena. The document explained the importance that historic Jewish cemeteries be held as sacred spaces that must not be disturbed, defended the eternal quality of Jewish burials, and provided guidelines on how to proceed when human remains are found: the federation must be immediately informed, archaeologists must preserve the individual bodies separately, and the remains should be reburied under the direction of a rabbi in the same location in which they were found, or, if that is not possible, transferred to the closest Jewish cemetery (FCJE, "Protocolo").

A few days later, on July 27, the Catalan government ordered the remains transferred to the Jewish cemetery of Collserola, in Barcelona, under rabbinic supervision. From the perspective of the Tárrega archaeologists, the decision was a mistake that prevented them from completing the excavation and the study of the remains. Three archaeology associations appealed the decision and mobilized their members and public opinion to protest it. Since the FCJE had referred to the Cooperation Agreement of 1992 as one that protected Jewish cemeteries as sacred spaces, the archaeology associations replied that such protection referred to cemeteries in use, not to medieval ones that haven't been used for five hundred years and that should be considered archaeological sites (Colet Marcé and Saula Briansó 244–48). This mobilization was successful in lobbying the Catalan government to reach a new agreement with the FCJE and resulted in the continuation of the excavation in August of the same year and in the anthropological study of the human remains found between August and December 2007 (Colet Marcé and Saula Briansó 249).

The dispute in Tárrega had a precedent in the controversy surrounding the medieval Jewish cemetery in Montjuïc, Barcelona. After the 1391 destruction of the Jewish community, most of the tombstones were reused as building material in the city of Barcelona. In 1945, 171 Jewish graves were discovered, 114 burials were studied, and personal ornaments found were transferred to museums before the area was transformed into a clay pigeon–shooting range and an amusement park. During the mid-1970s, these facilities fell into disuse (Colomer, "Approaching" 82). In connection to the sweeping renovation and gentrification many areas of the city underwent for the 1992 Olympic Games, Barcelona's municipal government planned a beautification project to construct a new public park in the area occupied by the cemetery. An archaeological survey in 2001 found 557 tombs and revealed an older, unexcavated section. According to the archaeologists involved, the park would not disturb the site or the tombs, "taking into account its special historic and religious significance" (Colomer, "Approaching" 82). However, when details of the planned project were revealed in 2006—especially that a restaurant and public bathrooms were to be built as part of the public park, right above the cemetery—the three Jewish congregations of Barcelona successfully petitioned the municipal government to designate the area a Historic Site of National Interest and to stop the project (see Centro de estudios Zahkor, "El cementerio").

One of the leaders of the effort was Dominique Tomasov Binder, a Jewish architect born in New York and raised in Argentina who has lived in Barcelona since 1991. Tomasov has been a pioneer in the promotion of Barcelona's Jewish heritage, offering educational tours of Jewish Barcelona through her company Urban Cultours since 1999.[15] In 2008, she cofounded with David Stoleru the Zakhor Center of Studies for the Protection and Transmission of Jewish Heritage. One of the main objectives of the center, which closed in 2012, was the protection of medieval Jewish cemeteries in Spain. In this role, it monitored and collaborated in the excavations of Tárrega's mass graves.[16]

As a result of these controversies, Barcelona's Museum of History organized the international conference "Archeological Intervention in Historic Necropoles: Jewish Cemeteries" on January 15–16, 2009. Archaeologists and curators of Jewish heritage from France, Israel, and the United States, together with representatives of the governments of Catalonia and Barcelona and a representative of the FCJE, were invited to discuss the pressing issue of how to treat human remains in newly discovered Jewish cemeteries. As part of the conference, a group of anthropologists and archaeologists issued a declaration stating that ancient burial sites are central and irreplaceable evidence to be used for accurately reconstructing the past and defending the right of scientists (specifically anthropologists and archaeologists) to study the human remains found in these sites ("Declaración").

In an article published in the Jewish publication *Raíces,* entitled "Antiguos cementerios judíos de España: La necesidad de un diálogo" [Old Jewish cemeteries in Spain: The need for dialogue] the Zahkor Center responded to the Barcelona conference and its conclusions by stating that the conference was not a true dialogue with a diversity of opinions because the vast majority of the archaeologists invited shared the same point of view and the sole representative of Spain's Jewish communities, Dalia Levinsohn, was relegated to a round table discussion (Centro de estudios Zahkor, "Antiguos cementerios" 77).

In his talk at the conference, Neil A. Silberman, from the Center for Heritage and Society of the University of Massachusetts–Amherst, did try to find common ground. Relating the cases of old Jewish cemeteries to those concerning Native American burial sites, he explained how these conflicts rest on two maximalist positions that are difficult to reconcile: on the one hand, communities claim complete ritual control over the human remains, which are seen as human beings intimately connected to their contemporary community and their memory. On the other hand, archaeologists claim unlimited scientific access to the remains, seen as a unique source of data and information about the past. Government officials are usually caught in the middle. The only way to get beyond this zero-sum game of ownership, he argued, is a negotiation in which both parties recognize their rights and responsibilities in civil society. Scientists must see human remains as more than data and respect a community's sense of identity in connection to those remains. After a certain period of time, bones need to be given some sort of cultural return (Silberman 33–36, 40). Communities must accept the right of scientists to study the bones and, "perhaps most challenging of all . . . recognize that cultural continuity is never direct, complete and unequivocal" (Silberman 41).

Several of the participants in the conference, however, engaged precisely in this maximalist discussion over ownership rights in an attempt to delegitimize any Jewish claim to continuity with the remains. Laia Colomer i Solsona, from the Barcelona History Museum, argued against the FCJE's assumption that Jewish medieval cemeteries constituted sacred places. There is no historical continuity in property or use, she said, of cemeteries that "had been abandoned and handed over more than 500 years ago." Historical Jewish heritage, she argued, is public cultural property that belongs to everybody as an expression of a shared past (Colomer i Solsona, "La arqueología" 226–27). Anna Colet Marcé and Oriol Saula Briansó also insisted that because the cemetery had not been in use for more than 500 years, "it should be considered what it is: an archeological site." They also explicitly delegitimized the authority of the Jewish representatives who had stopped the excavation in Tàrrega: the complaints, they argued, were voiced by "a small collective from a religious minority" who "don't respect the laws of the country"; they were "a strict and radical branch" of the Catalan Jewish community who "took Jewish law to the extreme" (Colet Marcé and Saula Briansó 248).[17] In the prologue to the Tàrrega exhibition catalog, Paul Salmona, director of the Musée d'Art et d'Histoire du Judaïsme, Paris, bluntly asked, "Can a minority prohibit a whole nation access to its past?" (363).

In order to bolster their case, archaeologists and museum authorities used a surprising argument: the remains, in fact, belong to Tàrrega (and to other Spanish cities) because it was very possible that owing to the massive conversions of Jews to Christianity in the fourteenth and fifteenth centuries, these cities' current inhabitants were descendants of conversos. Vicent Lerma, a Valencia archaeologist, argued that "*conversos* and their descendants" could in fact have more legitimacy as "heirs" than Sephardi Jews ("Debate" 252). This idea was expanded in the prologue to the Tàrrega exhibition's catalog: "Nowadays, do the Catalan Jews, without any family links to the victims of 1348, have any 'particular right' over these [human remains]? In contrast, would it not be better for the 'rights' of possible descendants of the converts who remained in Tàrrega after the edict of expulsion in 1492 to prevail, currently unaware of their Jewish origins but potentially linked, from the genealogic point of view, to the deceased in the Jewish necropolis of Les Roquetes?" (Salmona 363). Salmona also summarized the controversy about Tàrrega's human remains stating that the *Tragèdia* exhibit "unequivocally demonstrates that the best way to respect the victims is to study their remains as scientifically as possible, as we would for a crime committed nowadays, [to] know their fate accurately . . . [and] give them back their dignity with a symbolic burial before giving them a physical burial" (363).[18]

How does the exhibit speak about the tragedy it attempts to represent, then? The display is part of the larger Museu Comarcal de l'Urgell-Tàrrega, a "site of glory" museum for the culture, art, and history of the town. In terms of history and economic evolution, Tàrrega is quite similar to Ribadavia, Béjar, Tarazona, and other midsize towns with newly opened Jewish museums. Like them, Tàrrega grew in the shadow of a castle to become a regional market town. It developed into a small but significant industrial center (traditionally of textiles and eventually of farm machinery) and saw its economy decline with the globalization of manufacturing in the late twentieth century. Tàrrega also boasts of having a well-preserved walled historic center containing an area locally known as the Jewish Quarter. Located in a seventeenth-century urban mansion, the Perelló house, the museum reopened in this location in the 1980s and shows collections of fossils, paintings by local artist Antoni Alsina and archaeological objects excavated from a nearby Iber settlement, as well as the colorful rococo interior decoration in the main living quarters of the mansion.

The *Tragèdia* exhibit, with its immediate connotations of a site of shame, is not only conceptually at odds with the rest of the museum, it is also severed from it physically. Located in the dark and stone-walled basement of the building, its cavernous atmosphere stands in stark contrast to the colorful luminosity and open spaces that characterize the museum's two main floors. A series of large panels divide the space into six small partitions. As visitors meander through this miniature labyrinth, they see the now familiar juxtaposition of bare ancient structural elements (exposed stone, bricks, and wooden beams) and sleek panels, vitrines, backlit transparencies, and audiovisual projections. Again, this labyrinthine layout implicitly resonates with the stereotypical notions of Judaism as mysterious, secret, and remote. The sleek display techniques and panels connect Tàrrega to the efforts we have seen in other museums to reconcile tradition and modernity. Yet in the context of the local massacre chronicled in this exhibit, a new layer of meaning arises from these structural motifs that we can now sense as a latent presence in other museums. The labyrinth becomes a symbol of the game of revelation and concealment to which the events of the massacre are subjected in the exhibit and, by extension, to the tortuous alternation of approaching and distancing, of calculated strategy and affective longing that characterizes the relationship this town and the rest of Spain have to its Jewish past. The setting and display techniques reveal the struggle between efforts to tame the negative affects that are bound to emerge when this difficult past is reexamined and the hopes that this time the barbaric past would be critically confronted.

The narrative content and objects further amplify this process of resignification the *Tragèdia* exhibit operates on the narratives of Spain's Jewish past. Surprisingly, given the contrary evidence it provides, the exhibit as a whole remains committed to the convivencia narrative and does so by adopting a scientific tone in the explanations. This turn to science parallels the position that archaeologists took in the public discussion about the proper way to deal with the human remains found in the mass graves. The rooms showing the archaeological and documentary materials related to the massacre are embedded within two "site of glory" rooms that precede and close the exhibit as a kind of symbolic safety belt. Together, these rooms situate the massacre as a brief interruption to an otherwise tolerant and diverse local community life. An introductory panel named "Mosaic of Cultures" depicts the climate of "relative tolerance" in the village, "despite Christian hegemony," and speaks about the golden age experienced by the Jewish community under the crown of Aragon. The room is dominated by a set of early fourteenth-century life-size Gothic sculptures representing five of the Apostles. They are not just one more "tile" in the village's medieval cultural mosaic. Their towering presence—a panel next to them describes the hegemonic power of the Catholic Church—seems to give the exhibit Christian approval. The size and solidity of these granite sculptures also has the effect of emphasizing the minute, fragile, and fragmentary nature of Jewish material remains. At the other end of the exhibit, the convivencia narrative reappears in a large panel dedicated to the life and work of Moixé Natán (Moshe Nathan in English texts), a prominent local Jew introduced as "an erudite, poet, writer, moneylender, and survivor of the events of 1348."

In between these two attempts to reconnect with the idea of convivencia, four smaller rooms gradually introduce us to what the exhibit refers to as "The Crisis." The second room depicts the years leading to the massacre as a period in which increasing scarcity and hunger created a tense atmosphere. Christian ecclesiastical discourse, states the panel "In the Name of God," becomes radicalized, reaching apocalyptic levels. Jews are stigmatized and blamed for the Black Death. Discriminatory measures are imposed against them, including limiting their access to fresh food. The panel includes visual representations of Jews with long noses and peculiar hats.[19] The next room, the virtual midpoint in the exhibition, is a narrow corridor where the whole length of a wall is covered by a panel entitled "The Assault," which includes a short text and a large photograph. The text describes the attack on the Jewish Quarter, stating "Men, women and children are violently, brutally and indiscriminately killed." The photograph shows one of the mass graves found in 2007; a group of over a dozen skeletons lying at the bottom of a trench (see fig. 4.10).

In an effort to soften the documentary impact of the photograph, the image has been modified by adding layers of ocher and red colors as if suggesting the light of a sunset or the bloody stains of violence. The result recalls the aesthetic meditation on the inevitability of death in a vanitas painting and connects formally to politically motivated art such as Goya's black paintings. But it also directly connects, in the Spanish imagination, to the exhumation photographs from the victims of the Spanish Civil War and the ensuing Francoist repression that have surfaced and circulated widely in the last few years thanks to the work of the Association for the Recovery of Historical Memory.[20] Many photographs and videos without "artistic touchup" are included in the exhibition as well: for example, aerial views of the mass graves and anthropologists at work

Figure 4.10. "The Assault" Panel, with photograph of one of the mass graves found at Les Roquetes. *Tragèdia al call: Tàrrega 1348,* Museu de l'Urgell, Tàrrega. ©Museu de l'Urgell, Tàrrega.

next to the remains. The images are nearly identical to those of the exhumations of Francoist mass graves. In fact, when Les Roquetes began to be urbanized in 2000 and the first human remains were found there, they were assumed to be remains from the Civil War. They were thus reburied in the municipal cemetery without contacting the museum (Colet and Saula 243).

The next two rooms gather the small material objects found in the excavation. They appear carefully arranged as if they were precious pieces in a jewelry collection: sitting inside vitrines embedded on the walls, elevated on minute transparent pedestals, and illuminated by strong direct lighting (see figs. 4.11 and 4.12). The presence of these objects, so personal that they accompanied their owners to their graves, is bound to raise immediate questions in the viewer: who was the owner? What hopes, joys, and fears made these objects cherished by their owners? What memories lie dormant in them? The surrounding explanatory texts, however, displace the viewer's attention to other more "scientific" questions. First the objects are presented as evidence that Tàrrega has a "unique and singular archaeological site" since, as a panel informs us, it represents the best documented mass burial among those connected to the numerous Black Death persecutions that took place throughout medieval Europe. In this way the nationalist local narrative reemerges: these Jewish objects

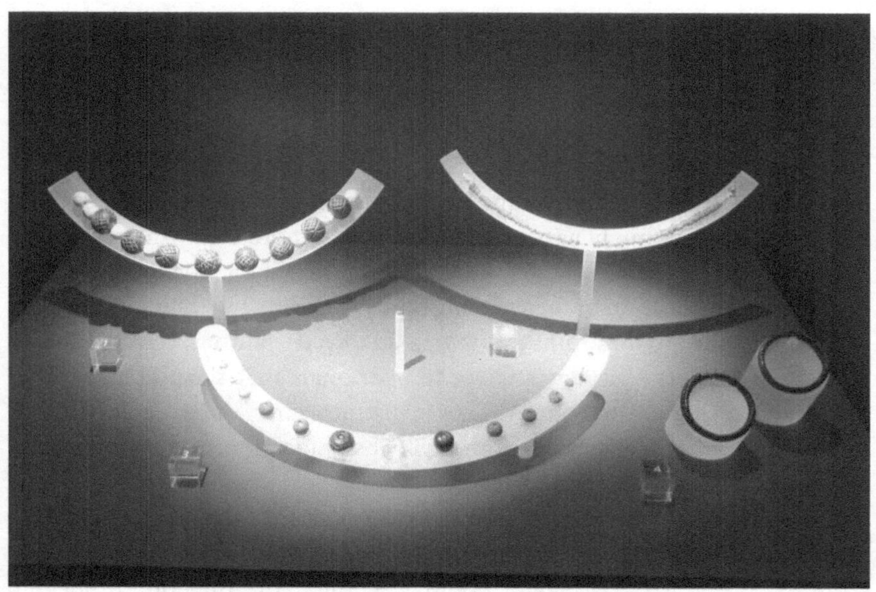

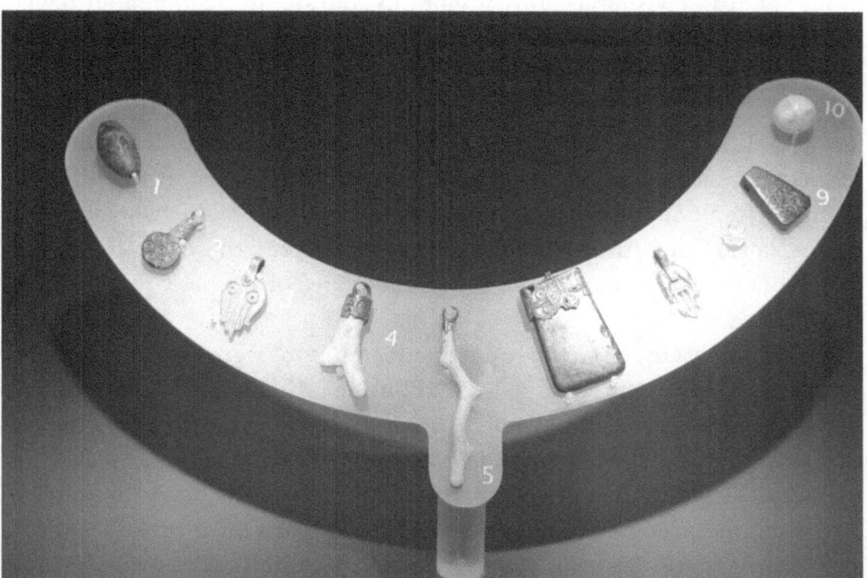

Figures 4.11 and 4.12. Personal objects exhibited in *Tragèdia al call: Tàrrega 1348*, Museu de l'Urgell, Tàrrega, July 2017. ©Adrián Pérez Melgosa.

speak of Tàrrega's connection to and exemplary significance within Europe. Then, presented in small groups, the objects become the basis for ethnographically reconstructing medieval Jewish life and discussing the craftsmanship of local Jewish artisans.

But this effort to redirect the objects' significance to their archaeological and historical value does not fully tame the violent memory embedded in them. If silence and absence might have helped other museums re-create their presently desired pasts, the event at the center of the *Tragèdia* exhibit does not fully lend itself to any idealization or repurposing for the present. The direct links to the events embedded in these diminutive trinkets, beads, buttons, ceramic housewares, and amulets resist any attempt to instrumentalize the past for present gain. The way they are exhibited reveals in distinct clarity the struggle between celebration and atonement, local and global signification, and converso and normative religious epistemologies.

If the massive tombstones shown in Toledo and Girona implicitly inscribed medieval Jews into a rhetoric of death by positioning them in a remote and closed past, these objects embody human life and point to specific affections, fears, and hopes. Whereas the ritual objects displayed across the other Spanish Jewish museums attempt to educate the visitor about Jewish religious practices through objects from the Sephardi diaspora, these objects point to a rich nonreligious life and (in the case of the amulets) hint at popular beliefs in magic shared with their neighbors. Because of their familiar design and materials, their easily understandable utilitarian functions and refined aesthetics, they resist any pull toward exoticization. And unlike the many written documents that remain from the medieval Jewish past, most of them legal briefs, property titles, and royal decrees, these humble objects of personal use depict a web of human affections, of aesthetic pleasure, and everyday care.

Other objects in the Girona and Toledo museums were also found in Jewish cemeteries. But the fact that this exhibition is thematically centered on a massacre, the fact that these objects are directly connected to the violence that interrupted the lives of their owners, recontextualizes and resignifies the objects beyond their counterparts in other museums. As Antonio Monegal explains in relation to objects found at Francoist mass graves, "Objects ... are made to speak within the discourse of an exhibition, and thus become readable thanks to the context that frames them" (240). In a video shown as part of the exhibition, *Site of Roquets: The Graveyard of the Jews (Tarrega)*, we can see the objects as they were found, next to the human remains (see fig. 4.13). These images become powerful carriers of the link between the

Figure 4.13. Still from exhibit's video *Site of Roquets: The Graveyard of the Jews (Tarrega)* showing jet-stone necklace next to the human remains where it was found. Museu de l'Urgell, Tàrrega, July 2017. ©Adrián Pérez Melgosa.

violence of the past and its present visualization. The contextualization of these objects provided by the video, its "process of semioticization" (Monegal 243), presents them as not only physical traces but also witnesses of the massacre. They were there: their position is similar to that of an eyewitness (Monegal 243). So powerful is the resignification of these necklaces and bracelets that, after visiting this exhibition, similar objects at the museums of Toledo or Girona could also become resignified for the visitor, as they were for us.

These objects embody the haunting quality of the story told in the exhibition, and they speak of the past's hold on the present and point to an outstanding debt. The final section of the exhibition catalog describes the physical evidence of violence found in each body, to conclude: "Both the localization and characteristics of the traumatisms [as] the number identified on each skeleton (up to twenty-two traumatisms on a single body) clearly show the intentionality and cruelty used and, by extension, the aim of exterminating the population of the Jewish quarter" (Colet Marcé, Ruiz Ventura and Subirà de Galdàcano 401–2). In a revealing passage at the end of the essay, the researchers move away from the controversy over who owns the remains and who can be identified as descendants of the victims to ponder on the responsibility for the perpetrators' actions: "It is precisely these differences and the gaps in the written sources finally that encourage the researcher to fill in the gaps in history, both the recent and ancient, in order not to forget, mask or overlook any of the events featuring those who, through their acts, have brought us to where we are, although the discovery of some of the passages of our history involve a sad memory, as has happened with the study of the mass graves at Les Roquetes in Tàrrega" (Colet Marcé, Ruiz Ventura and Subirà de Galdàcano 402). The common inheritance of the discovery would consist not only in claiming a more nuanced understanding of "who we are" but also in understanding that the violence of the attacks against medieval Jews, and more recent episodes of violence, are a constituent part of "where we are." This link of ancient and more recent violence and the opening up of the memory of this violent past are examined in the next chapter.

NOTES

1. These three new museums—in Berlin, Moscow, and Warsaw—are the largest Jewish museums in Europe. They are highly ambitious, multimedia, multimillion-dollar installations employing local and international scholars, architects, and designers. See Rothstein's "In Berlin" and Young's chapter 6 of *At Memory's Edge* for Berlin, Gershenson for Moscow, and Kirshenblatt-Gimblett's "Inside the Museum" for Warsaw.

2. For the results of a recent survey of European Jewish museums conducted by the Rotschild Foundation, see Sion.

3. Before the referendum, the village was called Castrillo Matajudíos, a name of medieval origin that in modern Spanish could be translated as "little hill fort kill Jews," although other less apparent possibilities, such as "little village on the grove of the Jews," are also plausible.

4. The documents relating the disputation of Barcelona speak of the presence of a Bonastruc Sa Porta and of Nahmanides. Many historians contend that both names refer to a single individual, the former in Catalan, and the latter in Romance transliteration from Hebrew. There are some scholars, however, who think of these names as belonging to different individuals.

5. This Star of David, photographed in many of the promotional materials of the museum, was there before the museum opened, as a decoration on the patio floor of a restaurant owned by local entrepreneur Josep Tarrés i Fontan. The restaurant was named "after a provincial kabbalist named Isaac the Blind (Isaac el Cec in Catalan). In addition to the food services, Tarrés i Fontan hosted expositions and celebrations of Sephardi culture in the building. . . . However, as the Isaac el Cec restaurant became more popular locally and gained attention

from scholars of Sephardi history, officials in the city government noted some concerns about the business . . . the government (Nadal in particular) determined that the restaurant, while promoting topics of Jewish culture, focused too heavily on making a profit" (Nadel 5). In 1987, the city began buying the buildings to build the Center Bonastruc ça Porta.

6. See chapter 3 for a discussion of what is lost in this "peeling off" of the layers of history of these buildings.

7. This link between Catalans and Jews is not new. In his article "On Universalist Particularism: the Catalans and the Jews," Edgar Illas discusses the articulation of an aesthetic-political linkage between the Catalans and the Jews from the late nineteenth century to the present. In the early twentieth century, explains Illas, Catalan writers Salvador Espriu and Josep Pla established a profound and positive identification with the Jewish people, the state of Israel, and the use of the Hebrew language. Jordi Pujol, who was president of the Generalitat de Catalunya from 1980 to 2003 elaborated on the Jewish-Catalan affinity for the forging of his own brand of Catalan nationalism. Illas also traces the ways in which anti-Catalanism and antisemitism often are conflated in reactionary texts that position both groups as a threat to law, unity, and order in Spain.

8. The distinction is historically justified. Medieval Jews saw their identity as mainly tied to their city of origin and occasionally to a region. The notion of Sepharad as encompassing the whole Iberian Peninsula, in terms of geography and shared culture, existed only among the rabbinic elites, who wanted to assert a continuity with the achievements of Jewish intellectuals of al-Andalus. The boundaries of what exactly constituted the Sephardi cultural sphere varied over time (Ray, "Images" 195–200).

9. In the later part of this chapter, in our discussion of Tárrega, we address some of the controversies regarding the medieval Jewish cemetery in Montjuïc.

10. See A. Baer, "Between Old and New Antisemitism" and Baer and López, "The Blind Spots of Secularization" for qualitative and quantitative analysis of Spanish antisemitism and Spanish public opinion about Jews and Israel.

11. See Judith Cohen, "Bringing It All Back" and "Constructing" for the evolution of this festival and her role in it as musicologist and performer of Sephardi music. As do many other initiatives regarding Jewish heritage in Spain, her analysis of this festival suggests that a genuine curiosity for Ribadavia's past and the possibilities of its recuperation coexist with commercialization, opportunism, and cultural appropriation.

12. His *Crónica burlesca del Emperador Carlos V* is considered the masterpiece of court jester literature in Spain. See Roncero López.

13. In her article "La Sefarad cautiva y reinventada, o los retos de la arqueología y la divulgación del patrimonio cultural," Flocel Sabaté describes how some archaeologists have been pressured to hurry their conclusions in order to prove that a "Jewish treasure" useful for tourist promotion has been found.

14. The controversy that ensued the following year surrounding the discovery of part of the Jewish cemetery in a school outside of Toledo was even stronger and more embarassing for the Spanish authorities due to its international dimension: unflattering reports appeared in international newspapers and protests were staged in front of the Spanish Embassies in New York, Israel, and Canada (see Burnett for the *New York Times* coverage of the story, Ruiz Taboada for the perspective of the archaeologist in charge of the Toledo excavation).

15. See Linhard, *Jewish Spain* 160–65 for an analysis of the different initiatives that compete for tourists' attention in Barcelona's Jewish quarter. As Linhard explains, Tomasov Blinder's Urban Cultours is unique in that, in contrast to Casa de l'Espai Call, a center for interpretation linked to the city's history museum, it offers information not only about Jewish life in medieval Barcelona but also about Barcelona's Jewish present, "about currently functioning synagogues, and where to purchase Kosher food and celebrate Jewish holidays" (164). Tomasov criticizes the municipal government, which sponsors Casa de l'Espai Call, as lacking a Jewish perspective and not being interested in Barcelona's Jewish present (Linhard, *Jewish Spain* 162–63).

16. See their website, http://www.zakhor.net/1presentacio_cas.html.

17. Ironically, she mentioned ATID Barcelona (Tomasov's congregation) as the "radical" and "orthodox" organization that was behind the halt to the excavation. The irony stems from the fact that ATID is actually a progressive organization, close to the principles of Reform Judaism. See Vándor for the history of Barcelona's Jewish community and its two main congregations, CIB (Comunidad Israelita de Barcelona) and ATID (Comunidad Judía ATID de Cataluña). This characterization reveals, at best, a lack of interest in finding out who their Jewish interlocutors are and, at worst, a willingness to use the terms *Orthodox* and *religious* as disqualification. The position of many archaeologists when arguing for science and secularism against (Jewish, also Muslim) religion seems blind to the encompassing influence and power that the Catholic Church and religion still exert in Spain.

18. The official catalog contains academic articles written by historians, archaeologists, and anthropologists in Catalan, Castilian, and English versions. We quote from its English section.

19. See Sara Lipton's *Dark Mirror: The Medieval Origins of Anti-Jewish Iconography* for an analysis of the social functions of images of Jews in Christian art. These images, she explains, are not based on actual Jews but speak about Christian preoccupations regarding the visible world, knowledge, perception, and spiritual truth (Lipton 6–11).

20. See the introduction to this volume for more on this association and its role in the landscape of memory politics in contemporary Spain.

FIVE

MEMORY ENTANGLEMENTS: HERVÁS'S JEWISH INHERITANCE AND THE FRANCOIST REPRESSION

SINCE 1997, THE TOWN OF Hervás, in the province of Cáceres, Extremadura, has hosted an annual popular festival called "Los Conversos," in which town residents stage a play about the local Jewish past, re-create a medieval "Jewish market," and dress up "as Jews." Looking at the evolution of the festival over the last twenty years, this chapter analyzes the local memory entanglements of the Francoist repression and anti-Jewish persecutions. It argues that memory of the Jewish medieval past has been anachronistically borrowed, adapted, and rearticulated in order to explain and displace more recent social and ideological divisions and reenact specific forms of violence. In the introduction to this book, we discuss how in the 1990s in Spain there was a temporal coincidence in the reemergence and development of different memories. This landscape of memory includes the reengagement with the memory of Jewish Spain, the arrival from the outside of a discourse of memory and commemoration of the Holocaust, and the emergence of a critical reevaluation of the democratic transition and activism about the previously unrecognized victims of the Civil War and Francoist repression.

The analysis of the Los Conversos festival in Hervás illustrates how these memories function as a tangled complex. The relationship between them can be understood through the interrelated concepts of "multidirectional memory" (Rothberg 2009), "travelling memory" (Erll 2011), and "entangled memory" (Feindt et al. 2014). As we note in the introduction, Michael Rothberg developed the concept of *multidirectional memory* to refer to "the dynamic transfers between diverse places and times in the process of remembrance." Memory, he explains, is "subject to ongoing negotiation, cross-referencing, and borrowing" (Rothberg 11, 3). Rothberg's main examples come from his study of the way in which memory discourses about the Holocaust provided key elements for the articulation of anticolonial movements. The tendency of memory discourses to migrate and reemerge in other cultural and temporal contexts becomes for Astrid Erll the key element in understanding complex events that cannot be fully understood just by considering "hard facts" (5). Drawing on James Clifford's concept of "travelling culture," Erll reflects on the transcultural movements of memory. Erll explains how "memories do not hold still—on the contrary, they seem to be constituted first of all through movement" and invites us to analyze those movements: their carriers, media, contents, practices, forms, and routes (11). By tracing the changing times and geographies in which a memory appears, says Erll, it is possible to establish how "old" mnemonic forms can be used to explain "new" and different experiences (14). Feindt et al. speak of the interrelational, plural, and dynamic character of memory and of the entangledness of acts of remembering in synchronic and diachronic terms: synchronic because every act of remembering inscribes an individual in multiple social frames and because concurrent interpretations of the past coexist; diachronic because we have constant reconfigurations of acts of remembering and changing mnemonic patterns (43).

In this chapter, we examine the travels and multidirectional entanglements of Hervás's local memory of its Jewish past. A town of four thousand people, Hervás lies in the valley of Ambroz at the northern limit of the province of Cáceres. In 1966, in the midst of Spain's tourism boom and Francoist dictatorship, it set out to gain official recognition from Spain's Ministry of Education and Science for the "historic and artistic" value of its Barrio Judío [Jewish Quarter]. Also known locally as the Barrio de Abajo [Lower Quarter], this neighborhood consists of a group of narrow labyrinthine streets and a group of ragged old buildings overlooking the Ambroz River. Today, tourist guides and street signs consistently refer to this area as Hervás's Jewish Quarter, emphasizing in their descriptions the meandering layout of its streets and the local architectural style of its adobe and wood houses. The area is presented as a rare well-preserved example of high-medieval popular Spanish architecture and as a standing vestige of the village's foundational era. This is precisely the argument that Hervás presented to the Ministry of Education and Science in 1966. The application included a map of twelve streets with accompanying texts that characterized them as the town's medieval Jewish Quarter. As evidence, the document pointed to the "Jewish-sounding names" of some of the streets and the fact that the layout and building structures had suffered no significant modifications from the time when Jews supposedly inhabited them (see fig. 5.1).

By 1969, Hervás had succeeded in obtaining the title "Conjunto Histórico Artístico de Interés Nacional" [Historic Artistic Site of National Interest], a

Figure 5.1. Street in Hervás's Lower Quarter, July 2008. ©Adrián Pérez Melgosa.

title that provided access to special national funds for the area's preservation and promotion. In 1985, the then newly formed Autonomous Government of Extremadura awarded Hervás's Jewish Quarter the title of "Site of Cultural Interest" and restated the theory of the area's Jewish origins. In 1987–88, this regional goverment approved a "Special Project for the Protection and Rehabilitation of the Old Town and Sephardi Quarter," agreeing to the necessity of preserving and restoring the quarter (de Hervás, "La invención" 180–82). Each of these designations repeated and sanctioned the quarter's ties to a medieval Jewish community as a historical reality and entitled Hervás to regional, national, and eventually European funds to restore and promote it.[1]

The irony, as detailed by local historian Marciano de Hervás, is that not a single documented source identifies the existence at any time of a segregated Jewish quarter either as a juridical or as an urban entity in the village. Jews and gentiles shared the urban space as a mixed settlement. The myth began at the end of the nineteenth century, when A. Manzano Calzado, a schoolteacher, argued that the village's "calle Sinoga" (which he identified as Synagogue Street) was proof that there had been a Jewish temple on that street. He went on to interpret the expression "en Hervás, judíos los más" [in Hervás, mostly Jews] to mean that the village must have been home to an important and large Jewish community. These assumptions, written in 1886 and published in the *Revista de Extremadura* in 1907, became the seed from which a growing number of authors branched into an ever-more-detailed and unsupported myth of the existence of an ancestral, large, and powerful Jewish community in Hervás, with influential local bankers who lent to noblemen and even to the Castilian kings (de Hervás, "La invención" 178–79, 187). The saying "en Hervás, judíos los más," which enshrines a historical suspicion of crypto-Judaism among Hervás's Christian converts, has transmuted into a celebratory tourist slogan that "proves" Hervás's rightful place in Jewish heritage matters (de Hervás, "La invención" 193–94). In its new role, this refrain appears cited in every tourist guide and brochure that promotes Hervás as a prime location in which to find the heritage of Jewish Spain.[2]

Against the tide of this growing mythologization and after extensive research in local and national archives, Marciano de Hervás concluded that indeed there were Jews in Hervás but that their presence was limited in time, modest in size and means, and never segregated within the village. The first textual evidence of Jewish presence in Hervás comes from administrative documents related to the expulsion of the Jews by the Catholic Monarchs in 1492 (de Hervás, *Los judíos* 8). A census carried out that year names forty-five Jews (either persons or families) who lived in Hervás. Of these, as recorded in the list, twelve did not own any property (de Hervás, "La invención" 187). It is not positively known where those Jews came from or when they moved to Hervás, although the most plausible answer is that they might have been exiles from Andalucía and Castilla in the aftermath of the 1391 persecutions (de Hervás, *Los judíos* 14), a time when many Jews left larger cities and settled in the countryside, specially in areas within proximity of the border with Portugal.

Marciano de Hervás has found references to several Jewish-owned vineyards and houses, all left behind after the expulsion of 1492, and to a synagogue owned by a Rabbi Simuel, although its specific location has not been identified. There is also documentation related to the existence of an extensive building complex that served as the institutional home to the converso brotherhood that was located in the currently named "calle de la Amistad Judeo-Cristiana" [Judeo-Christian Friendship Street]. Sinoga Street itself, the basis of many of the mythologizing claims, appears in the municipal records for the first time in 1872 (de Hervás, "La invención" 178, 185–86).[3] Calle Rabilero, on which oral tradition situates the synagogue, has been interpreted as a corruption of the word *rabino* or *rabí* [rabbi], but it may also derive from the Arab *rabid*, meaning *arrabal, rabalero* [slum] (de Hervás, *Judíos y Cristianos* 359–60).

The much-marketed peaceful convivencia of Jews and Christians in Hervás, if it was real at all, must have been very short, and it would stand in sharp contrast to the documented persecutions that local conversos suffered after 1492. Some documents suggest that in the hundred or so years of Jewish presence in Hervás before the expulsion, the town experienced a period of economic bounty that, perhaps, facilitated the absence of major conflicts between Jewish and Christian communities (de Hervás, *Los judíos* 19). Beginning in the 1480s, this situation rapidly deteriorated. In 1492, the regional nobleman, the Duke of Béjar, announced that all properties belonging to the Jews forced into exile were to be his, and he prohibited selling, exchanging, or giving them away. It seems, however, that many Jews found a way around this expropriation plan, for although some properties were plundered and robbed (among them, the synagogue), most seem to have been passed on to the Jews who converted and stayed in Hervás. Thus, the town's conversos inherited and preserved most of the Jewish physical patrimony of those who left in 1492. Because conversos are known to have resided on Corredera, Collado, and Plaza Streets in the sixteenth century, de Hervás concludes that it is very possible that those were the same houses where they had lived as Jews before 1492 or that they were houses that conversos inherited from exiled Jews. The irony of this quite plausible argument is that those streets—Corredera, Collado, and Plaza—are not in the Lower Quarter like Rabilero and Sinoga Streets but in the Upper Quarter, an enclave traditionally identified as the Christian neighborhood (de Hervás, *Los judíos* 18–27).[4]

In the aftermath of the expulsion and conversions of 1492 and following the edict of return in 1494 (to which we will come back later in this chapter), local conversos were repeatedly targeted by the Inquisition and found guilty of a variety of charges, from profanation of the Host to crypto-Judaism, and then condemned in several autos-da-fé (de Hervás, *Los judíos* 22–24). By 1578, Hervás was divided into two distinct political and professional factions, the *mercaderes* [merchants], mostly New Christians and well-off Old Christians, who lived in the Upper Quarter, and the *labradores* [farmers], mostly Old Christians, who lived in the Lower Quarter (de Hervás, *Judíos y Cristianos* 366). The irony of these findings is that the highly publicized and promoted Jewish Quarter of Hervás, a founding member of the Network of Jewish Quarters of Spain, seems to have been mostly, in fact, home to Old Christian peasants. This leads Marciano de Hervás to conclude, humorously,

> Si los judíos cacereños, por cuestiones históricas, fueron compelidos a la conversión al cristianismo en 1492, en el siglo XXI estamos asistiendo al fenómeno de la reconversión forzada, por cuestiones meramente turísticas, del patrimonio material cristiano en un legado material judío ficticio.
>
> [if the Jews of Cáceres, due to historical reasons, were compelled to convert in 1492, in the twenty-first century we are witnessing the phenomenon of the forced reconversion, merely for touristic reasons, of the Christian material patrimony into a fictional Jewish material legacy]. (*Judíos y Cristianos* 358)

A further irony is that the current (poor) state of preservation of the medieval structures in the majority of the Lower Quarter's houses seems to have been the result of their occupants' lack of economic resources. Stigmatized as an undesirable area of town, possibly because of its steep streets and its closeness to the cold dampness of the river, the Lower Quarter has provided living space to a succession of people who did not have the means for significant remodeling or upgrades to their homes. In our interviews, several people in Hervás explained to us that this quarter was, even until the 1970s, a ghetto in terms of social class, lacking basic services such as paved streets, reliable electric service, running water, and a sewage system. Living there carried a great social stigma until very recently, and still today, after all its intrumentalization as a tourist attraction, the area lags well behind the rest of the town in public services and social esteem. As recently as 2010, the neighbors of the quarter petitioned for the installation of proper street signage, house numbers, trash cans, and street cleaning.[5]

Underpinning this reconversion from working-class Christian neighborhood to Jewish-themed tourist attraction is a complex entanglement of two difficult sets of memories: those of the 1492 expulsion and subsequent persecutions of conversos and those of the violence against the town's Republican sympathizers during the Spanish Civil War and the resulting Francoist dictatorship.

During the Civil War and its aftermath, this quarter was inhabited by the peasants, workers, and day laborers who supported the Republic and who would become victims of Francoist repression. Franco's regime extended the brutal and systematic persecution and elimination of his enemies for many years after the Civil War ended. A great number of victims of Nationalist violence lay in unmarked mass graves all over Spain's countryside. In the local language of Hervás, the sympathizers of the left were known as *berzas* (collard greens)—an allusion to either their agricultural work, their poor diet, or both—while the Falangists (those belonging to Falange Española, Spain's fascist party) and their sympathizers were known as *virutas* (shavings), perhaps an allusion to the wood factories some of them owned. The Lower Quarter, thus, has been associated not only with the Jewish past but also with a disadvantaged part of Hervás's society, many members of which identified as Republicans or Republican sympathizers in the Civil War.

These facts about the Lower Quarter stand in sharp contrast to the explanation offered by the organizers of the Los Conversos festival, which uses the Jewish Quarter as its centerpiece, backdrop, and stage. A promotional brochure of the festival claims that the quarter's preservation is the result of the community's love and pride in its tradition: "El mérito de que el conjunto [de viviendas] haya llegado hasta nuestros días hay que atribuirlo a sus propios moradores, que han sabido mantener y conservar sus raíces" ["Credit for having preserved this group (of houses) today must be given to their own residents, who have known how to maintain and safeguard their roots"] ("Conversos"). Here the concepts *preservation* and *roots* are purposely left vague, but uninformed visitors can very well conclude what they imply: that keeping the quarter's structures intact for hundreds of years was the result of the inhabitants of Hervás's Jewish Quarter having been faithful to their Jewish roots. As we have seen, and as everyone in Hervás very well knows, this is not the case.

GONZÁLEZ DE HERVÁS'S POETRY AND CHRISTIAN/JEWISH RECONCILIATION

The collapsing of the identities of the inhabitants of the Lower Quarter—poor laborers, most of them Republicans—and medieval Jews and the split between Republicans and Nationalists as an iteration of the ancient split of the village between Jews and Christians appear crystallized in a 1953 poem by Emilio González de Hervás.[6] González de Hervás was a prominent local intellectual, who successfully lobbied the Francoist government for the 1969 recognition of Hervás's Lower Quarter as a Historic Artistic Site of National Interest. The poem "Hervás: Canto al verdadero amor" [Hervás: Song to True Love] constitutes what Marita Sturken has called a technology of memory—that is, objects that embody and generate memory: "not vessels of memory in which memory passively resides so much as objects through which memories are shared, produced, and given meaning" (Sturken 9–10). Written by a celebrated local personality, the poem disseminated and consolidated local legends about the Jews and Jewish/Christian relations in the town. Its enduring appeal and circulation became clear in 2008, when, at a critical juncture in the history of the Los Conversos festival, it was used by local playwright Miguel Murillo as the main literary source for a new play, as we will see later in this chapter.

The poem was first published in the local magazine *Revista de Ferias y Fiestas de Hervás* [Magazine of fairs and festivals of Hervás], a yearly almanac widely circulated in Hervás and its surrounding region. Dedicated to the city council of González de Hervás's "dear town," the poem relates the tragic love story between the daughter of a rabbi and a young Christian man. In 1971, eighteen years later, a revised version (Marciano de Hervás calls it a "censored" edition) appeared in González de Hervás's compilation *Mis versos de ayer y de hoy* [My poems of yesterday and today] published in Madrid. In this new 1971 version the poem is entitled "La hija del rabí" [The rabbi's daughter], and appears modified in crucial ways. One of the most striking differences is the omission of the introductory lines that in the 1953 version served to contextualize the setting of the poem within Hervás's post–Civil War social climate. In the original 1953 poem published in *Revista de Ferias y Fiestas de Hervás*, these lines read,

> Sé muy bien la triste historia
> de ese odio tan maldito que divide a nuestro Hervás,
> ese antagonismo mudo, anticristiano y brutal
> que sin saber el por qué no podéis desarraigar
>
> [I know very well the sad story
> of that damning hatred that divides our Hervás,
> that mute antagonism, anti-Christian and vicious
> that, without knowing the reason, you are unable to uproot]
> ("Hervás," v. 15–18, p. 7)

During the 1950s, the "damning hatred that divides our Hervás" had an immediate referent in the bitter Civil War and the prolonged postwar Francoist repression. The adjective "anti-Christian," with its ambiguous condemnation of this "damning hatred" as not good Christian behavior but also as having Christians as its main targets, opens the possibility for a transhistorical connection. González de Hervás was drawing from a rhetoric that the far right had articulated repeatedly when, among other justifications, they presented their 1936 rebellion as a Crusade to save Catholic Spain.

Emulating the structure of a popular romance, the poem introduces medieval Hervás as an Edenic town originally founded by hardworking Jews who settled in the Lower Quarter. This peaceful existence comes to an end when a group of Christians from Galicia settles in the Upper Quarter. The poem suddenly takes sides with the Christian newcomers and blames the Jews for instigating hatred against Christians and avoiding any contact with them because the mere presence of the newly built humble Christian Church reminds them of their deicide (González de Hervás, "Hervás," v. 63–66, p. 8). One Sunday, a young Jewish woman, the rabbi's daughter, approaches the Christian area of the town and confides to a young Christian man her interest in his religion. He agrees to "teach her," and in their ensuing meetings, the rabbi's daughter receives an education in both Christian doctrine and romantic love. A local Jew informs the rabbi that a Jewish woman is revealing "the secrets of their race" to a Christian. Enraged and unaware that the girl is his daughter, the rabbi finds the couple and kills them. After discovering the crime, the local priest confronts the town's Jews. He accuses them of killing Christ first and now these "two Christians" and commands them to convert. Miraculously, the whole Jewish community responds by falling to their knees and begging to be baptized.

Predictably, given the plot, the poem is laced with antisemitic stereotypes. It establishes a clear contrast between the brutality of the rabbi, who stabs the lovers seven times, and the depiction of the priest as "humilde, estoico, valiente, el venerable eremita" [humble, stoic, brave, the venerable hermit] (González de Hervás, "Hervás," v. 119–20, p. 9). Surprisingly, given the depiction of conversion as atonement for the murders, the final coda presents the story as proof that "el odiar es inhumano y amar al prójimo es / lo primordial del cristiano" [to hate is inhuman and to love one's neighbor is / primary for a Christian] ("Hervás," v. 145–49, p. 10).

These rhetorical contradictions appear throughout the poem. Their ambivalence and ambiguity convey an underlying struggle between near and distant collective memories. Thus, the Jews are initially presented as an Edenic community but soon after as prone to secrecy, jealousy, and violence. They are said to be "racially" entrenched in their anti-Christian sentiments, yet they immediately follow the priest's orders to convert. Poignantly, rather than depicting the conversion as a scene of Catholic triumph and glory, the poem paints it as a gruesome spectacle where "a gritos inacabados y arrastrando sus rodillas / cual dantescos alocados, bautismo, por Dios, pedían" [with eager screams and dragging their knees / like deranged Dantean creatures, (Jews) begged God for baptism] (González de Hervás, "Hervás," v. 139–40, p. 10).

As a whole, the poem begins with a call for reconciliation but actually delivers an antisemitic story of massive conversion as a just response to Jewish crimes. The poem justifies violence against Jews as deserved punishment, repeatedly accusing them of deicide, depicting rabbis as angry executioners and blaming them for harboring inhuman hatred against Christians. By inventing a mythical, primal, communal, and voluntary conversion of Jews to Christianity after their having committed a violent crime, the poem circumvents any kind of historical Christian responsibility for the events that characterize Christian/Jewish relations in the area. While Jewish conversions to Christianity throughout the Iberian Peninsula took place mostly under duress, as a way for Jews to guarantee their personal safety, especially during the widespread attacks of 1391, this poem posits that Jews were actually the initiators of both the violence (the rabbi's killing of the two lovers) and its consequence, the conversions (the Jewish young woman takes the initiative of wanting to learn about Christianity and the Jews beg for conversion after the murders). The underlying anxiety seems to be centered, then, on identifying and locating responsibility for the circumstances of Jewish conversions.

The resolution of social tensions through conversion does not seem a proper example of "Christian neighborly love." Rather, it seems to contain a warning for those in a minority position that they must accommodate to the views of the majority. This irony stretches even further when we realize that the massive conversion did not end "that damning hatred that divides our Hervás" since, as the opening lines suggest, it was alive in the 1950s, if not between Christians and Jews, then transmuted into a conflict at this time between the victorious Nationalists and the defeated Republicans. The multidirectionality of this memory reaches into the past to interpret the present, but all it finds is more ambiguity and indetermination.

These contradictory takes on the meaning of conversion, reconciliation, and intolerance have become basic features of Jewish/Christian relations as interpreted today in Hervás. Thus, the promotional tourism literature of the town describes the restoration of the Lower Quarter as an act of recovery of Hervás's Jewish heritage. González de Hervás's poem has been a foundation for this certainty as it evokes, constructs, and disseminates, with great success, a local memory of this area as being both Hervás's Jewish Quarter and the materialization of the true essence and origin of the town ("Hervás," v. 2–3, 7). The poet describes himself as "un hervasense que adora tu calle Abajo" [a Hervasene who adores your Lower Quarter] and sings proudly of its "enchanting" and "millenary" streets and houses, with their "Sephardi taste" ("Hervás," v. 12–13, v. 1, p. 7). Glossing over the neglect and privation that have kept the neighborhood in an unrenovated state, this characterization romanticizes the precarious architecture as an ancient treasure and invents an exotic Jewish identity for its historical inhabitants. Spearheaded by González de Hervás himself, this is the version of the Lower Quarter that would find its way to the 1969 petition to the ministry.

Within the magazine *Revista de Ferias y Fiestas de Hervás*, the original poem appeared preceded by a piece titled "Plegaria al Santísimo Cristo de la Salud" [Prayer to the Most Holy Christ of Health] written by José Luis Cotallo, a priest and cultural affairs representative for the regional Francoist government. Linked to the poem as its conceptual framework, the prayer contextualizes the "hatred that divides our Hervás" in the current year 1953 as a simultaneously social, ideological, and religious schism. Father Cotallo asks God to help bring together the town's factions, clearly inscribing in the geography of the town the two warring factions of the recent Civil War: "Te pido, Cristo bendito, porque se abracen los que hasta ahora se odian . . . por la justicia y la paz social entre los de arriba y los de abajo" [I ask you, blessed Christ, that those who continue to hate each other might join in an embrace . . . that there may be justice and social peace between the ones from on high and those below] (Cotallo 6). In political terms, these two groups represented respectively those who supported or were part of the Francoist establishment and those who had resisted it and had been punished for it. This preamble allows for a reading of the poem as an explanation of both the past and the present: the Christian/Jewish confrontation and violence it depicts renders meaningful the political confrontation and violence of the Civil War and its aftermath as a reiteration of an ancestral geographical confrontation between the two parts of the town, the upper and lower sides.

The dichotomies staged in the poem between deicidal, resentful, violent, and intolerant Jews who ask for conversion and a forgiving priest and town ready to accept them parallel the roles of those who have abandoned the Christian faith and Father Cotallo's self-appointment as the understanding priest who pleads for their return to the fold. Cotallo says, "Yo te adoro, Cristo bendito, por cuantos, siendo hijos tuyos, dejan de hacerlo, sin ver que con ello te vuelven a crucificar . . . perdón, Señor, por tus hijos que te olvidan" [I worship you, blessed Christ, for those who, being your children, act as if they were not, without realizing that by doing this they crucify you again . . . I ask for forgiveness, Lord, for those among your children who forget you] (Cotallo 4–5). This transhistorical connection posits a legendary account of Jewish/Christian frictions from the past as the origin of the town's political and social divisions in the 1950s. This sorting out of historical blame, the collusion of Jewish/Republican identities and the desire of redemption through Christian "reconciliation" would be reproduced in later poems and would find their way to the present-day festival of Los Conversos.

Emilio González de Hervás celebrated the 1969 proclamation of Hervás's Lower Quarter as a Historic Artistic Site of National Interest in his poem "Nuevamente amanece en el valle de Ambroz" [Dawn breaks again in the Ambroz Valley, 1970], included in his collection *Mis versos de ayer y de hoy*. The poem interprets the national recognition as an opportunity to usher in a new era of reconciliation between contemporary Hervás and its past Jewish inhabitants. Like "Hervás: Canto al verdadero amor," this poem travels back and forth not only in time but also among the derisive and admiring portrayals of Jews and between condemnation and celebration of their actions. The admonitions in which the absent ones, those expelled, are suddenly blamed for instigating their own victimization can be fully understood only if read against the background of the ideological and social split that Spain experienced in the 1930s and the aftermath of the violence and repression staged in this town during and immediately after the Civil War.

The entanglement of memories resurfaces early in the poem through its foregrounding of the word *decree*, placing the tourism-related recognition of the Jewish Quarter at the same legal level as the 1492 document that commanded the expulsion of the Jews. In the view of the poet, this humble new decree recognizing the artistic value of a group of buildings erases the edict of Granada and brings about a reconciliation of centuries of conflict. In the first stanza, it states, "Las burlas incultas solapadas / borra el decreto que promulga España [The ignorant, veiled offenses / are erased by the decree that Spain has issued]. The second stanza explains, "Antiguos odios de raza vulnerada / obstruían la Luz en las estancias" [Ancient hatreds of an abused race / obstructed the Light in the dwellings] (González de Hervás, *Mis versos*, v. 3–6, p. 206).

The poem is laced with ambiguity as it celebrates the Lower Quarter and its supposed ancestral Jewish inhabitants while simultaneously assigning them blame for the town's divisions. Thus it is not clear whether the town's Jews are the subjects or the objects of the "ancient hatreds" running through the town. The "abused race" reference can refer to Jews and their long history of victimization or to the conversos, seen as crypto-Jews who, symbolically, prevented the "light" of the Christian God to enter their houses. Another interpretation, one that bridges these contradictory meanings, appears when these lines are read as speaking about the situation of Francoist Spain at the time. Spain's recognition of Hervás's Jewish Quarter would silence the "offenses" that the inhabitants of the Lower Quarter are subjected to. Those inhabitants, the marginalized and economically pressed day laborers and farmers, would be linked in the poem with the Jews or conversos as exhibiting "ancient hatred." They would also be linked by their not accepting the light of Christian salvation, and of Franco's Nationalist credo, to enter their dwellings—as the prayer from Father Cotallo indicated.

Surprisingly, when the poem turns to imagine the "new era" ushered in by this reconciliation, it re-creates a supposedly "pure" Sephardi community in the "salvaged" Jewish Quarter. The poem proceeds to summon a spectral presence of the Jews to emerge and exhorts them to open their windows, let in the air (González de Hervás, *Mis versos*, v. 9–12, v. 22–25, p. 206–7), and, presumably, resume practicing their religion (or what González de Hervás understood as such) overtly: "Comed los panes ázimos"; "Cantad . . . los salmos de la Cábala"; "Abrid la sinagoga"; "Prended las siete llamas" ["Eat the unleavened bread"; "Sing . . . the psalms of the Kabbalah"; "Open the Sinagogue"; "Light the seven flames"] (*Mis versos*, v. 27–33, 40–44, p. 207).

The poem's linking of the national recognition of the Jewish Quarter, as such, to an internal reconciliation of the town with its past Jewish population is imbued with the logic of convivencia. By this convivencia logic, the spectral return of those banished in the past redeems the present divisions in the village. After describing the "liberation" and reemergence of Jewish practices, the poet proclaims: "¡Vamos a redimirnos / de históricos pecados!" [Let us redeem ourselves / of historical sins!] (González de Hervás, *Mis versos*, v. 47–48, p. 207). The poem ends with the euphoric prediction that this new union of Jews and Christians will make the town an example for the world, placing Hervás in the highest of positions (v. 54–61, p. 207–8). The actual "redemption" ushered in, in 1969, came through the state's seal of approval for the town's wider tourist exposure. At a time when the town's wood and textile industrial base had suffered significant erosion due to Francoist policies fostering concentration in larger urban areas, the decree, as people like González de Hervás understood very well, represented a triumph of their efforts to "put Hervás on the map," with the implicit promise of economic benefits and dividends this repositioning implied.

But the poem's references to a "redemption of historical sins" evoke not only the violence and sins perpetrated in the town against medieval Jews, but also more recent "sins," the violence committed in Hervás in the Civil War and its aftermath. Within Hervás, the split that divided Spain into Republican constitutionalists and Nationalist rebels became understood, through cultural "carriers" of traveling memory such as these poems, as an iteration of the ancient split of the village between Jews and Christians. In 1936, Hervás was a fairly prosperous community of 4,800 inhabitants, with a significant number of wood processing and textile manufacturing industries and well-developed agriculture in specialty products like cherries, grapes, and chestnuts. During the war, the village saw no actual battles. The Nationalists took control of the town on July 21, 1936, only three days after the rebellion, and found almost no resistance, as happened in the rest of Cáceres province as well. However, the ensuing repression was ferocious and long-lasting. As described by local schoolteacher Francisco Moriche Mateos in his account of the oral testimonies given to him by survivors and their families, what took place was "la acción incivil, injusta, innecesaria, cruel y desproporcionada de unos hervasenses sobre otros" [the uncivil, unjust, unnecessary, cruel and disproportionate violence of some hervasenses against others] (Moriche Mateos 40). Dozens of workers, peasants, and municipal officials connected to the Republic were tortured and arbitrarily executed by local Falangist militants with either the complicity or the tacit approval of the authorities. Black lists were made by local bosses and in some cases by the village's priests

(Moriche Mateos 74). Dead bodies were abandoned at the curb of local roads, along walking trails, or by the cemetery's wall (Moriche Mateos 19). Other people were executed after court-martials. Still others were jailed, "depurated" (fired from their administrative jobs), or banished from the town, their possessions seized and themselves humiliated, with continued interrogation and police monitoring for years. Their families were left terrified until well into the 1960s (Moriche Mateos 103–4). The commander of the Civil Guard in Cáceres characterized this repression as "the sweeping purge of undesirables" (Preston 180).

In many of these episodes, the violence stemmed from a mixture of ideological differences, personal vendettas, and crimes of opportunity. Two events carry special significance for our purposes. The first one took place on the night of Sunday, March 29, 1936, a short month after the victory of the Popular Front in the general elections. That day, a fire destroyed the altar and part of the building of the church of Santa María in Hervás. The tabernacle and the holy chalice disappeared from the church, and a few witnesses said that they saw "leftist men" using the chalice to drink wine at a local tavern. Soon these men were accused of having started the fire and having stolen the chalice and desecrating it. In 1939, they were sentenced to twenty years in prison. Right before dying, Tomás Ordoñez "Chinín," one of the nine men accused, provided a different version of the events, stating that town Falangists tortured and forced him to accuse himself and others of starting the fire (Moriche Mateos 98, 161). According to Moriche Mateos, the chalice appeared years later in Hervás in the house of a prominent local Francoist (64–65).

While there remain many questions about what actually happened that day, the narrativization of the events was constructed, perhaps subliminally, through and by the memory of a case the Inquisition investigated in the area in 1506. At that time, Juan Sastre, a local Old Christian, was accused of stealing consecrated Hosts from the church of Aldeanueva del Camino in order to sell them to a group of conversos from Hervás. Both Sastre and the conversos were convicted of profanation and burned at the stake (de Hervás, "La invención" 195).

Over the years, the story of this sixteenth-century Inquisition case has been repeated in a good number of documents, books, and popular oral traditions, even into the twentieth century to become part of local folklore. By the time José Sendín Blázquez reproduced it in his 1987 book *Tradiciones Extremeñas,* Juan Sastre had become Jewish; the conversos had thrown the Hosts into boiling water; a painting of Jesus had miraculously begun to sweat, giving the conversos away; and other Hosts buried in manure caused a figure of the Virgin of the Assumption to cry until they were recovered (Marciano de Hervás, "La invención" 196–97). It should not be surprising, then, that the March 1936 social and political conflicts that would lead to the Civil War in July of that year found expression in the town's memory of the sixteenth-century narratives of confontation between New and Old Christians. Central to the time travel of this memory is the accusation of desecration of Catholic religious symbols as an undeniable marker of the gravity of the crime. In this interpretation of the events, the Republicans were forced into a narrative of anti-Christian religious desecration, a role traditionally assigned to Jews and conversos. This parallel between Republicans and Jews, as expressed in the double accusations of desecration, was not exclusive of Hervás. It obeys the logic of the very successful right-wing propaganda of the 1930s inspired by the *Protocols of the Elders of Zion*. Fascist ideologues posited, in apocalyptic terms, that the Second Republic was part of an international Jewish conspiracy to take over the world and destroy Christianity (see Preston 5–10, 42).

Both memories also share the ambiguity about the actual perpetrators of the crime. In 1506, were the guilty ones Old Christians, Jews, or conversos? In 1936, were they leftists or Falangists? Certainly, the disapearance of the Hosts in 1506 must have contributed more to furthering the agenda of the Inquisition than to easing the everyday life of local conversos. Similarly, the burning of the church seemed to advance the cause of the Catholic Church and Falangists more than that of the Popular Front sympathizers. The debates about the actual meaning of these events hold a strong presence in the memory of the town. In 2013, Los Conversos festival staged a new play based on the sixteenth-century Host desecration accusations and Inquisition trial entitled *La calumnia* [The slander], to which we will return later in this chapter.

Another series of events with strong resonances in the memory of Hervás was the postwar treatment of women and girls who were socially humiliated for having leftist ideas or being married or related to Republican men. One of the gendered strategies of shaming used by the victorious Nationalists consisted of shaving their heads and giving them castor oil laxatives and forcing them to walk through town while soiling themselves, singing "Cara al sol," the Falangist hymn. People were called to witness these parades and encouraged to insult, boo, and spit on the women. Children were sometimes taken out from school so that they could watch and participate in the shaming (Moriche Mateos 105). Most of the victims would never talk publicly about it. The testimonies gathered in Hervás by Moriche Mateos come mostly from their descendants.[7]

These shaming parades were repeated throughout Spain as the Nationalist troops advanced into new towns. Only recently have scholars begun to gather oral testimonies regarding these acts and interpret them as part of a Francoist backlash against the gains that women had obtained during the Republic, as punishment to women who had expressed a "perverse" desire to participate in the public sphere and to return them to the "proper" private space of the home and its servitude (Cobo Romero and Ortega López 64–65). Critics coincide in interpreting the head shaving as taking away the victims' feminity, while the castor oil purge implied the "cleansing" of the victim's Republican ideas.[8] These ritual shamings had an undoubtedly gendered form. But the processions, the public humiliation, and the requirement to don ridiculous garb and carry symbols from the defeated Republic also contained echoes of Inquisitorial practices of public humiliation, such as the donning of the sanbenito, historically carried out against conversos accused of Judaizing. Within Hervás's multifaceted history of the divide between the Upper and Lower Quarters, the Inquisitional resonances of this public shaming become more poignant as the victims were women from the Lower Quarter, which popular belief already identified as the Jewish part of town.

In his description of the multidirectionality of memory, Rothberg discusses Freud's conceptualization of "screen memory" as a "more innocent" memory that replaces other memories that are too painful to retrieve. He explains how "while screen memory might be understood as involving a conflict of memories, it ultimately more closely resembles a remapping of memory in which links between memories are formed and then redistributed." He also reminds us of the inevitability of displacement and substitution in all acts of remembrance (Rothberg 14). He concludes, "It is precisely that convoluted, sometimes historically unjustified, back-and-forth movement of seemingly distant collective memories in and out of public consciousness that I qualify as memory's multidirectionality" (Rothberg 17).

In the case of Hervás, we can think of the neighbor-to-neighbor violence, the dehumanization of state violence, and the protracted marginalization of those who lost the Civil War and survived the postwar as the more painful, recent memory that, until only a short while ago, was never publicly articulated. The more "innocent" memory emerges from the narrativization of a romanticized past of "tolerance" in which Hervás is depicted as a safe haven for Jews and a model of medieval convivencia. But as Rothberg explains, memory is an associative process, in which the content of a memory "takes on meaning precisely in relationship to other memories in a network of associations" (16). As Hervás has begun to put its Jewish Quarter and narratives of idealized convivencia on display for tourist consumption, the entanglement between the memory of the events of the Civil War and the popular legends about the history of confrontation between Christians, Jews, and conversos acquires a new set of transcultural resonances. The Los Conversos festival reserves the display of stories of violence and betrayal between Christians and Jews for the fictional domain represented in the plays performed nightly. But even if the initial intention is to celebrate the village's history and to create a sense of common heritage, the festival does not manage to fully contain and repress the echoes awakened by the stories of denunciation, complicity, fratricidal violence, and revenge it puts on display.

Alejandro Baer has explained how in Spain the memorialization of the Holocaust constitutes a kind of cultural matrix for the various forms of production, circulation, and consumption of traumatic memory in relation to the Civil War and the Francoist repression. He has also shown how, through official commemorations of the Holocaust, the memory of the Jewish genocide paved the way, at least symbolically, for an institutional recognition of Republican victims of Francoism (A. Baer, "The Voids").[9] In a similar way, in Hervás, "Jewish memory"—at the center of which stands the recognition of the Lower Quarter as a historically Jewish site—even if historically inaccurate, has been the vehicle through which this historically marginalized neighborhood has been physically restored, officially rehabilitated, and incorporated into the rest of the town. Through a displacement or entanglement with local Jewish memory, the inhabitants of this Quarter now performatively embody the town's history of violence through their theatrical performances of Jewish and Christian characters who are secular victims and perpetrators of intolerance and violence.

LOS CONVERSOS FESTIVAL

The most recent wave of "rediscovery" of Hervás's Jewishness began in 1996, when Juan Ramón Ferreira and Mercedes Belmonte, respectively Hervás's mayor and culture councilor at the time, saw a performance of Calderón's *El alcalde de Zalamea* [The mayor of Zalamea] in Zalamea de la Serena, Badajoz, by local Zalameans. Behind the project was Miguel Nieto, a well-known theater director from Madrid who specializes in popular performances by nonprofessional actors. Ferreira asked Nieto for ideas about how to organize the staging of a play in Hervás in order to revitalize the cultural life of the town and attract tourists. This happened at the same time that Ferreira was seeking to increase Hervás's visibility through the creation of the Network of Jewish Quarters of Spain, of which Hervás, through Ferreira, was to become a founding member. Miguel Nieto was introduced by the authorities to Hervás's Jewish claims and to the tourist potential of the Jewish Quarter. Coincidentally, Nieto happened to be very interested in Spain's Jewish past, and he suggested staging the play *Los conversos*, written in 1985 by Solly Wolodarsky, an Argentine Jewish

Figure 5.2. Inhabitants of Hervás dressed up as "medieval Jews," July 2008. ©Adrián Pérez Melgosa.

playwright who had been living in Spain since 1969. Although the play was highly experimental and had been intended for an audience that was knowledgeable about Jewish culture and history, the production, directed by Nieto and performed by nonprofessional actors from Hervás, was a success with an audience initially primarily composed of people from the village and surrounding areas. Eventually, the audience grew to include people from other parts of Spain as well as international visitors. The play, performed over three consecutive summers, became the central event of and gave its name to the festival. The four-day-long event occurs with the participation and attendance of most of the community. It consists of the nightly performance of a play—several plays have been staged, as we will see—and a "reconstruction" of medieval Jewish life throughout the Lower Quarter with reenactments of "medieval Jewish culture" (see fig. 5.2), exhibiting and selling local crafts and food, and performing live chess matches and Sephardi music concerts.[10]

The festival is fascinatingly fraught with contradictions, especially in terms of the desire to showcase, through numerous activities and symbols, the positive cultural capital of religious and ethnic tolerance. In promotional materials for the festival, these events are marketed as a historical re-creation of the fifteenth century, in which the participants "rememoran, en un día de mercado la mutua tolerancia y lazos familiares entre los judíos y cristianos en el Hervás de antaño" [remember, on a market day, the mutual tolerance and family ties

Figure 5.3. Lower Quarter stage where Hervás's festival plays are performed, July 2008. ©Adrián Pérez Melgosa.

between Jews and Christians in the Hervás of the old days] ("Conversos"). However, as we see in chapter 2, this deployment of the convivencia concept as a particular characteristic of a town has to constantly narratively reinterpret the historical fact of the destruction of this supposedly convivial life, the absence of any significant material remains, and the lack of a present-day local Jewish population.

The play that initiated the festival, Solly Wolodarsky's *Los conversos*, has been subsequently replaced by three other plays that develop their plots out of González de Hervas's poetry and a cluster of local legends about Jews. If Wolodarsky's play foregrounded Spain's Jewish history as a way to articulate a reflection on contemporary questions of Jewish identity, the subsequent plays rewrite and stage local stories of Christian/Jewish violence in order to make them fit into present-day celebrations of tolerance. The set where these plays have been staged, for several nights every summer in front of thousands of spectators, is the Lower Quarter itself, which has become the stage, literally, of a town that has transformed its Jewish past into a tourist destination (see fig. 5.3). We will read these four plays against each other and in relation to their respective performances as we have witnessed them in Hervás. This analysis helps us trace the past twenty years of the festival's evolution in relation to broader trends in the process of Spain's working through the memory of its Jewish past.

SOLLY WOLODARSKY'S *LOS CONVERSOS* (1997–1999)

Wolodarsky's play *Los conversos*, staged in Hervás from 1997 till 1999, brought to Hervás's memory entanglements not only the past history of medieval Iberian Jews but also present-day discussions about Jewish identity in the diaspora that emerged as Sephardi and Ashkenazi Jews brought back Judaism to Spain in the late twentieth century.

Samuel, the play's protagonist, is a Latin American Jewish tourist visiting the Synagogue of the Transit in Toledo in the late twentieth century. To emphasize his role as an everyman, when the play begins, the actor playing Samuel enters the scene among the spectators while they are looking for their seats. Like the others, he is casually dressed, "as a tourist in spring time strolling through Toledo." While contemplating the synagogue's historic Great Prayer Room, Samuel reconsiders a question that haunts him: why should he, as an agnostic intellectual, continue identifying as a Jew? Immersed in his thoughts, Samuel dreams that he is in front of Daniel of Toledo, a fifteenth-century rabbi who decided to go into exile in 1492 to preserve his faith and is the second protagonist of the play. Daniel's brother Isaac is the third protagonist. In contrast to Daniel, he remained in Toledo and converted to Christianity. Samuel wants to hear directly from Daniel and Isaac about the reasons behind the decision each made when confronted with the choice of exile or conversion. He is confident that their answers will help him solve his personal dilemmas as a secular Jew. As the brothers explain and justify their lives and choices to Samuel, their apparently opposite positions begin to show their interdependence.

As a whole, the play emphasizes the fundamental importance of the conversos to the history of relations between Jews and Christians in the Iberian Peninsula. From the very first dialogue between Samuel and Daniel the play undertakes the work of making visible and reevaluating the converso historical memory (or rather, the historical silence and vilification surrounding conversos). Samuel explicitly tells Rabbi Daniel that he wants to know about those "others" who converted, because "son una realidad, incluso si no quieres hablar de ella, incluso si eludes nombrarla, o evitas pronuciar sus nombres" [they are a reality, even if you do not wish to talk about it, even if you avoid naming it, or avoid pronouncing their names]. Isaac, the converso brother, starts his testimony by stating how things are not "as white and black" as they seem. Afraid that Samuel, like Daniel did, may also condemn him, he warns that there are "many truths in the world."

To the brothers' surprise, Samuel confesses that he has also often thought about the possibility of choosing to stop being Jewish. He explains, describing his experiences as an immigrant: "¿Por qué no? Son países nuevos, tierras de aluvión. Todo se mezcla en la gran olla que hierve. Nadie tiene pasado. . . . Acabar con todo lo que en nosotros huele a judío. . . . ¡Cuántas veces no hemos pensado si no era lo mejor!" [Why not? They are new countries, not fully formed lands. Everything is mixed in their big melting pot. Nobody has a past. . . . To end everything in us that smells Jewish. . . . How many times have we thought if this wouldn't be better?] (36). Daniel, however, only sees betrayal and cowardice in this decision and accuses Isaac of having betrayed his people only to keep the family's fortune. While the play focuses in more detail on Isaac's reasons to convert, it neither condemns nor romanticizes his actions. On the one hand, we learn how, ironically, it was thanks to Isaac's "betrayal" that he was able to send money to Daniel so he could to complete his spiritual education and his pilgrimage to the Promised Land. The play also reveals the shadows of Isaac's moral pragmatism when we see him as an informer, exposing Judaizing converts when the Inquisition directly threatens his family.

Isaac's testimony dismantles the binary logic that opposes the heroism of those who maintained their Jewish identity, by going into exile or practicing Judaism in secret after converting, to the supposed treason of the assimilated converso. As the play continues to unveil the complexity of the converso condition, it deploys the term *converso* beyond religion, into the realms of culture. Thus, when Rabbi Daniel accuses Isaac of having broken his covenant with God, allowing his children to marry Christians and erasing their lineage through the purchase of noble titles, Isaac exclaims, pointing to the audience: "¡Ahí tienes a mis descendientes! ¿Cuántos con mi sangre encuentras hoy en las calles de toda España? Tienen una patria cierta, no ambulante. Poseen un linaje, una religión que no los diferencia. . . . ¡Ahí están los frutos de mi sacrificio!" [Behold my descendants! How many people with my blood do you find today in every street of Spain? They aren't nomads, but have a secure homeland, they are not exiles. They have a lineage, a religion that does not set them apart. . . . There you have the fruits of my sacrifice!].

The openness with which Isaac articulates his response contrasts with the reductionism of Daniel's argument, which remains enclosed in the tradition or treason dichotomy. What at first glance seems a cowardly and selfish decision of Isaac's reveals itself as the path that ensured the life, security, and social stability of both his and Daniel's descendants, both converts and exiles in their family. His words attempt to conjure up the converso component in Spanish society, a group largely silenced, both because its existence bothered practicing Jews and Christians and because its survival depended on the strategic erasure of their tradition and memory. Surviving, says Isaac, is the indispensable condition for maintaining a tradition. By making this converso component visible, both Isaac and the play connect today's Spain with the Jewish identity that the country sought to eradicate after 1492.

From a perspective similar to Wolodarsky's Isaac, Jacob Hassán has exposed the idea that the Jewish presence in Spain ended in 1492 with the expulsion as a fallacy:

> La sociedad española de los siglos de oro estaba marcada por el profundo conflicto social entre cristianos viejos y cristianos nuevos . . . sin darse cuenta ni unos ni otros de que no eran propiamente ni lo uno ni lo otro, sino las primeras manifestaciones de esa síntesis de ambas que ha conformado la sociedad española de nuestro tiempo
>
> [Spanish society of the Golden Age was marked by deep social conflict between Old Christians and New Christians . . . without these groups realizing it they were properly neither one nor the other, but the first manifestations of this synthesis of both that has shaped the Spanish society of our time] (Hassán, "Realidad" 357)

If, for Isaac, his conversion was the price he paid to ensure his descendants' life, for Hassán, the synthesis between Christians and conversos shaped the formation of Spain.

The play's conceptualization of conversion dialogues with a case Wolodarsky was familiar with: the cultural debates surrounding the incorporation of Jewish immigrants to Argentina. In 1910, Alberto Gerchunoff, the pioneer of Argentine Jewish literature, wrote the now classic *Los gauchos judíos* [The Jewish gauchos of the pampas], a fictionalized history of the settlement of Jewish immigrants in the Argentine agricultural heartland. As Edna Aizenberg and Leonardo Senkman explain, Gerchunoff created a Sephardi mythology for the Russian and Polish Yiddish-speaking Ashkenazi immigrants who were trying to find a place for themselves in Argentina. He used Sephardi heritage to link Judaism and Hispanism, "to give the Ashkenazi immigrants a sense of belonging but, just as important, to convince their non-Jewish neighbors that they indeed belonged" (Aizenberg 132–33), lending Jewish immigration to Latin America cultural legitimacy (Senkman 35). The Jewish gauchos were therefore adapting to their new environment by inserting themselves within local mythologies (embracing the gaucho mystique) while simultaneously providing a new genealogy for themselves and their presence in Argentina by means of the history of Sephardi Jews.

In the 1980s, at the time that Wolodarsky wrote *Los conversos*, Jewish immigrants in Spain were also debating appropriate modes of inserting themselves within a national community that was undergoing an accelerated process of modernization, democratization, and secularization. Wolodarsky was witness the negotiations about Jewish identity that emerged as Sephardi and Ashkenazi Jews brought back Judaism to Spain in the later part of the twentieth century. Moroccan Jews began arriving in Spain in significant numbers after Morocco's independence in 1956, and, especially, following the Six Day War in 1967. These Moroccan immigrants rapidly became a numerical majority and organized the structures of today's official Jewish community in Spain based on the principles of Orthodox Judaism. A few years later, significant numbers of Argentine Jews emigrated to Spain as part of a larger group of political exiles escaping from the persecution of the military dictatorship established in Argentina in 1976. A second and larger wave of immigrants arrived following the 2001 Argentine economic crisis, looking for better economic and professional opportunities. Because of their different origins and paths of incorporation into Spanish society, these two groups, Moroccans and Argentines, brought with them diverging visions about questions of religious observance, cultural norms, and social integration (see Garzón, "El retorno a Sefarad"; Álvarez Chillida, *El antisemitismo*; Rein and Weisz).

In this intra-Jewish context, the play *Los conversos* participates in the discussion about contemporary Jewish identity in Spain by interpellating its Spanish audience. The play confronts this group with the "conversions" they have undergone in order to survive. When, at the end, the play addresses the audience directly to point out Spain's ancestral converso legacy, converting, in the sense of surviving their own historical circumstances, including immigrating and adapting to a new environment, becomes not the exception but the common experience that Samuel, Daniel, Isaac, and the audience share. Implicitly, this redefined "conversion" becomes the common ground that today's Jews share with the rest of the population in Spain. In the context of a country in which Judaism has been, and still is, a suspect identity associated with foreignness—much like it was in Gerchunoff's time in Argentina—*Los conversos* refashions Spain, and its Jewish legacy, as a legitimate home for each of these three groups.

The play's 1997 performance in Hervás, the first time the festival was held, took place in the town's bullring. The event became a whole-town affair, with neighbors filling the bleachers and families bringing their children. The play's script was modified to localize its action and characters within the town's geography and history. Thus, in Hervás, Samuel does not daydream in the Synagogue of the Transit in Toledo but in "the probable location" of the town's Talmudic school. Rabbi Daniel and his brother Isaac become naturalized as Hervás Jews working for regional noblemen. In this new context, the play's symbolic equation of Toledo and Hervás (much like the modification of Borges's poem in Béjar's museum, as we saw in the previous chapter) becomes a vehicle for the town's desire to rewrite its rather tenuous medieval Jewish history as a key episode in Spain's Jewish history. In turn, this historical reinscription supports the town's right to figure as a prominent destination for Jewish tourism in the present. This desire appears performatively fulfilled in the opening scene, as a tour guide leads a group of international tourists through the streets of Hervás as if visiting an archaeological site.

In a subtler way, this rhetoric of localization also affects those scenes that reference physical suffering and anti-Jewish violence. In Hervás's mise-en-scène, Samuel's references to how he has at times felt as if a cold knife were slitting his throat is given verisimilitude in its on-stage representation. A stage direction calling for an allusive abstract representation of Inquisitorial interrogation becomes a full-fledged display of violent physical torture. In the final scene, where the script calls for a vivid representation of gallows and a burning stake, the performance further developed it into a detailed representation of a scene of shaming with sanbenitos and a prolonged triple burning of the three protagonists at the stake. These graphic representations of violence have the effect of transforming the central subtext of the play, the debate about contemporary Jewish identity, into a spectacle of intolerance and cruelty. The denunciation of intolerance as the opposite of convivencia has been a widely used vehicle for calling for social and political consensus by a variety of social actors in Spain. In Hervás, this same denunciation of intolerance, in a most general way, has become one of the central ways of gaining wide support for the festival among the different social groups that make up Hervás society. This focus on intolerance, together with the transhistoric and transcultural elements included in the play's plot, carries the added effect of contextualizing Hervás's difficult histories as part of a worldwide history of atrocity. Paradoxically, this rhetoric of localization ends up transmuting the "damning hatred that divides our Hervás" into the currency with which one purchases cosmopolitanism and modernity for the town. The complexity of Wolodarsky's *Los conversos*, however, seems to have resisted complete appropriation.

SOLLY WOLODARSKY'S *LA CONVERSA DE HERVÁS* [THE CONVERT WOMAN FROM HERVÁS] (2000–2007)

In the year 2000, moved by the enthusiastic reception of his play in Hervás, Wolodarsky decided to write a play specifically tailored for the town, with the action set in its streets and local historical references incorporated into the plot. Thus was born *La conversa de Hervás*, the central piece of the festival from 2000 to 2007. This play uses theatrical conventions of the cloak-and-dagger comedies from the Spanish Golden Age to tell the story of Manuel Alvarado, a prominent local converso who represents the interests of Tomás Coronel, a powerful businessman from Toledo, in Hervás. Tragedy ensues as Teófilo, another local converso, denounces Manuel to the Inquisition for Judaizing. The text of the play emphasizes the inclusion of Don Manuel and his family in the cultural, social, and religious life of the town, presenting them not as conversos who happen to live in Hervás but rather as people from Hervás who are conversos. Tragedy occurs as a result of human greed: the professional zeal of Don Lope, a new official of the Inquisition in search of a case that may provide a breakthrough in his career, and the economic need of Teófilo, who seeks a reward that might alleviate his poverty after the Inquisition confiscated his property and its tortures rendered him unable to work. The accusation of Judaizing becomes a smokescreen every social group uses to cover up secret ambitions and desires.

From 2000 to 2006, Miguel Nieto, the play's director, worked with a script that closely followed Wolodarsky's text. He understood the play as revealing class conflicts, "a defense of the expelled Jews, against Carlos V and the Inquisition."[11] In 2007, however, Hervás's city council asked Nieto to step down. He was replaced by two of the main actors, Jesús Sanabria and Teddy Ramírez, who took up the role of codirectors. As a result, the 2007 performance transformed the meaning of the play from a denunciation of Jewish scapegoating to a virtual justification of it. This was done through subtle and not-so-subtle changes in the script and its representation.

In an early scene of the play, for example, Ana and Josefina, her maid and former wet nurse, run into Diego. He informs them that he is leaving for Flanders to look for glory in battle, which he hopes will help him gain official recognition as the rightful heir to his father's title, which, in turn, might convince Manuel Alvarado that he is a worthy husband for Ana. Ana and Josefina tell Diego that his efforts will be in vain, since Manuel has arranged Ana's marriage to Tomás Coronel. According to the original written text, when asked by Diego if she will really marry someone she does not know, Ana, "determined, without hesitation," tells him: "Sí, . . . Las decisiones de mi padre yo no las discuto. . . . Siempre quiere lo mejor para mí" [Yes, . . . I do not question my father's decisions. . . . He always wants the best for me] (*La conversa* 17). In later performances, however, Ana and Diego's interchange takes the tone of a melodramatic rendition of Romeo and Juliet, while Manuel becomes a tyrannical father who forbids the young lovers' wish to be together. Ana cries inconsolably, grabbing Diego's clothes and shoulders, something not called for in the written version of the play. Manuel's decision to separate them connects the performance to the legend narrated in González de Hervás's poem, that of the rabbi who killed his daughter when he discovered her with her Christian lover.

The performance also eliminates key moments from the original play that present Manuel's actions as the result of his attachment to the town. In the original version, for example, when Ana begs him to move to Toledo with her, Manuel refuses, saying, "Aquí he nacido, aquí yacen mis padres, está la tumba de tu madre. . . . Esta es mi patria, hija" [I was born here, my parents lie here, here is your mother's grave. . . . This is my homeland, daughter] (*La conversa* 26). This dialogue, like others that underline Manuel's belonging to Hervás, was omitted in the 2007 production.

Another crucial scene that was significantly modified shows Lisandro, the overseer of a nobleman's herd of sheep, meeting Manuel to ask for an advance on the wool that will be sheared by the end of the year. The play emphasizes the inter-Christian conflict generated by the Mesta system, in which the owner of pastures has the right to all the wool produced by the sheep that feed on them, even if the herd is not his. Manuel, understanding Lisandro's difficult economic position, accepts the deal proposed by the shepherd so that both of them could keep some of the benefits that, according to the law of the Mesta, would rightfully belong only to the marquis. By this arrangement Lisandro would get to keep the wool from three hundred of the sheep he owns. In the original text, the scene emphasizes complicity and familiarity between the two local characters at the expense of the nobility, which is characterized repeatedly as uncaring, foreign, and incompetent (Wolodarsky, *La conversa* 19–21).

However, as the scene was played in 2007, this meeting becomes an unpleasant Christian-Jewish confrontation in which Lisandro successfully outsmarts Manuel at bargaining. The complicit smiles between the two that are called for in the stage directions and the references to "our business" (Wolodarsky, *La conversa* 20–21) are transformed into raised voices, veiled threats, and forceful gestures of disagreement. These changes concern three aspects of Manuel's character that, in the original play, challenge traditional, stereotypical notions of Jewish intransigence, disloyalty, and usury by offering alternative narratives.

In the latter production, however, the Jewish protagonist is forced back into the narrow confines of the stereotype. This process generates narrative gaps that render incoherent the succession of events in the rest of the performance. Why would Ana feel so utterly distressed about Diego's departure while readily accepting her father's decision? Why would Manuel have so much love for a village in which he has only business interests? Why would Manuel, who, as the lender, has no need to risk his money, surrender to the haggling demands of Lisandro, who, from his economic status as a shepherd, would have extremely restricted influence?

In the production, these gaps are addressed by recourse to common narratives of romantic love and Diego's heroism. Thus, the ending shifts the play's emphasis on Manuel as an exemplary Jewish father to Diego as an exemplary Christian lover. In the original play, Manuel, mortally wounded, begs to receive a Christian death as his last effort to ensure the future well-being of his daughter in a society obsessed with purity of blood (*La conversa* 64). In the revised performances post-2007, Manuel's action conveys not so much a father's concern for his daughter as the fear of a converso who is guilty of secretly practicing Judaism in the presence of the Inquisition. The action in this case is further driven by the romantic love between Ana and Diego and by Diego's heroism, as he, even though badly wounded, kills Ana's would-be torturer. But while in the original play Diego stabs the Inquisitor in the back, a cowardly deed by chivalric standards (*La conversa* 65), in the newer performances he stabs him from in front. In order to further clarify the play's new meanings, the production ends not with the laments of several characters mourning Manuel's death but with the addition of a sung poem that highlights Manuel's guilt, explaining that "los lugareños de Hervás . . . / pensaban que don Manuel / no tiene buena semilla" [the locals of Hervás . . . / thought that Don Manuel / was a bad seed]. In addition, the last stanza completes the portrait of a heroic Diego, describing Ana and Diego's escape to Portugal, with the words, "la niña llora que llora / los gitanos van cantando / y don Diego del Casar / pronto la va consolando" [the girl cries and cries / the gypsies singing along / and don Diego del Casar / goes quickly to console her].[12]

How are we to understand, then, the return of scapegoating within the context of a festival conceived precisely to undo centuries of protracted silence about the history of the local Jewish and converso families? When Hervás promotes its Jewish heritage and positions itself as a beacon of convivencia, it also resurrects unresolved questions about its past and present identities. Are the current residents of Hervás descendants of Jews and conversos? Are they descendants of those who, actively or passively, contributed to or took advantage of their expulsion and persecution? There is no single, clear answer to this question. In either case, there is much to lose. Explicitly claiming Jewish ancestry, even at the collective level, is a step still fraught with difficulty in contemporary Spain, where antisemitism stubbornly persists. But not claiming Jewish heritage would preclude, for Hervás, the possibility of celebrating anything at all in its festival. The transformations in the 2007 play, as well as the references in brochures and other promotional materials, try to reconcile the two mutually exclusive positions in an attempt to provide the most advantageous answer. Repeatedly, every event in the festival singles out individual intolerance as the problem and Hervás's communal solidarity as the solution. But by emphasizing "Manuel's religious intransigence" (a phrase from the promotional brochures that is also highlighted in the play's performance), the festival blames the local Jews for ruining the community's convivencia, though they are the same collective that made the concept possible.

MIGUEL MURILLO'S *LA ESTRELLA DE HERVÁS* [THE STAR OF HERVÁS] (2008–2012)

Hervás appears to have settled on a growing effort to focus the festival on the generalized evils of religious intransigence, portrayed as something that any religion can fall into. The festival's evolution away from Wolodarsky's first play conveys the delicate negotiations between an autarchic drive—Hervás's Jewish past as proof of its idiosyncratic uniqueness—and a desire to position the village within cultural tourism circuits in order to attract an international, cosmopolitan clientele. After the 2007 production of *La conversa de Hervás* under the direction of Sanabria and Ramírez, Wolodarsky pushed for Miguel Nieto to be reassigned as director. Festival organizers chose instead to commission a new play based on local legends from Miguel Murillo, an Extremeño author. His being Extremeño seems to have been a decisive factor in his selection. Promotional materials for the 2008 festival made repeated references to Murillo's origin and his being "comprometido con su tierra" [committed to his birthplace] ("La leyenda" 19). Most of the people we interviewed in 2008 in Hervás, including the actors, were very excited that the local stories they knew, and someone from Extremadura, were the sources of the play this time.

In the first publication of the Network of Jewish Quarters of Spain—the tourist guide *Routes of Sepharad,* analyzed in chapter 2—these legends are characterized as part of Hervás's "Jewish legacy" and as transmission of "Jewish traditions." The guide speculates that Jews must have inhabited Hervás for a long period of time, since "it is not possible that a short stay of this culture among us should have left such a deep cultural influence in us" (*Routes* 59). The guide further explains: "In Hervás, Jewish traditions come to the surface everywhere. There are many legends about them that carry with them all the reality that every legend comprises." And "the cultural legacy that Hervás received from the Jewish people was a great one and remains in popular traditions. There are many legends about them, like the one about the rabbi who killed his daughter for having love relations with a Christian" (*Routes* 59). The existence of these stories in local folklore justified, in the minds of those seeking to promote Jewish tourism, Hervás's rightful place in a Jewish heritage route. These legends, argued the guide, reflect the reality of Jewish life in Hervás. Later tourist guides would keep reproducing this idea, using the legends as "proof" of Hervás's Jewish legacy.[13]

However, far from being proof of Jewish-Christian relations in Hervás, the legend of the rabbi who kills his daughter fits the narrative pattern of countless medieval tales about "the beautiful Jewess." As Louise Mirrer explains, two fates are available to this literary type: one is her happy conversion to Christianity and the other is her tragic death. We find the first option in the story of Marisaltos, a popular Castilian folktale that appears in Gonzalo de Berceo's *Milagros de Nuestra Señora* (1260) and in the *Cantigas de Santa María*, attributed to Alfonso X (1221–84). In this folktale, a Jewish girl is being thrown from a cliff by Jewish leaders as punishment for having had sex with a Christian man. She asks the Virgin Mary for help, and the Virgin saves her. The second option appears in the legend of the "bitter well" in which the beautiful Raquel tragically dies after her affair with a Christian man is discovered (Mirrer 31–33). Hervás's version of these popular and well-disseminated legends—much like Gustavo Adolfo Bécquer's "La rosa de pasión"—mixes both of these fates. She tragically dies, and after the fact, we find out she had converted to Christianity. While Christian salvation did not save her on time, as in Marisaltos's story, it saves the whole town's Jewish population, which, as in González de Hervás's poem, converts en masse after the lovers' tragic deaths. Thus, the basic moral of Marisaltos's story applies to the Hervás one; it is "a fairly common message of Christian forgiveness (and divine favor) over and against Jewish harshness and obstinacy" (Ray, "Beyond" 7). Marisaltos, preferring a Christian over a Jew and rendering ineffectual Jewish men's punishment and authority by turning to the Virgin, is also "a metaphor of the triumph of Christianity" over Judaism (Mirrer 40–41).[14] Hervás's legend conveys the same message, accentuating "Jewish harshness" by having the rabbi kill the lovers and emphasizing Christian forgiveness by having the whole Jewish population voluntarily convert. It is thus deeply ironic and troubling that these Christian antisemitic legends would figure in Hervás's promotional literature as its Jewish legacy and proof of the town's Jewish traditions.

Utilizing the beautiful Jewess legend as narrative basis, in just over a month's time, Murillo wrote a tragedy entitled *La Estrella de Hervás*. While the organizers justified the change to a new play as the result of the village's call for a renovation of the festival, the change also meant a push away from plays written by a Jewish author with a lifelong commitment to the study of Jewish issues in Spain. This localism was a new attempt to provide a coherent narrative to the threads of Hervás's Jewish and converso history that acquired new visibility through the celebration of the festival.

The main plotline of the new play had two main sources. The first was González de Hervás's poem, "Hervás: Canto al amor verdadero," which, as we have seen, has been a pivotal embodiment and generator of memory. The play also used elaborations and variations on the legend that were introduced in the 1980s by José Sendín Blázquez. In his "Amor y sangre en la judería" [Love and blood in the Jewish Quarter], included in his volume of collected legends from Extremadura, Sendín Blázquez describes the character of the rabbi, whom he calls Ismael, as an "hombre soberbio, poseído de su cargo e influencia, intransigente, fanático, que sostenía a pulso el poderío de la grandeza de su raza" [arrogant man, infatuated with his position and influence, intransigent, fanatic, who upheld with a steady hand the power of the glory of his race] (114). When "a jealous Jew" tells him that his daughter is having an indecent relationship with a young Christian man, his reaction shows his "arrogance and pride": without any investigation, he orders their deaths (Sendín Blázquez 116). After the two have been killed, "cruelmente fue mucho más lejos . . . para demostrar su inocencia e integridad religiosa, mandó enterrar los despojos de su hija fuera del cementerio judío, para que no se contaminaran las cenizas de sus antepasados" [cruelly, he went much further . . . to demonstrate his innocence and religious integrity, he ordered his daughter's body to be buried outside the Jewish graveyard, so that their ancestors' ashes would not be contaminated] and "prohibió expresamente cualquier señal que significara el descanso eterno de aquella inocente criatura" [expressly forbade any sign that would bring eternal rest to the innocent creature] (Sendín Blázquez 118).

As in the legend's previous version, it is the Jews who do not want to mix with the Christians and who show intransigence, excessive pride, cruelty, and hatred. Curiously, however, in contrast to the 1953 poem, the evangelizing element is completely absent, and the story does not end in conversion. The primacy of religious love in González de Hervás's poem disappears here, transformed into romantic love, although we are told that it remained "chaste." Instead of the

Jewish young woman's desire to learn about Christianity, this tale portrays a more conventional narrative of the Christian young man's taking the initiative of teaching her after having fallen in love "with her beauty and candor" (Sendín Blázquez 114–16).

Murillo's play follows this path, shaping the legend into a Romeo and Juliet–like story of romantic love and infatuation. *La Estrella de Hervás* distances itself from the most explicitly antisemitic elements of the legend while following it closely enough that the local audience can still recognize it.[15] To this end, Murillo removes the negatively charged figure of the rabbi, replacing him with a father who is enraged when he hears of his daughter's involvement with a Christian boy, but who neither kills nor orders the killing of the two lovers. The responsibility for the murders is evenly distributed between a Christian and a Jew, both acting out of jealousy: Labán, a Jew who wants to marry Myriam, the Jewish young woman, kills her Christian lover, Álvaro; and Gil, a Christian friend of Álvaro's who is also secretly in love with Myriam, kills her. The play also erases the conversion. However, the play does reiterate the depiction of Jews as the intransigent ones, together with the underlying notion that there are intrinsic traits, both biological and psychological, that clearly differentiate them from Christians. Baruch, Myriam's father, is not a vengeful killer, but he indirectly contributes to the crime through his intransigence by insisting, again and again, that Jewish law prohibits him from accepting Don Gonzalo de Béjar's offer to buy his lands and vineyards. Labán, the Jewish killer, had been promised Myriam's hand by Baruch, so he accepts a deal proposed by Gonzalo, by which, after killing Álvaro, he would marry Myriam, become rich by selling the lands to Gonzalo, and then disown her. Myriam's father shows his intransigence by not accepting the good deal that Gonzalo proposes and, as in the case of the converso Manuel in *La conversa de Hervás*, by arranging a different marriage for his daughter and forbidding her to marry the man she loves.

Moreover, the Jews are persistently shown as seeking to distance themselves from Christians and, in an ironic historical twist, spatially forcing the Christians out: in one of the first scenes, Labán orders Alvaro to get off the path where Alvaro is talking to Myriam, saying, "estás en una senda judía" [you are on a Jewish path]. Later, when Don Gonzalo and his men go to Baruch's household to convince him to sell his property, they are told by the Jews, "Estamos celebrando un rito sagrado al que no podéis asistir" [We are celebrating a sacred rite that you cannot attend]. In terms of the relationship between Myriam and Álvaro, it is she, as a young Jewish woman, who is the most convinced that their love is impossible and who constantly reminds him of the barrier between her

Jewishness and his Christianity, although, after much hesitation, she finally accepts a relationship with him.

The notion of Jews and Christians as racially separate, expressed by Emilio González de Hervás in his poem as "razas tan distintas" [races so different], is characterized in *La Estrella de Hervás* as "dos pueblos, dos culturas muy diferentes" [two nations, two very different cultures]. This notion of fundamental difference seems to be easier to uphold than the intrinsic ambivalence that arises from the figure of the converso. The erasure of the converso issue highlights the basic structural contradiction of the festival: the desire to identify Hervás's essence in its Jewish heritage and, at the same time, to make sure that Jewishness is something contained and easily distinguishable from a Christianness that is synonymous with Spanishness and normalcy. However, the festival holds onto its original name, Los Conversos, inspired by the title of Wolodarsky's first play, which specifically dealt with the conflict of identity in the converso subject and the possibility of current Spaniards' being descendants and heirs to conversos and their conflict of identity. But the festival organizers refuse to come to terms with the conflict this name entails. Interrogating the converso condition and the town's plausible converso identity would place Hervás and its current identity in a much more complex position than does the current narrative implicit in the celebrations. This narrative imagines a sequence of events in which there were Jews in Hervás, the town treated them very nicely, lived side by side with them, and, then, the Jews left.

The festival draws territory and identity boundaries: the Jewish Quarter is contained within clearly demarcated streets, as are the pseudo-Jewish clothing and rituals staged as part of the show. It represents Jewishness as an Other, from a position of paternalistic superiority, as in the following quote from the festival's promotional materials: "El esfuerzo y la generosidad por acercarse y comprender al 'otro' se dan cita estos días en Hervás" [The effort and generosity of approaching and understanding the "other" can be seen these days in Hervás] ("Conversos").

HERVÁS: IMÁGENES DE SU HISTORIA [HERVÁS: ITS HISTORY IN IMAGES] BY MIGUEL GÓMEZ ANDREA AND ANTONIO ROA CILLO

In 1996, as Hervás joined the Network of Jewish Quarters of Spain and began to prepare the first edition of Los Conversos, a comic book entitled *Hervás: Imágenes de su Historia* described this "generosity" toward the Jewish past. This limited first edition was further disseminated through a second edition in 2013.

Both editions prominently exhibit the logo of the festival on their back covers. They were prepared with the collaboration of Hervás's city council, through its councilwoman for culture, and financed by seventeen local businesses (Gómez Andrea and Roa Cilla 32). The comic's plot depicts Hervás's tourism success and imagines it as part of a larger phenomenon that will result in a "return" of its former Jewish inhabitants. The comic book's authors, Miguel Gómez Andrea and Antonio Roa Cilla, define it as a historical comic with didactic intentions. The first two pages are dedicated to the description and explanation of the Expulsion Decree of 1492. The panels culminate in a close-up of Maruxa, a young Jewish woman who is torn because she neither wants to abandon her parents' religion nor wants to leave her hometown, Hervás (Gómez Andrea and Roa Cilla 4). Immediately after, a sequence of panels transports us to contemporary Hervás, where two tourists, mother and son, stroll the streets and stop by monuments while reading a tourist guide about Hervás. The mother seems stunned and lost in thought.

Suddenly, the mother feels dizzy and confides that she has had "a vision," but we do not yet know what it is (Gómez Andrea and Roa Cilla 13). When they bump into Félix, a local man who is writing an article about Hervás history, they introduce themselves as Rocío and Simón Hamiz, Sephardim from Bulgaria, who now live in Madrid and like to visit "the Jewish quarters of Sepharad" and "discover the traces of Jewish life in Spain" (14). As staged in Los Conversos, mother and son performatively embody the wish for the emergence of Jewish tourism in Hervás. When hearing about the Jewish identity of the visitors, Félix observes, "Here, we respect you a lot." Simón validates this assessment: "Ya hemos visto que proclaman con orgullo su pasado judío" [We have already seen that you proudly proclaim your Jewish past" (Gómez Andrea and Roa Cilla 14). Félix joins them and becomes their guide. He paints a rosy picture of Hervás's industrial development and downplays the events of the Civil War: "en el siglo XX, Hervás, a pesar del triste paréntesis de la guerra civil, siguió mejorando" [in the twentieth century, in spite of the sad parentheses of the civil war, Hervás continued its progress] (Gómez Andrea and Roa Cilla 29).

At the end of the comic, the story reveals the link between the narrative threads of past and present. Stopping in front of one of the houses of the Lower Quarter, Rocío, astonished, exclaims that she has seen this same house in the strange visions she has been having. Félix offers a solution to this enigma. Hamiz, remembers Félix, is one of the family names of the Jews who once lived in Hervás. Perhaps, he concludes, she is their descendant. The sequence ends with a close-up of Rocío's astounded face, reminding readers of the similar close-up of Maruxa (her ancestor, we presume) a few pages earlier. The next panels, on the last page of the book, confirm the link between the two: in a ship headed for Turkey in 1492, Maruxa promises to one day return to Hervás (Gómez Andrea and Roa Cilla 29-30).

This comic book's emphasis on the narrative of return confirms the shift that the festival took after distancing itself from Wolodarsky's first play. *Los conversos* emphasized the impact of memory on the identities of those Jews who remained in Spain and became present-day Spaniards. But like the comic, the festival turned its eyes to Jews as past inhabitants who left (Maruxa) or present-day foreign Jews who may want to visit (Rocío), leaving aside the question of the local conversos and their memory. Despite lending their name to the festival, conversos gradually disappeared from its celebrations until 2013, when a new play incorporated them again through another local legend.

LA CALUMNIA [THE SLANDER] BY MIGUEL MURILLO (2013–15)

In 2013, a new play, *La calumnia*, was staged in the festival. As in Wolodarsky's first play, in *La calumnia* we find the thematic conflict of Jews' having to choose either to convert or to leave Spain. But contrary to in *Los conversos*, the focus here is not the Jewish condition and the identity conflict that converting supposes. *La calumnia*'s main focus is on portraying Hervás as an essentially good village whose inhabitants love their town and protect their neighbors. Rather than presenting the destruction of local Jewish life as a challenge to this goodness, the play blames it on the greed and cruelty of a fringe group of deplorable criminals.

The raw material for the play was the aforementioned case the Inquisition investigated in the area in 1506 and the subsequent local legends that developed around it. The scant information that exists about the case is the accusation against Juan Sastre, a local Old Christian. He was accused of stealing consecrated Hosts from the church of Aldeanueva del Camino, a small village four miles from Hervás, in order to sell them to a group of Hervás conversos. Both Sastre and the accused conversos were convicted of profanation and burned at the stake. Following the model of *La Estrella de Hervás*, the play explicitly acknowledges and pays homage to local legends. It is subtitled, "Obra dramática basada en la leyenda de Hervás 'La forma profanada' [Dramatic play based on Hervás's legend 'The desecrated Host'].[16]

The play positions the proclamation of the 1492 Edict of Expulsion as the originating event from which the plot will unfold. It shows the fear and confusion the edict causes in Hervás's Jewish population, who loudly wonder why they are receiving such punishment. A "Jewish Chorus" affirms the Jews' condition as eternal exiles, exclaiming, "La Tierra no es lugar para nosotros!" [Earth is no place for us!]. When Jewish landholders attend a meeting called by the Duke of Béjar in order to negotiate the sale of their properties, the duke imprisons them, prohibiting them from abandoning Spain and demanding their conversion to Christianity as the price of their liberation. Once and again, we hear Jewish characters express their love for Hervás as the land of their ancestors, a land they worked with their hands and that they do not wish to leave. When several families leave Hervás, the Jewish Chorus repeatedly proclaims that the village "will never be erased from our hearts." Jews take the keys of their houses so that "in the future, one of our descendants could return to our home." Later, in the second part of the play, the truthfulness of this love materializes when several of those families have literally returned to the village a few years later and the mythical keys are again used to open the doors to their homes. The script explains that they have done so under the protection of decrees of repatriation that allow them to return if they have converted to Christianity.

At the center of the story are Jacob and Raquel, two young Jewish lovers who explain the changes in the town to the audience in a dialogue in which Raquel asks Jacob why people have suddenly turned against them. Jacob answers that "ambition and greed" are to blame. Soon, we meet the characters who exemplify the best and the worst of Christian Hervás: Hervás's (and Christianity's) goodness is personified in Francisco Saysilero, who offers himself and his men as escort, guide, and safeguard to the Jews fleeing the village. He is a good, honorable Christian who respects, protects, and helps Jews. Jews themselves testify to this fact, saying, "If your religion predicates love . . . you are its worthy representative, Francisco" and "May your name be remembered from generation to generation."

On the opposite end of the spectrum, the antagonists of the play are a group of men characterized as "ganapanes malvados" [villainous louts]. These thugs are cruel to the point of becoming caricatures. Crouching behind corners and bushes, they wait for the Jews' departure to burglarize their houses. Unfailingly, they insult and humiliate Jews and conversos who cross their path. When young Jacob runs into them, they thrash him until he is close to death. Most importantly for the plot, they are the ones who conceive the scheme that triggers the play's main event: they steal a consecrated Host and hide it in the property of a converso family to then denounce conversos to the Inquisition for having stolen it. Through these thugs, the play gives voice to a cluster of different antisemitic legends depicting Jews' performing a number of sacrilegious actions. Thus, it is the thugs who say they have seen conversos boiling the Host, urinating in the cooking pot, and dancing around the fire. They also announce that a statue of Christ in Hervás's church is bleeding, as if indicating that it is being killed once again.

The play restores the Old Christian identity of these thugs, altering the modern versions of the story that had depicted them as conversos (Sendín Blásquez; Gómez Andrea and Roa Cilla). The play's performance adds a crucial element not present in the script: the thugs also boast about having violently murdered a young Jewish girl. Spectators witness the anguish and suffering of the girl's mother looking for her daughter and, later in the performance, the mother's confronting them about the crime. In case the audience had missed it, this event confirms the character of these *ganapanes* as essentially evil. They are the negative portrait of Hervás's essence as an Edenic location, home to a tolerant and happy community.

The play's climax takes place during an Inquisition trial in which the conversos are formally accused of stealing and desecrating the Host. Crucially, the trial takes place in front of the Church of Santa María, the location of the 1936 violent incident in which a group of local Republicans were accused of burning the church and stealing the holy chalice and the tabernacle. As described earlier in this chapter, one of the accused men who was condemned to prison in 1939 explained years later how the police and local authorities had forced him to accuse himself and others. The reference to these thugs as ganapanes, a word that characterizes them as poor day laborers, also resonates with local characterizations of the marginalized inhabitants of the Lower Quarter. In the play, the Inquisitor reminds the conversos that the crime for which they are accused is of the utmost gravity and that they should confess if they hope to save their souls. Echoing both the title of the play and the 1936 episode, the conversos respond that they are victims of a false accusation, a slander, and that Juan Sastre had found something on their property because he himself had hidden it there. An unexpected twist happens at this point in the play, though: Francisco Saysilero appears and attests on behalf of the conversos that he saw Sastre hide the Host. But the duke himself had already signed off the denunciation of Sastre as guilty of stealing the Host, and Sastre is thrown in jail with the conversos.

The play's ending centers on the actions of Francisco. We casually learn that Sastre and the group of conversos were condemned by the Inquisition and that all, except Jacob, have died. Jacob has not, thanks to Francisco, who not only manages to bring Sastre to justice but also saves Jacob from jail, helping him escape and reunite with Raquel. Echoing the performance of Wolodarsky's second play, *La conversa de Hervás*, the two young lovers escape to Portugal and promise to return to Hervás. Raquel explicitly clarifies that it is thanks to Francisco's good deeds that they might return one day and be embraced by a town that would be transformed in Francisco's image: "Ojalá esta acción tuya sirva para que un día podamos regresar de nuevo y ver cómo todos los cristianos como tú se abrazan a nosotros sin recelo" [Hopefully this action of yours will one day help in our return and we will see how all the Christians embrace us without suspicion, as you do].[17] The current inhabitants of Hervás are supposed to be these future people who, like Francisco, are exemplary Christians who value and embrace Hervás's Jewish legacy. They can feel good about themselves and their town by contemplating themselves in the mirror image of Francisco.

This message about the type of town that Hervás should be is predicated on the notion of a past convivencia sustained by people like Francisco and the transferring of responsibility for its destruction to "a few bad apples" like Juan Sastre and his henchmen. The focus on Sastre's extreme cruelty and malice, accentuated in the performance by the addition of the assassination of the Jewish girl plot element, dilutes any possibility of imagining collective responsibility.[18]

And it is precisely these issues of complicity and denunciation that bring us back to Hervás's political and social climate of the late 1930s and beyond. In the last few years, historians of twentieth-century Spain have begun to examine the deeply uncomfortable matter of civil complicity during the war and postwar periods. As Peter Anderson explains, the mass killing and incarceration of those suspected of supporting the Republic was possible because common citizens were exhorted to denounce their neighbors when a town was occupied by Nationalist troops and they did so: "the widespread practice of denunciation proved crucial in selecting those who suffered execution or imprisonment" (Anderson 8). This practice of ordinary citizens' active collaboration with the authorities in the implementation of political repression is exemplified in the aforementioned case of the leftists who were accused by their neighbors of starting the fire and desecrating the Host at Hervás's Church of Santa María and were sentenced to jail in 1939. When *La Calumnia* defines a clear line between the compassionate behavior of Francisco Saylisero as representative of Hervás and the criminal behavior of a few thugs, it is not only trying to gloss over the history of civil collaboration with the Inquisition in medieval Hervás, but it is also attempting to restrict responsibility for the widespread violence against those suspected of supporting the Republic to a small group of uncontrollable thugs.

Since its first edition in 1997, Los Conversos has contained a messy entanglement of memories. The plays at the center of the festival can be understood as a sequence of reenactments of episodes of violence, betrayals, and denunciations between neighbors. They depict what today we would call hate crimes and also attempt to find acceptable narratives for the civil complicities that made them possible. In the performances of the festival's plays, the town's inhabitants perform a script written by a playwright but they also embody and reenact the town's collective memory. These are the stories they have heard over and over, stories about Jews and conversos who are represented as guilty of their own victimization and simultaneously as perpetrators and victims. As these plays strive to depict a local-nationalist version of Hervás as a product for tourist consumption, a welcoming and tolerant village, a beautiful and generous land never forgotten by those who experience it, the plays' tales of violence, social stigmatization, slander, and injustice cannot help but awaken more recent memories of victimization. The effects of the specific multidirectionality of these memories can be perceived in the successive plays and their shifting perspectives, each more localized than the previous, each more focused on rescuing a romanticized version of Hervás's difficult memories. While they are not scripted in the plays, Hervás's collective memories of stigmatization and shaming become reenergized within each performance, even if displaced to the painful events surrounding the town's Jewish past. In a similar manner to the 1953 poem "Hervás: Canto al amor verdadero" in which references to a medieval "damning hatred that divides our Hervás" were also alluding to the more recent memories of the Civil War, the plays are also doing more than "performing" the town's distant past. In them, past and present enter into a dance of memory in which each period becomes both shown and concealed, its conflicts mobilized and contained once again. While these entanglements may potentially serve to add another layer of memory erasure, they also carry the possibility of further engagement and critical explorations of Hervás's and Spain's difficult pasts and unstable presents.

NOTES

1. These efforts at conservation and tourist promotion have been well recognized both at the regional and national levels since the end of the 1950s. José María Castellano explains how, in 1959, Hervás's mayor received the Governor's Honorary Prize for Beautification after the city council paved the streets of the Barrio Judío. In 1972, the town received the National Prize for Beautification and Conservation, given by the Ministry of Science and Education and, in 1981, the Golden Oscar for the best tourist promotion (Castellano 17).

2. To disguise the traditional antisemitic connotation of this refrain, the rest of the rhyme where this sentence appears has been edited out. The complete refrain characterizes the inhabitants of Hervás and three neighboring towns by stating: "En Hervás, judíos los más / En Aldeanueva, la judería entera / En Baños, judíos y tacaños / y en Béjar, [judíos] hasta las tejas" [In Hervás, mostly Jews / in Aldeanueva, the complete Jewery / in Baños, Jews and misers / and in Béjar, (Jews) up to the roof tiles].

3. Marciano de Hervás explains that the naming of this street as "Sinagoga" took place in the context of the First Republic, at the same time that the subject of religious tolerance was being debated in the Spanish Courts (de Hervás, *Judíos y Cristianos* 360).

4. In the fifteenth century, several individuals suspected of involvement in the robbery and semilegal acquisitions of Jewish houses also owned properties situated in Corredera Street (de Hervás, *Judíos y Cristianos* 361).

5. In 2005 a group of neighbors from the Lower Quarter formed an association, the Asociación de Vecinos del Barrio Judío de Hervás, to request appropriate sewage and water services (Asociación de Vecinos).

6. As we saw in chapter 1, the identification of Republicans as Jews and as part of a Jewish international conspiracy to destroy Christianity was a staple piece of right-wing propaganda that informed the uprising against the Second Republic in 1936 and the Francoist view of its enemies as a "Judeo-Masonic-Bolshevik" conspiracy. See Preston.

7. For an explanation of this silence prolonged over several generations as a strategy of survival, see Jo Labanyi, "Languages" and "Entrevista a Emilio Silva." Labanyi explains how the victims and their relatives have had to wait until the twenty-first century, decades after the reestablishment of democracy, "for suitable conditions of reception to exist for their stories" ("Languages" 28).

8. See Cobo Romero and Teresa María Ortega López; González Duro.

9. Alejandro Baer explains how, in the first commemorative ceremony organized by the Jewish community of Madrid, representatives of the Jewish communities were joined by a Republican survivor of the Nazi camps and a Roma representative ("The Voids" 100–103).

10. The structure of the festival has similarities with the one celebrated in Ribadavia, in the province of Ourense, Galicia. As Judith Cohen observed in her analysis of this festival, a genuine curiosity about the town's past and the possibilities of its "recuperation" coexist with commercialization, opportunism, and cultural appropriation. See Cohen, "Bringing It All Back Home" and "Constructing a Spanish Jewish Festival."

11. Miguel Nieto explained his role as director and his vision for the play in an interview we conducted in Madrid in July 2007.

12. We could say that although the play's title points to Ana, the play's protagonist is, without a doubt, Manuel Alvarado. This is confirmed by Wolodarsky's extension of the play as the 2007 novel, *El judío de Hervás* [The Jew from Hervás].

13. *Viaje por la España judía* [Travel in Jewish Spain], from 2002, says that a trip to Hervás should begin by learning this local legend about the historical Jewish Quarter (thus giving credence to its claim of Jewishness). The legend, the authors argue, "gives true, passionate expression to Jewish-Christian relations in the town" (Aradillas and Íñigo 262).

14. Jonathan Ray also explains that "the sense of Jewish outrage at such relationships present in these folktales is not without historical merit." Rabbinic authorities were, indeed, "most alarmed by Jewish sexual liaisons with gentiles." These tales speak about Jewish anxiety over the very attractive option that Hispano-Christian society presented to medieval Sephardim (Ray, "Beyond" 7–8). Mirrer also sees that "the threat from within (symbolized by Marisaltos, who is intimate with a male Christian) could be far more destructive to the Jewish community than the threat from without" (Mirrer 44). But Ray's and Mirrer's reflections about the reality of Jewish authorities' alarm over Jewish-Christian intimate relations and about sexual attractiveness as part of and metaphor for Christian society's attractiveness for Jews, does not mean that these legends are factually true, as Hervás's narratives promoting tourism pretend.

15. Murillo explained in an interview that when asked by Hervás's authorities to write a new play to replace Wolodarsky's, he requested information about local stories and legends that he could use. By reviewing the legend of the two lovers, he said, one can see its antisemitism ("*La leyenda*" 19).

16. Our quotes come from the screenplay written by Murillo and followed in the performance. We thank the city council of Hervás for providing us with a copy of the unpublished script the actors used for the play. We indicate when the performance of the play we saw in July 2014 deviates from this text.

17. Raquel's mention of one day returning to Hervás explicitly alludes to Hervás's current tourism efforts, as we have seen explicitly in the historical comic *Hervás: Imágenes de su Historia.*

18. Hervás's festival keeps evolving. As we were revising this chapter, a new play entitled *Alma Negra* [Black soul] was premiered at the festival's twentieth anniversary in July 2016. Written by Miguel Gómez Andrea "Gol," the coauthor of the comic *Hervás: Imágenes de su Historia,* and directed by José A. Raynaud, it seems to follow in the footsteps of *La calumnia* in terms of placing the blame for the end of convivencia on "a few bad apples" and away from the town as a whole. Its author explains, in a promotional release for the play,

> Siempre me ha llamado la atención la facilidad con la que unos pocos pueden envenenar la convivencia pacífica en una localidad, o incluso en un país. . . . La gente vivía en paz y de repente un energúmeno o energúmena podía encender los ánimos de los, hasta hace un momento, pacíficos ciudadanos y convertirlos en asesinos
>
> [My attention has always been attracted by the ease with which a few individuals can poison peaceful coexistence in a locality or even in a nation. . . . People could be living in peace and suddenly a raging lunatic could stir up those that until recently were peaceful citizens and turn them into murderers] (Gómez Andrea)

SIX

RETURNS TO SEPHARAD

THE INCREASED VISIBILITY OF "THINGS Jewish" chronicled in this book has reenergized, and in certain cases awakened for the first time, a wide array of desires to explore modes of reconnection to Spain's Jewish inheritance. The concept of "return," with its appeal to a right of origin and connotations of reconnection to a forgotten truth, has become a common term to describe this highly diverse array of identifications that carry the symbolic connotations of the term Sepharad in many directions, both within and outside of Spain.[1] What does it mean to return to Sepharad in contemporary Spain? What are the means of return for different groups in Spain today?

In this final chapter, we discuss several ways through which different people in Spain provide answers to these questions. We examine several narratives, discourses, and artistic representations of desired returns to the Jewish past, to Judaism and to Sepharad, to tease out the identitary, political, and aesthetic work performed by them. We analyze how Esther Bendahan, a Spanish writer of Sephardi-Moroccan descent, conceptualizes the return to Sepharad in her fictional work, followed by the diverse modes of personal reconnection with Judaism and Jewishness being articulated by people in Spain who self-identify as descendants of conversos. We reflect on contemporary artistic elaborations of the Iberian Jewish past in the work *Shoah 1492–1945* by Wolf Vostell, a German-born pioneer of installation art who from the 1950s until the mid-'90s lived intermittently in Malpartida (Cáceres) and in the series *Sephardi Portraits* created in the last twenty-five years by one of the leading figurative painters in Spain, Daniel Quintero.

Appeals to any kind of return are frequently grounded in sentiments of nostalgia for something lost. At work in the narratives, paintings, and life stories examined in this chapter are diverse combinations of the restorative and reflective modes of nostalgia which Svetlana Boym identifies as a byproduct of modernity. Boym argues that nostalgia performs a symbolic shift presenting itself as "longing for a place, but it is actually a yearning for a different time" (Boym, "Nostalgia" 8). What different times, and by whom, emerge within these yearnings for Sepharad? Narratives of "return to Sepharad" have proven to be prolific, and it would be impossible to account for their multiple manifestations. The works of Bendahan, Vostell, and Quintero, together with the narratives of self-discovery of those identifying as descendants of conversos contain emblematic examples of the yearnings for different temporalities and the attempts to articulate acts of obligation that have emerged around the concept of return. Because of their conceptual richness and multiple perspectives, the cases studied here become key markers in a cartography of the expanding imaginary territory of contemporary Sepharad. They offer a guide to the possibilities of engagement through which different groups of people from different subject positions within Spain attempt to come to terms with the unresolved questions engendered by engagement with Spain's Jewish past and its memory.

RETURNS TO SEPHARAD IN THE WORK OF ESTHER BENDAHAN

Born in Tetuán within a Sephardi family and community, Bendahan moved as a child to Madrid with her family in the early 1970s and has lived there ever since.[2] Her experiences as a Sephardi Jew born in Morocco and raised in Spain occupy a central place in Bendahan's work as a fiction writer. Bendahan has also been the director of cultural programming at the Centro Sefarad-Israel since its inauguration in the year 2007, and as such she has played a key role in Spain's official efforts to strengthen diplomatic and cultural links with Judaism, the Sephardi diaspora, and Israel. Bendahan's writing captures with particular poignancy the difficulty of avoiding well-established clichés when speaking for and about Sephardi Jews in contemporary Spain. Bendahan is critical of the origin and use of the romantic myths of historic loyalty and love for an Iberian homeland, the Spanish language, and the idealization of convivencia that emerge in public discourse when the name Sepharad is invoked. Yet she is also aware that these myths often provide the means through which the experience of Sephardi Jews finds articulation and a degree of visibility within contemporary Spain.

In an article in *El País* in 2007 in which Bendahan refers to her role in the Centro Sefarad-Israel, she expresses her hopes that her work would help dispel myths and clichés about Sephardi Jews and more accurately educate the public about Sephardi culture as something alive and integral to Spain. Later in this same article, however, she characterizes Sephardi Jews as "exiliados españoles que mantuvieron el judeo-español durante siglos, conservando su lengua y su identidad a pesar de haber sido expulsados" [Spanish exiles who maintained Judeo-Spanish for centuries, preserving their language and identity in spite of having been expelled] ("Sefardistán"). Ángel Pulido's romanticized and Hispano-centric view of Sephardi Jews resonates in these words and their redeployment of timeworn myths. In the article "Memoria rota de los judíos de Marruecos" [The broken memory of Moroccan Jews], Bendahan characterizes Sephardi Jews as "true Spanish ambassadors," a term that was common currency among Spanish philosephardists in the early twentieth century.[3] But Bendahan is acutely aware of the multiple meanings these mythologies hold for the different social actors involved and of their strategic usefulness for Jews' search for belonging in contemporary Spain. Her work explores this tension between the need to fully normalize the Jewish presence within contemporary Spain and the desire to dispel the many prejudices and misconceptions that still circulate about them. As connected as these two goals might seem, in practice, however, the price of expediting integration has often entailed the perpetuation of a romanticized Hispano-centric view of Sephardi Jews.

We can argue that for some Sephardi Jews in Spain today, a group that includes Bendahan herself, this discourse of ancestral love for Spain, the often-repeated formulation "la conciencia de regreso," something like "an awareness/understanding of their journey to Spain as a return," has become the most expedient and, at times, the only available rhetorical instrument to articulate a claim of legitimacy, belonging, and authority.[4] Within Spain, participating in the country's mythologies of medieval convivencia and of Sephardi Jews as zealous preservers of Spanish culture and language provides a social right to inhabit a shared space. These time-sanctioned myths still provide the available grammar through which it is possible to speak, and to be listened to, as Jews in Spain.[5] Frequently, Bendahan's narratives inhabit these commonplaces and deploy their grammar. Yet as critics like Campoy-Cubillo observe, Bendahan's fiction stays away from essentialist definitions of identity (Campoy-Cubillo 87). Her writing also embarks in critical explorations of these received notions, exposing their mythical nature. These critical moments appear in the form of narrative voices that interrogate characters' notions of genealogy, identity, and national belonging, and invite us to reconsider long-held notions of historical and cultural identity. Bendahan's literature explores and negotiates with this "available grammar."

Bendahan's first novel, *Soñar con Hispania,* written with Israel-based Chilean Jewish writer Ester Benari, undertakes such exploration through the identification, deployment, and demythologization of the multiple forms of return that Sepharad offers to a number of different people. Each of the two parts of the novel focuses on one of the two protagonists, José de la Villa, a Spanish professor of medieval amatory literature, and Sofía Corzo, an Israeli computer programmer. The first part of the novel, written by Bendahan, follows José as he researches the life stories of the authors of two letters written in the fifteenth century by two Jewish women, Sara Laredo, whose maiden name was Corzo, and Miriam Corzo. The second part, written by Benari, retells much of the story from the perspective of Sofía, who, after becoming a widow, has taken an interest in the origins of her last name and maintains a genealogical website dedicated to the Corzo family. As José and Sofía develop their correspondence through email, their messages provide a symbolic connection between contemporary Spain and Israel and between them and fifteenth-century Jewish Iberia and North Africa, specifically the city of Tetuán.

As José advances in his research, he interprets any new finding as a confirmation of philosephardi mythologies. First, he discovers that both Sara and Miriam were from the town of Laredo, the same town where he was born, and that the two became separated when, in 1492, Sara was forced into exile while Miriam, Sara's younger niece, converted and stayed. With this knowledge, José begins to see his hometown in a new light, and imagines connections with her: Sara, he thinks, "vivía aquí mismo, hace quinientos años. Paseaba por estas calles . . . como lo hago yo" [lived precisely here, five hundred years ago. She would go for a walk in these streets . . . as I do] (26); "Sara debía cocinar en una cocina como ésta, con ese mismo verde alrededor" [Sara must have cooked in a kitchen like this one, with the same green surrounding it] (33).

This reemergence of a once forgotten past, his realization that Laredo was the town that Sara, Miriam, and their families had called home, makes José look at his familiar surroundings differently: "las propiedades, las casas, los objetos siguen existiendo: parecen pertenecer realmente a alguien, hasta que le dejan de pertenecer y el nuevo propietario es dueño, como si lo hubiera sido siempre. Pero los espacios, las casas, los documentos, la tierra tienen su propia identidad" [properties, houses, objects continue existing: they seem to truly belong to somebody, until they stop belonging to that person and the new holder becomes owner, as if he had always been that. But spaces, houses, documents, land have their own identity] (27). These familiar surroundings appear now connected to the history he begins to uncover through the study of Sara and Miriam's letters. The deciphering of the letters, and of the local past, makes José begin to question the belonging and ownership of spaces, houses, and objects.

When, browsing through internet pages, he discovers a genealogy site dedicated to the Corzo family maintained by Sofía, José, and the readers along with him, imagine her as a descendant of the two women José is researching. In José's imagination, present-day Sofía and fifteenth-century Sara "se configuraban en el mismo rostro. Detrás de Sofía, en susurros, se escondía Sara" [took shape in the same face. Behind Sofía, Sara was hidden in whispers] (17). José never doubts that there is a genealogical line going straight from Sara to Sofía. The most important thing about Sofía is that "ella es Corzo como la familia de Sara" [She is a Corzo like the rest of Sara's family is] (24). His assumption about a genealogical straight line connecting them participates in current understandings, such as those promised by commercial DNA tests, that posit supposed origins as explanations of present interrogations of identity. As we will see, the novel playfully comments on the fallacy of José's—and perhaps the readers'—assumption.

The narrative of return from a protracted exile gets further reinforced when José travels to Tetuán in search of information about Sara Laredo. The text highlights Tetuán's connection to Spain as the city founded by those who went into exile in 1492 (87). It is also significant that it is at this point, during his visit to Tetuán, that José completes his efforts to decipher Sara's letter, and that he mails a transcription to Sofía from there. The letter explains the difficulties faced by both Miriam and Sara in the years immediately following 1492. It explains how the family's properties went to a Christian woman in payment for helping Miriam during a protracted illness (75). Sara details her long journey along with her family and their eventual arrival in Tetuán, where, she says, people are surprised to hear that they do not harbor any rancor toward Spain (76–77). Furthermore, in Tetuán, José finds a document that speaks about the first families that arrived from Spain and mentions a woman who repeatedly expressed her longing to return to Sepharad and how she believed this return was her right (107). This woman, José imagines, could have been Sara.

Up to here, the first part of the novel becomes almost an official wish list for everything Spain wants from Sephardi Jews, a narrative that captures the preferred version of the Iberian Jewish past disseminated by tourist initiatives like the Network of Jewish Quarters of Spain: before the expulsion, Jews lived prosperous and happy lives in their communities. After the expulsion, they remained unfailingly faithful to their Iberian origins, harbored no rancor, and legitimately transferred their properties to those who helped them.

The perceived added value this past provides contemporary Spain becomes literally ingrained in the narrative when, at the end of this first part, José looks for a picture of himself to send to Sofía. After feeling unsatisfied by many attempts, José finds "his face" in a portrait of himself inside Tetuán's synagogue. As he sends this picture to Sofía, we can see a parallelism between this portrait of José with Jewish backdrop and how Spain currently deploys the country's Jewish past as a framework from which to portray itself to the international community for, assumedly, political and economic advantage.

The parallelism between José's fantasies and recent Spanish history gets further reinforced when José invites Sofía to come to Laredo by telling her "to come home," a reference that points not only to his house but also to Spain and to Sepharad as shared homes. This is the same metaphoric use of the term *home* frequently invoked by Spanish authorities in official ceremonies welcoming Sephardi Jews. Spain is your "home," as in King Juan Carlos's landmark speech in 1992 or King Felipe's in 2015 (see introduction). The way these same tropes are embraced by José in the novel leaves us far from certain whether Sephardi Jews' yearning for Spain was ever true, or if it has really been fulfilled by the law of nationality. What we can be certain of in terms of this novel is that José is the one who dwells in a very peculiar nostalgia, one for a past he hopes can provide a background against which he may revalue his present.

In the second part of the novel, we find Sofía's version of events. Sofía's husband has died recently and the website has become one of her ways to mourn his loss. Initially she is skeptical about José's story and his reasons for researching the history of the Corzo family (118). But in the course of reading the content of the sixteenth-century letters José forwards her, she feels deeply moved and begins to identify with the story of Miriam (170). When she finally receives José's picture, Sofía feels as if she already knew him; she "recognizes" in his features those of "a Spanish nobleman or a Jew" (173). If in José's section he imagined Sara as Sofía, it is now Sofía who imagines traces of Miriam's features as José's: "La cara de José, finalmente visualizada, se le sobreimprimía a la de Miriam, en la imaginación, y los rasgos de ambos se le entremezclaban en un puzzle inquietante" [José's face, visualized at last, superimposed itself on Miriam's in her imagination, and the features of both would mix together in a disconcerting puzzle] (173–74).

This imaginary joining together of José and Miriam by Sofía appears in the text right after we read the rest of Miriam's letter in which she describes her transformation from reluctant convert to sincere Christian (although she also reveals her physical aversion to meat, which may be pointing at her keeping

Jewish dietary laws). The imaginary link of Miriam's and José's features hints at the possibility of seeing José, and current inhabitants of Spain, as descendants of conversos. Upon Sofía's arrival in Spain, these echoes of Jewish presence in Spain get reinforced: at Madrid's airport, people's interactions and faces remind Sofía of Tel Aviv's (177). Seeing José for the first time, she feels as if she had always known him; he reminds her of a Corzo (178–79).

Soon, an authorial voice bursts José's, and the readers', romantic bubble regarding Sofía's genealogical link to Sara. Sofía herself, we learn, is not a Corzo. The Corzos are not her ancestors, but those of her deceased husband. Her maiden name is Livne, and she comes from an Ashkenazi family (175, 179–80). As the novel draws to a close, Sofía and José become romantically involved and one last letter is decoded, revealing a nun's report on the death of Miriam from an illness caused by a long walk in the rain. Addressed to a rich benefactor who had once rescued Miriam, the letter explains that the rumors about Miriam's having escaped from Spain in order to reunite with her family and return to Judaism are not true (191–200). Sofía and José thus conclude what the readers of the novel are supposed to conclude: that we have no way to know what really happened to Miriam or which were her true religious convictions. Like Sofía, we might be inclined to believe that what the letter insists in negating must be true: that Miriam did escape, that she returned to Judaism, that the soaking in the rain was not an accident but a purification ritual (195). But as José remarks, there is nothing in the documents that tells us this might be the case. We do not know.

Shortly after this revelation, Sofía feels that by putting together the pieces of Miriam's puzzle she has also solved her own puzzle; her fascination with the memory of her husband's family, she now understands, is related to the sense of void in her own eastern European family decimated by the Holocaust. Her husband's premature death by a landmine before they were able to have children meant that this void subsequently extended to her biological future (198). Thus, the Sofía Corzo we meet at the beginning of the novel through José's eyes, the keeper of the internet site dedicated to the Corzo last name and its ancestral memory, is transformed into an Ashkenazi Tsofía Livne who "dreams of Hispania" as a personal quest for an identity anchor. Her ties to Spain and to the Sephardi identity of the Corzos are not genealogical but affective and affiliative; they don't belong to a past accurately described in a family tree but to the hopes for the present she was building with her husband before his premature death. José de la Villa, who knows nothing about Judaism, finds its ghostly traces in his own hometown of Laredo and perhaps in himself. It is through his imagining and conjuring the story of the two sixteenth-century Jewish women from Laredo that he makes peace with his own family history and the tragedy of his parents' death when he was a child.

José comes to understand his own link with the histories of these Jewish women from the past as fluid and alive, a connection that affects the past and the present. He explains:

> No quería coleccionar conocimientos como mi tío coleccionaba mariposas. Pasar alfileres sobre el dato dictado rompe la historia, mata su continuo fluir . . . ahora [mi vida] debe seguir adelante, dejar la vida de Sara, dejar que su grito recorra el presente como si lo acabara de dar, no mi grito sino rescatar el suyo. . . . Así permitiremos volar a las mariposas, conociéndolas, dándolas nombres pero dejando los alfileres y los cartones. Las mariposas vivas de la historia que van del ayer al hoy.

> [I did not want to collect knowledge like my uncle collected butterflies. Putting pins through pieces of information breaks history, kills its continuous flow . . . now [my life] must continue, I must leave Sara's life, allow her scream to reach the present as if she had just now screamed it, not my scream but rescuing hers . . . this way we will allow the butterflies to fly, getting to know them, giving them names but leaving aside the pins and cardboard boxes. The living butterflies of history that go from yesterday to today.] (108–9)

The living butterflies that connect present and past are the connections José traces with Sara, Miriam, and his town's Jewish history. These are not exactly his families' memories, or we do not know if they could be. Like Sofía's, they are affiliative connections. Marianne Hirsch developed the concept of "affiliative postmemory" to speak of a connection to the past "mediated not by recall but by imaginative investment, projection, and creation" (Hirsch, *The Generation* 5). As Hirsch explains, memories can be transmitted within the family, but they can also be acquired through "structures of mediation that would be broadly appropriable, available, and indeed, compelling enough to encompass a larger collective in an organic web of transmission" (Hirsch, "The Generation" 114–15).[6]

As a whole, *Soñar con Hispania* articulates a kind of pragmatic remythologization of the return to Sepharad. In the second part of the novel, when we read Sofía's version of events, we find an explicit mention of the novel's title in a letter she sends to José. She explains that "Soñar con Hispania" [Dreaming about Hispania] is a phrase used in the Talmud to mean "hacer castillos en el aire . . . soñar con cosas lejanas o irreales" [to make castles in the air . . . to dream about things far away or impossible] (167). Hispania was, geographically, the furthermost province of the Roman Empire at the time of and from the perspective of those who compiled the Babylonian Talmud. In the context of the novel, this allusion seems to point to the insurmountable distance separating the protagonists not geographically from Spain but from Sepharad: chronologically from the medieval and early modern periods and conceptually from being able to "return" in the sense of apprehending or grasping what really happened or was felt by those Jews who left, converted, or both.

In a complex counterpoint, the narrative first inflates and later bursts the bubble of these myths. It starts by fully deploying the mythologies of an immanent and material presence of the Jewish past in cities in Spain, echoing Sephardi yearning for a return to Spain and reproducing a genealogical fallacy, all of them articulated from Spanish and Ashkenazi-Israeli perspectives. Eventually, by revealing Sofía's non-Sephardi origins, and by leaving Miriam's story and motivations unresolved, the novel reveals the status of these myths as myths. Yet the fact that both José and Sofía end up finding in these myths the tools they need to conjure their personal crises and start a new chapter in their lives points to an underlying belief in the usefulness of these myths even when knowing that they are just projections from our problematic present onto a past that is impossible to fully reconstruct. The search for ancestry and return are thus revealed as projects anchored in the needs of the present and the future, not as clear-cut answers that repair wounds or inoculate us from the past. Genealogical links are not direct or straightforward, and affective, affiliative connections are varied and unexpected.

Bendahan expands her reflection on the paradoxes of the myth of return in her 2006 novel *Déjalo, ya volveremos,* through the story of a Moroccan Sephardi family who leaves Tetuán for Madrid in the late 1960s. With clear autobiographical overtones, the novel is extremely aware of the way the average reader in Spain may see Jews and Judaism.[7] It uses the perspective of a child narrator who tells us of her family's life in Tetuán, her arrival in Madrid, and her progressive adjustment to her new home. The unusual title, "Déjalo, ya volveremos" [Leave it, we'll come back] is a phrase that is repeated in the novel by the protagonist's father. It is an unfulfilled promise of return to the space of childhood and the safety of home. In very concrete terms, it refers to the closet that Reina, the child protagonist, had in her room in Tetuán. This closet served the crucial purpose of helping the girl control her fears and the chaos around her. The title's phrase appears in Reina's memory in one of the most poignant scenes of the novel, at the beginning of part 2. Shortly after their arrival in Madrid, Reina realizes what she calls "the truth" about her new country, the widespread ignorance and prejudice about Jews and

Judaism. This realization comes after a confrontation at school: "Is it true that you are Jewish?" asks a girl from her class. Another one answers, "Eso es mentira, no se es judío . . . judío no se puede ser, no se puede, es un insulto" [That is a lie, you cannot be Jewish . . . you cannot be that, you can't, it is an insult] (102). This is not the first time that Reina becomes aware of her Jewishness as a difference—the novel has already mentioned confrontations with Moroccan Muslim characters to describe the mounting climate of tension that had resulted in Reina's family leaving Morocco for Spain. But the novel makes clear that the family thought that moving to Spain would result in a considerable improvement in that situation. When leaving Morocco, the father had told Reina and her siblings that they were going to a beautiful place (93).

Her classmates' remarks make Reina consider that what her new friend Pilar tells her might be right: "que nunca tendría país, que los echarían siempre, y que ser judío no sólo era un insulto sino que era ser echado" [that she would never have a country, that they would always be kicked out, and that being Jewish was not only an insult but also to be kicked out] (109). In Madrid, she comes to understand her exclusion not as an exception due to the complex geopolitical circumstances of Morocco but as an intrinsic part of her Jewish identity. As if confirming this insight, she remembers how back in Morocco her aunt had once told her, "No somos del todo de aquí, no somos de ningún lado" [We are not completely from here, we do not belong anywhere] (73).

Back home from school after that confrontation, Reina decides not to share with her family what just happened: "Ellos seguían en casa entre ellos y preparaban Rosh Hashaná, y no sabían nada de dónde estaban, ni las sombras de este nuevo país y no quería ser ella quien descubriera esa verdad cruel" [They were still at home among themselves and they were preparing Rosh Hashana, and they did not know anything about where they were, or about the shadows of this new country and she did not want to be the one to unveil that cruel truth] (106). When her mother hugs her, Reina thinks of what she left behind. She remembers asking her father, as they were leaving Tetuán, about what would happen to her closet, and his response, "Déjalo, ya volveremos."

At the very end of the novel, Reina remembers this premonitory dialogue again. Time has passed and she has matured. She feels more comfortable both in her own skin and in Madrid. But the words of her father have now acquired deeper resonances as a foundational condition of her identity:

> A veces recordaba su armario. "Déjalo. Ya volveremos," decía su padre en su recuerdo, "ya volveremos," y sabía que ya no había vuelta posible; al salir volvían y si se marchaban sería como volver otra vez, como si siempre

> estuvieran volviendo.... Algún día regresarían, pero ya habían vuelto. Y si tenían que irse, sería para llegar a un lugar al que estaban volviendo.
>
> [Sometimes she remembered her closet. "Leave it. We will come back," her father would say in her memory, "we will come back," and he knew that there was no way back anymore; by leaving, they were returning and if they left it would be like returning again, as if they were always returning.... One day they would come back, but they were already back. And if they ever had to leave, it would be to arrive at a place to which they were returning]. (238–39)

This reflection purposely plays on the ambiguity of the lack of place referent. *Morocco, Spain, Sepharad* are exchangeable terms of reference for the acts of leaving and returning. They are all home and yet never completely home; to arrive in these places can be seen as a return but always in an oblique way, as something never completely realized. In her work on nostalgia, Boym explains that homecomings, or returns, are "riddled with contradictions and zigzags, false homecomings, misrecognitions" (Boym, *Future* 8). The nod to the cliché of Spain as a place of return, as an ancestral home, which is also a nod to the Spanish audience that would buy and read the novel, is tinged with feelings of ambivalence and nostalgia for other lands and other paths.

The ambivalence about the degree of Spanishness of Sephardi Jews remains equally unresolved in the text. When Reina, in Spain, hears of Rabí Yehudáh Halevy as "a poet who lived in Spain in the eleventh century," she wonders, "Así que no eran los primeros, entonces: ¿por qué tenía la sensación de inaugurar algo?" [So they were not the first, but then: why did she have the feeling of inaugurating something?] (117). To Reina, the presence of her family in Madrid feels like a new arrival. Their experience does not seem to bear out the seamless continuity of the past and the present, of medieval Jews in al-Andalus and contemporary Sephardi Jews in Spain that the mythology of Sephardi Jews as "Spanish exiles" espouses. And yet, Spain is not just any place to them. When at the end of the novel Reina finds out that she will have a new cousin, her family says that this baby will be the first Spaniard in the family: "luego añadían que ellos eran sefarditas, que eran españoles de siempre y que además también habían nacido en el protectorado, que era una manera de estar y ser de España.... Pero de cualquier manera repetían que era el primero de la familia en la península" [then they would add that they were Sephardi Jews, that they had always been Spaniards and that on top of that they had been born in the Protectorate, which was a way of being in and being from Spain.... But, in any case, they repeated that the baby was the first of the family on the Peninsula] (238). In this dialogue about their family's identity, the literal belonging of the new baby to Spain sets up a back-and-forth discussion about what kind of Spaniards they are, marking the limits and margins, or the extension of the continuum of metaphorical and literal belongings and the spaces in between that they themselves inhabit. As Dalia Kandiyoti explains in her book *Migrant Sites,* the homeland is far from being an uncontested space and source of identification (37). Indeed, "the condition of multiple rediasporization that characterizes the trajectories of many communities may make the assumption of a single place of origin impossible or moot" (Kandiyoti, *Migrant Sites* 38). Kandiyoti uses the oxymoronic formulation "migrant sites" to characterize these dwelling places, a term that encompasses both the local and the translocal, the national and the transnational, fixity and mobility (*Migrant Sites* 39).

The mythologies of Sepharad—and Spain's persistent antisemitism—are confronted with disarming humor and irony by Bendahan in "Condecoración" [Homage]. This short story belongs to the collection *Una hora solamente, de la orilla del día,* published in 2016. The story takes place in 2015, the year, we are reminded, of the law that "restores" Spanish nationality to Sephardi Jews. The language of "restoration" is essential here, echoing the characterization of the law by both Spanish officials and the leaders of the Federation of Jewish Communities of Spain as bringing closure to a five-hundred-year-long situation of injustice.

The short story is narrated from the point of view of a Spanish trade advisor who is Jewish and works at the Spanish embassy in Greece. The other two main characters are a young Spanish ambassador in his first diplomatic position and an old Greek Jew who ceremoniously introduces himself to the ambassador and the advisor as "Excmo. Señor Solal Saltiel, *bar mitzvah* con honores. Embajador de Sefarad en tierras griegas" [Excellency Mr. Solal Saltiel, *bar mitzvah* with honors. Ambassador of Sepharad in Greek lands] (113). Mr. Saltiel is Bendahan's homage to Albert Cohen's iconic literary characters, as she explains through one of her characters in *Soñar con Hispania* (99–100).[8] Self-appointed "ambassador of Sepharad," and, as we will see below, "Spaniard for hundreds of years," he echoes and embodies the characterizations of Sephardi Jews explained throughout this book.

In an interview with the Spanish ambassador, Mr. Saltiel proposes the organization of a ceremony to honor himself. He speaks of Spain as "our motherland" and quotes Borges's poem "La llave en Salónica."[9] As Mr. Saltiel explains it, he has brought honor to Spain's name all over the world, spreading the word about the literary achievements of Spain's Jewish writers and creating "the Sepharad brand." The ambassador fears being the victim of a prank. Attempting to get rid of the "intruder," he tells Mr. Saltiel, "Yo siempre he admirado a su pueblo. Son unos visitantes que cuando se marchan dejan mejor la casa que cuando llegaron" [I have always admired your people. You are those visitors who, upon departing, leave the house in better condition than they encountered it]. Offended, Mr. Saltiel answers with a reproduction of the language of Sephardi love and attachment to Spain as their eternal home, "¿La casa? ¿Visitantes? Señor, yo soy español desde hace cientos de años. Soy un nacionalista, no olvidé su lengua por vínculo con su tierra y la mía" [The house? Visitors? Sir, I have been a Spaniard for hundreds of years. I am a nationalist, I have not forgotten its language because of its link with your land and mine] (114).

The tongue-in-cheek exchange brings us back to Spain's ambivalent embracing of and welcoming Sephardi Jews "home." It reveals Sephardi Jews—or some of them—as complicit in the mythologization and "branding" of Sepharad, but also reveals the extremely old prejudices that make Sephardi Jews "others" to Spaniards: the ambassador deems the idea of the homage absurd; Mr. Saltiel "seems a character out of a novel." He states, speaking of Jews, "they killed God and want medals" (116). The last word of the story belongs to the Jewish trade advisor, who, upon witnessing the conversation and being charged with the task of "very diplomatically" rejecting the idea of the homage, herself rejects the ambassador's rejection of Mr. Saltiel's idea and writes a memo soliciting (in another ironic and humorous twist) "the Medal of Isabel the Catholic" for Mr. Saltiel as "a symbol in the year of the restoration of Spanish nationality to Sephardi Jews, condemned after the expulsion to being ambassadors of nothing" (117).[10]

With her final words and actions, the trade advisor pays homage to Mr. Saltiel's person, underlining his exilic identity as "ambassador of nothing," in a way similar to the simultaneous presentation and dispelling of the myths and romantization of Sephardi identity in *Soñar con Hispania* and *Déjalo, ya volveremos*. He has been "ambassador of nothing," but nevertheless becomes a symbol in the year of the law of nationality for Sephardi Jews. This is not surprising, since, as we have seen, the 2015 law in fact embraces the precise mythologization of Sephardi Jews embodied in and parodied by the figure of Mr. Saltiel. The short story "Condecoración," as do Bendahan's novels, participates in this return to Sepharad in contemporary Spain by incorporating Sephardi characters that both embody and dispel romanticized notions of Sephardi Jews and showing varied possible affiliations with the Iberian Jewish past. Bendahan's work uses these myths, and the tension between these positions, to both facilitate Sephardi Jews's visibility in present-day Spain while articulating a space from which to pay homage, like the trade advisor in the short story, to the injustices, multiple attachments, and homes that make up their diverse histories.

CONVERSO DESCENDANTS: RETURN FROM WITHIN

In parallel to the returns to Spain exemplified and narrated by Bendahan, a small, yet significant and growing number of people in Spain have begun to identify themselves as having Jewish converso ancestry. In contrast with the discreet, unassuming, almost self-effacing presence of Spain's Jewish communities, many of these self-identified converso descendants have embraced their reclaimed Jewish identity with passion. They publicly proclaim their "Jewish lineage," organize conferences to research their past, connect with associations of descendants in Latin America and the United States, and actively pursue a variety of ways to obtain recognition of their Jewishness from Jewish organizations in Spain and abroad. These converso descendants, some of whom identify themselves as Anusim, are a local manifestation of a much wider phenomenon.[11]

The Iberian Jewish past, with its irrevocable destruction, its exilic dislocation, and its internal concealment appears trapped in a "pastness" embedded in the fragmentary nature of its vestiges and a widespread "offensive amnesia," as Cansinos Assens called it in the short story referenced in the introduction. This amnesia refuses to acknowledge the status of these vestiges as traces. Every so often, however, traces become unavoidably visible: a fragment of a Hebrew inscription on a repurposed stone, a random mention of Jews within a local tradition, an unexplained family routine that resounds with Jewish rituals. But these fragments from a distant past appear surrounded by the many layers of ambiguity they have acquired as their performers, uses, identities, and locations have changed over time. When these fragments reemerge from oblivion, there appears the temptation to foreclose their multifaceted ambiguity and to endow them with a clear, undisputed meaning as a direct path to a reliable recovery of a univocal past. The interpretations gravitate to two opposite extremes. Either these traces are taken as signs of the existence of an inherent Jewishness marking the identity of those connected to the fragments (a person, a town, a region, the whole of Spain), or they are appraised as curious leftovers of a long-gone and exotic past surrounded by an inscrutable mystery that serves to spice up present fantasies.

Emmanuel Levinas defines a trace as "a presence of that which properly speaking has never been there, of what is always past" ("The Trace" 358). He pushes the trace beyond its primary indexical relation to an absent referent that remits to an indefinite past, the footprints on the sand that point to the person that once walked on that beach. For him the very presence of the trace becomes evidence of the existence of an absolute Other stemming from an unrecoverable past. In this sense, the trace, he argues, is like a sign in that it points to a meaning, but unlike a sign, it refuses disclosure (Levinas, "The Trace" 357).[12] The trace is a presence that refuses to fully reestablish its relation to that which originated it. In Levinas's argument, the human face becomes the ultimate incarnation of his concept of trace. He points to the inherent abstractness of our faces and their ultimate resistance to disclose that which they are a trace of.

It is worth remembering that the emergence of the Inquisition in Spain is intimately related to an anxiety of indifferentiation. After the unprecedented mass conversions of 1391, the Catholic Church panicked at its inability to distinguish, just by looking at a face, who was a Christian and who was a Jew. The Inquisition's main charge was to reestablish the boundaries that conversion and coexistence had blurred (Nirenberg, "Mass Conversion" 10–12).

In modern and contemporary Spain, antisemitism has developed in spite of the near absence of Jews, the systematic oblivion about their pre-1492 presence, and the strategies of gradual erasure and silencing undertaken by conversos and their descendants. In this context, the newly gained, yet tentative, visibility of Spain's Jewish past has ignited a wide array of identifications, misidentifications, and what Levinas calls the acts of "obligation." At times obligation presents itself as an epiphany that reveals the presence of "humanity as a whole, in the eyes that look at me" (Levinas, *Totality* 213). These eyes, and the face, are for Levinas "the living presence" of another person as an undeniable expression, a discourse that "speaks to me and invites me to a relation" (*Totality* 66, 198). Those eyes are the face and the presence, and they are also the trace.

As the claims of those self-identified as converso descendants concern a biological understanding of personal, cultural, and at times even religious identity, there is always the temptation of undertaking a search for origins. Against Levinas's warning, some see in the trace an invitation to disclose its genotypic referent. Thus, some of the people identifying as converso descendants engage in a genealogical search for what they understand as the actual origins of their family, bolstered by genetic studies that argue that descendants of Sephardi Jews today compose about 20 percent of Spain's population (Jobling). In most cases the search will become unworkable, and ironically it will deploy the same genealogical mentality the Inquisition used to identify its victims. Even if, as commercial DNA tests now claim, it would be possible to discern that a person has converso ancestors, five hundred years is a long stretch of time to have kept a straight lineage, especially under constant social and political pressure to disavow one's heritage. Indeed, genealogical models suggest that given that the number of ancestors that a person has grows exponentially with each successive generation—to amount to millions—it is quite possible that most Jews today, Ashkenazi and Sephardi, would have one or more ancestors with a genealogic link to the expelled Jews of Spain (Weitz 1). As Jonathan Freedman has noted in the context of the American Southwest, converso and crypto-Jewish identities are "fundamentally unverifiable" (Freedman 194). Thus, and with very few exceptions, for every converso forebear any person may have, he or she will also have many more Christian ancestors.

In her analysis of converso return narratives, Kandiyoti explains that a reencounter with the Iberian Sephardi past is actually impossible and returns are often marked by failure. But this impossibility does not prevent many social actors from "returning" and finding, or producing, remnants of that past or seeing themselves, through the revelations of genetic ancestry testing, as remnants, even where other people might see nothing (Kandiyoti, *Converso's Return*).[13] In Cansinos Assens's novel *Las luminarias de Janucá* (1924), the novel's protagonist, Rafael Benasar, sees himself precisely this way, as a remnant, and so do his friends. Doctor Salomon (whose character in the book stands in for Abraham Shalom Yahuda) tells Rafael, "por todas partes, en España, me salen al encuentro los vestigios de la tradición de nuestra raza. Piedras antiguas, vestigios de templos y de juderías y *reliquias vivas*, como usted mismo, me acogen en este país" [everywhere, in Spain, I meet with vestiges of our people's tradition. Old stones, vestiges of temples and Jewish quarters, and *live remnants*, just like yourself, meet me in this country] (Cansinos Assens, *Luminarias* 183, my emphasis).[14] Rafael, an alter ego of Cansinos Assens, explains in the novel that he cannot have absolute certainty about his Jewish ancestry but that he does not need it. Just the possibility that it might be true is enough for him to accept a lineage and a legacy that "he cannot refuse" (*Luminarias* 44–46).

Kandyoti notes that in the last few decades, the legacy of the conversos has resulted in two developments that stand in sharp contrast with each other: on the one hand, a group of scholars have studied the crypto-Jewish experience as a metaphor that helps them theorize the multilayered and fragmentary complexity of current identities within a globalized world. On the other hand, most of the actual people who claim to be converso descendants do not see themselves as examples of any theoretical identitary debate. Their claim contains a gesture to recover what they see as an authentic and clearly delimited identity for themselves (Kandiyoti, *Converso's Return*). In an ironic conceptual dance, the desire to claim a univocal, authentic identity ends up providing evidence of our cultural inheritance's irrevocable status as fragmented, complex, and mixed.

Official Jewish institutions and organizations and the laws of Israeli nationality recognize a mix of tradition and family heritage as keys to Jewish identity. Orthodox Jewish institutions like the official Federation of Jewish Communities of Spain do not recognize these converso descendants as Jews. In the opinion of its former president, Jacobo Israel Garzón, "if a group of people have lived for more than five hundred years away from Jewish religion, culture, and society, they are not Jewish."[15] But increasingly, different social actors, especially in Israel and the United States, are lobbying for their inclusion. Among them, Shavei Israel is an Israeli-based organization that has been quite active in Spain. Created in 2002 by Michael Freund, it encourages people who identify as B'nei Anusim worldwide to officially return to religious Judaism through a process officially recognized by the state of Israel. Representatives of Shavei Israel estimate that about seventy people from Spain so far have completed this conversion process with their help (email communication, December 2017). Non-Orthodox synagogues in Madrid and Barcelona welcome descendants as well and accompany them in their different paths of return, which may or may not include conversion.[16]

An anxiety to distinguish between "real" and "fake" Jews appears in some evaluations of this phenomenon. If we consider these people gentiles performing or appropriating Judaism, they may be seen as a case of multidirectional memory gone awry, in which people embrace the identity and memory of an Other formerly excluded from their very society. Ruth Ellen Gruber referred to this phenomenon as the emergence of a "virtually Jewish" set of practices in contemporary Europe. These "virtual Jews" embrace and display a variety of cultural expressions of what they consider to be Jewish traditions: fashion accoutrements, idioms, music, and cuisine. As noted by Erica Lehrer, even in her more recent reevaluation of these cultural manifestations as part of what she calls a "new-authentic," Gruber builds her interpretation on the alignment between cultural expression and a conventional understanding of the identity of its performers (Gruber, "Beyond"; Lehrer, "Virtual").

In the 1990s, Y. Michal Bodemann emphasized the importance of the performative character of identity not in opposition to heritage but as a parallel phenomenon. Bodemann spoke of the emergence of a "Judaizing terrain" in Germany made up of recent converts to Judaism, members of Jewish-themed cultural associations, and "professional almost-Jews." Yet he argued that even if they are understood as "absolute fake," as "a culture that is not lived, that draws heavily from the museum," these cultural manifestations are "still no less genuine" (Bodemann, "Reemergence" 57–58). In a way, deepening any inquiry into questions of authenticity is bound to show the actual constructedness, variation, and indefinability of anything that consensually and/or conventionally has been termed Jewish or, by that measure, of any other cultural identity throughout history.

More recently, Lehrer has proposed a more functional approach to the analysis of the status of Jewish cultural and identitary heritage.[17] Studying the emergence of a variety of ways to relate to Judaism in postsocialist Poland, Lehrer interviews three groups of people whom she terms "vicarious Jews": some are descendants from Jewish families who were adopted and raised within Catholic families, others are non-Jews working in Jewish-themed tourism enclaves who have become experts in local Jewish history, and the last group is gentile Poles who, in their everyday lives, have adopted a variety of cultural practices that they identify as Jewish ("Bearing" 87). Rather than attempting to delimitate the frontier between "true" and "fake" Jewishness, Lehrer analyzes the way these people and their actions function within a contemporary Poland where, she argues, "the presence of Jewish 'blood' is not the significant element in being treated as marked by Jewishness. Jewish identification in Poland is a risk for all who engage in it" ("Bearing" 103).[18] In bearing witness to the tragedies of others, concludes Lehrer, these contemporary "vicarious-Jews" are also opening an alternative way in which Poland may bear witness to its own Jewishness ("Bearing" 103).

As happens in Poland, embracing Jewish identity in contemporary Spain is not an obviously advantageous path to take. It goes against the tide of a society where the central concern is to fully arrive in a Europe conceived as modern, secular, and cosmopolitan. Unlike those in Poland, the events to which self-identified descendants in Spain attempt to bear witness took place well beyond the span of their personal memory or that of their immediate and even distant forebears. If in less than a century and with many direct witnesses still alive or able to register their testimony, Jewish absence has developed a wide array of forms of vicarious Jewishness in Poland, we can only imagine how much more complex, distorted, elaborated, and multidirectionally entangled the domestic memory of the Iberian Jewish past may have gotten in over five hundred years. Following Lehrer's and Kandiyoti's lead, we do not attempt to determine the "real" or "fake" nature of the converso descendants' memory. Rather, we look at the kinds of narratives they articulate and the symbolic cultural work they engage in as they negotiate their self-identification within their family and community and vis-à-vis Spanish and Jewish identity formations.

This phenomenon challenges entrenched notions of who does and does not belong in certain groups. Within Spain, and merely by claiming Jewish lineage, these groups directly question traditional understandings of Jews as foreigners. Implicitly their presence conveys an unequivocal message of Jewish belonging to Spain: We are Jews, we did not leave, we have "always" been here. This message unsettles the very ideas of linguistic, religious, and territorial unification that lay behind the events of 1492 and were used to build traditional notions of Spanish national identity. The emergence of the identification of converso descendants also affects existing notions of normative Jewish identity, as Kandiyoti explains in *The Converso's Return*. Implicit in their desire to be identified as Jews runs an aspiration that their exilic story in regard to Jewish religion and Jewish lived culture be included as a legitimate constituent of the history of Judaism. From a variety of perspectives running from converting to Judaism, through different Christian allegiances, to the most agnostic secularism, they express a desire to participate in transforming the scope of Jewish identity and in defining what Jewishness means today.[19]

To demonstrate their Jewish lineage, converso descendants offer a variety of evidence, from concrete testimonies of family transmission to the most intangible forms of intuition and revelation. Equally diverse are the paths different people take once they assume their Jewish identity. If there is a common thread to these stories, it is the presence of a narrative of return and restoration. In an interview we conducted in 2007, José Manuel Laureiro, president of Tarbut Madrid (a local section of a larger organization, Tarbut Sefarad, founded in 2007 to promote Jewish culture in Spain), vividly remembered the moment in which his family's Jewish identity was transmitted to him: when he was ten or eleven years old, he sat watching the news on TV. When the screen showed some Israeli Jews, his grandfather said to him, "We are part of them." In a book published in 2011 by Santiago Trancón, the author explains about Laureiro, "Fue su abuelo el que le confesó, solo a él, que estaba circuncidado, y aunque no era religioso, sino masón y anticlerical, él se sentía diferente y le transmitió a José Manuel ese miedo" [It was his grandfather who confessed, only to him, that he was circumcised and that, although he was not religious . . . he felt different and transferred that fear to José Manuel] (Trancón 441). Laureiro has not converted, though: as he said to us, he wants to be a secular Jew and not renounce many of the customs, like eating Spanish ham, that he also considers part of his inheritance. Anun Barriuso, vice president of Tarbut Madrid and married to Laureiro, explained to us, and also explains in Trancón's book, that in her family everybody knew they were descendants of Jews and that small traditions had persisted: covering the mirrors when someone died, having a different plate and knife for the cheese so it would not get mixed with the meat, and so on (Trancón 441–42).

Others gradually reached the conclusion that they descended from Jewish families. María Teresa Llurba, the owner of the bookstore and Judaica store in Toledo we discuss in chapter 2, described to us in 2007 how her "relationship with Judaism is the result of a long journey of spiritual search through many countries and many cultures." At a point in her journey, she traveled to Gaza as part of a Spanish humanitarian mission. As she put it, "When we lived among Palestinians, they thought we were Israeli spies. How about that! They knew we were Jewish before we did. Then we began to do research until we realized we had Jewish blood."[20] Other people, like María Luisa García Verdugo and Oscar Carbajo Anaut, speak of a deeply transformative experience of revelation.[21] María Luisa describes her awakening to her Jewish identity in terms of a feeling first and a revelation later: "I feel, I sense that my family, in a certain way, may have been conversos . . . getting closer we began to feel something pulling us, pulling us, towards Judaism, as if we heard a call telling us that the truth was in that direction" (in Matittiahu). Oscar explains how during his childhood "I did not feel any affinity towards the people of Israel, like a normal child of the 1970s in Spain." He then proceeds to relate a sudden personal transformation: "What came as a shock to us in our lives is a revelation, so to speak, a revelation through the word written in the Bible about who the people of Israel are and what that means in our lives" (in Matittiahu).

A distinct group of people with probable ancestral links to Jews are the *xuetas* of Mallorca, who were marginalized and ostracized for centuries and maintained a high degree of endogamy vis-à-vis the rest of Mallorca society.[22] While contemporary reactions among the xuetas are also highly divergent, a variety of notions of return run through them.[23] The organization Shavei Israel has been very active among the xuetas in Mallorca, encouraging them to return and, in the words of its founder, Michael Freund, "correct the historical error committed against them" (Freund). Antonio Piña, for example, a well-known chef specializing in traditional Mallorcan cuisine, completed his conversion to Judaism in 2013 with Freund's help. Piña describes this process as an act of reparation to his forebears: "I hope that my return may help the souls of my ancestors who were converted by force" (Freund and Birnbaum 43).

The converso descendants' embrace of a minority identity perceived as both exotic and rooted in genealogical grounds both stems from and challenges the mix of new traditionalism and cutting-edge modernity, regional nationalisms and cosmopolitanism, anti-clericalism and alternative religious revivals that characterizes contemporary Spain. It exists in parallel to the (larger in number) phenomenon of converts to Islam. In both cases, the identification or conversion stems from a particular understanding and interpretation of the medieval Iberian multireligious past. In the case of New Muslims in Spain, their most frequent historical referent is the idealized image of a tolerant and culturally sophisticated al-Andalus. This idealized legacy is, in a way, their "spiritual home," what they convert *to* (Abend 138). As analyzed by Mikaela H. Rogozen-Soltar, the presence of these New Muslims bolsters the celebratory narrative of Spain's Arab legacy institutionalized in Spain, especially in Andalucía. But in their claiming a return to their Muslim roots as a way of belonging in Andalucía, these converts also point at the fissures in Spain's national formation as an ostensibly homogeneous Catholic nation (Rogozen-Soltar 97, 83). In the case of those who identify as descendants of Jewish conversos, their instrumentalization or collaboration in the celebration of a glorious past is potentially more difficult, since their spiritual home is not idealized convivencia but, more explicitly than for New Muslims, the intolerance and violence that existed alongside tolerance and resulted in their ancestors' forced conversions.

The self-identification of converso descendants adds yet further complexity to the debate about who owns Jewish memory and heritage, who has the right to identify as Jewish, and what constitutes an acceptable way to feel and act Jewish in Spain. Surprising resonances can result from the claims and interactions of people inside and outside Spain who claim an ancestral relationship with Iberian Judaism and current initiatives related to the Iberian Jewish past. One such occurrence involved German-born artist Wolf Vostell, whose exhibition at the Sephardi Museum of Toledo in 2014 is analyzed next.

WOLF VOSTELL AND *SHOAH* AT THE SEPHARDI MUSEUM

In 2014, coinciding with the many cultural activities related to the four hundredth anniversary of the death of El Greco, the Sephardi Museum organized an unprecedented exhibition entitled *El Greco y Vostell, dos forasteros en las Españas* [El Greco and Vostell, two strangers in the Spains (*sic*, an archaizing majestic plural that addresses Spain as both a large and diverse country)]. While the Casa del Greco exhibited the paintings of Domenico Theotocopuli, across the street, the Sephardi Museum exhibited Vostell's large-format triptych *Shoah 1492–1945: En memoria de la expulsión de los judíos españoles y de las víctimas del Holocausto* [Shoah 1492–1945: In memory of the Spanish Jews expelled and the victims of the Holocaust]. The rationale for the comparison was that both artists were foreigners who decided to move to Spain in periods of Spanish authoritarian rule: El Greco lived in Spain during the counter-Reformation period in the late sixteenth century; Vostell made it his home in the Francoist late 1950s.[24] As explained in the exhibition's dossier, both artists were unrecognized in Spain at first but went on to become celebrated artists and left profound traces in Spain and in the places they lived. Toledo and Malpartida, Cáceres (the village where Vostell settled), are now forever intertwined with El Greco and Vostell and the way they represented each of these places in their works. The 2014 exhibition at the Sephardi Museum had as its objective to "link them together in an imaginary sense in twenty-first-century Toledo, as an homage to the genius of both artists" (Mateos Paramio). The Sephardi Museum exhibited Vostell's canvas in front of the eastern wall of the Great Prayer Room of the synagogue with explanatory panels about El Greco and Vostell on either side.

The date chosen for the opening of the exhibition was not random: it was January 27, the Official Day of Remembrance of the Holocaust. Vostell's expressionist painting, a 2.7-by-6.6-meter acrylic-and-concrete canvas, is an explicit homage to Picasso's *Guernica* in terms of content, style, and dimensions. Both mural paintings denounce acts of political brutality and their inflicting of human suffering. Vostell's uses this highly allusive format to link the horrors of the 1492 expulsion to those of the Nazi Holocaust. He has explained that, as in the case of *Guernica,* his painting's title explicitly points to its referent. In his case, the dates following the word *Shoah,* 1492 and 1945, obviously allude to the Expulsion of the Jews from Spain in 1492 and the end of World War II in 1945 (Vostell 11). *Shoah* features a concrete gray-and-black structure along its surface, "a hybrid between a Catholic cross and a swastika" (Lépicouché 44). Its overwhelming presence appears to crush with its weight a group of abstract humanoid and animal-like forms (see fig. 6.1).

Vostell has explained the origin of *Shoah* as the result of an "inner order" to remember, something he felt compelled to carry out at the time of the fifth centenary of 1492: "En el caso de la expulsión de los judíos españoles . . . me vi obligado en 1992, por un encargo interno y en conmemoración de los 500 años transcurridos, a recordar los padecimientos de estos judíos españoles incluyendo en mi recuerdo a las víctimas del Holocausto" [In the case of the expulsion of Spanish Jews . . . I felt compelled in 1992, as a personal imperative and in commemoration of the past 500 years gone by, to remember the suffering of these Spanish Jews by including in my remembrance the victims of the Holocaust] (11). Further explanation of the painting's meaning is included in the exhibition's panels, in the form of quotes from Vostell himself:

> El cuadro recordatorio "Shoah" (gran desgracia) no pudo concluirse hasta 1997, y dibuja un arco entre 1492 y 1945, sin proponerse establecer jerarquías ni valoraciones sobre lo sucedido. Lo que me importa es usar como tema el infinito puente de más de 500 años sobre ese mar de lágrimas de las víctimas sojuzgadas, expulsadas, perseguidas y masacradas

Figure 6.1. Exhibition of *Shoah 1492–1945*, Great Prayer Room, Sephardi Museum, Toledo. ©Daniela Flesler.

[The commemorative painting "Shoah" (great catastrophe) couldn't be completed until 1997, and it draws an arc between 1492 and 1945, without intending to establish hierarchies or assessments of what happened. What matters to me is to use as a subject the infinite bridge of more than 500 years over that sea of the tears of the subjugated, expelled, persecuted and massacred victims] (Vostell, exhibition panel)

Vostell sees this painting as—problematically—connecting different memories.[25] But the travels of memory between 1492 and 1945 that it enacts are not obvious. The links between the suffering of medieval Jews and the suffering of Jews in the Holocaust are intimately tied with one of Vostell's primary works—the construction of his own persona. Born in 1932, a few months before Hitler seized power in Germany, Vostell's presentation of his life story conveys a defensive attitude and a conflictive sense of personal identity in regard to his German nationality. In a 1982 interview with Kristine Stiles, when she asks about his personal experience of the war, his first statement is, "I was with the children," meaning he was a child and therefore innocent. He then says, "My family is half Jewish but not in recent history." Upon Stiles's follow up of "You yourself are not Jewish?" he responds, "I am Jewish. Of course, we got persecuted but not directly because in our papers it all came up; when the Germans had to look at the papers, they saw that we had Jewish influence precisely from Spain" (Stiles 40). When Stiles pressed him as to whether he was raised as a Jew, he said he wasn't but that his mother was very afraid and they escaped early in the war to Czechoslovakia, where they lived in hiding, moving from village to village.

In the interview, Vostell seems to conflate the justifiable fear of a German family in the middle of war, who survived bombardments, hunger, and widespread violence and destruction, with the very specific fear of a Jewish family targeted for genocide. However one might construe this, Vostell chooses to narrate his war story as if from the perspective of a Jewish family—note, for example, his reference to "Germans," as opposed to "the police," who looked at the family's papers, as if he weren't German—when it is not clear at all that this, his being part of a Jewish family, was the case. As Erin Hanas observes in her study of Vostell, even though the family's fear was justified in terms of the war itself, there is no evidence that they were ever persecuted or targeted as being Jewish or having Jewish ancestry. Hanas explains that Vostell's father worked as a railroad guard, although it is not clear when he was hired and what exactly his duties were. Since Vostell hardly ever spoke about his father and the war, Hanas speculates that he might have been ashamed of acknowledging a direct relationship with the Nazi national railway, the logistical support and means of transportation that facilitated the Holocaust. Hanas recounts a 1981 interview in which Vostell explained, "[My] father was constantly underway with trains. He often took us along and brought the family out of the dangerous zones. We were brought here and there the entire time. I saw a lot of horrible things as a child." Subsequently, trains, so saturated with meaning related to the Nazi genocide, became a key motif in his work (Hanas 266).

As Hanas also explains, Vostell's relationship to Jewishness (and to Germany) was deeply complex: in the 1950s, he changed his birth name, Schäfer, connected with his father and possibly with the recent Nazi past, and adopted his mother's maiden name, Vostell (Hanas 262). He believed this name, and his mother's family, had Sephardi origins, connecting him to the Jews expelled from Spain in 1492 (Hanas 267). A few years later, he also adopted what he imagined or thought was his maternal family's ancestral home, moving to Spain after his marriage to Mercedes Guardado Olivenza in 1959.

Vostell's decisions seem to follow the pattern described by Gabrielle Schwab (95) for German children like herself as "the internalization of guilt and shame and concomitant wholesale affective rejection of one's [German] heritage." Vostell's belief in having Sephardi Jewish ancestry certainly seems to have been energized by his experiences growing up in Germany during World War II and in the aftermath of the Holocaust. The attempt to reconstruct or claim Jewish ancestry is not unique to Vostell, and as we have seen in the cases of converso descendants, complex factors contribute to the phenomenon. In the case of Vostell, the decision to identify with his mother's side of his family while silencing that of his father seems to have served the same kind of exculpatory function that Schwab identifies as an aspiration in postwar German youth.

However, Vostell also made of this troubled identity a deep political commitment and a rich source of material for his artistic practice, which extended to his own public persona. The memory of the Holocaust, and Germany's difficulty in coming to terms with its past, played a central role in his art projects (Langston 135). In his happenings of the 1960s, in particular, he sought to implicate his audience in the process of unveiling the links between postwar Germany's present and its fascist past (Langston 152–53). His artistic practice about memory and the Holocaust also extended to his own body. As Hanas explains,

> By the late 1960s he was captured on film occasionally wearing a black fedora reminiscent of those typically worn by Lubavitscher Jews, and by the 1970s he also began wearing what appeared to be a kippah rimmed with fur, but what was really a cap that his wife, Mercedes, had knit per his specifications. He also grew long, curled side-locks, and often wore a white button-down shirt, black pants, and a black coat. In short, Vostell affected the appearance of a Hasidic Jew until his death in 1998. He did not, however, practice Judaism, or any other religion, and he was not raised as a Jew. The German-born artist's carefully constructed Jewish appearance became his artistic persona. (263)

Hanas sees this careful staging of his physical appearance as part of the artistic project of Vostell, who would be "deploying his constructed identity as a memorial to the Holocaust and as an embodied performance that transmitted social knowledge and memories about the crimes of the fatherland" (266–67). He certainly seems to have perceived this project, his physical appearance, as an inherent part of the process by which he left his father's name, and Germany, behind and adopted his mother's name and supposed ancestral home, Spain. When Stiles asked him about the motivations behind taking the appearance of an Orthodox Jew, he answered, seemingly unaffectedly, "I am now a Sephardi Jew. My family coming from Spain were Sephardi Jews" (41).

In the painting *Shoah*, Vostell further connects his personal rejection of his father's world to his belief that Germany has a collective obligation to remember the victims of the Holocaust. In Stiles's words, Vostell "wore his guilt as a commitment to Jews for the rest of his life, dedicating his life to alerting the world to the human and planetary devastation of destruction and violence."[26] As a conclusion to his war memories, Vostell told Stiles, "After the war as a child I have told [*sic*] myself that I have to do everything so this doesn't happen again" (Stiles 41). Vostell's answer is aligned with the consensus about German collective responsibility explained by Jürgen Habermas as the obligation "to keep alive the memory of the suffering of those murdered at the hands of the Germans" (44). This has to be done, said Habermas, "through a reflective and keenly scrutinizing attitude towards one's own identity-creating traditions" (47).[27]

While Vostell may have understood his settling in Spain as a return to the land of his mother's ancestors, his self-fashioning of a quasi-Jewish persona for himself and his work about the memory of Spanish Jews performs a different kind of return, one in which Spain and its Jewish history serve as points of departure for him to explore the Holocaust from a longer historical perspective. Vostell spoke of the origin of his painting *Shoah* in 1992, on the anniversary of the expulsion of the Jews from Spain, as an "inner order and in memory of the 500 years past, to remember the suffering of these Spanish Jews." He was thus enacting this sense of responsibility for collective Spanish memory at a time, 1992, when Spain was not accepting any sense of collective responsibility for the devastating consequences of 1492 for Jews, Muslims, and the indigenous peoples of the Americas. Thus, while we find problematic his historical collapsing of the expulsion and the Holocaust, we can read this work as an intervention in the particular context of 1992 Spain. As we saw in the introduction, Spanish authorities in charge of the 1992 commemorations showed a remarkable reluctance to critically explore the underside of 1492 in celebrations that emphasized a celebratory view of Columbus's voyage to America and characterized this event not as the onset of a prolonged conquest that would decimate the native population of the Americas but rather as an "encounter of cultures." We have also discussed how the movement for the recuperation of historical memory in Spain has used a transnational human rights conceptual frame and language for its claims of public recognition of Francoist victims. In its explicit parallel to the Holocaust and the 1492 Expulsion, Vostell is extending this human rights frame to argue that a crime against humanity was committed in 1492.

Just as Vostell's motivations for creating *Shoah* run counter to the types of commemorations that dominated Spanish public discourse in 1992, the exhibition of this painting at the Sephardi Museum in 2014 runs counter to the kinds of discourses deployed by national institutions in Spain to speak about Jewish issues. It defies the prevalent Spanish official discourse of idealized convivencia, a discourse that bolsters a nationalistic understanding of Spain as a great nation where medieval Christians, Jews, and Muslims lived in peace and produced outstanding cultural achievements. Although referencing the 1492 expulsion is almost mandatory in terms of any narrative account that aspires to be historically credible, the more complex side of the history of the Jews in Spain, including persecutions and scapegoating is usually narrated with the impersonal third-person plural of "historical vicissitudes," as we saw in chapter 3. Within this official frame of reference, convivencia, comparing the persecution of Jews in Spain to the Nazi Holocaust is unthinkable. In fact, what we frequently find in Spain is the use of the Holocaust as a comparative measure that exculpates Spain.[28]

In contemporary Spain, as Alejandro Baer argues, the memory of the Holocaust triggers a particularly poignant and paradoxical set of effects. On the one hand, the debates about the Holocaust and its memorialization draw attention to the country's unresolved Francoist past and promotes sympathy toward the Republican victims of fascism. Yet, continues Baer, "the very uniqueness of the Holocaust" allows Spain to dissociate Nazism and Francoism and, thus, to remember the Holocaust without probing its own past. At the same time, pointing to atrocities committed in other countries can serve an exculpatory function for Germany, while emphasizing the Holocaust's singularity becomes a self-critical gesture (A. Baer, "The Voids" 106). What Vostell's painting demonstrates, however, is that once the link between these events and times becomes established, even if exculpatory factors are at play, the link in itself produces an uncomfortable confrontation with issues that most people in Spain today would rather not think or talk about.

In this sense, this exhibition's not shying away from the possibility of controversy and discomfort is courageous and potentially productive. Its succinct and unapologetic linking of 1492 and 1945 invites precisely the kind of reckoning with the past that the celebrations of 1992 wanted to prevent.[29] As conveyed to us in an interview in July 2014, Santiago Palomero Plaza, the museum's director, thought that the museum should provoke questions and surprise its visitors, even make them uncomfortable. This exhibition seems to have done precisely that. Palomero Plaza reported receiving numerous complaints from people who found the painting's connection between the 1492 expulsion and the Holocaust wrong and plainly offensive. The great majority of comments written in the museum's visitors' books are extremely positive, speaking about how much they have learned from their visit, how beautiful the synagogue is, and how they appreciate the message of peace and tolerance the museum conveys. But all the comments written specifically about the Vostell exhibition during 2014 were negative.[30] Visitors complained about the "horrible" modern painting obstructing the view of the "beautiful" old synagogue and preventing their enjoyment and found particularly offensive the connection between the 1492 expulsion and the Holocaust. The discomfort expressed in these reactions implies that an unwritten cultural pact had been broken. The irruption of the Holocaust produced a sharp dissonance in a space that, as we describe in this book, is usually shown to the general public through the framework of idealized convivencia.

Exhibited in the Great Prayer Room, a few yards in front of, and running parallel to its lavishly decorated eastern wall, this installation was the first thing visitors saw as they entered the main room of the museum. Framed by the magnificent surroundings of the Great Prayer Room, the contrast and dissonance between the color-filled modernist painting depicting utmost destruction and suffering and the comforting splendor of the old restored synagogue made the sight all the more remarkable. The disrupting contrast between painting and background highlighted the simultaneous reality of loss and survival that this museum embodies.

Another temporary exhibition at the Sephardi Museum, *Daniel Quintero, Sefarad: Memoria Escondida* [Daniel Quintero, Sepharad: Hidden Memory] further illustrates the capacity of the visual arts to provide complex performative modes of negotiation of the legacies of medieval Jewish Iberia and the current effects of the ongoing rediscovery of that past. Shown from November 2017 to February 2018, this exhibition illustrated and creatively intervened in many of the concerns explored throughout this book. At first sight, the work of Quintero seems to stand in the starkest of contrasts with that of Vostell. Where the German artist employs abstract expressionism to denounce well-known contemporary atrocities, Quintero works in two of the most traditional of painting modes, the portrait and the still life, and can easily be read as apolitical. Yet like Vostell, Quintero connects history and the immediate present, proposing that while a return to that Sepharad constructed by nostalgia may not be achievable, its legacy has never completely abandoned Spain. His goal is to provide visual presence to the connection between the Iberian Jewish past and present.

THE DANCE OF MEMORY IN DANIEL QUINTERO'S SEPHARDI PAINTINGS

Born in Málaga in 1949, Daniel Quintero is a leading figurative painter who for over fifty years has been exploring what he describes as an "abstract naturalist" visual style. He has painted official portraits of the Spanish royal family, as well as leading figures in the realms of culture, science, and politics, including film director Pedro Almodóvar, writer Manuel Vicent, Manuela Carmena—painted in 1993 during her time as a judge, before she became Madrid's mayor (2015–19)—and former presidents Adolfo Suárez (1976–81) and Leopoldo Calvo Sotelo (1991–92).

In contrast with these portraits of contemporary public figures, his *Sephardi Portraits* stand out as a project deeply embedded in a sustained and intentional exploration of a single topic, the larger process of Spain's "reconnection" with Jewish history, culture, and practices. The project encompasses complementary groups of paintings on which Quintero has worked since the early 1990s. The first group portrays contemporary religious and political leaders of Sephardi communities in France and Spain. The second group consists of imaginary portraits of historic figures in medieval and early modern Iberian Judaism. Besides these two, a third group is composed of still lifes of food arrangements and material symbols of traditional Jewish celebrations. While thematically these paintings belong to three distinct temporalities (the present implied in the contemporary portraits, the past evoked by the historic portraits, and a transhistorical dimension embodied in symbols and rituals captured in the still lifes), they all show a remarkable convergence in terms of themes and style.

Composed through a careful interplay of past and present temporalities, these paintings embody the unstable and symbolically rich in-betweenness of Sephardi and converso identities in the Iberian Peninsula. Rather than a source of anxiety, this in-betweenness becomes in Quintero's work a revelatory space, one that forces viewers to confront the offensive amnesia denounced by Cansinos Assens. But these paintings are neither about a remote difficult past whose injustices may be brushed aside as the fault of others living in another time, nor do they present a biological genealogy. Through contemporary models who lend their faces to prominent Jews of the past, and by showing Jewishness as a constitutive part of what has been traditionally understood as Spanish culture, Quintero's paintings construct a social and cultural genealogy of lived experience. This creatively anachronistic link connects situations of injustice and everyday violence that are both part of Spain's past and still present today.

Quintero's interest in Jewish culture and Sephardi history has been a constant throughout his life. At age twelve, he became fascinated by Hebrew letters and calligraphy: "From my first contact with it, I was drawn to that writing, so compact and abstract. It was like a world asking me to immerse myself in it" (Jarque). This early fascination with Hebrew calligraphy denotes an experience of revelation not unlike those expressed by the converso descendants in their testimonies. But if for many of the former this revelation results in a radical transformation of personal identity, for Quintero this revelation becomes mainly an aesthetic and epistemological search. He converted to Judaism but does not claim to be a descendant of conversos, nor does he make his religious beliefs into a significant part of his public persona. It is his work that carries an implicit and complex reflection on the present inheritances derived from the historic Jewish presence in Spain. This reflection addresses Spain's offensive amnesia toward its Jewish past, its converso history, the prolonged exile of Sephardi Jews, and the contemporary claim of converso descendants.

Compositionally, the portrayed subjects appear enveloped in an evanescent atmosphere that fades away toward the frame of the canvas. The color palette, characterized by a revealing, celebratory luminosity conjures a sense of contemporary immediacy and material presence. By contrast, the titles and garments identify the portrayed subjects as coming from remote times, distant places, or overlooked marginal proximities. This subtle play with temporality reappears in the paintings at the formal and thematic levels. Through this creative anachronism, Sepharad becomes in these paintings simultaneously a trace of the past and a contemporary presence.

The portraits explore the resonances of Spain's Jewish past in the present, as well as construct a gaze that, from the present, invites a reimagining of the past. They establish a relationship between a past that remains in the faces, gazes, and gestures of those who forgot it, or never could have known it, and a present that works to make those traces visible.

In order to read these portraits through the prism of a reengagement with the memory of Jewish Spain, we are experimenting with what Shelley Ruth Butler and Erica Lehrer call "curatorial dreaming." Curatorial dreaming is "an innovative method of engaged cultural analysis and critique," a way for critics and scholars to "curate our arguments" through imagining exhibitions of our own (Butler and Lehrer 4). As Butler and Lehrer argue, "exhibits naturalize particular ways of looking at the world. They can also clear paths for new ways of seeing" (Butler and Lehrer 6).

Our dream exhibition places Quintero's paintings in dialogue with the great Spanish masters. We view his portraits as formally embracing and intervening in many of the conventions explored by painters such as Diego Velázquez, Francisco Goya, and José de Ribera. They all belong to a peculiarly Spanish tradition of developing the portrait as a tool of social commentary. Similarly, his still life paintings contain frequent allusions to the classical bodegón paintings of the Spanish baroque by artists such as Pedro Acosta, Blas de Ledesma, Juan Sánchez Cotán, Francisco de Zurbarán, and Pedro de Medina Balbuena. Like them, Quintero's paintings endow everyday foods and wares with a sense of symbolic immanence. While being intensely material in their realism, their composition and status as representation endows them with a mystical dimension. Yet this group of paintings also pushes these classical Spanish visual traditions into a conceptual territory that they had all but overlooked: explicitly, Quintero embraces the Iberian Jewish past and present.

Like Velázquez and Goya, Quintero's equal artistic treatment of both the social elite and the downtrodden implicitly humbles the powerful and dignifies the marginalized. If Velázquez focused his eye on the dignity of the court jesters and Goya rescued the figures of street children and the old, poor, and infirm, Quintero turns his attention to present-day inhabitants of Spain, or who are in close proximity to Spain, and who in different ways occupy positions of marginality and to medieval Iberian Jews who have been relegated to the margins of history. While Quintero has painted the portraits of some of the most powerful members of the political and cultural elite, his "Sephardi portraits" focus attention on groups of people who do not have a high degree of social visibility within contemporary Spain.

Quintero's portraits of contemporary Sephardi Jews imply a welcome home qualified by equal parts of symbolic aesthetic restitution, joyful discovery, and acknowledgement of their experiences gathered and delivered from the diaspora. Quintero's conscious update of the visual rhetoric of the Spanish classical and baroque both honors these Sephardi subjects and inserts them into the long list of portraits of kings, queens, noblemen, saints, and common Spanish folk portrayed by the great Spanish masters. This subtle aesthetic embrace inserts the portraits starkly into the center of Spain's visual tradition. Historically, successive and self-interested Spanish politicians and governments have performed eager gestures of welcoming back of Sephardi Jews to the Spanish flock, from Ángel Pulido's characterization of Sephardi Jews as "Spaniards without a homeland" through the famous 1992 declaration by King Juan Carlos that in Spain "Jews are in their own home" and on to the legal recognition offered in the 2015 law of nationality. Unlike these political gestures, Quintero's paintings embody acts of homecoming that do not flatten or erase either the identity or the multiple attachments of Sephardi Jews, but rather embrace the complexities entailed in this recognition. The portraits contain a symbolic inclusion, but also an acknowledgment of the protracted distance and respect for difference.

For example, the painting *Anglo Sefarad* (oil, charcoal, and tempera on Japanese paper, 2007; fig. 6.2) shows a life-size full-body portrait of an elegant young man from Madrid's Jewish community who stands in front of us returning our gaze. The composition reminds us of Goya's portraits of aristocratic figures like the similarly arranged *Duque de San Carlos* (1815). Unlike the dark, ominous tones that surround Goya's portraits, a set of luminous hues of blue and white place the subject of *Anglo Sefarad* in an inviting atmosphere, fully open for the viewer to enjoy. Within it, however, hints of the Sephardi layers of history and experience emerge symbolically from the dandy-like cane, top hat, white tallit with blue stripes, and sobriety of the black-and-white attire. These elements become indexes of the subtle historical and cultural distance differentiating the young man in the painting from the average Spanish viewer.

Similarly, *Rav Knafo* (oil on board, 2009; fig. 6.3) portrays the rabbi of Bayonne's community, a community that holds a strong historical connection to the Jews expelled from Spain. Again, the composition resonates with joy and lightness. The smiling Rabi Knafo holds a book in a pose that closely resembles Velázquez's portraits of humble people as philosophers and wise men. In particular, we can look at the aesthetic filiation with his portrait of *Esopo* (Aesop, 1640) similarly holding a book, although in much darker, tenebrous tones. Rabbi Knafo's portrait provides a sense of dignity to the subject and of immediacy and closeness to the viewer. But the subject is not immediately apprehensible: the Hebrew characters on the book, the unshaven face, and the simplicity of the suit and the black hat provide reminders that the Jewish difference is not to be flattened out. The paintings do not represent Sephardi Jews as "Spaniards without a homeland." They do not erase the multiple attachments of Sephardi Jews or downplay the uncomfortable difference that Sephardi Jews, as Jews, bring with them to Spain.

The book is a leitmotif of several portraits of contemporary Sephardi men, all of whom appear joyfully reading and studying their books, as we can see in

Figure 6.2. *Anglo Sefarad* (Daniel Quintero, 2007). ©Daniel Quintero.

Figure 6.3. *Rav Knafo* (Daniel Quintero, 2009). ©Daniel Quintero.

Figure 6.4. *Rabino estudiando Torá* ("Rabbi studying Torah," Daniel Quintero, 2013). ©Daniel Quintero.

Rabbi Baruj Garzón (2007) or *Rabino estudiando Torá* [Rabbi Studying Torah, 2013] (fig. 6.4). In this last portrait, Rabbi Moshe Bendahan, who presides over the Jasdei Leah Sephardi synagogue in Madrid, appears against a blue background that Quintero characterizes as "Moroccan blue," Morocco being the place from where the Bendahan family migrated to Spain in the 1960s.

If these portraits of present-day Sephardi Jews insert their subjects into a quintessentially Spanish classical visual tradition and become thus subjects of Spanish culture, Quintero's Sephardi still lifes take this idea of a joyful and respectful welcome one step further. Composed using many of the conventions of the Spanish baroque still lifes, the paintings implicitly reflect on the complex shared ritual and symbolic practices that crisscross Spanish and Sephardi religious celebrations. The similarities are so striking that at first sight these might be perceived as Jewish renderings of a Catholic Iberian tradition. Yet, more powerfully, they reveal the Jewish elements present in classic Spanish mysticism, which both inspired and achieved expression through the baroque still life. Thus, in *Acerca de Pesaj* [About Pesach, 1990] (fig. 6.5) the traditional food elements of the Passover feast appear represented with the characteristic classic Spanish still life's frugality and careful attention to the composition's geometric balance.

Figure 6.5. *Acerca de Pesaj* ("About Pesaj," Daniel Quintero, 1990). ©Daniel Quintero.

In fact, the painting draws from the style of two mystical painters in this tradition: Juan Sánchez Cotán (1560–1627) and Francisco de Zurbarán (1598–1664). Cotán's intense attention to the food at its most humble materiality (see *Bodegón de caza, hortalizas, y frutas*, 1602) combines with Zurbarán's emphasis on the depiction of tableware (trays, cups, dishes) in such detail that the objects of the painting appear materially palpable (see *Bodegón con cacharros*, 1650). *Acerca de Pesaj* adds two narrative references placed at opposite corners of the composition. One depicts an Egyptian pyramid on the prayer book's cover; another image, adorning the cup that holds the haroseth, displays a tiled-roof whitewashed house resembling a traditional southern Spanish home. The Passover meal serves as the bridge connecting these two symbols of the Exodus and Jewish life in Iberia.

La noche de la Mimona [The night of Mimouna, 1998], (fig. 6.6) also emphasizes foods and tableware, but its style has moved away from classicism into expressionism and abstract naturalism. The Mimona festival, celebrated by Moroccan Jews on the last night of Pesach, is a Sephardi holiday with origins in the mid-eighteenth century. The mystical dimension reappears here in the translucent quality of the objects portrayed. Discernible thanks to the contours, reflections, and decorative fringes indicating their North African origin, the foods symbolizing hope and redemption and drinking glasses appear as ethereal presences floating on a water-like "Moroccan blue" fluid background.

Norman Bryson argues that the classical Spanish painters' still lifes (like those of Zurbarán and Cotán) create a space in which the mundane transmutes

Figure 6.6. *La noche de la Mimona* ("The night of Mimouna," Daniel Quintero, 1998). ©Daniel Quintero.

into the supermundane and show the "interpenetration of the ordinary and unassuming with what is exalted and sacred" (Bryson 79). By situating themselves in relation to these classical paintings, *Acerca de Pesaj* and *La noche de la Mimona* show the ease with which Sephardi traditions converse with the mystical Catholicism the still lifes represent. In effect, this dialogue makes visible the possibility that the interpenetration of mundane and supernatural in the baroque bodegones was possible because of the existence of another interpenetration, another hybridity: that of the shared symbolic universes that emerged among Jews, Christians, and conversos in medieval and early modern Spain. Quintero has explained how, "Siempre, desde el principio, he trabajado el retrato, incluso a través de otros géneros como el bodegón" [From my beginnings, I have always worked the portrait genre, even by means of other genres such as the *bodegón*] (Bujalance). Through looking at these still lifes as portraits by other means, *Acerca de Pesaj* and *La noche de la Mimona* come to be seen as portraits of Sephardi Jewish subjects steeped in both Jewish and Catholic traditions and of the mystical threads that run between them. In these still lifes, we can see the representation of North African Jewish cultural objects through the conventions of the Spanish baroque. As a result, in these paintings it is impossible to maintain any kind of binary opposition between Sephardi and Spanish. In doing so, these "portraits by other means" gesture to the Jewish elements that had lain invisible as frames of reference for many of Spain's most traditional ways of constructing its national identity.

Quintero's conscious update of the visual rhetoric of the Spanish classical and baroque traditions in the still lifes and the portraits of contemporary

Sephardi Jews finds a complementary gesture in his portraits of contemporary people embodying historical figures of the Iberian Jewish past. Along with his working on Sephardi contemporary figures, Quintero has been carefully selecting models to portray historical figures of medieval and early modern Iberian origin. Quintero's portraits bring these historical characters back from oblivion and invisibility by reimagining them in the faces of his contemporaries, more specifically, in the case of some of these models, people who have undergone experiences of marginalization, injustice, or exile. He sees in them characteristics that transcend their physical appearance. By looking at their physiognomy as a landscape shaped not so much by genetics but by their thought, life, and history, Quintero finds in their features a cartography shaped by experiences commensurate with those of the historical figures he wants to represent. He is not exactly painting a person but composing a retrospective construct of these historical figures. This construct would be the byproduct of the experiences and works of these individuals, based on the traces of their lives that have reached us and that we have access to hundreds of years later.

Some of those lending their faces to the portraits are themselves Jewish; others are not. Symbolically, these Jewish and non-Jewish portraits of the present remember, or become traces of, their Sephardi heritage. In them, the debts of past and present violence merge together, one resounding on the other. They invite today's inhabitants of Spain to acquaint themselves with Spain's Jewish past from the perspective of its present embodiment in themselves. The implication of a possible genetic continuity is there—this is in the sense that some people in Spain today believe it's possible that they could have Jewish ancestry. The portraits indirectly hint at this possibility. But they also establish a link between past and present that is one of both rupture and commensurate experience. The experiences of those posing for these portraits in the present speak to the experience of medieval and early modern historical figures evicted from their homes and removed from traditional Spanish history.[31] And the experiences of these historical figures speak to contemporary inhabitants of Spain. The resulting portraits interrogate how to recompose the faces of a community that has been made invisible through a prolonged and deliberate historical process: what traces remain of that which disappeared with those expelled or converted? How to see again that which could not be seen for centuries? Through these visual juxtapositions of past and present, contemporary notions of Spain shift by looking at these notions through the genealogy of Sepharad. These paintings bring this genealogy to the forefront by inserting the subjects of offensive amnesia at the heart of Spain's visual tradition.

Figure 6.7. *Emiliano Maté como Maimónides* ("Emiliano Maté as Maimonides," Daniel Quintero, 1991). ©Daniel Quintero.

In one of the earliest paintings in this series, *Emiliano Maté como Maimónides* (*Emiliano Maté as Maimonides*, oil on canvas, 1991; fig. 6.7), a homeless man, Emiliano Maté, lends his face to Maimonides, the prominent philosopher, doctor, and rabbi from twelfth-century Cordoba. For several years, Quintero had noticed Maté sleeping on a public bench in Cuatro Caminos in downtown Madrid. He learned that Maté had to quit his job as a draftsman to care for his chronically ill aging mother. Eventually Maté's inability to pay his co-op's expenses as the area gentrified led his neighbors to take over his apartment and forced him into homelessness. As a form of protest, Maté made the sidewalk across the street from his former apartment his new home. He sat there as a homeless man for thirty years. Quintero felt drawn to him and his story. After speaking with him several times, he convinced Maté to come to his studio and pose for him for several sessions. They spoke about Maimónides, whom Maté already knew about. In the portrait that resulted from these sessions, the traces of resigned suffering in Maté's persona, the weight of his story as reflected in his body, allow us a glimpse into Maimonides's experience of religious persecution

Figure 6.8. *Retrato de Samuel Ha-Leví* ("Portrait of Samuel Ha-Leví," Daniel Quintero, 2000). ©Daniel Quintero.

and recurrent exile. The portrait simultaneously vindicates Matés's dignity and intelligence and Maimónides's legacy. The homeless philosopher of the past meets the destitute homeless philosopher of the present.

Perhaps it is the portrait *Retrato de Samuel Ha-Leví* (oil on canvas, 2000; fig. 6.8) that best exemplifies the hopes implicit in this group of paintings and, more generally, of Spain's reencounter with Sepharad. The painting, owned by the Sephardi Museum, portrays Halevi, the treasurer and diplomat from the fourteenth century who built the Synagogue of the Transit in Toledo and was executed by the king he served, Pedro I. The model for the portrait was Máximo Cajal López (1935–2014), the Spanish diplomat who acquired notoriety in 1980 as ambassador in Guatemala when a group of indigenous Guatemalan peasants occupied the Spanish embassy to protest their harrowing working conditions. With the embassy surrounded by the police and armed forces, Cajal offered himself as negotiator to find a peaceful solution to the occupation. The Guatemalan government, however, decided to raze the embassy, which eventually burned. Thirty-nine people died, including Spanish diplomats, Guatemalan opposition politicians, and indigenous leaders (Sebastián). Cajal escaped through a window and survived with third-degree burns over most of his body. At that time, Spain was consolidating a mostly peaceful transition to democracy after the death of dictator Francisco Franco in 1975. Cajal's calls for dialogue during the occupation of the embassy in Guatemala were emblematic of the recent lessons of Spain's transition to democracy, seen at this time as an example of how to reach consensus through dialogue among highly divergent political views.

After returning to Spain, Guatemalan and Spanish right-wing groups tried to discredit Cajal. Guatemalan sources close to the positions of General Lucas García, Guatemala's president at the time, accused Cajal of being a communist who had collaborated with the peasants to organize the assault. Nevertheless, Cajal continued a successful diplomatic career. However, upon the publication of his 2003 book arguing for the need to return Spanish cities of Ceuta and Melilla to Morocco, many Spanish political figures questioned his loyalty to Spain. The public uproar escalated to the point that his party, the PSOE, revoked his membership (see Cajal). Although not literally, like Halevi, Cajal was also sacrificed by the government he had served.

While painting the ambassador's official portrait, Quintero was inspired by Cajal's face, in which he perceived traces of the gravity left by these events. Cajal, says Quintero, fully embraced the idea of embodying Samuel Halevi and participated very effectively in the creative process, resulting in "a perfect symbiosis" between the two figures.[32] In linking Halevi to this contemporary Spaniard, the diplomat who embodied the values of a newly democratic Spain in the 1980s, the painting invites us to reimagine the death of the medieval Jewish royal treasurer in relation to the courageous life of Cajal. The painting blends the plight of the two men: Halevi, the Jew condemned to death by the king he served, whom Christians were taught to hate, becomes reimagined in Cajal, the contemporary diplomat who tried to avert tragedy through dialogue, endured criticism by many of the people for whom he worked, and banishment from his political party. Present and past come to illuminate and intervene in each other.[33]

The portrait further invites viewers to contemplate themselves as part of a democratic society that defends tolerance and dialogue. Red, a color associated with the bloodshed of violence, becomes here the ethereal substance from which Halevi's head and hands emerge. In its transhistoric condensation of dual historical periods and people, the painting helps us entertain an alternative vision of Spanish identity. Cajal provides visible presence to Halevi, and through it, to the silenced history of Jewish Spain. Halevi, in turn, suggested not only by the countenance of the portrait but also in the clothing and the color red, allows us to historicize Cajal's role in Spanish political history.

If these portraits performatively represent the experiences of contemporary people in Spain as "traces" of past figures of Iberian Judaism, the portraits of today's Sephardi Jews perform a reciprocal genealogical connection by representing figures of the Sephardi diasporic present through Quintero's conscious update of the quintessentially Spanish visual tradition. These portraits and the still lifes as "portraits by other means" present Sephardi identity as both internal and external to Spain, as part of Spain but not subsumed by it.

As we state in the introduction, the implementation of initiatives to reevaluate Spain's relationship to its Jewish heritage has brought to the fore several interrelated issues. Vostell's poignant exhibition at one of the very few surviving medieval synagogues in Spain encapsulates the power of the resonances of the memory of Iberian Jews beyond the borders of Spain and over a prolonged time span. If the myth of an ancestral nostalgia for Sepharad has become one of the narratives that, as Esther Bendahan's works illustrate, has become most productive for Jews currently living in Spain in their facilitating public acceptance of their presence, the Jewish/ Christian identity of the conversos has become one of the means by which different communities in Spain can claim Sepharad as their own inheritance. In Quintero's portraits, most poignantly in their exhibition at the Sephardi Museum (see fig. 6.9), they can find traces of the Jewish past on their own bodies and histories. The portraits' traces of the past in the present and of the present in the past attempt to open up a space in which to reimagine not only the Iberian Jewish past, but also the post-1492 Iberian Jewish futures that never were and a present constituted by all of them.

As they move away from the offensive amnesia denounced by the protagonist of Cansinos Assens's short story by exploring the current resonances of the Iberian Jewish past, these literary, personal, and artistic explorations are haunted by a set of historical paradoxes. The premodern Jewish presence appears as memories and fragments that have been dislocated, scattered, and repurposed to the point that they can be rearranged into multiple narratives of

Figure 6.9. *Memoria escondida/Hidden Memory* exhibition, Sephardi Museum, Toledo. ©Daniel Quintero.

glory and shame, loss and rescue, invention and recuperation. Casinos Assens's protagonist confronts the deep effect these paradoxes have had on the people he meets. He notes their amnesia with disappointment,

> No sabían decirle más y se encogían de hombros. Habíase perdido ya toda tradición del judío, de su figura, de su religión, de sus supuestos crímenes; y él, tipo característico de la raza, encontraba en uno su rostro moreno y su nariz nazarena en aquellas gentes que no sabían ya descifrar aquel jeroglífico vivo.
>
> [They did not know what more to say and they shrugged. All and every tradition of the Jews, of their figure, of their religion, and of their supposed crimes had been lost; and he, a characteristic type of that race, noticed in one person his own dark complexion and his Natharentian nose, in those people who did not know how to decipher that living hieroglyph anymore]. (Cansinos Assens 160)

The story's protagonist looks into the faces of his interlocutors and sees in them a mirror of his own, but it is an empty mirror that does not return any sense of recognition. Their inability to decipher his/their own features redoubles his unease and becomes further proof of the offensive amnesia he had denounced before. What we see in the phenomena in this chapter is the generative ability of these traces to formulate versions of the Jewish past that intervene directly and critically in the personal, religious, and social points of fracture of today.

NOTES

1. See Tabea Linhard's book *Jewish Spain: A Mediterranean Memory* for the currency of this myth in relation to narratives that depict the survival of Jews in or because of Spain in World War II, and Dalia Kandiyoti's forthcoming book *The Converso's Return*.

2. Bendahan is one of the very few Moroccan Sephardi writers in Spain today. She grew up speaking Haketía (a mix of Spanish, Hebrew, and Arabic) at home, but her first schooling in Tetuán (the capital of the Protectorate) was in French, in one of the schools of the Alliance Israelite Universelle. The Jewish communities in northern Morocco were re-Hispanized at the time of the establishment of the Spanish Protectorate (1912–56). See Jacobo Israel Garzón's *Los judíos hispano-marroquíes (1492–1973)*.

3. See Adolfo Campoy-Cubillo (90–93) for an analysis of this article by Bendahan and the polemic response to it by Edmon Amran El Maleh.

4. As we note in chapter 4, this is the phrase that was used in the debate over whether Spain's Jewish community had a right to claim ownership of the human remains found in excavated medieval Jewish cemeteries.

5. In interviews with the sociologist Camargo Crespo, Moroccan Sephardi Jews embrace this mythology: they tell Crespo that they feel like Spaniards returning to their ancestral home and are very proud of their connection to Spain's medieval Jewish past and the continuity with this past through language, culture, and religious ritual they see themselves as embodying. See Camargo Crespo, "Una aproximación sociológica a la población judía madrileña." From his interviews with Turkish Sephardi Jews living in Spain, Albert Sabanoglu draws a very different picture: his interviewees say they did not grow up hearing stories about Spain as a place of origin and that Spain was not part of their mental map, at least not until the 2015 law of nationality. Their only connection to Spain was the Judeo-Spanish language spoken by their grandparents.

6. While Hirsch speaks of postmemory in terms of the literal second generation (both the familial transmission from parents to their children, and the "intra-generational horizontal identification that makes that child's position more broadly available to other contemporaries" ("The Generation" 114–15),

we follow Dalia Kandiyoti's argument that Hirsch's concept is also useful to describe the affiliative connections of contemporary actors (in Bendahan's case, literary characters) in relation to the centuries-removed Iberian Jewish past (*The Converso's Return*).

7. In 2016 Bendahan published the book *Tetuán*, recounting her memories of the city and her recent trips there. Even more explicitly than *Déjalo, ya volveremos*, this book emphasizes the identity ties between the Jewish community of the Moroccan Protectorate and Spain and the Spanishness of Bendahan's family.

8. Bendahan wrote her PhD dissertation about the novelist and diplomat Albert Cohen (1895–1981), who was born in Corfú, Greece in a Romaniote Jewish family, moved to France as a child, and later to Switzerland. Solal is the name of the main character of several of his novels. Bendahan's revised dissertation was published as a book: *Sefarad es también Europa. El otro en la obra de Albert Cohen* [Sepharad is also Europe. The other in the work of Albert Cohen].

9. This is the same poem reproduced in the Museum of Béjar analyzed in chapter 4. As we note there, the poem's key stands for the impossibility of return—there is no door that it can open—and for the multiple experiences of loss and exile (from Sion, from Spain, from Salonica).

10. The short story "Requiem por la sombra de mi tía Blanca" [Requiem for the shadow of my aunt Blanca] by Israeli Moroccan writer Mois Benarroch also uses irony and humor to tell the story of its Sephardi narrator's visit to the museum Casa de Sefarad in Córdoba. Having historically been labeled guests who overstayed their welcome, says the story, Sephardi Jews are now being welcomed in their own home but having to pay an entry ticket to get in.

11. The term *Anusim* derives from the rabbinic point of view regarding the conversos and their descendants. At the time of the conversions, these Jewish authorities saw the conversos as still Jewish. As the sixteenth century progressed, however, second and third generations of exiled Jews began to see conversos who had stayed in the Iberian Peninsula with suspicion, "less like beleaguered *anusim* than willing apostates" (Ray, *After Expulsion* 126–28). See Kandiyoti, *The Converso's Return*, for an in-depth analysis of this phenomenon and its literary manifestations in the Americas, Europe, and Turkey in the last few decades. One of the novels she studies, *Mi nombre es Jamaica* (José Manuel Fajardo 2011) has as its protagonist a history professor from Spain who discovers his Jewish ancestry.

12. In his words, "Disclosure which reinstates the world and leads back to the world, and is proper to a sign or a signification, is suppressed in traces" (Levinas, "The Trace" 357).

13. Similar ambivalences and misrecognitions occur in the case of contemporary returns to al-Andalus and Spain's Arab past. See

Martin-Márquez's *Disorientations*, Flesler's *The Return of the Moor*, Doubleday and Coleman's *In the Light of Medieval Spain*, Calderwood's *Colonial al-Andalus*.

14. See chapter 1, note 46, for Yahuda.

15. Personal interview, Madrid, December 2016. Jacques Laredo, advisor to the president of the FCJE, says something similar to Garzón in the documentary *The Sephardi Legacy of Segovia, Spain: Pentimento of the Past*: "They might have been Jewish 500 years ago, but they cannot pretend to be Jewish today" (Regan, dir).

16. In his dissertation, Charles McDonald examines the conversion phenomenon and different types of return to Judaism among self-identified converso descendants and "Jews by choice" in Madrid and Barcelona.

17. The Polish case studied by Lehrer presents a rich point of comparison with which to discern the peculiarities of the situation in Spain. Both countries had large, significant, and constitutive Jewish communities integrated within a Catholic majority. Notwithstanding the historical distance and important differences between the 1492 Iberian Jewish expulsion and the murder of Polish Jews in the Holocaust, both Spain and Poland went from having a thriving Jewish presence to an almost complete absence of Jewish society in a very short time. The experience of conversion is also present in both societies, as is the prevalence of a society-wide forgetfulness about anything Jewish. Since the 1990s, both countries have ventured into the repurposing of their Jewish past to, among other things, foster heritage and cultural tourism. Although the Jewish presence that Spanish initiatives seek to recover is five hundred years old, Spain's engagement with its Jewish heritage is, as we have seen, closely connected to and modeled on Polish and European-wide initiatives related to the memory of the Holocaust.

18. Lehrer borrows Dominique LaCapra's conceptualization of extreme trauma to explain how these are experiences that "are not entirely 'owned' as 'one's own' by any individual or group. If they haunt a house (a nation, a group), they come to disturb all who live in . . . that house" (quoted in Lehrer, "Bearing" 103).

19. In her analysis of Sephardism within US Latina literature, Kandiyoti explains that Sephardism reconfigures both Latinx identity and the dominant Ashkenazi Jewish–US imaginary. Sephardi Latina stories add a dimension of secrecy and unknowability to existing formulations of both conventional and radical Latinx identities ("Sephardism" 237). These stories suggest a genealogical link, a connectivity, between the histories of Latinx and Jewish people through a shared past involving conversos ("Sephardism" 240).

20. Interview conducted by the authors in 2007 at the Casa de Jacob bookstore in Toledo. As we detail in chapter 2, the store opened in 2000 and became a target of local neo-Nazi groups. Often its facade appeared covered with

antisemitic messages, and once it suffered an arson attack. The store closed in 2010 and reopened with the same name in Barcelona later that year.

21. These testimonies appear in the documentary *Toledo: El secreto oculto* [Toledo: The hidden secret], directed by Jack Matittiahu (Madrid: Prima Luz Productions, 2008).

22. The Catalan term *xuetas* is the pejorative name by which this group of families were known. It derives from *juetó*, the diminutive pejorative of *jueu* (Jew), although it might also be related to the term *xuia* (pork) in the same way that *marrano* was used in Castilian to derogatorily refer to conversos. Fifteen last names were considered xuetas, corresponding to last names that were published after people belonging to these families were condemned for Judaizing by the Inquisition in the seventeenth century. Prejudice and discriminatory measures against them lasted well into the twentieth century (Álvarez Chillida, *El antisemitismo* 78–79; Joan Tous). The xuetas have been an object of fascination for special interest groups in Israel for a long time. They were discovered in 1961 by the Israeli press, which wrote many articles about them, characterizing them as crypto-Jews. While their ancestors perhaps were such, this characterization was extremely misleading in the 1960s. The xuetas were undoubtedly Catholic; however, a representative of the Jewish agency traveled to Mallorca and informed the Israeli public that as many as two hundred xuetas wished to move to Israel. In the end, twenty-four people, including children, traveled to Israel in 1966, but twenty-three of them returned to Spain within days. This episode produced great scandal both in Israel and Spain (Lisbona 241–42). See Leite and Kandiyoti's *The Converso's Return* for the case of the Belmonte converso descendants in Portugal.

23. The range of possibilities of self-identification among the xuetas is exemplified by Cayetano Martí Valls, who acquired media notoriety in Spain. Martí Valls was a humble worker from Inca (Mallorca) who dedicated his life to propagating the idea that the xuetas, like himself, were the first to bring the teachings of Christ to the island in the early first century. In his view, these teachings emphasized the individual relationship to God and empowered the workers, the poor, and the needy. Since the 1950s and until his death, Martí Valls presented his religion as a "return to primitive Christianity based on Jewish traditions" and was at odds with both Jewish and Catholic official institutionalized religions.

24. Wolf Vostell (Leverkusen, 1932–Berlin, 1998), a longtime admirer of Goya, Picasso, and Zurbarán, first visited Spain in 1958. In 1959, he married Mercedes Guardado Olivenza and moved to Cáceres, Extremadura. He was a pioneer of video art, installations, and happenings in the 1960s. In 1976, he founded the Museo Vostell Malpartida, managed by the government of Extremadura since 1994.

25. Problematically because, as Nirenberg (*Communities of Violence* 4–7) explains, these continuities (as in Vostell's title uniting 1492 and the Holocaust) often imply a teleology and a simplified "persecutory landscape" leading to the Holocaust.

26. Kristine Stiles, email communication, November 8, 2014.

27. Carl Jung introduced the phrase *collective guilt* into German discourse in 1945, when he said that all Germans, either actively or passively, consciously or unconsciously, were participants in the atrocities of the Holocaust and therefore psychologically guilty (Olick, "Guilt" 110). In 1947, Karl Jaspers, in *The Question of German Guilt*, wrote of the collective responsibility of Germans, both the perpetrators who had committed the crimes and bystanders who failed to do anything about it (Habermas 43). Olick describes "the politics of regret" as a new principle of political legitimization at work today in Germany and other nations, grounded in the principle of responsibility for the wrongs of the past.

28. Joshua Goode explains this exculpatory use of the comparison with Germany in relation to the racial thinking and crimes of Francoism (3).

29. As we reference in the introduction, diplomatic documents explain that Spain wanted to make sure that the preparations for 1992 did not "stir up negative elements like the memory of the expulsion, Inquisitorial persecution, intolerance, and negative aspects of the colonial past" (Lisbona 351).

30. We thank Santiago Palomero for giving us access to these visitor books in July 2015.

31. In an article in *El País* about Quintero's portrait of Maimónides using a homeless man as a model, writer Manuel Vicent talks about "personajes sefardíes de la Edad Media que fueron desahuciados de la historia española" [Sephardi figures that were evicted from Spanish history].

32. Email communication with Daniel Quintero, August 21, 2015.

33. For a discussion of the power this legend still holds today, see our discussion of the commemorations of Halevi's figure in Toledo's public plaques and monuments in chapter 2.

CONCLUSION

Memory and the Future

THE MEMORY OF JEWISH SPAIN as a marker of nostalgia and utopia has been busy at work for many centuries. It has served Sephardi Jews as a strategic marker of exilic identity, of distinct cultural heritage and intra-Jewish difference. During the twentieth century, it was deployed as an instrument of Spain's colonial ambitions in Morocco and as a way to erase the Francoist regime's collaboration with Nazi Germany. More recently, in the democratic period, it has been redeployed as a means of exorcising the lingering ghosts of intolerances old and new and, continuing a long tradition, as a tool of international relations and diplomacy. As chronicled throughout this book, this memory continues to be rediscovered and reenergized by different social actors for different purposes both inside and outside of Spain.

In Toledo, a short two hundred yards to the north of the Sephardi Museum, stands the Sinagoga of Santa María la Blanca [Synagogue of Saint Mary the White]. Like the smaller Synagogue of the Transit, this second surviving synagogue's name also evokes the particular complexities of its converso identity. The building stands today as a precious yet self-effacing trace of the living presence of an unresolved past. Like many traces of pre-1492 Jewish material culture in Spain, this building has experienced several conversions (built in the second half of the thirteenth century in the Mudéjar style to become Toledo's major synagogue, it became a church during the anti-Jewish riots incited by the 1411 visit of preacher Saint Vincent Ferrer), variations in use (becoming consecutively a monastery for repentant prostitutes, military barracks, and a storage facility for a steel factory), and changes in ownership (the state declared it national patrimony in 1856, and in 1939, Franco donated it to the Catholic

Figure Concl.1. Interior of Sinagoga Santa María la Blanca, Toledo. December 2015. ©Adrián Pérez Melgosa.

Church). Behind high walls, surrounded by a small courtyard and a humble exposed-brick-and-wood exterior stands its elegant structure and interior. A forest of octagonal columns with capitals forming arches sustains its five naves, conveying simultaneously a feeling of infinity and intimacy. Its whitewashed walls and humble red-clay ceramic floor suggest simplicity and lightness (see fig. Concl.1).

Since our first visits to Toledo, we have found the paradoxes of the splendor, destruction, and fragmentary survival of Jewish Spain best encapsulated in this synagogue. Subtly beautiful, decayed, and empty, this space and its voids have always resonated in a powerful, emotional way with both of us. The fact that its emptiness is directly related to that history of destruction and loss make it all the more meaningful. In contrast to its neighbor the Synagogue of the Transit, owned by the Spanish state and transformed into the Sephardi Museum, this synagogue belongs to the Archdiocese of Toledo and its presentation to the public is outdated and careless. The museographic information provided is limited to a sign in its entrance that erroneously identifies it as originating in the twelfth century. Yet the space remains magnificent in spite, or perhaps because, of the apparent neglect in which it stands.

While the Synagogue of the Transit/Sephardi Museum is earnestly filled with cultural activities, educational courses, workshops, historical information, and guides, Santa María la Blanca remains all but empty.[1] Both Andreas Huyseen and James Young have eloquently written about the architectural project of Daniel Libeskind's giving form to the historical void of the destruction of Jewish life in Germany (Huyssen, *Present Pasts*, 66). Libeskind's design for Berlin's new Jewish Museum is premised on the very idea of the void, a void to be experienced by the public as absence embodied by empty spaces (Young, *At Memory's Edge* 8, 165). In contrast to this void produced in order to awaken the public's consciousness, the emptiness of Santa María la Blanca has not been intentionally produced in order to stand for the destruction of Jewish life in Spain. Its void is only the result of that destruction. And yet, at least for us, this space resounds with loss and persistent splendor in an emotionally powerful way precisely because the lack of care in its present use and presentation, its emptiness, directly relates to the absence left by the purposeful destruction of Jewish life in Spain. This loss, and Spain's Jewish past, has always been ripe for resonances with other histories of destruction and loss. It is not surprising that so many people have come to embrace the possibilities offered by it, to fill it with desires, anxieties, and hopes.

About fifteen years ago, at a stop for gas on a car trip from Barcelona to Burgos, we found a tourist brochure announcing Tarazona's rediscovery of its Jewish past. After visiting Tarazona's Jewish Quarter, and many subsequent visits to dozens of cities' Jewish sites—former cemeteries, possible synagogues, maybe mikvehs, and museums of all sizes and characteristics—and conversations about newly discovered Jewish last names and newly interpreted quasi-Jewish traditions, we still feel a high degree of ambivalence about the meaning of these reencounters. Are they tourist traps? Can they become the unheroic starting point of a Benjaminean illumination of a barbaric past? Do they open up the possibility of exploring more complex histories and imagining better futures? Yes.

In his book with Erica Lehrer, *Jewish Space in Contemporary Poland*, Michael Meng explains how "many of the carriers of Jewish memory in contemporary Poland and in post-Holocaust Europe more broadly often invest memory with profound political and social aspirations" (Meng 82). Building on Svetlana Boym's conceptualization of restorative and reflective modes of nostalgia (Boym, *Future* 41), Meng argues that this "cosmopolitan memory" has two iterations: redemptive cosmopolitanism "symbolically reincorporates Jewishness into the present as a marker of achieved tolerance and multiethnicity in the new Europe ... [it is a] self-celebratory narrative of democratic redemption" (83). On the other hand, "reflective, critical cosmopolitanism ... recalls the past to transform and improve democratic societies in the future [in order to] engender more historically conscious and tolerant citizens . . . [and to] construct more egalitarian and open societies in the future" (Meng 82; see Huyssen, *Present Pasts* 27 for a similar argument). As Boym argues, nostalgia is not just retrospective but can also be prospective and "have a direct impact on the realities of the future" ("Nostalgia" 8).

Like Boym, Meng recognizes that these two iterations are tendencies: "redemptive and reflective cosmopolitanism should not be seen as distinctly opposite; rather, they may circulate, if in tension with each other, in the same memory project" (83). As in the Polish case, both the reflective and the redemptive impulses arise from the variety of practices of remembrance of the Jewish past in which Spain and its regions, towns, and citizens have become invested. But unlike the post-Holocaust Poland Meng has in mind, a wider time gap separates the present from the events addressed by the memories of medieval Jewish Spain, enabling a wider repertoire of "memory work" practices. These memories often reappear as a foundational experience against which succeeding experiences of violence are compared and interpreted. The complexity derived from the long temporality of this memory gets further complicated by the tenuous, unverifiable, yet compelling challenge of the converso experience. This paradoxical experience simultaneously "erased" Jewishness from Spain and ensured its permanence. The prolonged history of erasures and presences, of oblivion and remembrance, imprints the iterations of redemptive and reflective cosmopolitanism within an even longer chain of signification.

In January 2014, while the new law of nationality for Sephardi Jews was being discussed, Josh Nathan-Kazis wrote an account of his trip to Spain for *Haaretz* and *The Forward* entitled "My Spanish Inquisition: A Jewish Reporter Exercises His Right of Return." His thirteen-part account, filled with humor and insights, begins by establishing what at first seem to be stable categories of identity: he is an American Jew proud of his Sephardi roots, one of his ancestors was named Abraham de Lucena, and Spain, after hundreds of years, wanted to make amends. It seems like a fair deal, says Nathan-Kazis. He will go to Spain and "see about becoming Spanish." In part 2 of his account, "The Real Spain," he observes, "when you spend weeks preparing for a trip about Jews, it's easy to forget that the country is really, really Catholic. The dead piglet in the café was a good reminder." He reacts defensively when these Catholic Spaniards talk about having Jewish roots: "it felt like they were cutting in on my territory ... they were all grabbing at something I had thought was mine." The climax of the story occurs in part 9, when he visits Lucena, the town whose name became part of his family's lore, perhaps the hometown of his ancestor. There, he is both mortified at the shameless exploitation of Jewish heritage for tourism dollars and taken with the story he is told about Lucena's being full of conversos who needed to flaunt their Christianity in order to survive the Inquisition. Suddenly, the piglet in the café might have another layer of meaning. The history of the conversos makes him rethink his positioning regarding the ownership of Spain's Sephardi heritage:

> What right did one tiny sliver of a fraction of a blood tie give me to this place? Sure, the burger-hawkers were sons of the inquisitors—but they were also sons of conversos. And while my people had gone across the ocean and bought land and seats at a synagogue, theirs had stayed in Lucena and made sure everyone could recognize them through their Holy Week masks so that they wouldn't be burned at the stake. And if their 15th-generation descendants had lost their jobs at the furniture factories and wanted to hustle some sentimental Jewish suckers into buying Star of David–shaped cookies and weird aural tours, who was I to get offended? Maybe their claims to the Jews of pre-Inquisition Spain were just as strong as mine. Maybe they really were as Sephardi as I was. (Nathan-Kazis)

As we have seen throughout this book, claims to Spain's Jewish inheritance have been articulated by Sephardi Jews around the world, by Spain's current Jewish communities, and also by a variety of civil actors and institutions inside and outside of Spain. As these groups deploy specific notions of heritage and patrimony to articulate their claims, they also find that the very act of connecting themselves to this memory and experience implicates them in larger questions of cultural identity. These processes may produce unexpected filiations, as it occurred to Nathan Kazis in Lucena. In the introduction, we quoted Stuart Hall's definition of identities as "the names we give to the different ways we are positioned by, and position ourselves within, the narratives of the past" (225). It is in this sense of an intervention in a much larger process of reevaluation of cultural identity that we see the potential of Spain's reencounters with its Jewish past. The very material of these cultural processes is the memory work of Jewish Spain.

NOTE

1. The exception is the Christian messianic sect, Fraternidad Nuestra Señora de la Mañana [Fraternity of our Lady of the Morning], which was given "spiritual custodianship of the synagogue" by the archbishop of Toledo in the year 2000 (see Perez Colomé). The events organized by this fringe religious group include art exhibitions of its founder's mystical, psychedelic, magic-realist paintings; Catholic prayers held during Jewish holidays; and talks on the links between Jewish and Christian mysticism. Spain's Jewish leaders have unsuccessfully petitioned the archbishop for return of the synagogue to the Jewish community.

WORKS CITED

Abend, Lisa. "Spain's New Muslims: A Historical Romance." *In the Light of Medieval Spain: Islam, the West and the Relevance of History*, edited by Simon R. Doubleday and David Coleman, New York, Palgrave Macmillan, 2008, 133–56.

Afinoguénova, Eugenia, and Jaume Martí-Olivella. "A Nation under Tourists' Eyes: Tourism and Identity Discourses in Spain." *Spain Is (Still) Different: Tourism and Discourse in Spanish Identity*, edited by Eugenia Afinoguénova and Jaume Martí-Olivella, Lexington Books, 2008, xi–xxxviii.

Aguilar Fernández, Paloma. *Memoria y olvido de la Guerra Civil española*. Madrid, Alianza, 1996.

Aizenberg, Edna. "Sephardism and Neo-Sephardism in Latin American Literature." *Sephardism: Spanish Jewish History and the Modern Literary Imagination*, edited by Yael Halevi-Wise, Stanford UP, 2012, 129–42.

Alberola, Miquel. "El Rey, a los sefardíes: 'Cuánto os hemos echado de menos!'" *El País*, Nov. 30, 2015, http://politica.elpais.com/politica/2015/11/30/actualidad/1448887588_869275.html. Accessed April 2, 2020.

Aliberti, Davide. *Sefarad: Una comunidad imaginada (1924–2015)*. Madrid, Marcial Pons, 2019.

———. "Volviendo a Sefarad desde la diáspora: Las leyes de 2015 para la naturalización de los judíos sefardíes en España y Portugal; Un análisis comparado." *Bulletin d'Histoire Contemporaine de l'Espagne*, vol. 53, forthcoming.

Álvarez Chillida, Gonzalo. *El antisemitismo en España: La imagen del judío, 1812–2002*. Madrid, Marcial Pons, 2002.

———. "Presencia e imagen judía en la España contemporánea: Herencia castiza y modernidad." *El otro en la España contemporánea: Prácticas, discursos y representaciones*, edited by Silvina Schammah Gesser and Raanan Rein, Sevilla, Fundación Tres Culturas del Mediterráneo, 2011, 123–59.

Álvarez Delgado, Yasmina. "Excavaciones en torno a la sinagoga de Samuel Halevi (Sinagoga del Tránsito): Toledo." *El legado material hispanojudío*, edited by Ana María López Álvarez and Ricardo Izquierdo Benito, Cuenca, Universidad de Castilla–La Mancha, 1998, 341–45.

Amador de los Ríos, José. *Historia social, política y religiosa de los judíos de España y Portugal*. Madrid, Aguilar, 1960.

———. *Toledo pintoresco o descripción de sus más célebres monumentos*. Madrid, Imprenta y librerías de D. Ignacio Boix, 1845.

Amelang, James S. *Parallel Histories: Muslims and Jews in Inquisitorial Spain*. Louisiana State UP, 2013.

Anderson, Peter. "Singling Out Victims: Denunciation and Collusion in the Post–Civil War Francoist Repression in Spain, 1939–1945." *European History Quarterly*, vol. 39, no. 1, 2009, 7–26.

Aradillas, Antonio, and José María Íñigo. *Viaje por la España judía*. Barcelona, Laertes, 2002.

Aragoneses, Alfons. "Convivencia and Filosefardismo in Spanish Nation-Building." *Max Planck Institute for European Legal History Research Paper Series*, vol. 5, 2016, 1–34.

Armengou, Montse, and Ricard Belis. *Las fosas del silencio ¿Hay un Holocausto español?* Barcelona, Debolsillo, 2005.

Ashtor, Eliyahu. *The Jews of Moslem Spain*. Philadelphia, Jewish Publication Society, 1992. 2 vols.

Ashworth, Gregory J. "Heritage, Tourism and Europe: A European Future for a European Past?" *Heritage, Tourism, and Society*, edited by David T. Herbert, London, Mansell, 1995, 68–89.

Ashworth, Gregory J., and J. E. Tunbridge. *The Tourist-Historic City: Retrospect and Prospect of Managing the Heritage City*. New York, Routledge, 2011.

Asociación de Vecinos del Barrio Judío de Hervás. http://asociaciondevecinosdelbarriojudio.blogspot.com/p/historia.html. Accessed April 15, 2020.

Assmann, Jan. *Moses the Egyptian: The Memory of Egypt in Western Monotheism*. Cambridge, MA, Harvard UP, 1997.

Avilés Amat, Antonio. *Guía del Museo Judío David Melul*. Museum leaflet.

Avni, Haim. *Spain, the Jews, and Franco*. Jewish Publication Society of America, 1982.

Baer, Alejandro. "Between 'Just Punishment' and 'Unthinkable Fascist Crimes.' Reactions to Kristallnacht in Civil War Spain." *Violence, Memory and History: Western Perceptions of Kristallnacht*, edited by Nathan Wilson and Colin McCullough, New York, Routledge, 2014, 73–89.

———. "Between Old and New Antisemitism: The Image of Jews in Present-Day Spain." *Resurgent Antisemitism: Global Perspectives*, Indiana UP, 2013, 95–117.

———. "Tanques contra piedras: La imagen de Israel en España." *Raíces: Revista judía de cultura* 72, 2007, 26–31.

———. "The Voids of Sepharad: The Memory of the Holocaust in Spain." *Revisiting Jewish Spain in the Modern Era*, edited by Daniela Flesler, Tabea Linhard, and Adrián Pérez Melgosa, special issue of the *Journal of Spanish Cultural Studies*, vol. 12, no. 1, 2011, 95–120.

Baer, Alejandro, and Paula López. "The Blind Spots of Secularization: A Qualitative Approach to the Study of Anti-Semitism in Spain." *European Societies*, vol. 14, no. 2, 2012, 203–21.

Baer, Alejandro, and Natan Sznaider. "Ghosts of the Holocaust in Franco's Mass Graves: Cosmopolitan Memories and the Politics of 'Never Again.'" *Memory Studies*, vol. 8, no. 3, 2015, 328–44.

———. *Memory and Forgetting in the Post-Holocaust Era: The Ethics of Never Again.* New York, Routledge, 2017.

Baer, Yitzhak. *A History of the Jews in Christian Spain.* Jewish Publication Society, 1992. 2 vols.

Bal, Mieke. *Double Exposures: The Subject of Cultural Analysis.* New York, Routledge, 1996.

———. "Exhibition as Film." *(Re)visualizing National History: Museums and National Identities in Europe in the New Millennium*, edited by Robin Ostow, U of Toronto P, 2008, 15–43.

Balfour, Sebastian. *Deadly Embrace: Morocco and the Road to the Spanish Civil War.* New York, Oxford University Press, 2002.

———. "The Loss of Empire, Regenerationism and the Forging of a Myth of National Identity." *Spanish Cultural Studies: An Introduction; The Struggle for Modernity*, edited by Helen Graham and Jo Labanyi. Oxford UP, 1996, 25–31.

Barke, M., and L. A. France. "The Costa del Sol." *Tourism in Spain: Critical Issues*, edited by M. Barke, J. Towner, and M. T. Newton, Wallingford, Oxon, UK, Cab International, 1996, 265–308.

Barke, M., and J. Towner. "Exploring the History of Leisure and Tourism in Spain." *Tourism in Spain: Critical Issues*, edited by M. Barke, J. Towner, and M. T. Newton, Wallingford, Oxon, UK, Cab International, 1996, 3–34.

———. "Urban Tourism in Spain." *Tourism in Spain: Critical Issues*, edited by M. Barke, J. Towner, and M. T. Newton, Wallingford, Oxon, UK, Cab International, 1996, 343–73.

Baudrillard, Jean. *The System of Objects.* London, Verso, 2005.

Baxandall, Michael. "Exhibiting Intention: Some Preconditions of the Visual Display of Culturally Purposeful Objects." *Exhibiting Cultures: The Poetics and Politics of Museum Display*, edited by Ivan Karp and Steven D. Levine, Washington, DC, Smithsonian Institution Press, 1991, 33–41.

Beckwith, Stacy N., editor. *Charting Memory: Recalling Medieval Spain*, Garland, 2000.

———. "Facing Sepharad, Facing Israel and Spain: Yehuda Burla and Antonio Gala's Janus Profiles of National Reconstitution." *Sephardism: Spanish Jewish

History and the Modern Literary Imagination, edited by Yael Halevi-Wise, Stanford UP, 2012, 169–88.

———. "Transitions Back to Sepharad in Spanish Historical Novels from 1985 through 2001" (unpublished manuscript).

———."With Sepharad as a Void: Recent Reckoning with the Holocaust in Spanish Fiction." *Spain, the Second World War, and the Holocaust Spain, the Second World War, and the Holocaust: History and Representation*, edited by Sara J. Brenneis and Gina Herrmann, Toronto UP, 2020, 536–51.

Behar, Ruth. *Traveling Heavy: A Memoir in Between Journeys*. Duke University Press, 2013.

Benarroch, Mois. "Requiem por la sombra de mi tía Blanca." *Ufrán. Relatos de autores judíos del Norte de Marruecos*, Madrid, Hebraica, 2010, 45–67.

Bendahan, Esther. *Déjalo, ya volveremos*. Barcelona, Seix Barral, 2006.

———. *Sefarad es también Europa. El otro en la obra de Albert Cohen*. Prensas de la Universidad de Zaragoza, 2016.

———. "Sefardistán." *El País*, February 8, 2007. http://elpais.com/diario/2007/02/08/opinion/1170889205_850215.html>. Accessed April 12, 2020.

———. *Tetuán*. Antequera, Confluencias, 2016.

———. *Una hora solamente, de la orilla del día*. Salamanca, Confluencias, 2016.

Bendahan, Esther, and Esther Benari. *Soñar con Hispania*. Santander, Tantín, 2002.

Bertz, Inka. "Jewish Museums in the Federal Republic of Germany." *Visualizing and Exhibiting Jewish Space and History*, edited by Richard I. Cohen, Oxford UP, 2012, 80–112.

Bodemann, Y. Michal. "Reconstructions of History: From Jewish Memory to Nationalized Commemoration of Kristallnacht in Germany." *Germans, Jews, Memory: Reconstructions of Jewish Life in Germany*, edited by Y. Michal Bodemann, U of Michigan P, 1996, 179–223.

———. "A Reemergence of German Jewry?" *Reemerging Jewish Culture in Germany: Life and Literature Since 1989*, edited by Sander L. Gilman and Karen Remmler, NYU Press, 1994, 46–61.

———. "The State in the Construction of Ethnicity, and Ideological Labour: The Case of German Jewry." *Critical Sociology*, vol. 17, no. 3, 1991, 35–46.

Bodian, Miriam. *Dying in the Law of Moses: Crypto-Jewish Martyrdom in the Iberian World*. Indiana UP, 2007.

———. *Hebrews of the Portuguese Nation: Conversos and Community in Early Modern Amsterdam*. Indiana UP, 1999.

Botín, Gonzalo. "El rey Juan Carlos inaugura la reforma del Museo Sefardí, que ha durado ocho años." *El País*, June 2, 1994.

Boym, Svetlana. *The Future of Nostalgia*. Basic Books, 2001.

———. "Nostalgia and Its Discontents." *Hedgehog Review*, vol. 9, no. 2, 2007, 7–18.

Brauch, Julia, Anna Lipphardt, and Alexandra Nocke. *Jewish Topographies: Visions of Space, Traditions of Place*. Hampshire, UK, Ashgate, 2008.

Braude, Benjamin. "The Myth of the Sefardi Economic Superman." *Trading Cultures: The Worlds of Western Merchants; Essays on Authority, Objectivity, and Evidence*. Turnhout, Belgium, Brepols, 2001, 163–91.

Brenneis, Sara J. *Spaniards in Mauthausen: Representations of a Nazi Concentration Camp, 1940–2015*. U of Toronto P, 2018.

Bryson, Norman. *Looking at the Overlooked: Four Essays on Still Life Painting*. London, Reaktion Books, 1990.

Buhalis, Dimitrios. "The Tourism Phenomenon: The New Tourist and Consumer." *Tourism in the Age of Globalization*, edited by Salah Wahab and Chris Cooper, New York, Routledge, 2001, 69–96.

Bujalance, Pablo. "Daniel Quintero abre en el Episcopal la mirada más amplia a su pintura." *Málaga Hoy*, January 24, 2008. http://www.malagahoy.es/ocio/Daniel-Quintero-Episcopal-amplia-pintura_0_116388808.html.

Burnett, Victoria. "School Built on Cemetery Provides Lesson in History." *New York Times*, July 1, 2009. http://www.nytimes.com/2009/07/02/world/europe/02toledo.html. Accessed April 10, 2020.

Bush, Andrew. "Amador de los Ríos and the Beginnings of Modern Jewish Studies in Spain." *Revisiting Jewish Spain in the Modern Era*, edited by Daniela Flesler, Tabea Linhard, and Adrián Pérez Melgosa. Special Issue of the *Journal of Spanish Cultural Studies*, vol. 12, no. 1, 2011, 13–33.

Butler, Shelley Ruth, and Erica Lehrer, eds. "Introduction: Curatorial Dreaming." *Curatorial Dreams: Critics Imagine Exhibitions*. Montreal, McGill-Queen's UP, 2016, 3–23.

Cabanillas García, Mercedes. "Introducción a la *Comisaría Regia de Turismo*: La figura del Marqués de la Vega Inclán como comisario regio." Archivos web del Museo del Romanticismo. http://museoromanticismo.mcu.es/web/archivos/documentos/comisaria_regia.pdf. Accessed April 10, 2020.

Cabo Aseguinolaza, Fernando, and Santiago Fernández Mosquera. "Prólogo." *Execración contra los judíos*, edited by Francisco de Quevedo, Barcelona, Crítica, 1996, ix–lix.

Cadiñanos Bardeci, Inocencio. "Precisiones acerca del *Tránsito de la Virgen* de Juan Correa de Vivar." *Boletín del Museo del Prado*, vol. 24, no. 42, 2006, 6–13.

Cajal, Máximo. *Sueños y pesadillas: memorias de un diplomático*. Barcelona, Tusquets, 2010.

Calderwood, Eric. *Colonial al-Andalus: Spain and the Making of Modern Moroccan Culture*. Cambridge, Harvard UP, 2018.

Camarasa, Santiago. "Turismo, Toledo, Greco." *Boletín de la Real Academia de Bellas Artes y Ciencias Históricas de Toledo*, vol. 30, 1927, 4–28.

Camargo Crespo, Oscar. "Una aproximación sociológica a la población judía madrileña." *Raíces*, vol. 42, 2000, 17–32.

Campoy-Cubillo, Adolfo. *Memories of the Maghreb: Transnational Identities in Spanish Cultural Production*. Palgrave, 2012.

Cansinos Assens, Rafael. "Amnesia ofensiva." *Los judíos en Sefarad*, edited by Jacobo Israel Garzón, Madrid, Hebraica Ediciones, 2006, 159–63.

———. *Las luminarias de Janucá: Un episodio de la historia de Israel en España*. Madrid, Arca Ediciones, 2011.

Cantera Burgos, Francisco. *Sinagogas españolas: Con especial estudio de la de Córdoba y la Toledana de El Tránsito*. Madrid, Instituto Arias Montano, 1955.

Caro Baroja, Julio. *Los judíos en la España moderna y contemporánea*. Madrid, Istmo, 1961. 3 vols.

Carrera, Esteve. "Els calls catalans s'independitzen." *El Punt Avui*, May 31, 2016. http://www.elpuntavui.cat/territori/article/10-administracions/972206-els-calls-catalans-sindependitzen.html. Accessed April 16, 2020.

Casa de Sefarad website. http://www.casadesefarad.es/. Accessed April 16, 2020.

Castaño, Javier. "Entre la visibilidad y el escepticismo: los restos materiales de los judíos de Sefarad y su interpretación." *¿Una Sefarad Inventada? Los problemas de interpretación de los restos materiales de los judíos en España*, edited by Javier Castaño, Córdoba, El Almendro, 2014, 69–86.

Castellano, José María. *Hervás: Guía Histórica Ilustrada*. Madrid, Celeste, 2000.

Castillo Iglesias, Belén. "Tesorillos judíos de Briviesca." *Catálogo de la Exposición Memoria de Sefarad*, edited by Isidro Gonzálo Bango Troviso, Toledo, Sociedad Estatal para la Acción Cultural Exterior (España), 2002, 99–103.

Castro, Américo. *España en su historia: Cristianos, moros y judíos*. Barcelona, Crítica, 1984.

Castro, Rafael. "Sebastián de la Obra: 'La dificultad de identificar la tradición judía es un reto.'" *Diario de Córdoba*, February 8, 2017. https://www.diariocordoba.com/noticias/contraportada/sebastian-obra-la-dificultad-identificar-tradicion-judia-es-reto_1121253.html. Accessed April 16, 2020.

Cembrero, Ignacio. "El Rey celebra en la sinagoga de Madrid 'el encuentro con los judíos Españoles.'" *El País*, April 1, 1992.

Centro de estudios Zahkor. "Antiguos cementerios judíos de España: la necesidad de un diálogo." *Raíces: Revista judía de cultura*, vol. 78, March 2009, 76–78.

———. "El cementerio de Montjuïc en Barcelona. Una oportunidad y un desafío para dignificar un pasado común." *Raíces: Revista judía de cultura*, vol. 76, October 2008, 77–80.

Cervilla, Paloma. "Adquirir la nacionalidad española, el último obstáculo de los judíos sefardíes." *ABC*, October 8, 2016. http://www.abc.es/sociedad/abci-adquirir-nacionalidad-espanola-ultimo-obstaculo-judios-sefardies-201610082021_noticia.html. Accessed April 16, 2020.

Charnon-Deutsch, Lou. "Exoticism and the Politics of Difference in Late Nineteenth-Century Spanish Periodicals." *Culture and Gender in Nineteenth-Century Spain*, edited by Lou Charnon-Deutsch and Jo Labanyi. Oxford, Clarendon, 1995, 250–70.

———. "The Narrative Work of the Jewish Conspirator in Mid-Nineteenth Century European Literature." *Revisiting Jewish Spain in the Modern Era*, edited by Daniela Flesler, Tabea Alexa Linhard, and Adrián Pérez Melgosa. New York, Routledge, 2013, 34–49.

———. *The Spanish Gypsy: The History of a European Obsession*. Pennsylvania State UP, 2004.

"Cinco propuestas de rutas judías." *Viajar por Aragón*, vol. 20, 2002, 24–25.

Cobo Romero, Francisco, and Teresa María Ortega López. "Francoist Antifeminism and the Violent Reversal of Women's Liberation, 1936–51." *Mass Killings and Violence in Spain 1936–1952*, edited by Peter Anderson and Miguel Ángel del Arco Blanco. New York, Routledge, 2015, 59–71.

Cohen, Judith R. "Bringing It All Back Home: Sephardic Re-creation in a Galician Town." *Donaire*, vol. 6, 1996, 98–106.

———. "Constructing a Spanish Jewish Festival: Music and the Appropriation of Tradition in Imagined Iberian Jewish Communities." *The World of Music*, vol. 41, no. 3, 1999, 95–114.

Cohen, Mark R. *Under Crescent and Cross: The Jews in the Middle Ages*. Princeton UP, 1996.

Cole, Peter. *The Dream of the Poem: Hebrew Poetry from Muslim and Christian Spain 950–1492*. Princeton UP, 2007.

Colet, Anna, et al. "The Black Death and Its Consequences for the Jewish Community in Tàrrega: Lessons from History and Archeology." *The Medieval Globe* inaugural issue. *Pandemic Disease in the Medieval World: Rethinking the Black Death*, edited by Monica H. Green, vol. 1, 2014, 63–94.

Colet Marcé, Anna, and Oriol Saula Briansó. "La influencia del componente religioso en la excavación del cementerio de los judíos de Tàrrega." *La intervenció arqueològica a les necròpolis històriques: Els cementiris jueus (actes del colloqui del 15 i 16 de gener de 2009)*. MUHBA i Ajuntament de Barcelona, Institut de Cultura, 2012, 243–49.

Colet Marcé, Anna, Jordi Ruiz Ventura, and Eulàlia Subirà de Galdàcano. "The Mass Graves: the Archaeological and Paleoanthropological Evidence of the Riot of 1348." *Tragèdia al call-Tàrrega 1348*, coordinated by Oriol Saula Briansó, Exhibition Catalog, Museu Comarcal de l'Urgell-Tàrrega, 2014, 399–402.

Colmeiro, José F. "Exorcising Exoticism: *Carmen* and the Construction of Oriental Spain." *Comparative Literature*, vol. 54, no. 2, 2002, 127–44.

Colomer i Solsona, Laia. "Approaching Montjuïc as Part of the Historic Legacy of Barcelona." *Museum International*, vol. 62, nos. 1–2, 2010, 81–85.

———. "La arqueología de las necrópolis antiguas judías, entre las reivindcaciones religiosas y la res publica." *La intervenció arqueològica a les necròpolis històriques: Els cementiris jueus (actes del colloqui del 15 i 16 de gener de 2009)*. MUHBA i Ajuntament de Barcelona, Institut de Cultura, 2012, 219–30.

"Comienzan a instalar las placas de calles escritas en hebreo." *Lucena Hoy*, October 19, 2012. https://www.lucenahoy.com/articulo/ocio/azulejos-calles-judias/20121019082500002130.html. Accessed April 16, 2020.

"Con nombre propio. Acto de restitución de la memoria, homenaje a los quemados por la Inquisición de Córdoba desde 1483 hasta 1731." https://www.youtube.com/watch?v=AsFNq8ibyzo&feature=related&gl=IL&hl=en. Accessed April 16, 2020.

"Conociendo a nuestros visitantes. Museo Sefardí." Informe del Laboratorio Permanente de Público de Museos, Secretaría de Cultura. http://www.culturaydeporte.gob.es/msefardi/home.html. Accessed April 16, 2020.

"Conversos. En el barrio judío de Hervás representan sus vecinos esta obra teatral y coral." Festivales y eventos culturales de Extremadura. http://www.escenaextremadura.com/Programa.asp?id_festival=24. Accessed July 5, 2015 (site discontinued).

Coro Elí Hoshaná website. http://www.coroelihoshana.com/. Accessed April 16, 2020.

Cossío, Manuel Bartolomé. *Una excursión a Toledo: 14 de Abril, 1913*. Madrid, Blas y Cía, 1913.

Cotallo, José Luis. "Plegaria al Santísimo Cristo de la Salud." *Revista de Ferias y Fiestas de Hervás*, 1953, 4–6.

Crumbaugh, Justin. *Destination Dictatorship: The Spectacle of Spain's Tourist Boom and the Reinvention of Difference*. Albany, SUNY Press, 2009.

Cuartas, Javier. "Felipe de Borbón recibió con emoción y los brazos abiertos a los judíos sefardíes." *El País*, October 19, 1990.

"Cultural Routes of the Council of Europe." https://www.coe.int/en/web/cultural-routes. Accessed April 16, 2020.

"David Melul y sociedades judías donan 50.000 euros al museo." C. D. Bejar Industrial, February 21, 2004. https://www.i-bejar.com/noticias/cultura/david-melul-sociedades-judias-donan-50000-euros-museo-1588.htm. Accessed April 16, 2020.

de Certeau, Michel. *The Practice of Everyday Life*. U of California P, 1988.

de Hervás, Marciano. *Judíos y Cristianos Nuevos en la Historia de Trujillo*. Badajoz, don José María Pérez de Herrasti y Narváez, 2008.

———. "La invención de la tradición: leyendas apócrifas sobre los judíos de Hervás." *Revista de Dialectología y Tradiciones Populares*, vol. 52, no.1, 1997, 177–203.

———. *Los judíos de Hervás*. Hervás, Cáceres, El Lagar, 2001.

"Debate." *La intervenció arqueològica a les necròpolis històriques: Els cementiris jueus (actes del colloqui del 15 i 16 de gener de 2009).* MUHBA i Ajuntament de Barcelona, Institut de Cultura, 2012, 250–55.

"Declaración de Barcelona sobre la intervención arqueológica en las necropolis históricas." *Evista ph. Instituto Andaluz del Patrimonio Histórico,* vol. 71, 2009, 10–11.

Díaz-Mas, Paloma. "Judíos y conversos en la narrativa española de los años 80 y 90." *El legado de Sefarad: Los judíos sefardíes en la historia y la literatura de América Latina, España, Portugal y Alemania,* edited by Norbert Rehrmann, Salamanca, Amarú, 2003, 167–80.

———. *Sephardim: The Jews From Spain.* U of Chicago P, 1992.

Doubleday, Simon R. "Introduction: 'Criminal Non-Intervention'; Hispanism, Medievalism, and the Pursuit of Neutrality." *In the Light of Medieval Spain: Islam, the West and the Relevance of History,* edited by Simon R. Doubleday and David Coleman, Palgrave Macmillan, 2008, 1–31.

Doubleday, Simon R., and David Coleman, eds. *In the Light of Medieval Spain: Islam, the West and the Relevance of History.* Palgrave Macmillan, 2008.

Efron, John M. "Scientific Racism and the Mystique of Sephardic Racial Superiority." *Leo Baeck Institute Yearbook,* vol. 38, 1993, 75–96.

"El rabino Meir Gabay destaca la relevancia de la necrópolis judía, que puede atraer a miles de visitantes de esta religión, y considera que Lucena es más importante en la historia del judaísmo que Toledo y otras ciudades españolas." *Lucena Digital,* March 7, 2012. http://www.lucenadigital.com/turismo/3919.html. Accessed January 8, 2015 (article discontinued).

"El Tránsito de la Virgen." Museo Nacional del Prado, Galería online. https://www.museodelprado.es/coleccion/galeria-on-line/galeria-on-line/obra/el-transito-de-la-virgen-1/. Accessed April 16, 2020.

Elliott, J. H. *The Count-Duque of Olivares: The Statesman in an Age of Decline.* Yale UP, 1986.

Endelman, Todd M. "Benjamin Disraeli and the Myth of Sephardi Superiority." *Jewish History,* vol. 10, no. 2, 1996, 21–35.

"Entrevista a David Melul." *Radio Sefarad,* March 18, 2004.

"Entrevista Sebastián de la Obra." *Cordoba PTV,* January 2014. https://www.youtube.com/watch?v=GDbzl_1fZio. Accessed April 16, 2020.

Erll, Astrid. "Travelling Memory." *Parallax,* vol. 17, no. 4, 2011, 4–18.

Escudero Ríos, Antonio. "David Hatchwell, Presidente Comunidad Judía de Madrid, conoce y se emociona al visitar Castrillo Mota de Judíos." *Diariojudío.com,* June 20, 2016. http://diariojudio.com/noticias/david-hatchwell-conoce-y-se-emociona-al-visitar-castrillo-mota-de-judios/201005.

"Estadística de Movimientos turísticos en fronteras (Frontur) Diciembre 2018 y año 2018: Datos provisionales." *INE (Instituto Nacional de Estadística),*

February 1, 2019. http://www.ine.es/daco/daco42/frontur/frontur1218.pdf. Accessed August 3, 2019.

Estow, Clara. *Pedro the Cruel of Castile, 1350–1369*. New York, Brill, 1995.

FCJE (Federación de comunidades judías de españa). "Aprobada la ley de nacionalidad Española a sefardíes-Comunicado de la Federación de Comunidades Judías de España." June 11, 2015. Esefarad.com

———. "Protocolo de actuación para la exhumación de restos humanos de necrópolis judías historicas." Madrid, July 22, 2007. http://www.observatorioreligion.es/upload/76/08/Protocolo_de_actuacion_para_la_exhumacion_de_restos humanos_de_necropolis_judias_historicas__FCJE_.pdf.

Feindt, Gregor, et al. "Entangled Memory: Toward a Third Wave in Memory Studies." *History and Theory*, vol. 53, no. 1, 2014, 24–44.

Feliu, Eduard. "Some Clarifications on Several Aspects of the History of Jews in Medieval Catalonia." *Catalan Historical Review*, vol. 2, 2009, 49–64.

Feros, Antonio. *Speaking of Spain: The Evolution of Race and Nation in the Hispanic World*. Harvard UP, 2017.

Ferrándiz, Francisco. "De las fosas comunes a los derechos humanos: El descubrimiento de las desapariciones forzadas en la España contemporánea." *Revista de Antropología Social*, vol. 19, 2010, 161–89.

———. "Exhumaciones y políticas de la memoria en la España contemporánea." *Hispania Nova*, vol. 7, 2007. http://hispanianova.rediris.es/7/dossier/07d003.pdf.

Ferrándiz, Francisco, and Alejandro Baer. "Digital Memory: The Visual Recording of Mass Grave Exhumations in Contemporary Spain." *Forum Qualitative Sozialforschung*, vol. 9, no. 3, 2008, 621–40.

Filios, Denise K. "Expulsion from Paradise: Exiled Intellectuals and Andalusian Tolerance." *In the Light of Medieval Spain: Islam, the West and the Relevance of History*, edited by Simon R. Doubleday and David Coleman, Palgrave Macmillan, 2008, 91–113.

Flesler, Daniela. *The Return of the Moor: Spanish Responses to Contemporary Moroccan Immigration*. Purdue University Press, 2008.

Flesler, Daniela, and Adrián Pérez Melgosa. "Battles of Identity, or Playing 'Guest' and 'Host': the Festivals of Moors and Christians in the Context of Moroccan Immigration to Spain." *Journal of Spanish Cultural Studies*, vol. 4, no. 2, 2003, 151–68.

———. "Marketing *Convivencia*: Contemporary Tourist Appropriations of Spain's Jewish Past." *Spain Is (Still) Different: Tourism and Discourse in Spanish Cultural Identity*, edited by Eugenia Afinoguénova and Jaume Martí-Olivella, Lexington Books, 2008, 63–84.

Flesler, Daniela, Tabea Linhard, and Adrián Pérez Melgosa. "Introduction: Revisiting Jewish Spain in the Modern Era." *Journal of Spanish Cultural Studies*, Special Issue, vol. 12, no. 1, 2011, 1–11.

Fredriksen, Paula. *Augustine and the Jews: A Christian Defense of Jews and Judaism.* Yale UP, 2010.

Freedman, Jonathan. "Conversos, Marranos, and Crypto-Latinos: The Jewish Question in the American Southwest (and What It Can Tell US About Race and Ethnicity)." *Boundaries of Jewish Identity,* edited by Susan A. Glenn and Naomi B Sokoloff, U of Washington P, 2010, 188–202.

Freund, Michael. "El Master Chef de Mallorca Retorna al Judaísmo." Beit Haanusim. *El Blog de Shavei Israel.* November 24, 2013. http://casa-anusim.shavei.org/2013/11/24/el-master-chef-de-mallorca-retorna-al-judaismo/#more-2599.

Freund, Michael, and Eliahu Birnbaum. *¿Tiene usted raíces judías? Guía práctica para descubrir sus raíces.* Jerusalem, Shavei Israel, 2015.

Friedman, Michal. "Abraham Shalom Yahuda: A Jewish Orientalist among Sepharad, Zionisms, and the British Empire." *The Jewish Quarterly Review,* vol. 109, no. 3, 2019, 435–51.

———. "Jewish History as 'Historia Patria': José Amador de los Ríos and the History of the Jews of Spain." *Jewish Social Studies,* vol. 18, no. 1, 2011, 88–126.

———. "Reconquering 'Sepharad': Hispanism and proto-Facism in Giménez Caballero's Sephardist Crusade." *Revisiting Jewish Spain in the Modern Era,* edited by Daniela Flesler, Tabea Linhard, and Adrián Pérez Melgosa, Special Issue of the *Journal of Spanish Cultural Studies,* vol. 12, no. 1, 2011, 35–60.

———. "Reconstructing 'Jewish Spain': The Politics and Institutionalization of Jewish History in Spain, 1845–1940." *Hamsa: Journal of Judaic and Islamic Studies,* vol. 1, 2014, 55–67.

———. "Recovering Jewish Spain: Politics, Historiography and Institutionalization of the Jewish Past in Spain (1845–1935)." Dissertation, Columbia University, 2012.

Fuchs, Barbara. *Exotic Nation: Maurophilia and the Construction of Early Modern Spain.* U of Pennsylvania P, 2008.

Furst, Joshua. "Slouching through Catalonia One Jewish Site at a Time." *Forward,* September 2014. http://forward.com/culture/205065/slouching-through-catalonia-one-jewish-site- at-a-t/.

García Álvarez, Jacobo. "Paisajes nacionales, turismo y políticas de memoria: Toledo (1900–1950)." *Ería,* vols. 73–74, 2007, 193–212.

García Arenal, Mercedes. Review of María Rosa Menocal, *The Ornament of the World: How Muslims, Jews and Christians Created a Culture of Tolerance in Medieval Spain. Speculum,* vol. 79, 2004, 801–4.

García Atienza, Juan. *Caminos de Sefarad: Guía Judía de España.* Barcelona, Robin Book, 1994.

García Martín, Francisco. *La Comisión de Monumentos de Toledo (1836–1875).* Toledo, Ledoria, 2008.

García Mercadal, José, editor. *Viajes de extranjeros por España y Portugal.* Madrid, Junta de Castilla y León, 1999.

Garzón, Jacobo Israel. "El Doctor Pulido y los Sefardíes." *Los israelitas españoles y el idioma castellano,* edited by Angel Pulido, Madrid, Riopiedras, 1992, ix–xxiii.

———. "El retorno a Sefarad y los Judíos de España." *El Judaísmo: Contribuciones y presencia en el mundo Contemporáneo.* Cuadernos de la Escuela Diplomática Número 51. Madrid, Escuela Diplomática España y Centro Sefarad Israel, 2014, 329–61.

———. "Introducción." Rafael Cansinos Assens, *Los judíos en Sefarad.* Madrid, Hebraica Ediciones, 2006, 9–29.

———. *Los judíos hispano-marroquíes (1492–1973).* Madrid, Hebraica Ediciones, 2008.

———. "Rafael Cansinos Assens, el judaísmo y *Las luminarias de Janucá.*" Rafael Cansinos Assens, *Las luminarias de Janucá. Un episodio de la historia de Israel en España.* Madrid, Arca Ediciones, 2011, 9–24.

Garzón, Jacobo Israel, and Uriel Macías Kapón. *La comunidad judía de Madrid: Textos e imágenes para una historia (1917–2001).* Madrid, Comunidad Judía de Madrid, 2001.

Gerber, Jane S. *The Jews of Spain: A History of the Sephardic Experience.* Free Press, 1994.

Gershenson, Olga. "How Russia Created a Jewish Museum and Tolerance Center Even Vladimir Putin Can Tolerate." *Forward,* January 8, 2016. http://forward.com/culture/art/328682/how-russia-created-a-jewish-museum-and-tolerance-center-even-vladimir-putin/.

Gitlitz, David M. *Secrecy and Deceit: The Religion of the Crypto-Jews.* U of New Mexico P, 2002.

Gold, Hazel. "Illustrated Histories: The National Subject and 'the Jew' in Nineteenth-Century Spanish Art." *Journal of Spanish Cultural Studies,* vol. 10, no. 1, 2009, 89–109.

Goldman, Esther W. "Samuel Halevi Abulafia's Synagogue (El Tránsito) in Toledo." *Jewish Art,* vol. 18, 1992, 58–69.

Golob, Stephanie. "Volver: The Return of/to Transitional Justice Politics in Spain." *The Politics of Memory in Contemporary Spain,* Special Issue of *Journal of Spanish Cultural Studies,* vol. 9, no. 2, 2008, 127–41.

Gómez Andrea, Miguel. "Obra teatral *Alma Negra.*" Los Conversos, July 7–10, 2016. http://losconversos.com/obra-teatral-alma-negra/.

Gómez Andrea, Miguel, and Antonio Roa Cilla. *Hervás: Imágenes de su Historia.* Hervás, Estudio La Recua, 2013.

González, Allyson. "Abraham S. Yahuda (1877–1951) and the Politics of Modern Jewish Scholarship." *The Jewish Quarterly Review,* vol. 109, no. 3, 2019, 406–33.

González, Manuel. "Benjamín de Sefarad enseña el pasado judío de Lucena a alumnos de Córdoba y Sevilla." *Lucena Hoy,* April 28, 2015. http://www.lucenahoy.com/articulo/ocio/benjamin-de-sefarad-ensena-el-pasado-judio-de-lucena-a-alumnos-de-cordoba-y-sevilla/20150428231146007007.html.

González de Hervás, Emilio. "Hervás. Canto al amor verdadero." *Revista de Ferias y Fiestas de Hervás*, 1953, 7–10.

———. *Mis versos de ayer y de hoy*. Madrid, Aldus, 1971.

González García, Isidro. *El retorno de los judíos*. Madrid, Nerea, 1991.

———. "La cuestión judía y la crisis del 98." *Los judíos en la España contemporánea: Historia y visiones, 1898–1998*, edited by Uriel Macías, Yolanda Moreno Koch, and Ricardo Izquierdo Benito. Ediciones de la Universidad de Castilla–la Mancha, 2000, 25–44.

———. *Los judíos y España después de la expulsión*. Almuzara, 2014.

Gonzálvez Ruiz, Ramón. "Intervención del alcalde Ronquillo en un caso de difamación de limpieza de sangre (1538)." *Anales toledanos*, vol. 1, 1967, 57–71.

Goode, Joshua. *Impurity of Blood: Defining Race in Spain, 1870–1930*. Louisiana State UP, 2009.

Graham, Helen, and Antonio Sánchez. "The Politics of 1992." *Spanish Cultural Studies: An Introduction*, edited by Helen Graham and Jo Labanyi. Oxford UP, 1995, 406–18.

Gray, Beverly. "Holy Toledo! A Trove of Jewish Memories." *Jewish Journal*, Travel Section, January 5, 2006. https://jewishjournal.com/culture/arts/12490/. Accessed April 17, 2020.

Greer, Margaret R., Walter D. Mignolo, and Maureen Quilligan, eds. *Rereading the Black Legend: The Discourses of Religious and Racial Difference in the Renaissance Empires*. U of Chicago P, 2007.

Gruber, Ruth Ellen. "Beyond Virtual Jewishness: Monuments to Jewish Experience in Eastern Europe." *Framing Jewish Culture. Boundaries and Representations*, edited by Simon J. Bronner. Liverpool UP, 2014.

———. *Virtually Jewish: Reinventing Jewish Culture in Europe*. U of California P, 2002.

Gutiérrez Calvo, Vera, and Miguel González. "El gobierno vende en EEUU su gesto hacia los sefardíes." *El País*, March 15, 2014. http://politica.elpais.com/politica/2014/03/15/actualidad/1394895807_715302.html. Accessed April 17, 2020.

Habermas, Jurgen. "Concerning the Public Use of History." *New German Critique*, vol. 44, 1988, 40–50.

Halevi-Wise, Yael. "Introduction: Through the Prism of Sepharad; Modern Nationalism, Literary History, and the Impact of the Sephardic Experience." *Sephardism: Spanish Jewish History and the Modern Literary Imagination*, edited by Yael Halevi-Wise, Stanford UP, 2012, 1–32.

Hall, Stuart. "Cultural Identity and Diaspora." *Identity: Community, Culture, Difference*, edited by Jonathan Rutherford. London, Lawrence & Wishart, 1990, 222–37.

Hanas, Erin. "Wolf Vostell's Fluxus Zug, Model Museum, Academy, Archive." Dissertation, Duke University, 2013.

Hassán, Iacob M. "De tolerado a reconocido: un judío español, filólogo sefardí." *Estudios sefardíes dedicados a la memoria de Iacob M. Hassán*, edited by Elena Romero, Madrid, CSIC, 2011, 59–77.

———. "Los sefardíes como tópico." *Raíces*, 67, 2006, 41–47.

———. "Realidad y fantasía en las relaciones recíprocas España-Sefardíes." *España y la cultura hispánica en el sureste europeo*, edited by Juan González Barba, Athens, Presbía tis Ispanías, 2000, 355–70.

Heimann-Jelinek, Felicitas. "Thoughts on the Role of a European Jewish Museum in the 21st Century." *Visualizing and Exhibiting Jewish Space and History*, edited by Richard I. Cohen, Oxford UP, 2012, 243–57.

Hillgarth, J. N. *The Mirror of Spain, 1500–1700: The Formation of a Myth*. U of Michigan P, 2000.

Hirsch, Marianne. *The Generation of Postmemory: Writing and Visual Culture after the Holocaust*. Columbia UP, 2012.

———. "The Generation of Postmemory." *Poetics Today*, vol. 29, no. 1, 2008, 103–28.

Holo, Selma. *Beyond the Prado: Museums and Identity in Democratic Spain*. Washington, DC, Smithsonian Institution Press, 1999.

Hosta y Rebés, Assumpció. "Red de Juderías-Caminos de Sepharad: Proyecto en construcción." *E-rph: Revista Electrónica del Patrimonio Histórico*, vol. 5, 2009, 1–14. https://revistaseug.ugr.es/index.php/erph/article/view/3363. Accessed April 17, 2020.

Hutcheson, Gregory S. Guest editor, Critical Cluster, "Inflecting the *Converso* Voice." *La Corónica*, vol. 25, no. 1, 1996, 3–68.

Huyssen, Andreas. *Present Pasts: Urban Palimpsests and the Politics of Memory*. Stanford UP, 2003.

———. *Twilight Memories: Marking Time in a Culture of Amnesia*. New York, Routledge, 1995.

Illas, Edgar. "On Universalist Particularism: The Catalans and the Jews." *Revisiting Jewish Spain in the Modern Era*, edited by Daniela Flesler, Tabea Linhard, and Adrián Pérez Melgosa, Special Issue of the *Journal of Spanish Cultural Studies*, vol. 12, no. 1, 2011, 77–94.

Ingram, Kevin, editor. *Conversos and Moriscos in Late Medieval Spain and Beyond*. Vol. 1. Leiden, Brill, 2009.

"International Tourist Arrivals Reach 1.4 billion Two Years Ahead of Forecasts." January 21, 2019. UNWTO (United Nations World Tourism Organization). https://www.unwto.org/global/press-release/2019-01-21/international-tourist-arrivals-reach-14-billion-two-years-ahead-forecasts. Accessed April 17, 2020.

Israel, Jonathan I. *European Jewry in the Age of Mercantilism 1550–1750*. 3rd ed., London, Littman Library of Jewish Civilization, 1997.

Jameson, Fredric. *Politics of Post-Modernity; or, the Cultural Logic of Late Capitalism*. Duke UP, 1991.

Jarque, Fietta. "Daniel Quintero recrea sus emociones ante la cultura sefardí." *El País*, September 6, 2000. http://elpais.com/diario/2000/09/06/cultura/968191209_850215.html. Accessed April 17, 2020.

Jerez Farrán, Carlos, and Samuel Amago. *Unearthing Franco's Legacy: Mass Graves and the Recovery of Historical Memory in Spain*. U of Notre Dame P, 2010.

Jiménez-Landi, Antonio. *La Institución Libre de Enseñanza y su ambiente. Tomo III: Periodo Escolar 1881–1907*. Madrid, Editorial Complutense, S. A., 1996.

Joan Tous, Pere. "Los chuetas de Mallorca: textos persecutorios, negociación del stigma y reivindicación literaria." El antisemitismo en España, edited by Gonzalo Alvarez Chillida and Ricardo Izquierdo Benito. Cuenca, Ediciones de la Universidad de Castilla-La Mancha, 2007, 127–64.

Jobling, Mark A., et.al. "The Genetic Legacy of Religious Diversity and Intolerance: Paternal Lineages of Christians, Jews, and Muslims in the Iberian Peninsula." *American Journal of Human Genetics*, vol. 83, 2008, 725–36.

Judt, Tony. "From the House of the Dead: An Essay on Modern European Memory." *Postwar: A History of Europe since 1945*. Penguin Books, 2006, 803–31.

Julbe, Barbara, and Sara Sans. "Aumentan los turistas judíos en las ciudades con judería." *La Vanguardia*, April 30, 2012. http://www.lavanguardia.com/vida/20120430/54286701939/aumentan-turistas-judios-ciudades-juderia.html. Accessed April 17, 2020.

Juris, Jeffrey S. "Los Caminos de Sefarad." *Revista de Antropología Social*, vol. 14, 2005, 241–79.

Kandiyoti, Dalia. *The Converso's Return: The Afterlives of Conversion in Contemporary Literature and Culture*. Stanford UP, 2020.

———. *Migrant Sites: America, Place, and Diaspora*. UP of New England, 2009.

———. "Sephardism in Latina Literature." *Sephardism: Spanish Jewish History and the Modern Literary Imagination*, edited by Yael Halevi-Wise, Stanford UP, 2012, 235–55.

Karp, Ivan. "Culture and Representation." *Exhibiting Cultures: The Poetics and Politics of Museum Display*, edited by Ivan Karp and Steven D. Levine. Washington, DC, Smithsonian Institution Press, 1991, 11–24.

Kelly, Dorothy. "Selling Spanish 'Otherness' since the 1960s." *Contemporary Spanish Cultural Studies*, edited by Barry Jordan and Rikki Morgan-Tamosunas. London, Arnold, 2000, 29–37.

Kirshenblatt-Gimblett, Barbara. *Destination Culture: Tourism, Museums, and Heritage*. U of California P, 1998.

———. "Inside the Museum: Curating between Hope and Despair; POLIN Museum of the History of Polish Jews." *East European Jewish Affairs*, vol. 45, nos. 2–3, 2015, 215–35.

———. "Why Do Jewish Museums Matter? An International Perspective." Keynote address delivered at the annual meeting of the Association of

European Jewish Museums in 2011 London. Published January 13, 2012, online at https://www.aejm.org/site/assets/uploads/2014/07/Barbara-Kirshenblatt-Gimblett_Why-Do-Jewish-Museums-Matter-An-International-Perspective_Keynote-2011.pdf. Accessed April 17, 2020.

Kovadloff, Santiago. "Judíos españoles, la hora de la reparación." *La Nación*, October 8, 2014. http://www.lanacion.com.ar/1733727-judios-espanoles-la-hora-de-la-reparacion. Accessed April 17, 2020.

"La judería estrena señalización." *La Tribuna de Toledo*, August 16, 2012. https://www.latribunadetoledo.es/noticia/ZE5CCFC12-9C74-C3B5-FCD0D47D0B273A01/20120816/juderia/estrena/se. Accessed April 17, 2020.

"La leyenda de un amor imposible representada para Los Conversos" (entrevista a Miguel Murillo). *La Aldaba*, Periódico de Hervás, April 2, 2008, p. 19.

Labanyi, Jo. "Entrevista con Emilio Silva." *The Politics of Memory in Contemporary Spain*, edited by Jo Labanyi, *JSCS* Special Issue, vol. 9, no. 2, 2008, 143–55.

———. "The Languages of Silence: Historical Memory, Generational Transmission and Witnessing in Contemporary Spain." *Journal of Romance Studies*, vol. 9, no. 3, 2009, 23–35.

———. "The Politics of Memory in Contemporary Spain." Introduction to *Journal of Spanish Cultural Studies*, Special Issue, vol. 9, no. 2, 2008, 119–25.

Lacave, José L. "De cómo se judaízan unos baños: Mallorca." *Raíces: Revista judía de cultura*, vol. 6, 1989, 29–31.

Langston, Richard. *Visions of Violence: German Avant-Gardes after Fascism*. Northwestern UP, 2008.

The Launching of the European Route of Jewish Heritage. Conference Proceedings. Luxemburg, June 18–20, 2004. Edited by B'nai B'rith Europe, European Council of Jewish Communities and Red de Juderías de España. Luxembourg, Ka Communications, 2004. http://www.redjuderias.org/upload/imagenes/CERJH2004en.pdf. Accessed August 12, 2015 (document no longer accessible).

Lebovics, Herman. *Bringing the Empire Back Home: France in the Global Age*. Duke University Press, 2004.

———. *True France: The Wars over Cultural Identity, 1900–1945*. Cornell University Press, 1992.

Lefebvre, Henri. *The Production of Space*. Wiley, 1992.

Lehrer, Erica. "Bearing False Witness? 'Vicarious' Jewish Identity and the Politics of Affinity." *Imaginary Neighbors: Mediating Polish-Jewish Relations after the Holocaust*, edited by Dorota Glowacka and Joanna Zylinska, U of Nebraska P, 2007, 84–109.

———. *Jewish Poland Revisited: Heritage Tourism in Unquiet Places*. Indiana UP, 2013.

———."Virtual, Virtuous, Vicarious, Vacuous? Toward a Vigilant Use of Labels." *Framing Jewish Culture: Boundaries and Representations*, edited by Simon J. Bronner. Liverpool UP, 2014, 383–95.

Lehrer, Erica, and Michael Meng, editors. *Jewish Space in Contemporary Poland.* Indiana UP, 2015.
Leite, Naomi. *Unorthodox Kin: Portuguese Marranos and the Global Search for Belonging.* U of California P, 2017.
Lépicouché, Michel Hubert. "Llanto por las rosas perdidas de Sefarad." *Wolf VostellShoah 1492–1945: En memoria de la expulsión de los judíos españoles y de lasvíctimas del Holocausto.* Badagoz, Editora Regional de Extremadura, 1998, 39–46.
Levinas, Emmanuel. *Totality and Infinity: An Essay on Exteriority.* Boston, Kluwer Academic Publishing, 1991.
———. "The Trace of the Other." *Deconstruction in Context,* edited by Mark C. Taylor, U of Chicago P, 1986, 345–59.
Levy, Daniel, and Nathan Sznaider. *Human Rights and Memory.* Penn State UP, 2010.
———. *Memory and the Holocaust in a Global Age.* Temple UP, 2006.
Levy, Daniel, Michael Heinlein, and Lars Breuer. "Reflexive Particularism and Cosmopolitanization: The Reconfiguration of the National." *Global Networks,* vol. 11, no. 2, 2011, 139–59.
"Ley 12/2015, de 24 de junio, en materia de concesión de la nacionalidad Española a los sefardíes originarios de España." *BOE* (Boletín Oficial del Estado) 151–7045, June 25, 2015, 52557–64.
"Librería judaica." Toledo Sefarad. Web Oficial del Toledo Judío. http://www.toledosefarad.org/COMPRAS/libreria.php. Accessed June 2, 2009 (site discontinued).
Linhard, Tabea. "Europe's Jewish Places." *Aschkenas,* vol. 25, no. 2, 2015, 209–20.
———. *Jewish Spain: A Mediterranean Memory.* Stanford UP, 2014.
———. "The Second Republic, the Jews, and the Uses of the Past." *Revisiting Jewish Spain in the Modern Era,* edited by Daniela Flesler, Tabea Alexa Linhard, and Adrián Pérez Melgosa, New York, Routledge, 2013, 91–105.
Lipton, Sara. *Dark Mirror: The Medieval Origins of Anti-Jewish Iconography.* Metropolitan Books, 2014.
Lisbona, José Antonio. *Retorno a Sefarad: La política de España hacia sus judíos en el siglo XX.* Barcelona, Riopiedras, 1993.
López Álvarez, Ana María, Yasmina Álvarez Delgado, and Santiago Palomero Plaza. "Nuevos datos sobre la Historia de la Sinagoga del Tránsito." *Sefarad,* vol. 52, no. 2, 1992, 473–500.
López Alvarez, Ana María, Santiago Palomero Plaza, and María Luisa Menéndez Robledo. *Guía del Museo Sefardí.* Madrid, Ministerio de Cultura, 2006.
———. *Guía del Museo Sefardí.* Madrid, Ministerio de Cultura, 2011.
"Los moriscos piden equipararse a los sefardíes y piden la nacionalidad española." *ABC,* February 17, 2014. http://www.abc.es/espana/20140217/abci-moriscos-sefardies-espana-201402171119.html. Accessed April 17, 2020.

"Los sefardíes podrán adquirir la nacionalidad española." *El Mundo*, November 22, 2012. http://www.elmundo.es/elmundo/2012/11/22/espana/1353599031.html. Accessed April 17, 2020.

Lustig, Sandra, and Ian Leveson. "Caught between Civil Society and the Cultural Market: Jewry and the Jewish Space in Europe; A Response to Diana Pinto." *Turning the Kaleidoscope: Perspectives on European Jewry*. Berghahn Books, 2006, 187–204.

Macías, Uriel. "Los cronistas de la Guerra de Africa y el primer reencuentro con los sefardíes." *Los judíos en la España contemporánea: historia y visiones, 1898–1998*, edited by Uriel Macías, Yolanda Moreno Koch, Ricardo Izquierdo Benito, Cuenca, Ediciones de la Universidad de Castilla-la Mancha, 2000, 45–60.

Maiztegui-Oñate, Concepción, and María Teresa Areitio Bertolín. "Cultural Tourism in Spain." *Cultural Tourism in Europe*, edited by Greg Richards, Wallingford, CAB International, 1996, 195–205.

Manzano Moreno, Eduardo. "La construcción histórica del pasado nacional." *La gestión de la memoria: La historia de España al servicio del poder*, edited by Juan Sisinio Pérez Garzón, Barcelona, Crítica, 2000, 33–62.

Marín, Manuela, editor. *Al-Andalus/España: Historiografías en contraste; Siglos XVII–XXI*. Madrid, Casa de Velázquez, 2009.

———. "Mujeres andalusíes: de la historia al presente." *Tulaytula: Revista de la Asociación de Amigos del Toledo Islámico*, vol. 12, 2005, 61–69.

Marquina, Antonio, and Gloria Inés Ospina. *España y los judíos en el siglo XX*. Madrid, Espasa Calpe, 1987.

Martin-Márquez, Susan. *Disorientations: Spanish Colonialism in Africa and the Performance of Identity*. Yale UP, 2008.

Martz, Linda. *A Network of Converso Families in Early Modern Toledo: Assimilating a Minority*. U of Michigan P, 2003.

Mateos Paramio, Alfredo. "El Greco y Vostell, dos forasteros en las Españas." *Shoah* Dossier. Exhibition Information. http://www.mcu.es/promoArte/Novedades/Shoah_MuseoSefardi.html.

Matittiahu, Jack (dir.). *Toledo: El secreto oculto*. Madrid, Prima Luz Productions, 2008. Video.

McDonald, Charles A. "Return to Sepharad: Citizenship, Conversion, and the Politics of Jewish Inclusion in Spain." PhD dissertation, New School for Social Research, 2019.

McGee, Suzanne. "Economic Boost? Sephardic Jews Contemplate a Return to Spain." *The Guardian*, November 26, 2014. www.theguardian.com/money/2014/nov/26/sephardic-jews-spain-economics. Accessed April 17, 2020.

McKercher, Bob, and Hilary du Cros. *Cultural Tourism: The Partnership between Tourism and Cultural Heritage Management*. Haworth Press, 2002.

Melul, David. "Reencuentro de dos Bejaranos después de 400 años." *Judíos y conversos en la historia de Béjar*. Béjar, Publicaciones del Museo Judío de Béjar, 2004, 29–38.

Menéndez Pelayo, Marcelino. *Historia de los heterodoxos españoles I*. Madrid: Consejo Superior de Investigaciones Científicas, 1992.

Meng, Michael. "Muranów as a Ruin: Layered Memories in Postwar Warsaw." *Jewish Space in Contemporary Poland*, edited by Erica Lehrer and Michael Meng, Indiana UP, 71–89.

Menny, Anna. "Entre reconocimiento y rechazo: Los judíos en la obra de Américo Castro." *Iberoamericana*, vol. 10, no 38, 2010, 143–50.

———. "Sepharad—Object of Investigation? The Academic Discourse about Sepharad and Sephardim in Spain." *Jewish Culture and History*, vol. 16, no. 1, 2015, 6–23.

Menocal, María Rosa. *The Ornament of the World: How Muslims, Jews and Christians Created a Culture of Tolerance in Medieval Spain*. Little, Brown and Company, 2002.

Meyerson, Mark D. *A Jewish Renaissance in Fifteenth-Century Spain*. Princeton UP, 2004.

Minder, Raphael. "5 Catalan Cities Step Away from Spain with New Jewish History Network." *New York Times*, June 7, 2016. https://www.nytimes.com/2016/06/08/world/europe/catalan-catalonia-spain-jewish-history.html. Accessed April 17, 2020.

Miranda Sánchez, Antonio. *Reconstrucción de la portada medieval de la sinagoga del Tránsito*. Toledo, Ledoria, 2012.

Mirrer, Louise. *Women, Jews, and Muslims in the Texts of Reconquest Castile*. U of Michigan P, 1996.

Monegal, Antonio. "Exhibiting Objects of Memory." *The Politics of Memory in Contemporary Spain*, edited by Jo Labanyi, Special Issue of *Journal of Spanish Cultural Studies*, vol. 9, no. 2, 2008, 239–51.

Monteverde, José Luis. *El Tesorillo de Bivriesca*. Zarauz, Editorial Icharopena, 1939.

Moreno, Manuel. "Intentan quemar con gasóleo la Librería & Judaica" *ABC.es*, January 19, 2007. https://www.abc.es/espana/castilla-la-mancha/toledo/abci-intentan-quemar-gasoleo-libreria-yamp-judaica-200701190300-163995690815_noticia.html. Accessed April 17, 2020.

Morgan, Tony. "1992: Memories and Modernities." *Contemporary Spanish Cultural Studies*, edited by Barry Jordan and Rikki Morgan-Tamosunas. London, Arnold, 2000, 58–67.

Moriche Mateos, Francisco. *Represión, silencio y olvido: Memoria histórica de Hervás y el Alto Ambroz*. Mérida, Asamblea de Extremadura, 2008.

Muñoz Herrera, J. Pedro. *Imágenes de la melancolía: Toledo (1772–1858)*. Ayuntamiento de Toledo, 1993.

Muñoz Solla, Ricardo. "El redescubrimiento de Maimónides y la cultura hispanohebrea en la primera mitad del siglo XX." *Et Amicorum: Estudios en honor al profesor Carlos Carrete Parrondo.* Salamanca, Universidad de Salamanca, 2019, 453–566.

Museo Judío David Melul website. http://www.museojudiobejar.com. Accessed April 17, 2020.

Nadel, James. "Rediscovering Sephardic Catalonia: Heritage and the Museum of Jewish History in Girona." *University of Michigan Working Papers in Museum Studies: Future Leaders,* vol. 2, 2016, 1–10.

Nathan-Kazis, Josh. "My Spanish Inquisition: A Jewish Reporter Exercises His Right of Return." *Haaretz* and *The Forward,* January 30, 2014. https://www.haaretz.com/jewish/my-spanish-inquisition-1.5317044. Accessed April 17, 2020.

Nirenberg, David. *Anti-Judaism: The Western Tradition.* W. W. Norton & Co., 2013.

———. *Communities of Violence: Persecution of Minorities in the Middle Ages.* Princeton UP, 1996.

———. "Mass Conversion and Genealogical Mentalities: Jews and Christians in Fifteenth-Century Spain." *Past and Present,* vol. 174, 2002, 3–41.

———. *Neighboring Faiths: Christianity, Islam, and Judaism in the Middle Ages and Today.* Chicago UP, 2014.

———. "Was There Race before Modernity? The Example of 'Jewish' Blood in Late Medieval Spain." *The Origins of Racism in the West,* edited by Miriam Eliav-Feldon, Benjamin Isaac, and Jiseph Ziegler, Cambridge UP, 2009, 232–64.

Novikoff, Alex. "Between Tolerance and Intolerance in Medieval Spain: An Historiographic Enigma." *Medieval Encounters,* vol. 11, nos. 1–2, 2005, 7–36.

Offe, Sabine. "Sites of Remembrance? Jewish Museums in Contemporary Germany." *Jewish Social Studies,* vol. 3, no. 2, 1997, 72–89.

Ojeda Mata, Maite. *Identidades ambivalentes: Sefardíes en la España contemporánea.* Madrid, Sefarad Editores, 2013.

———. "'Spanish' but 'Jewish': Race and National Identity in Nineteenth and Twentieth Century Spain." *Jewish Culture and History,* vol. 16, no. 1, 2015, 64–81.

———. "Thinking about 'the Jew' in Modern Spain: Historiography, Nationalism and Antisemitism." *Jewish Culture and History,* vol. 8, no. 2, 2006, 53–72.

Olick, Jeffrey K. "The Guilt of Nations?" *Ethics and International Affairs,* vol. 17, no. 2, 2003, 109–17.

———. *The Politics of Regret: On Collective Memory and Historical Responsibility.* New York, Routledge, 2007.

Pack, Sasha D. *Tourism and Dictatorship: Europe's Peaceful Invasion of Franco's Spain.* Palgrave Macmillan, 2006.

"Page apuesta por potenciar el turismo judío americano." *La Tribuna de Toledo,* June 3, 2012. http://www.latribunadetoledo.es/noticia/ZCBE7D7D7-02DC-DE76-D8B0CBDDF1E41BCA/20120603/apuesta/potenciar/turismo/judio/americano. Accessed December 2, 2016 (article no longer accessible).

"Palma abandona la entidad que reúne a todas las ciudades con legado judío." *Diario de Palma,* December 12, 2017. https://www.diariodemallorca.es/palma/2017/12/21/palma-abandona-entidad-reune-ciudades/1273919.html. Accessed April 17, 2020.

Palomero Plaza, Santiago. *Historia de la Sinagoga de Samuel Ha Leví y del Museo Sefardí de Toledo.* Madrid, Ministerio de Cultura, 2007.

Patronat Call de Girona website. http://www.girona.cat/call/eng/museu.php.

Peiró Menéndez, César. *Arte de conocer a nuestros judíos.* Barcelona: Imp. La Catalana, 1916.

Pérez Colomé, Jordí. "La sinagoga de la discordia." *El País,* February 19, 2017. https://elpais.com/cultura/2017/02/14/actualidad/1487073379_668229.html. Accessed April 12, 2020.

Pérez Higuera, María Teresa. "En torno al proceso constructivo de San Juan de los Reyes en Toledo." *Anales de historia del arte,* vol. 7, 1997, 11–24.

Pérez-Prendes, José Manuel. "El Nuevo marco legal: de la real cédula de 1802 a los acuerdos de 1992." *Los judíos en la España contemporánea: historia y visiones, 1898–1998,* edited by Uriel Macías, Yolanda Moreno Koch, Ricardo Izquierdo Benito, Cuenca, Ediciones de la Universidad de Castilla-la Mancha, 2000, 75–91.

Phillips Cohen, Julia. "El pasado como tierra ajena: imaginando Sefarad desde el Imperio Otomano." Paper presented at "Genealogías de Sefarad" Conference. Centro Sefarad-Israel, Madrid, July 2018.

Pi-Sunyer, O. "Tourism in Catalonia." *Tourism in Spain: Critical Issues,* edited by M. Barke, J. Towner, and M. T. Newton, Wallingford, Oxon, UK, Cab International, 1996, 231–64.

Pinto, Diana. "The Jewish Space in Europe." *Turning the Kaleidoscope: Perspectives on European Jewry,* edited by Sandra Lustig and Ian Leveson, Berghahn Books, 2006, 179–86.

Pluralismo y Convivencia Foundation. http://www.pluralismoyconvivencia.es/. Accessed April 17, 2020.

Preston, Paul. *The Spanish Holocaust: Inquisition and Extermination in Twentieth-Century Spain.* W. W. Norton & Co., 2012.

"Prime Minister of Spain Receives UNWTO/WTTC Open Letter on Travel and Tourism." January 28, 2015. UNWTO (United Nations World Tourism Organization). https://www.unwto.org/archive/europe/press-release/2015-01-28/prime-minister-spain-receives-unwtowttc-open-letter-travel-and-tourism. Accessed April 18, 2020.

Pulido, Ángel. *Intereses nacionales: Españoles sin patria y la raza sefardí.* Madrid, E. Teodoro, 1905.

———. *Los israelitas españoles y el idioma castellano.* Madrid, Riopiedras, 1992.

Purin, Bernhard. "Building a Jewish Museum in Germany." *(Re)visualizing National History: Museums and National Identities in Europe in the New Millennium,* edited by Robin Ostow. U of Toronto P, 2008, 139–56.

Quevedo, Francisco de. *Execración contra los judíos*. Edited by Fernando Cabo Aseguinolaza and Santiago Fernández Mosquera. Barcelona, Crítica, 1996.

Ray, Jonathan. *After Expulsion: 1492 and the Making of Sephardic Jewry*. NYU P, 2013.

———. "Beyond Tolerance and Persecution: Reassessing Our Approach to Medieval *Convivencia*." *Jewish Social Studies*, vol. 11, no. 2, 2005, 1–18.

———. "Images of the Jewish Community in Medieval Iberia." *Journal of Medieval Iberian Studies*, vol. 1, no. 2, 2009, 195–211.

———. *The Sephardic Frontier: The Reconquista and the Jewish Community in Medieval Iberia*. Cornell UP, 2006.

———. "Whose Golden Age? Jewish-Christian Relations in Medieval Iberia." *Studies in Christian-Jewish Relations*, vol. 6, no. 1, 2011, 1–11.

"Red 1995–2005." http://www.redjuderias.org/upload/imagenes/Red1995_2005.pdf. Accessed June 5, 2010 (document no longer accessible).

Regan, Kate (dir.). *The Sephardic Legacy of Segovia, Spain: Pentimento of the Past*. Princeton, Films for the Humanities and Sciences, 2007. Film.

Rein, Raanan. *Franco, Israel y los judíos*. Madrid, Consejo Superior de Investigaciones Científicas, 1996.

Rein, Raanan, and Martina Weisz. "Ghosts of the Past, Challenges of the Present: New and Old 'Others' in Contemporary Spain." *El Otro en la España Contemporánea: Prácticas, discursos y representaciones*, edited by Silvina Schammah Gesser and Raanan Rein. Fundación Tres Culturas, Sevilla, 2011, 161–86.

"Ribadavia registró un aumento del 15,62% de turistas en 2014." *Faro de Vigo*, January 31, 2015. http://www.farodevigo.es/portada-ourense/2015/01/31/ribadavia-registro-aumento-15-turistas/1175590.html. Accessed December 12, 2015 (article no longer accessible).

Richards, Michael. *A Time of Silence: Civil War and the Culture of Repression in Franco's Spain, 1936–1945*. Cambridge UP, 1998.

Rivière Gómez, Aurora. *Orientalismo y nacionalismo español: Estudios árabes y hebreos en la Universidad de Madrid (1843–1868)*. Madrid, Universidad Carlos III, 2000.

Robles, María Ángeles. "La Casa de Sefarad: el hogar de la cultura judeoespañola en el corazón de Córdoba." *eldiario.es*, February 1, 2019. https://www.eldiario.es/andalucia/pasaporte/Casa-Sefarad-cultura-judeoespanola-Cordoba_0_863014800.html. Accessed April 18, 2020.

Rogozen-Soltar, Mikaela H. *Spain Unmoored: Migration, Conversion, and the Politics of Islam*. Indiana UP, 2017.

Rohr, Isabelle. "Spaniards of the Jewish Type: Philosephardism in the Service of Imperialism in Early Twentieth-Century Morocco." *Revisiting Jewish Spain in the Modern Era*, edited by Daniela Flesler, Tabea Linhard, and Adrián Pérez Melgosa, Special Issue of the *Journal of Spanish Cultural Studies*, vol. 12, no. 1, 2011, 61–75.

———. *The Spanish Right and the Jews, 1898–1945. Antisemitism and Opportunism.* Brighton, UK, Sussex Academic Press, 2007.

Rojek, Chris. "Indexing, Dragging and the Social Construction of Tourist Sights." *Touring Cultures: Transformations of Travel and Theory,* edited by Chris Rojek and John Urry, New York, Routledge, 1997, 52–74.

Romeu Ferré, Pilar. "Sefarad ¿la 'patria' de los sefardíes?" *Sefarad,* vol. 71, no. 1, 2011, 95–130.

Roncero López, Victoriano. "Lazarillo, Guzmán and Buffoon Literature." *Modern Language Notes,* vol. 116, 2001, 235–49.

Ross, Chris, Bill Richardson, and Begoña Sangrado-Vegas. *Contemporary Spain: A Handbook.* Hodder Education Publishers, 2002.

Roth, Cecil. "A Hebrew Elegy on the Martyrs of Toledo, 1391." *The Jewish Quarterly Review,* vol. 39, no. 2, 1948, 123–50.

Rothberg, Michael. *Multidirectional Memory: Remembering the Holocaust in the Age of Decolonization.* Stanford UP, 2009.

Rothstein, Edward. "In Berlin, Teaching Germany's Jewish History." *New York Times,* May 1, 2009. http://www.nytimes.com/2009/05/02/arts/design/02conn .html. Accessed April 18, 2020.

———. "The Problem with Jewish Museums." *Mosaic,* February 1, 2016. https:// mosaicmagazine.com/essay/2016/02/the-problem-with-jewish-museums/. Accessed April 18, 2020.

Routes of Sepharad: Cáceres, Córdoba, Girona, Hervás, Ribadavia, Segovia, Toledo, Tudela. Cáceres, Patronato para la promoción del turismo y la artesanía, 1996.

Rozenberg, Danielle. *La España contemporánea y la cuestión judía: Retejiendo los hilos de la memoria y la historia.* Madrid, Casa Sefarad-Israel and Marcial Pons, 2010.

Rueda Laffond, José Carlos, and Carlota Coronado Ruiz. "Historical Science Fiction: From Television Memory to Transmedia Memory in El Ministerio del Tiempo." *Journal of Spanish Cultural Studies,* vol. 17, no. 1, 2016, 87–101.

Ruiz Souza, Juan Carlos. "Sinagogas sefardíes monumentales en el contexto de la arquitectura medieval hispana." *Memoria de Sefarad. Catálogo de Exposición.* Toledo, Seacex, 2002. 225–39.

Ruiz Taboada, Arturo. "La gestión de los cementerios históricos: la muerte como disputa." *Complutum,* vol. 25, no. 1, 2014, 203–15.

Ruiz Torres, Pedro. "Los discursos de la memoria histórica en España." *Hispania Nova,* vol. 7, 2007. http://hispanianova.rediris.es/7/dossier/07d001.pdf. Accessed April 18, 2020.

Sabanoglu, Albert. "Impresiones de un retorno: Experiencias de sefardíes turcos en la España de hoy." Paper given at ALCES Siglo XXI Conference, Zaragoza, Spain, July 6, 2017.

Sabaté, Flocel. "La Sefarad cautiva y reinventada, o los retos de la arqueología y la divulgación del patrimonio cultural." *¿Una Sefarad Inventada? Los problemas* *de interpretación de los restos materiales de los judíos en España*, edited by Javier Castaño, Córdoba, El Almendro, 2014, 29–67.

Salmona, Paul. "A Key Discovery for the History of Medieval Europe." *Tragèdia al call-Tàrrega 1348*, coordinated by Saula Briansó, Oriol, Exhibition Catalog, Museu Comarcal de l'Urgell-Tàrrega, 2014, 363.

Schapkow, Carsten. *Role Model and Countermodel: The Golden Age of Iberian Jewry and German Jewish Culture during the Era of Emancipation*. Lexington Books, 2015.

Schmidt-Nowara, Chris. "'This Rotting Corpse': Spain between the Black Atlantic and the Black Legend." *Arizona Journal of Hispanic Cultural Studies*, vol. 5, 2001, 149–60.

Schorsch, Ismar. "The Myth of Sephardic Supremacy." *From Text to Context: The Turn to History in Modern Judaism*. Brandeis UP, 1994, 71–92.

Schwab, Gabrielle. *Haunting Legacies: Violent Histories and Transgenerational Trauma*. Columbia UP, 2010.

"Se inaugura Museo Sefardí de Toledo." *ABC*, June 15, 1971.

Sebastián, Pablo. "En el asalto a la Embajada de España murieron 39 personas porque lo quiso el gobierno de Guatemala: Declaraciones del Embajador Máximo Cajal en el primer aniversario de la tragedia." *El País*, January 25, 1981. https://elpais.com/diario/1981/01/25/internacional/349225201_850215.html. Accessed April 18, 2020.

Sendín Blázquez, José. *Leyendas Extremeñas*. León, Everest, 1987.

Senkman, Leonardo. *La identidad judía en la literatura argentina*. Buenos Aires, Pardes, 1983.

Shinan, Nitai. "Emilio Castelar y los judíos: una reevaluación." *Miscelánea de estudios árabes y hebreos*, vol. 65, 2016. http://www.meahhebreo.com/index.php/meahhebreo/article/view/891/1032. Accessed April 18, 2020.

———. "Estudio preliminar." José Amador de los Ríos, *Los Judíos de España: Estudios históricos, políticos y literarios*. Pamplona, Urgoiti, 2013.

Silberman, Neil A. "Who Should Take Care of the Dead? Scientific Method, Human Rights, Heritage Ethics and Community Beliefs." *La intervenció arqueològica a les necròpolis històriques: Els cementiris jueus (actes del colloqui del 15 i 16 de gener de 2009)*. Barcelona, MUHBA i Ajuntament de Barcelona, Institut de Cultura, 2012, 33–41.

Sion, Brigitte. "A Survey of Jewish Museums in Europe." The Rothschild Foundation (Hanadiv) Europe, 2016. https://rothschildfoundation.eu/wp-content/uploads/2017/02/Jewish-Museums-in-Europe-Report.pdf. Accessed April 18, 2020.

Smith, Paul Julian. "La Celestina, Castro and the *Conversos*." *Representing the Other: 'Race,' Text and Gender in Spanish and Spanish American Narrative*. Clarendon UP, 1992, 27–58.

Soifer, Maya. "Beyond Convivencia: Critical Reflections on the Historiography of Interfaith Relations in Christian Spain." *Journal of Medieval Iberian Studies*, vol. 1, no. 1, 2009, 19–35.

Soja, Edward W. *Thirdspace*. Blackwell, 1996.

Soyer, Francois. "The Anti-Semitic Conspiracy Theory in Sixteenth-Century Spain and Portugal and the Origins of the Carta de los Judíos de Constantinopla: New Evidence." *Sefarad: Revista de estudios hebraicos y sefardíes*, vol. 74, no. 2, 2014, 369–88.

Stavans, Ilan. "Repatriating Spain's Jews." *New York Times*, April 1, 2014. https://www.nytimes.com/2014/04/02/opinion/repatriating-spains-jews.html?register=google. Accessed April 18, 2020.

Stiles, Kristine. "Wolf Vostell in Conversation with Kristine Stiles." August 27, 1982. Malpartida de Cáceres, Spain. Unpublished manuscript.

Stoller, Robin, and Alejandro Baer. "A Survey to Deny a Problem." *Jerusalem Post*, October 17, 2010.

Sturken, Marita. *Tangled Memories: The Vietnam War, the AIDS Epidemic, and the Politics of Remembering*. U of California P, 1997.

"Tarazona, el retorno de Sefarad." *Viajar por Aragón*, vol. 20, 2002, 8–21.

Trancón, Santiago. *Memorias de un judío sefardí: La verdadera historia de Dan Kofler*. Madrid, Infova Ediciones, 2011.

Travel and Tourism Economic Impact 2018, Spain. WTTC (World Travel and Tourism Council). March 2018. https://www.wttc.org/economic-impact/country-analysis/country-reports/#spain. Accessed April 18, 2020.

Tunbridge, J. E., and G. J. Ashworth. *Dissonant Heritage: The Management of the Past as a Resource in Conflict*. J. Wiley, 1996.

"Unfavorable Views of Jews and Muslims on the Increase in Europe." *The Pew Global Attitudes Project*. Pew Research Center Study, released September 17, 2008. http://pewglobal.org/reports/display.php?ReportID=262-. Accessed April 18, 2020.

Urry, John, and Jonas Larsen. *The Tourist Gaze 3.0* (3rd ed). London, Sage Publications, 2011.

Van Praag, J. A. "Los Protocolos de los Sabios de Sión y la Isla de los Monopantos de Quevedo." *Bulletin Hispanique*, vol. 51, no. 2, 1949, 169–73.

Vándor, Jaime. "Orígenes, desarrollo y presente de la Comunidad Judía de Barcelona." *Los judíos en la España contemporánea: Historia y visiones, 1898–1998*, edited by Uriel Macías, Yolanda Moreno Koch, and Ricardo Izquierdo Benito. Ediciones de la Universidad de Castilla–la Mancha, 2000, 307–21.

Vernon, Kathleen. "Re-viewing the Spanish Civil War: Franco's Film *Raza*." *Film & History*, vol. 16, no. 2, 1986, 26–34.

Vicent, Manuel. "Un mendigo llamado Maimónides." *El País*, November 10, 2017. https://elpais.com/cultura/2017/11/10/actualidad/1510348645_173248.html?id_externo_rsoc=whatsapp. Accessed April 18, 2020.

Villatoro, Vicenç. "¿De qué hablamos cuando hablamos de Israel?" *En defensa de Israel*, edited by Jaime Naifleisch, Pilar Rahola, and Horacio Vásquez-Rial. Sevilla, Certeza, 2004, 333–50.

Vinyes, Ricard, Montse Armengou, and Ricard Belis. *Los niños perdidos del franquismo*. Barcelona, Plaza y Janés, 2002.

Vostell, Wolf. "Sobre mi cuadro Shoah 1492–1945." *Wolf Vostell Shoah 1492–1945: Enmemoria de la expulsión de los judíos españoles y de las víctimas del Holocausto*. Badajoz, Editora Regional de Extremadura, 1998, 11.

Wacks, David. *Double Diaspora in Sephardic Literature: Jewish Cultural Production before and after 1492*. Indiana UP, 2015.

———. "Is Spain's Hebrew Literature 'Spanish'?" *Spain's Multicultural Legacies-Studies in Honor of Samuel G. Armistead*, edited by Adrienne L. Martín and Cristina Martínez-Carazo. Newark, Juan de la Cuesta, 2008, 315–31.

———. "Sepharadim/Conversos and Premodern Global Hispanism." *Journal of Spanish Cultural Studies*, vol. 20, no. 1–2, 2019, 1–14.

Weisz, Martina L. *Jews and Muslims in Contemporary Spain: Redefining National Boundaries*. Berlin, De Gruyter, 2019.

Weitz, Joshua S. "Let My People Go (Home) to Spain: A Genealogical Model of Jewish Identities since 1492." PLoS ONE, vol. 9, no. 1, 2014, 1–6. e85673. https://doi.org/10.1371/journal.pone.0085673.

Williams, A. M. "Mass Tourism and International Tour Companies." *Tourism in Spain: Critical Issues*, edited by M. Barke, J. Towner, and M. T. Newton, Wallingford, Oxon, UK, Cab International, 1996, 119–35.

Wolodarsky, Solly. *El judío de Hervás*. Madrid, Hebraica, 2007.

———. *La conversa de Hervás*. Madrid, La Avispa, 2000.

———. *Los conversos: pieza teatral en dos partes*. Madrid, La Avispa, 1985.

Yerushalmi, Yosef Hayim. *From Spanish Court to Italian Ghetto: Isaac Cardoso; A Study in Seventeenth-Century Marranism and Jewish Apologetics*. Columbia UP, 1971.

Young, James E. *At Memory's Edge: After-Images of the Holocaust in Contemporary Art and Architecture*. Yale UP, 2000.

———. *The Texture of Memory: Holocaust Memorials and Meaning*. Yale UP, 1993.

Zolberg, Vera L. "Museums as Contested Sites of Remembrance: The Enola Gay Affair." *Theorizing Museums*, edited by Sharon Macdonald and Gordon Fyfe. Blackwell Publishers, 1996, 69–82.

INDEX

Page numbers in italics refer to figures.

DANIELA FLESLER is Associate Professor and Chair of Hispanic Languages and Literature at Stony Brook University. She is author of *The Return of the Moor: Spanish Responses to Contemporary Moroccan Immigration* and editor (with Adrián Pérez Melgosa and Tabea A. Linhard) of *Revisiting Jewish Spain in the Modern Era*.

ADRIÁN PÉREZ MELGOSA is Associate Professor of Hispanic Languages and Literature and Director of the Humanities Institute at Stony Brook University. He is author of *Cinema and Inter-American Relations: Tracking Transnational Affect* and editor (with Daniela Flesler and Tabea A. Linhard) of *Revisiting Jewish Spain in the Modern Era*.

www.ingramcontent.com/pod-product-compliance
Lightning Source LLC
LaVergne TN
LVHW040756070826
844660LV00025B/1161